WOMEN, MODERNITY, AND LANDSCAPE ARCHITECTURE

Modernity was critically important to the formation and evolution of landscape architecture, yet its histories in the discipline are still being written. This book looks closely at the work and influences of some of the least studied figures of the era: established and less well-known female landscape architects who pursued modernist ideals in their designs.

The women discussed in this volume belong to the pioneering first two generations of professional landscape architects and were outstanding in the field. They not only developed notable practices but some also became leaders in landscape architectural education as the first professors in the discipline, or prolific lecturers and authors. As early professionals who navigated the world of a male-dominated intellectual and menial work force they were exponents of modernity. In addition, many personalities discussed in this volume were either figures of transition between tradition and modernism (like Silvia Crowe and Maria Teresa Parpagliolo), or they fully embraced and furthered the modernist agenda (like Rosa Grena Kliass and Cornelia Hahn Oberlander).

The chapters offer new perspectives and contribute to the development of a more balanced and integrated landscape architectural historiography of the twentieth century. Contributions come from practitioners and academics who discuss women based in USA, Canada, Brazil, New Zealand, South Africa, the former USSR, Sweden, Britain, Germany, Austria, France, and Italy. The book is ideal reading for those studying landscape history, women's studies and cultural geography.

Sonja Dümpelmann is Associate Professor of Landscape Architecture, Harvard University and **John Beardsley** is Director of Garden and Landscape Studies, Dumbarton Oaks, Washington, D.C.

WOMEN, MODERNITY, AND LANDSCAPE ARCHITECTURE

Sonja Dümpelmann and John Beardsley

Routledge
Taylor & Francis Group
LONDON AND NEW YORK

First published 2015
by Routledge
2 Park Square, Milton Park, Abingdon, Oxon OX14 4RN

and by Routledge
711 Third Avenue, New York, NY 10017

Routledge is an imprint of the Taylor & Francis Group, an informa business

British Library Cataloguing in Publication Data   1 0 0736 1723
A catalogue record for this book is available from the British Library

Library of Congress Cataloging in Publication Data
A catalog record for this book has been requested

ISBN: 978-0-415-74587-1 (hbk)
ISBN: 978-0-415-74588-8 (pbk)
ISBN: 978-1-315-73296-1 (ebk)

Typeset in Bembo
by Swales & Willis Ltd, Exeter, Devon, UK

Cover photo: Bullock's Fashion Square Santa Ana, 1969. Photo: Darrow M. Watt. Courtesy of Sunset Publishing.

FSC
www.fsc.org

MIX
Paper from
responsible sources
FSC® C013056

Printed and bound in Great Britain by
TJ International Ltd, Padstow, Cornwall

CONTENTS

CONTRIBUTORS

John Beardsley is director of garden and landscape studies at Dumbarton Oaks, a humanities research institute in Washington D.C., affiliated with Harvard University. Trained as an art historian, with an AB from Harvard and a PhD from the University of Virginia, he is the author of numerous books on contemporary art and design, including *Earthworks and Beyond: Contemporary Art in the Landscape* (fourth edition, 2006) and *Gardens of Revelation: Environments by Visionary Artists* (1995), as well as many titles on recent landscape architecture. Beardsley has taught in departments of landscape architecture at the University of Virginia, the University of Pennsylvania, and Harvard University, where he was an adjunct professor at the Graduate School of Design, from 1998 to 2013.

Bernadette Blanchon is a certified architect, associate professor at the École Nationale Supérieure de Paysage, in Versailles, and a research fellow at LAREP (Laboratoire de Recherche de l'École de Paysage). She has collaborated with Bureau des Paysages, led by landscape architect Alexandre Chemetoff. Her teaching and research work focuses on landscapes in the urban environment of the post-war era. She has contributed to various publications, including the *Dictionnaire des Femmes Créatrices* (2013), *Les Espaces Publics Modernes* (1997), *Landscape Research*, and *STRATES* N°13. She has lectured at international conferences and various universities and is a founding editor of the *Journal of Landscape Architecture*.

Kelly Comras is a landscape architect in private practice in Pacific Palisades, California. She holds an MLA from California State Polytechnic University, Pomona, and is a member of the California Bar Association. She is the author of a forthcoming book on Ruth Patricia Shellhorn (Library of American Landscape History, 2015). Comras chairs the editorial board of *Eden: Journal of the California Garden and Landscape History Society*; serves on the Stewardship Council of The Cultural Landscape Foundation; and conducts research, writes, and lectures on the work of mid-century landscape architects.

Sonja Dümpelmann is associate professor of landscape architecture at the Harvard Graduate School of Design. She holds a PhD from the University of the Arts, Berlin, and has held research fellowships at the German Historical Institute and at Dumbarton Oaks, Washington D.C. Her publications include a book on the Italian landscape architect Maria Teresa Parpagliolo Shephard (VDG Weimar, 2004) and, more recently, *Flights of Imagination: Aviation, Landscape, Design* (UVA Press, 2014), the edited *Cultural History of Gardens in the Age* *of Empire* (Bloomsbury, 2013), and the co-edited *Greening the City: Urban Landscapes in the Twentieth Century* (UVA Press, 2011).

Jeremy Foster is assistant professor of architecture at Cornell University. Trained as an architect, landscape architect, and cultural geographer, he is interested in the opportunities the landscape medium – simultaneously, an assemblage of material processes and practices, a space of representation, and a vehicle of discourse – offers for transdisciplinary study. In addition to design studios, he teaches courses on the history and theory of landscape and urban design; the interplay between cultural representations and material practices in the shaping of cities, landscapes, and territories; and the 'more-than-representational' aspects of place. His research focuses on the diverse ways landscapes are mobilized to project emergent ideas of culture, nature, and identity.

Susan Herrington is a professor in the School of Architecture and Landscape Architecture at the University of British Columbia, in Vancouver, where she teaches in the architecture, environmental design, and landscape architecture programs. She is the author of *Cornelia Hahn Oberlander: Making the Modern Landscape* (UVA Press, 2014) and *On Landscapes*, published as part of Routledge's Thinking in Action Series. Her book, *Landscape Theory in Design*, is forthcoming with Routledge in 2015.

Ulrike Krippner was trained as a landscape architect. Since 2001, she has been working at the Institute of Landscape Architecture at the BOKU Universität für Bodenkultur, Vienna. Her research focuses on twentieth-century landscape architecture in Austria. Her recent articles, papers, and presentations have focused on Jewish women in Austrian horticulture and garden architecture. She held a 2010 summer fellowship in Dumbarton Oaks, Washington D.C., where she pursued her research on exiled Austrian female garden architects.

Zeuler R. M. de A. Lima is a designer; author; and associate professor of history, theory, and design at Washington University in Saint Louis. He has won several Brazilian design competitions and awards. He holds a PhD from the Universidade de São Paulo and a postdoctorate fellowship in comparative literature at Columbia University. In 2007, he received the International Bruno Zevi Prize for architectural history and criticism. His numerous publications on modern and contemporary architecture, landscape architecture, urbanism, and art include the biography of the architect and designer *Lina Bo Bardi* (Yale University Press, 2013) and a co-edited anthology of texts by architects from Latin America (MoMA, 2015).

Iris Meder studied art history and literature. She works as an art and architectural historian and curator, focusing on modern architecture in Austria and Central Europe, theories of functionalism, post-war modern architecture, female photographers, and architects in exile. Her PhD thesis analyzed the work of Josef Frank, Adolf Loos, and the "Wiener Schule." Since 2008, she has been involved in research projects on the history of Central European landscape architecture.

Catharina Nolin holds a PhD in art history and is associate professor at Stockholm University, Sweden. She has received research grants from The Swedish Research Council and The Swedish Foundation for Humanities and Social Sciences. Her publications include a book on nineteenth-century urban parks in Sweden (1999); a book on Millesgården, home of sculptor Carl Milles (2004); a book on the landscape architecture of Lars Israel Wahlman (2008); and articles on Ester Claesson in *Die Gartenkunst* (2009) and on urban parks and national identity in *Public Nature: Scenery, History, and Park Design* (UVA Press, 2013). She is currently working on a book on Swedish female landscape architects, 1900–1950.

Alla G. Vronskaya is a postdoctoral fellow at the Institute for the History and Theory of Architecture (gta) at the Swiss Federal Institute of Technology (ETH Zürich). She holds a candidate of sciences degree from the State Institute for Art Studies in Moscow and a PhD from the Massachusetts Institute of Technology. Her research focuses on the interactions between psychology and architecture in the Interwar Soviet Union. She has been a recipient of research fellowships from Dumbarton Oaks, Washington, D.C.; the Getty Research Institute, Los Angeles; and the Canadian Center for Architecture, Montreal.

Thaïsa Way, BS University of California, Berkeley, M'ArchH UVa, PhD Cornell University, is a landscape historian teaching history, theory, and design in the Department of Landscape Architecture at the College of Built Environments, University of Washington, Seattle. She has published and lectured on feminist histories of design and, in particular, the role of women as professionals and practitioners. Her book, *Unbounded Practices: Women, Landscape Architecture, and Early Twentieth Century Design* (UVA Press, 2009), was awarded the J. B. Jackson Book Award. Her newest book, *From Modern Space to Urban Ecological Design: The Landscape Architecture of Richard Haag*, is forthcoming with UW Press.

ACKNOWLEDGMENTS

This book originated at a conference, held at the Harvard Graduate School of Design (GSD) on Women and Modernism in Landscape Architecture, convened by John Beardsley. We would like to thank Dean Mohsen Mostafavi and Charles Waldheim, chair of the Department of Landscape Architecture, for initiating and providing the opportunity for this conference in the first place and for supporting the publication of this book. We are grateful to the staff at the GSD for their most capable help in organizing the conference.

We owe abundant thanks to all of the conference speakers and to the scholars who agreed to contribute essays to this volume. During its production, we incurred many debts. Louise Fox and Sadé Lee at Routledge facilitated a smooth publication process, and Dalal Musaed Alsayer provided assistance in the last stages of compiling the entire manuscript. We are grateful to all of them.

INTRODUCTION

Women, modernity, and landscape architecture

Sonja Dümpelmann and John Beardsley

> June 1942 saw our last male contingent graduate . . . , someone had the bright idea of admitting women and by September 1942 in they came scrambling like the oysters who walked up the beach with the Walrus and the Carpenter in Alice in Wonderland. . . . The aegis under which they entered bore the words, "for the duration." They may end as the oysters did, or, they may be v-e-r-y difficult to dislodge.[1]
>
> *Bremer Pond, 1944*

The first women who entered the landscape architecture program at Harvard University in 1942 – as reported by Bremer Pond, Chair of the Department of Landscape Architecture at the time – followed earlier generations who had been trained in the architecture and landscape architecture programs at the Massachusetts Institute of Technology; the Lowthorpe School of Landscape Architecture for Women, founded in 1901 in Groton, Massachusetts, by Judith Motley Low; the Pennsylvania School of Horticulture for Women begun by Jane Haines in Ambler, Pennsylvania, in 1910; and the Cambridge School of Architecture and Landscape Architecture founded in 1915 by Henry Atherton Frost in Cambridge, Massachusetts. Once admitted to the landscape architecture degree program at Harvard in 1942, women were indeed "difficult to dislodge." Like the first generations of professional female landscape architects in the United States and abroad – many of whom were self-taught or merely attended horticultural training schools for women – the first female Harvard graduates went on to shape the landscapes we inhabit today, and to form a profession that has by the twenty-first century achieved significant acclaim.

However, the histories of twentieth-century landscape architecture, and especially of women's contributions to the field, are still being written. In the last decades, increasing attention has been paid to what might be described as underreported narratives: those based on regional or period differences, for instance, or attentive to environmentalist ambitions.[2] The pace of research on women in landscape architecture has also accelerated, after some first initiatives in the 1980s.[3] Several monographs, anthologies, and scholarly books on their contributions to the field have appeared, such that we now have the beginnings of a detailed picture of the role of women in landscape design at both the start and the conclusion of the twentieth century.[4]

FIGURE 0.1 Herta Hammerbacher designing in the office. Courtesy Architekturmuseum TU Berlin.

Yet, amongst the aspects of this story that are still largely unexamined, is the place of women in the emergence of modernist landscape architecture in the decades just before and just after World War Two, and, conversely, the role of modernist ideals and aesthetics in the work of female landscape architects at this time. For example, in 1964, the Museum of Modern Art published Elizabeth Kessler's book *Modern Gardens and the Landscape*; although prepared by a woman, the book included no women beyond a glancing reference to Gertrude Jekyll. The expanded 1984 version of the book still included no women. The anthology *Modern Landscape Architecture: A Critical Review*, which appeared in 1993, featured the work of only one female designer and of a decidedly later generation: the contemporary landscape architect Martha Schwartz. Even the more recent publication, *Women in Landscape Architecture* (2012), concentrates on the founding generations, and not on those associated with modernism in the pre- or, in particular, the postwar years. Moreover, none of these publications in English looks outside of North America and Western Europe.

FIGURE 0.2 Sylvia Crowe at Swanley Horticultural College, Kent (from: Geoffrey Collins and Wendy Powell, eds., *Sylvia Crowe* [Reigate, Surrey: Landscape Design Trust, 1999], 12. Courtesy of Simon Crowe).

Broadened horizons and new perspectives

In contrast, *Women, Modernity, and Landscape Architecture* seeks to begin broadening the view, offering material for a comparative perspective. It assembles essays that deal with the lives and work of female landscape architects in Germany, Britain, Italy, Sweden, Russia, Austria, France, South Africa, New Zealand, the United States, Canada, and Brazil. This comparative perspective shows that landscape modernism emerged at different times in different cultures: earlier in Europe than in the Americas and other colonial societies. Women were a strong force in modernist landscape design in Russia, Scandinavia, and Western Europe by the late 1920s and 1930s, while, in the United States, women were not generally engaged with modernist ideas until the years after World War Two. Yet, landscape modernism can also be read as a transnational project.

As a variety of contributions in this volume show, female landscape architects were part of the early and subsequently more established professional international networks that spanned continents and generations; many traveled extensively as part of their own educational and professional development; and some even practiced in different countries. The female landscape architects presented here were both part of a larger international community that included their male colleagues and a group of individuals who shared similar experiences because of their professional affiliation and gender, but who, nevertheless, cannot be reduced to this common identifier because they came to the profession in different ways and contexts. As this volume shows, despite significant attempts at self-help in terms of career advancement (for example, some female practitioners only hired other women), most women followed their own individual paths into the profession, leaving us with many different and very personal stories. Although this volume has assembled these stories, both to highlight the female presence in the profession and to further a more nuanced understanding of recent landscape architectural history, female practitioners cannot be considered as a group with a shared agency. The grouping presented here is constructed and, while many personal and professional relationships and networks are uncovered in the following chapters, more research on these as well as shared and differing experiences is required.

Women were engaged in cross-cultural training and work, from England to South Africa and from Europe to America; they were also prominent in building the modern educational and professional institutions of landscape architecture. Some contributed to landscape architectural education through lecturing and studio teaching at universities, like Miranda Magnoli in Brazil, Isabelle Auricoste in France, and Geraldine Knight Scott in the United States; or they even assumed positions as university professors as in the cases of Herta Hammerbacher in Germany and Elizabeth May McAdams and Florence B. Robinson in the United States. Many women established their own firms, including Rosa Kliass in Brazil, Cornelia Oberlander in Canada, Carol Johnson in the United States, Sylvia Crowe in Britain, and Maria Teresa Parpagliolo in both Italy and England. Others assumed leadership positions in the public realm. In France, Marguerite Mercier worked for the planning authority of the new town of Saint-Quentin-en-Yvelines near Versailles before joining the regional development agency for the coast of Aquitaine and then working for the regional public works department in Gironde. Two of the most prominent first-generation Soviet landscape architects – Militsa Prokhorova and Liubov' Zalesskaia – were women; they worked in the 1930s at the Office of Planning of the Moscow Park of Culture and Leisure, a showcase public park directed by another woman, Betty Glan. Other women found corporate clients. In South Africa, Joane Pim worked with big mining conglomerates remediating mining compounds, designing planting strategies for the spoils piles that dominated mining communities in South Africa's bleak interior and a master plan for the new mining city of Welkom in the Northern Free State (see Plate 0.1). In California, Ruth Shellhorn became the go-to person for Disneyland and Bullock's Department Stores.

Women, Modernity, and Landscape Architecture, therefore, seeks to revise current gendered and national readings of modernism and modernity, and to contribute to the development of a more nuanced, balanced, and integrated landscape architectural historiography of the twentieth century.[5] Although this book assembles essays on female practitioners, the aim is not to substitute a feminine view for a masculine one. Instead, by uncovering the hidden careers of some neglected female landscape architects in various regions of the world and by highlighting how they both collaborated with their male colleagues and stood their own ground, the essays in this volume also shed new light on heretofore little or entirely unknown parts of recent landscape architectural history. Thus, as shown in Sonja Dümpelmann's chapter, landscape historian Jeong-Hi Go's work on Herta Hammerbacher and the study of Maria Theresa Parpagliolo's career have uncovered new insights into German and Italian landscape architects' involvement in Nazi and fascist planning projects. These studies have also shown how landscape architecture offered women – whose role the chauvinist regimes sought to confine to homemaking, childbearing and child-rearing – a professional opportunity, despite the discrimination they faced. Besides the politicization of design, the politics of design are also revealed in Zeuler R. M. de A. Lima's essay in this volume. He shows that wealthy female activists played an important role in the design process of some of Brazil's signature landscape architecture projects like Roberto Burle Marx's Flamengo Landfill Project. Alla G. Vronskaya's chapter on pioneering female landscape architects in Soviet Russia and the Soviet Union brings to the fore the connection between kinesthetics, modernist functionalism, and public park planning in communist Russia, as well as professional landscape architecture's early twentieth-century association with urbanism and public urban landscapes in this country. By focusing on three female practitioners who reached maturity in the postwar years, Bernadette Blanchon uncovers landscape architecture's role in postwar modernist housing developments in France, also shedding light on the opening of landscape architecture to the social sciences that occurred in this period and that, for some, was based on the Marxist teachings of Henri Lefevbre. The postwar career of landscape pioneer Joane Pim, presented by Jeremy Foster, further expands this discussion by drawing attention to the often-overlooked relationship between labor relations and landscape architecture in the distinct geographical and political context of South Africa. While Foster shows how Pim considered landscape a means to improve not only devastated mining sites but also social relations in a country characterized by apartheid, Thaïsa Way's essay on female practitioners in the United States contributes to today's rising interest in the critical assessment of environmental ethics in landscape architecture.

Critical global and regional histories of landscape modernism

In comparison to many other professional women of their generation, pioneering female landscape architects tended to be comparatively mobile, thus defying the association of women with the local and women's history with localized histories.[6] Not only did they travel for educational purposes to study, explore sites and historic landscapes, and attend conferences (Figures 0.3 and 0.4), but also, like their male colleagues, they designed landscapes in various places, often traveling hundreds of miles for site visits. Because of the lack of training and education in their home countries, women, more often than men, were forced to live in other countries already known for their design and horticultural education. The stories of female landscape architects, therefore, require a global or transnational outlook that not only enables comparison but also an integration of individual stories into larger, international contexts. At the same time, histories of landscape architecture cannot be told without the study of the respective local contexts and environments. They are locally situated, or grounded. As elaborated on by Catharina Nolin in this volume, the lack of training facilities in Sweden led some young women from this country to train in horticultural training schools in Britain and in offices in Germany. When they returned to Sweden, the knowledge gained in these countries was adapted to their respective Swedish contexts (see Plate 0.2).

Thus, women actively contributed to the development of landscape architecture as a product of modernity and modernization characterized by a tension between the local and the global. We follow a by-now familiar practice of distinguishing modernization, revolutions in production, transportation, and communication characteristic of the modern world, from

FIGURE 0.3 Sylvia Crowe in front of the caravan that she and her colleague Brenda Colvin used to tour in Britain. Brenda Colvin Collection. Courtesy Museum of English Rural Life, University of Reading.

FIGURE 0.4 A program session of the 1956 IFLA Congress at the Swiss Federal Institute of Technology in Zurich. (Photograph by A. Jansen, published in Merel S. Sager, "International Landscape: The Formal Meetings of the Fifth IFLA Congress," *Landscape Architecture* 47, no. 1 [1957]: 232–325 [232].) Reprinted with permission from the American Society of Landscape Architects.

modernity, the cultural conditions that resulted from modernization, notably transformations in labor and social relations. And we distinguish both of these from modernism, the set of styles or cultural codes that came to be regarded as expressive of modernity.[7] We have been careful in the title of this volume to refer to modernity rather than modernism, for while all of the women presented in this anthology participated in some measure in modernity – especially in those aspects related to individual emancipation and growing professional opportunities for women – not all participated equally in modernism; not all, that is, worked in a style characterized by new formal expression and material innovation that might be described as modernist. Indeed, many employed what could be termed transitional or modernizing styles. For example, the *Wohngarten* paradigm was advanced by many pioneering European women in the early decades of their careers, especially in Germany and Austria; as Ulrike Krippner and Iris Meder show in this volume, the *Wohngarten* provided several Jewish women in Vienna the opportunity to grow their design practices. It might be described as an expression of vernacular modernism, or "naturalist modern." That is, it was a style that, in part, sought to imitate nature and was, therefore, little interested in the exploration of new, especially geometric formal expression, but which, nevertheless, addressed the modern human needs for active outdoor life and the continuity of indoor and outdoor space.[8] Yet, almost all the women presented in this book addressed the challenges of the modern world – notably, on the one hand, landscapes of infrastructure and industrial production and, on the other, public landscapes of an expansive urbanization. Many of them, like Miranda Magnoli and Rosa Kliass in Brazil, worked for, or were commissioned by, local park departments, thereby strengthening the commitments of urban governments to the public environment. Female landscape architects were also involved as consultants in large-scale land management projects and in the landscape planning and design of entire new urban neighborhoods. They did not stand behind their male colleagues when it came to broadening the professional field in the postwar years, and entering the urban realm, or public sphere.

This is not to say, however, that some of these women were not avowedly modernist. In postwar California, suburban house gardens modeled on the "Southern California Look" became pervasive, not least as a result of Ruth Shellhorn's design practice, which Kelly Comras presents in her chapter in this book. Other landscape modernisms developed, for instance, by Mina Klabin and Rosa Kliass in Brazil, testify to women's interest in the combination of the aesthetics and social purpose of design characteristic of the modern era. Modern designs that could, at the same time, fulfill their social purpose also lay at the heart of German-born Cornelia Oberlander's work in Canada. As presented by Susan Herrington in this book, Oberlander used design methodologies learnt during her studies at the Harvard Graduate School of Design in the 1940s. Applying and elaborating on these methodologies, which included abstraction and syncopation – i.e. spatial design that created moments of suspense and surprise – Oberlander developed a successful practice providing designs for private and public clients alike. Although many women began their careers firmly grounded in the history and horticultural knowledge of the profession, many quickly broadened their design vocabulary to respond to the changing tasks of the profession, or even became a "model modern," as Susan Herrington argues in the case of Oberlander.

Designing across spheres

Landscape design provided women with both a chance and a challenge, offering them opportunities to enter the male-dominated professional world. For many women, landscape design appeared as a logical choice, as it originated in garden design and horticulture, which, by the nineteenth century, were often seen as domestic pursuits coded female because of their association with the home and homemaking. Working with nature and creating place added an additional legitimization to women's work as landscape designers, as, of course, the female body has throughout history been identified with nature and the home.[9] This general coding, however, did not prevent their male colleagues from responding to the female entry into the professional work force with reactions that ranged from hesitation to disbelief and downright exasperation – even aggressive disapproval. In 1892, the director of the Arnold Arboretum in Boston, Charles Sprague Sargent, questioned women's abilities outside the small flower garden. He contended that landscape gardening on a large scale was "a masculine art" requiring "a certain manly vigor of treatment, an unhesitating despotism, that the gentler sex deprecate as cruel and unnecessary."[10] Two years later, his landscape architecture colleague Charles Eliot endorsed Marianna Schuyler Van Rensselaer's book *Art-Out-of-Doors* (1893), yet criticized its representation of the young profession. With its focus on gardens, shrubberies, and parks, he found the book neglected "the village, the factory, and the railroad yard" and ignored "the essentially virile and practical nature of the art and profession," which, as he explained, had to "be founded in rationality, purpose, fitness."[11] Around the same time in Germany, the garden journal *Möller's Deutsche Gärtner-Zeitung* launched attacks against the first horticultural schools for women and the women's movement more largely in the form of cartoons that illustrated what was considered by many an innate female unpreparedness for professional life in general and gardening in particular (Figures 0.5 and 0.6). Some decades later, opposition had softened somewhat; in 1930, the German arborist and garden architect Camillo Karl Schneider, in reference to the women-led American Garden Clubs, welcomed women's engagement in house garden design. Perceiving a lack of quality in many garden designs, Schneider argued that gardens had, until then, been designed "based upon male psychology."[12]

Yet, in the founding years of the profession, male colleagues and commentators at best relegated women's professional roles to house garden design and planting, enforcing the separation of male and female spheres that were associated with public life, production, and culture, on the one hand, and privacy, home, reproduction, and nature, on the other. However, it was this initial separation of spheres and the relegation of women to house garden design that provided some of them not only with an entry into the professional workforce in the first place, but also gave them a springboard into the expanded field of landscape architecture. Landscape design was a means for them to actively bridge the spheres.

Gebildete Gärtner-Damen.

FIGURE 0.5 Cartoon published in *Möller's Deutsche Gärtner-Zeitung*, titled "Educated female garden ladies." (*Möller's Deutsche Gärtner-Zeitung* 11 [1896]: 440–441.)

FIGURE 0.6   Cartoon published in *Möller's Deutsche Gärtner-Zeitung*, titled "Training of educated ladies in carrying liquid fertilizer." (*Möller's Deutsche Gärtner-Zeitung* 11 [1896]: 123.)

As shown by the professionals featured in this volume, female landscape designers have often avoided expressing feminist views openly, or they have not been interested in actively engaging in feminist agendas and politics. Some women, however, were implicit, or even more or less explicit, in voicing feminist positions. Perhaps because of the inherent nature of the profession that quite literally deals with natural features like plants and has its origins in the domestic sphere, many practitioners presented in this volume embraced both of the two prevalent feminist positions:[13] they turned their "otherness" into a strength on the one hand, and sought maximum equality on the other hand. However, a number either sided with the one or the other attitude more explicitly. Thus, some women actively embraced their "otherness" and women's values to push for physical transformations in design, and, in some cases, even societal change. They used their plant knowledge to good effect, like Mae Arbegast; they designed for women as users, like Marjorie Sewell Cautley (Figure 0.7); and they helped spread new design paradigms like the *Wohngarten*, as in the case of Anna Plischke and Helene Wolf. Others, like Herta Hammerbacher, Sylvia Crowe, and Isabelle Auricoste, worked against the historically constructed separation of spheres seeking to achieve total equality in a shared arena with men.

Yet, in 1944, even as the first female students were matriculating at Harvard and as the first generation of female landscape architects in Europe and the United States were reaching maturity in their careers, the Harvard women were seen as domesticating the studio environment. Thus, the landscape architecture department secretary Marion Kohlrausch reported in a letter to alumnus Charles Burns on "the feminine influence" remarking that, "They don't

FIGURE 0.7   Interior garden courtyard with playgrounds for small children at Sunnyside Gardens, Queens, NYC, designed by Marjorie Sewell Cautley. (Photograph published in Albert G. Hinman and G. Coleman Woodbury, "Landscape Architecture's Role in Modern Housing Projects," *American Landscape Architect* 1 [October 1929]: 9–15, 40 [11].)

seem to be too great a nuisance." The female presence was, however, sensed quite literally through the smell of bacon as a result of the women's initiative to cook breakfast in the basement drafting room:

> When they [the female students] first arrived they had what might be called a luncheon club – a coeducational one, where the male was broken gently to the mysteries of cooking soup, washing dishes all in collaboration, you understand with the alluring female, you know Jack and Jill did it one day and Mike and Mary the next, in groups, of course. It was great sport when the odors began to waft up to the first floor – it all took place in the basement drafting room. Sometimes they had breakfasts too. Perhaps you never realized it but there are times when the odor of bacon just doesn't fit – at least not with marble corridors, etc. Also, when they plugged in their electric apparatus, it usually blew out the lights in one of the professor's office – he was that type of snapping goldfish professor and he used to furnish a bit of excitement as he would come out on the roar – he didn't like to smell bacon at 10:45 in the morning either.[14]

Whereas female students were seen as domesticating the studio environment by "infesting" it with the smell of bacon, in the world of landscape architectural practice, women like Ruth Shellhorn built their careers by working on designs for the domestic sphere, actively fostering a group of female middle-class clients.

On the other hand, women were also among the first practitioners who embraced large public commissions and the design of public urban or even regional landscapes. In the 1920s and 1930s, Militsa Prokhorova and Liubov' Zalesskaia helped design the Moscow Park of Culture and Leisure. During World War Two, the German landscape architect Herta Hammerbacher produced landscape plans for towns in the annexed Eastern territories. Maria Teresa Parpagliolo was in charge of the planning team for the parks and gardens of the Roman World's Exhibition site planned for 1942.

These women actively began to shape the public sphere, space that had, until the early twentieth century, largely been considered a male domain. By the mid-twentieth century, in fact, the activity of female landscape architects in the public realm had led to a new situation: for the first time, women could inhabit urban space designed by and, in some cases, for women. *Women, Modernity, and Landscape Architecture* seeks to complement studies that have appeared in the last decades on women and urban history.[15] These publications have focused on women's institutions and their relationships to the city, especially in the second half of the nineteenth century and in the early twentieth century, and they have only marginally, or not until recently, offered further insights into how women have literally shaped the city through their own architecture.[16] *Women, Modernity, and Landscape Architecture* contributes individual stories that direct attention instead to the design and shaping of the open spaces and infrastructure networks of the city, to their actual making and materialization, and to the lives of their female creators. Focusing on the period of the inter- and postwar years, and on selected parts of the world, this book shows how women have contributed to urban modernization in very concrete ways.

Many of the pioneering female landscape architects were also vocal advocates and representatives of their profession, assuming leadership roles in national and international organizations like the International Federation of Landscape Architects (Figure 0.8). Although many were operating across national borders, attending conferences, going on study tours, and accepting commissions in different countries, the strategies and methodologies the women employed to reach their positions and hold their ground depended very much on distinct local contexts and their individual characters and interests. In some cases, women partnered with their husbands who worked as architects, or who, in rare cases, even supported their female partner's practice through other types of work. Other women built a female client base, or they supported each other by training younger generations and sharing workspaces and projects. Teaching and writing figured high in female landscape architects' chosen tasks. While these were activities traditionally associated with the female sphere they were also a necessary means for shaping and building a more robust foundation for a young profession. Using social conventions to achieve professional goals could be another way to circumvent more explicit discrimination, get the job done, and turn a challenge into an opportunity, as some of the chapters in this book show.

We hope that this book will add complexity and depth to understandings of the histories of women, modernity, and landscape architecture, and that these understandings might be valuable to the present. As more and more women enter the profession, it is essential for them and their male colleagues to know something of the women who went before them – the personal and professional challenges they faced, and the accomplishments they managed nevertheless. As younger practitioners claim authorship of innovative ideas in design, whether urbanist, infrastructural, social, or stylistic, it is important for them to know how these ideas were anticipated and articulated in the work of earlier generations. As sustaining and restoring biodiversity have increasingly emerged as crucial tasks for contemporary practice, and as knowledge of the relationships between human and nonhuman nature become ever more

FIGURE 0.8 Ulla Bodorff from Sweden (IFLA Honorary Treasurer), flanked by the American landscape architect Hubert B. Owens (left; IFLA Honorary Secretary), and the IFLA President René Pechère from Belgium (right), at the 1956 IFLA conference in Switzerland. (Photograph by Reinhart Besserer, published in Stuart M. Mertz, "An IFLA Exhibition at Zurich," *Landscape Architecture* 47, no. 1 [1957]: 326–327 [326].) Reprinted with permission from the American Society of Landscape Architects.

central to the discipline, there is much to be learned – by men and women alike – from the horticultural, ecological, and social aspects of women's practice in the modern era. We also hope that the book will inspire other comparable efforts at research. There is much still to be said, not only about the women in this volume, but also about others like them whose stories have yet to be told. And there are narratives from other parts of the globe that await recovery. What of those places in the world where the democratizing and emancipatory effects of modernization, especially with respect to women, have been slower to take hold? Who are the women working in landscape architecture or comparable professions and activities in these societies, and is design culture the richer for it?

Although we focus on women, our ambition here is to further a larger goal: to aid in uncovering neglected histories of landscape architecture altogether. The essays assembled here show that it remains an open question how far landscape architecture was an emancipatory occupation. Was landscape architecture in the modern era as beneficial socially and as progressive ideologically as its proponents sometimes claimed? Who did it serve, and to what ends? Within its modernizing agenda, did men and women play similar roles, or did women design differently from men? Under which circumstances did women take into account human needs that may have been neglected by men? By focusing on the inter- and postwar period, the contributions to this volume also shed light on the still relatively young history of landscape architecture itself, and on the emergent qualities and challenges of professional practice. Serving public and private interests of varying characters (some of which we might still embrace, while repudiating others), reacting to global developments, yet creating – and firmly grounding – humans in specific localities and places, the careers of the women presented here illustrate a developing practice that operated on a variety of scales and addressed a growing range of social and environmental challenges. We offer this anthology as a tribute to the women whom we know to have blazed trails in modern landscape architecture, to those whose histories are yet to be recovered, and to those women – and men – who today are still following in their footsteps. But it is also our hope that this volume might encourage further critical engagement with, and analysis and interpretation of, the larger histories of landscape architecture – still one of the least well known and arguably most underappreciated of the arts.

NOTES

1 Newsletter from Department of Landscape Architecture, December 5, 1944, signed by Bremer Pond. Correspondence with students and alumni, 1942−1946. UAV 322.442, Graduate School of Design, Harvard University Archives.

2 See, for example, Therese O'Malley and Marc Treib, eds., *Regional Garden Design in the United States* (Washington, D.C.: Dumbarton Oaks Research Library and Collection, 1995); Michel Conan, ed., *Environmentalism in Landscape Architecture* (Washington, D.C.: Dumbarton Oaks Research Library and Collection, 2000).

3 See, for example, Catherine R. Brown and Celia Newton Maddox, "Women and the Land: 'A Suitable Profession'," *Landscape Architecture* 72, no. 3 (1982): 64−69; Catherine M. Howett, "Careers in Landscape Architecture: Recovering for Women What the 'Ladies' Won and Lost," in *Feminist Visions*, ed. by Diane L. Fowlkes and Charlotte S. McClure (Tuscaloosa, AL: The University of Alabama Press, 1984), 139−148; Deborah Nevins, "The Triumph of Flora: Women and the American Landscape, 1890−1935," *Magazine Antiques* CXXVII (April 1985): 904−922; for the first symposium on women in landscape architecture, see the issue of *Landscape Journal*, introduced by Karen Madsen and John F. Furlong, "Introduction: Women Land Design: Considering Connections," *Landscape Journal* 13, no. 2 (1994): 88−101; Diane Kostial McGuire and Lois Fern, eds., *Beatrix Jones Farrand (1872−1959): Fifty Years of American Landscape Architecture* (Dumbarton Oaks Colloquium on the History of Landscape Architecture, VIII: Washington, D.C.: Dumbarton Oaks, Trustees for Harvard University, 1982).

4 See, for example, Susan Herrington, *Cornelia Hahn Oberlander: Making the Modern Landscape* (Charlottesville: University of Virginia Press, 2014); Judith K. Major, *Mariana Griswold Van Rensselaer: A Landscape Critic in the Gilded Age* (Charlottesville: University of Virginia Press, 2013); Kristine F. Miller, *Almost Home: The Public Landscapes of Gertrude Jekyll* (Charlottesville: University of Virginia Press; Amsterdam: [published] by arrangement with Architectura & Natura, 2013); Trish Gibson, *Brenda Colvin: A Career in Landscape* (London: Frances Lincoln, 2011); Thaïsa Way, *Unbounded Practice* (Charlottesville and London: University of Virginia Press, 2009); Cynthia Zaitzevsky, *Long Island Landscapes and the Women Who Designed Them* (New York: Society for the Preservation of Long Island Antiquities: in association with W. W. Norton & Co., 2009); Eran Ben-Joseph, *Against All Odds: MIT's Pioneering Women of Landscape Architecture* (Cambridge, MA: MIT, School of Architecture and Planning, 2006); Marta Isnenghi, ed., *Donne di fiori: paesaggi al femminile* (Milano: Mondadori Electa, 2005); Sonja Dümpelmann, *Maria Teresa Parpagliolo Shephard (1903−1974): Ein Beitrag zur Geschichte der Gartenkultur in Italien im 20. Jahrhundert* (Weimar: VDG, 2004); Anke Schekahn, *Spurensuche. 1700−1933, Frauen in der Disziplingeschichte der Frairaum- und Landschaftsplanung*, Arbeitsberichte des Fachbereichs Stadtplanung/Landschaftsplanung no. 144 (Kassel: Universität Gesamthochschule Kassel, 2000); Geoffrey Collens and Wendy Powell, eds., *Sylvia Crowe* (Reigate, Surrey, England: Landscape Design Trust, 1999); Judith B. Tankard, *The Gardens of Ellen Biddle Shipman* (Sagaponack, NY: Sagapress, 1996).

5 For a first call for a revisionist landscape architectural history and pointing out the role that attention to women in the profession can play in this history, see Heath Schenker, "Feminist Interventions in the Histories of Landscape Architecture," *Landscape Journal* 13, no. 2 (Fall 1994): 107−112.

6 For a discussion of female and male gendering and the local and the global, see Doreen Massey, *Space, Place, and Gender* (Minneapolis: University of Minnesota Press, 1994), 9.

7   See, for instance, Marshall Berman, *All That Is Solid Melts into Air: The Experience of Modernity* (New York: Simon and Schuster, 1982), especially the Introduction; and David Harvey, *The Condition of Postmodernity* (Cambridge, MA, and Oxford, UK: Blackwell, 1990), especially chapter 2, "Modernity and Modernism," and chapter 5, "Modernization."

8   For a definition of "naturalist modern" and other terms to describe twentieth-century designed landscapes, see Marc Treib, "Landscapes Transitional, Modern, Modernistic, Modernist," *Journal of Landscape Architecture* 8, no. 1 (2013): 6–15. Treib's essay is a good overview of the different levels of engagement with modernist ideas.

9   See, for example, Carolyn Merchant, *Reinventing Eden: The Fate of Nature in Western Culture* (New York: Routledge, 2013); Carolyn Merchant, *Earthcare* (New York: Routledge, 1996); Carolyn Merchant, *The Death of Nature: Women, Ecology, and the Scientific Revolution* (San Francisco: Harper & Row, 1989); Annette Kolodney, *Lay of the Land: Metaphor as Experience and History in American Life and Letters* (Chapel Hill: University of North Carolina Press, 1975). For the nature–culture/female–male binary in relation to landscape architecture, see Elizabeth Meyer, "The Expanded Field of Landscape Architecture," in *Ecological Design and Planning*, ed. by George F. Thompson and Frederick R. Steiner, 45–79 (New York: John Wiley & Sons, Inc.); and the overview by Karen Madsen and John F. Furlong, "Women, Land, Design: Considering Connections," *Landscape Journal* 13, no. 2 (Fall 1994): 89–101.

10 Charles Sprague Sargent, "Taste Indoors and Out," *Garden and Forest* 5, no. 233 (1892): 373–374.

11 Charles W. Eliot, ed., *Charles Eliot Landscape Architect* (Boston and New York: Houghton Mifflin, 1902), 546–547. See also Judith Tankard, "Women Take the Lead in Landscape Art," in *Women in Landscape Architecture*, ed. by Louise Mozingo and Linda Jewell (Jefferson, NC, and London: McFarland & Company, 2012), 84.

12 C[amillo]. S[chneider], "Um den kommenden Garten," *Die Gartenschönheit/Gartenwerk* 11, no. 1 (1930): 3–5 (5).

13 For the two prevalent positions see, for example, Carolyn Merchant, *Earthcare* (New York: Routledge, 1996), 183–184.

14 Miss K[ohlrausch], letter to Charles Burns, July 11, 1944. UAV 322.442, Graduate School of Design, correspondence with students and alumni, 1942–1946, Harvard University Archives.

15 See Daphne Spain, *How Women Saved the City* (Minneapolis: University of Minnesota Press, 2001); Daphne Spain, *Gendered Spaces* (Chapel Hill: University of North Carolina Press, 1992); Sarah Deutsch, *Women and the City: Gender, Space, and Power in Boston, 1870–1940* (Oxford and New York: Oxford University Press, 2000); Elizabeth York Enstam, *Women and the Creation of Urban Life: Dallas, Texas, 1843–1920* (College Station: Texas A & M University Press, 1998).

16 See Despina Stratigakos, *A Women's Berlin: Building the Modern City* (Minneapolis and London: University of Minnesota Press, 2008); Dolores Hayden, *The Grand Domestic Revolution* (Cambridge and London: The MIT Press, 1981).

1

CREATING NEW LANDSCAPES FOR OLD EUROPE

Herta Hammerbacher, Sylvia Crowe, Maria Teresa Parpagliolo

Sonja Dümpelmann

At the opening of the first International Conference of Landscape Architecture in London in 1948, which led to the foundation of the International Federation of Landscape Architects (IFLA), eight landscape architects sat on the podium: four men and four women (Figure 1.1).[1] This gender equality did not, however, reflect the true percentage of women and men in the profession at the time – women were and still are in the minority. Neither did it influence subsequent historiographies in which women have been largely neglected. However, it does attest to the fact that the still relatively young discipline of landscape architecture provided women with an opportunity to enter the professional world, despite discrimination and doubts on the part of many of their male colleagues. As Thaïsa Way has shown, women can be portrayed as "a force in landscape architecture" playing an active role in the profession's development rather than as passive professionals "helplessly subject to men."[2] In fact, as Karen Madsen and John Furlong pointed out in 1994, "garden and landscape architecture has also been a tool for women's emancipation."[3] The three women discussed in this essay were pioneers of the profession in Europe, and they both created and seized the opportunities of this young profession. The German landscape architect Herta Hammerbacher (1900–1985), and her British and Italian colleagues Sylvia Crowe (1901–1997) and Maria Teresa Parpagliolo (1903–1974), perceived landscape architecture as a chance to lead independent professional lives at a time when most women's activities were still limited to housekeeping and child-rearing in the shadow of their husbands' businesses and professional lives.

The international conference had been proposed in 1946 by another woman: Lady Allen of Hurtwood.[4] As Marjorie Allen, she had received some informal gardeners' training during the World War One years. After a diploma course in horticulture at University College, Reading, she had designed and promoted the establishment of roof gardens in the 1920s and 1930s and she was elected the first fellow of the British Institute of Landscape Architects in 1930. In the 1940s and 1950s, she campaigned for the implementation of adventure playgrounds in Britain, following the example of C. Th. Sørensen's first adventure playground in Emdrup, Denmark, in the early 1940s.[5] On the occasion of the 1948 conference, Allen shared the podium with the female landscape architects Brenda Colvin,[6] Maria Teresa Parpagliolo Shephard and Sylvia Crowe. Crowe had chaired the organizing committee, and her Italian-born colleague Maria Teresa Parpagliolo Shephard participated in the meeting in a variety of functions, including that of

FIGURE 1.1 Four female and four male landscape architects were on the podium at the inauguration of the first International Conference of Landscape Architects, in London in 1948. The Duke of Wellington, standing on the left, is opening the conference and exhibition. To his right are Walter Owen from the London County Council, the landscape architects Geoffrey A. Jellicoe, E. Prentice Mawson, Edward Wink and Sylvia Crowe. Seated in the front row from left to right are landscape architects Lady Allen of Hurtwood, Richard Sudell, the secretary of the Institute of Landscape Architects Mrs. Douglas Browne and the landscape architects Brenda Colvin and Maria Teresa Parpagliolo Shephard. (Russell H. Butler and Loutrel W. Briggs, "The International Conference with the Institute of Landscape Architects as Hosts," *Landscape Architecture* 39 (1949): 72–75 [72].)

translating, organizing the accompanying exhibition and leading some of the conference tours. Not present at the venue was the German landscape designer Herta Hammerbacher, whose work was influential in Maria Teresa Parpagliolo's early years as a professional. Like all her German colleagues, Hammerbacher was excluded from participation at the conference, due to Germany's role in World War Two. This chapter foregrounds relevant similarities in these women's careers, in their working methods and in their roles in furthering the profession. Concentrating on the years when these women's careers reached maturity in the 1950s, 1960s and 1970s, it also draws attention to specific events that led the lives of these women to converge directly or indirectly, even if only for short periods.

Hammerbacher, Crowe and Parpagliolo had many things in common.[7] They were of the same generation, born at the beginning of the twentieth century into liberal middle-class families. While their mothers had provided them with independent progressive female role models they found male mentors to introduce them to their prospective careers as landscape architects. Hammerbacher's first position was among male colleagues in the design studio of the tree nursery Ludwig Späth. With a degree from the horticultural school in Berlin-Dahlem, she prepared drawings and construction documents for designs by Otto Valentien (1897–1987) and Carl Kemkes (1881–1964), a position she soon considered unsatisfying.[8] Crowe trained for a while under the landscape architect Edward White (1872–1953) in London. Due to a lack of opportunities in her own country, Parpagliolo spent several months of training in the office of the British garden designer Percy Stephen Cane (1881–1976). The women began their professional education at horticultural colleges in the cases of Hammerbacher (Lehr- und Forschungsanstalt für Gartenbau Berlin-Dahlem) and Crowe (Swanley Horticultural College). Due to a lack of such colleges in Italy, Parpagliolo learned about botany and plants on her own. Their first works as landscape architects were closely related to the domestic sphere, focusing on planting and private house garden designs. However, this was the major area of occupation for European landscape designers in general at the time and, in many cases, women tended to acquire skills while working on house garden designs for members of their social networks. Although it was a woman – the German Countess Ursula Dohna – who, as early as 1874 under the pseudonym Arminius, drew attention to the necessity of "green rings" and other public open spaces in European cities, including kindergartens and playgrounds, the first garden designers to embark on the design of public urban parks and other public landscapes in Europe were men. Many of them had been trained on the job during their journeymen's years or had been educated in the first horticultural schools founded in the early nineteenth century, such as the royal gardener's training school near Berlin.[9]

Hammerbacher, Crowe and Parpagliolo were also prolific writers on a variety of subjects that included planting and garden design, and later urban design and broader environmental issues. Besides several commonalities in their biographies and careers, there were also points of direct contact among the three women. In fact, their paths crossed on a number of occasions, and they influenced each other in their work. For example, Parpagliolo's writings and designs in the 1930s show diverse references to Hammerbacher's house gardens and design philosophy. It appears that in 1933 she even copied the general layout of Hammerbacher's design for the 1931 garden of the Poelzig House in Berlin-Grünewald and adopted some of its design elements.[10] When the Italian visited Germany in 1936 and 1938, Hammerbacher very likely belonged to the group of German colleagues with whom she met. Furthermore, after Parpagliolo had married the Englishman Ronald Shephard in 1946, she moved to England and worked on projects in Sylvia Crowe's newly established London office. In the same year, she collaborated on the design and planting recommendations for dune gardens in Mablethorpe on the Lincolnshire coast, a project for the reconstruction of a shoreline that had been largely transformed during World War Two, due to the construction of fortifications. An event that all three women attended and that was to influence their work was the 1964 IFLA conference in Japan, on which both Hammerbacher and Parpagliolo subsequently reported.

Hammerbacher, Crowe and Parpagliolo represent a group of independent professional women who, by the postwar years, had established themselves and had gained a high profile in their respective countries, if not internationally. They actively seized the new opportunities the profession offered in the postwar years. This meant they became involved in a variety of large-scale projects as landscape architects and consultants. Hammerbacher and Crowe embarked on projects that involved them as landscape consultants and architects for the new towns, Harlow and Basildon (Crowe), and the International Building Exhibition Interbau in Berlin (Hammerbacher). In 1954, Parpagliolo was one of the first Italian landscape architects to work for an Italian development company. Although Catherine Howett and Thaïsa Way have observed for the United States that "feminine visibility in the profession declined radically" in the war and postwar years,[11] the women discussed here seized the new possibilities the profession offered after Word War Two and held representative, influential and visible positions. In fact, in 1946 Sylvia Crowe, together with her colleague Brenda Colvin, successfully argued against the merging of the Institute of Landscape Architects with the Royal Institute of British Architects.[12] Having approached the field from its horticultural side rather than from architecture, as many of their male colleagues did, Crowe and Colvin were perhaps more able and more interested in seeing and maintaining a division between the two disciplines. Crowe received various honors for her work and, in 1969, was elected the first female president of IFLA. Hammerbacher became the first female professor of landscape architecture at a German university, and Parpagliolo collaborated with Pietro Porcinai (1910–1986) in an attempt to found a school for landscape architecture in Italy, a first step that smoothed the way for the organization of a qualified and professional landscape architecture practice in that country.

Not uncharacteristically for professionals of their generation, Hammerbacher, Crowe and Parpagliolo embraced modernist agendas while remaining grounded in the past. The women achieved this grounding literally by their interest in garden history, on the one hand, and in planting design, on the other. And while all three women used their plant knowledge extensively, they also pushed the profession's boundaries by engaging in large-scale design and planning projects. They can, therefore, be described as figures of transition. Working on a variety of scales, their designs were works of synthesis that sought to elevate and promote the profession while, at the same time, firmly grounding it in its past.

Herta Hammerbacher: Hansaviertel and *Stadtlandschaft*

Creating a synthesis out of house and garden, landscape and city was the conceptual approach used by Herta Hammerbacher throughout her career (Figure 1.2). Born in 1900, she studied at the Höhere Lehr- und Forschungsanstalt für Gartenbau in Berlin-Dahlem from 1924 to 1926. Hammerbacher's subsequent work as a young landscape architect, leading up to and through the years of World War Two, predominantly involved domestic garden designs, some of which she used to illustrate her 1970s publication on house gardens in Berlin. In the years 1935–1948, she worked in partnership with her first husband Hermann Mattern and the plant breeder Karl Foerster, developing the design principles that would guide the small- and large-scale designs she produced throughout her career. Herbaceous plants and shrubs as well as ground modulation using s-curves were used to make space[13] and to establish connections between house and garden – perceived of as an outdoor room – and the larger landscape (Figure 1.3). The idea of blending house and garden into the surrounding landscape was later paralleled by the idea of merging landscape and city. Although being a woman prevented her from participating in the motorway projects promoted by the Nazi regime – a prestigious, well-paid and secure job – she engaged in other projects for the regime that led her to work in distant locations and on larger scales during the World War Two years.[14] The projects included work commissioned by the Nazi Operation Todt, such as the landscape planning for war worker housing and for towns in the occupied territories in Poland (Plate 1.1).

Despite her involvement with commissions for the regime, in 1946, she became a lecturer in landscape and garden design at the Department of Architecture and Urban Planning at the Technical University Berlin (TU Berlin); and in 1950 she was the first German woman to hold a professorship in the field and at the TU Berlin. Teaching architecture and urban planning students the principles of garden architecture and landscape planning enhanced her

FIGURE 1.2 Herta Hammerbacher (right) explaining a plan to her client Elsbeth Heddenhausen, 1930s. Courtesy Architekturmuseum TU Berlin.

own interest in broader urban planning issues.[15] She had developed the principle of merging the landscape with architecture on the intimate scale of her early house garden designs and, in the war and postwar years, began to apply it to her urban designs and plans, in the latter case using many of the ideas that had been promoted and further developed by urban planners and architects working for the Nazi regime. The "city landscape" (*Stadtlandschaft*), a paradigm coined and developed in the 1920s by the geographer Siegfried Passarge, had first been adopted and used by German urban planners in 1929.[16] From what had initially been a term to describe the zone of transition between the city and its hinterland, or periphery, and the relationship between urban form and rural surroundings, in urban planning *Stadtlandschaft* came to denote an urban landscape characterized by a dispersed settlement pattern. Planners under the Nazi regime used it to describe the urban design concept of the so-called "settlement cells" that was less vulnerable against aerial attack. The "settlement cells" were neighborhood units whose size corresponded to the organized units of the Nazi party. Based on

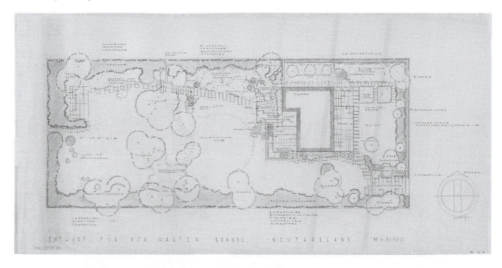

FIGURE 1.3   Herta Hammerbacher, design for the garden Brandl, Neu Fahrland, April 1937.
Pencil on trace paper. The design includes a swale in the open lawn (Rasenmulde),
a characteristic of many of her house gardens designs. Courtesy Architekturmuseum
TU Berlin.

an idea promoted by the German architects Hans Berhard Reichow, Wilhelm Wortmann
and Friedrich Heuer in 1940, it was subsequently used in the preparation for the 1944 master
plan (*Generalbebauungsplan*) for Hamburg.[17] Indeed, during and after World War Two, some
planners entertained ideas of reconstructing the cities of Berlin and Hamburg with dispersed
settlements surrounding large central park areas.[18] While these visions were never realized,
the "city landscape" paradigm nevertheless dominated much of the discourse at the time. In
1948, the landscape architect Reinhold Lingner, who served as director of the Municipal
Parks Department Berlin from 1945 until 1950 and helped draw up the 1946 reconstruction plan (*Kollektivplan*) for Berlin in 1946, argued that, in the "city landscape," the terrain
and natural features like creeks, rivers and woods should determine urban form. Greenways
encompassing fruit orchards, vegetable plots, pastureland, forests, as well as paths, roads and
railroads were to structure the city and cater to the citizens' recreation. The "city landscape"
could address the technical, economic, social and ecological, besides the aesthetic concerns of
urban development. Science could, according to Lingner, also lead to a satisfyingly pleasant
urban form.[19]

Hammerbacher's holistic and organic approach to city building, in which landscape was
supposed to form a unified whole with the urban fabric while at the same time ordering and
structuring it, was based on the "city landscape," a pervasive idea among designers engaged
in the reconstruction of German cities at the time. "City landscape" also played an important
role for the site and open space design of Berlin's Hansaviertel that Hammerbacher would
become involved in.[20] Like her garden designs, Hammerbacher's urban designs were guided
by the idea of a harmonious relationship between humans and nonhuman nature. To design
cities and urban neighborhoods, Hammerbacher argued, required taking into account the
topography, geology, climate and hydrology of the respective site and region. It was the "total
character" of the landscape that designers had to understand.[21] This "total character" of landscape had first been put forward by Alexander von Humboldt in his early nineteenth-century

landscape descriptions, in which he analyzed the relationship between topography, climate and plant cover and explored the perceived effects of the synthesis of these different factors.[22] The idea had been taken up and developed by early-twentieth-century geographers who, like Carl Troll and Josef Schmithüsen after World War Two, were in many cases able to resume their professorships at German universities despite their Nazi allegiance.[23] Hammerbacher's and many of her colleagues' work at the time quite uncritically built on these theoretical and conceptual understandings of landscape that, by the postwar years, had come to be seen both as a totality of appearances and effects and as a spatial system.[24]

Housing and urban fabric were to be embedded in and framed by green open space. A self-serving argument accompanied this design concept, described and promoted by Hammerbacher as "urban planning related to landscape" (*landschaftsbezogene Bauplanung*): she argued that, due to its focus on the landscape, landscape architects were to be involved in the urban planning process from the beginning. The characteristics of the landscape were to become evident in the urban form.[25] As Jeong-Hi Go has pointed out, Hammerbacher's work and argumentation led to the inclusion of landscape planning in the first West German federal building law of 1957.[26]

As faculty member at the TU Berlin, Hammerbacher quickly became involved in reconstruction planning for Berlin. One of the most prestigious and internationally acclaimed projects was the International Building Exhibition Interbau that opened in 1957 on a 44-acre site – the old Hansaviertel – adjacent to the northwestern part of Tiergarten. The Interbau was intended to tackle current urban planning and housing questions and to provide examples of technically and architecturally advanced construction.[27] The architects who were invited to contribute to the exhibition through the design of various housing types included Alvar Aalto, Le Corbusier, Oscar Niemeyer, Egon Eiermann, Max Taut, Wassili Luckhard and Werner Düttmann. "Flowing" green open space was to form a backbone and ordering structure of the Hansaviertel and was to connect the neighborhood with the surrounding landscape, in particular with the Tiergarten. In the vein of his colleague Lingner's explanations of "city landscape," the landscape architect on the Interbau's Directorial Committee, Walter Rossow, stressed the dependency of humans on nature, and the need for a harmonious relationship between humankind and its environment. Having overcome the anti-urban bias of the prewar years, Rossow, like Lingner, argued for the synthesis and equality of the agencies of nature and the intellect in the city.[28]

After she had already served on the jury for the urban design competition, Hammerbacher was also one of five German landscape architects out of a total of ten involved in the site designs of the Hansaviertel. Only architects and architecture students who were residents in West Germany or West Berlin had been allowed to participate in the urban design competition. In 1954, the organizing committee had determined that garden architects were to be involved in the actual site design at a later point,[29] a decision that was finally realized in 1956. While Hansaviertel's site design was already based on the idea of "city landscape," the garden architects were charged with actually creating the city landscape that unified the diverse housing typologies. Among the sixteen landscape architects shortlisted for commissions on this project were three women: Herta Hammerbacher, the Swedish landscape architect Inger Wedborn, and Maria Teresa Parpagliolo Shephard, together with her working partner H. F. Clark.[30] It seems likely that Clark and Parpagliolo's work on the 1951 Festival of Britain (see below) had gained them the recognition and renown necessary to be included in the shortlist. When Wedborn, with whom Hammerbacher had been paired initially, declined participation, the German remained the only woman in the group of landscape architects that was finally commissioned. Hammerbacher's subsequent collaboration with the Swede Edvard Jacobson did not work well, so they divided tasks. Hammerbacher designed the Hansaplatz, the plaza in front of the St. Ansgar church, and the open spaces surrounding the house designed by Oscar Niemeyer. She also developed an iconic paving design using granite slabs and Bernburger Mosaiksteine that connected all open spaces assigned to her and Jacobson, which subsequently became one of her signature design features (Figure 1.4, 1.5).[31] Although the paving was, of course, not "natural" green open space, conceptually, it unified the residential neighborhood by "flowing" through it. The paving's irregular edges also blended with lawns and other green open spaces so that the open-space system as a whole became a structuring device, as intended by the overall open-space scheme for Hansaviertel.[32] Hammerbacher established further connections between the new neighborhood and Tiergarten by planting groups of deciduous trees irregularly and modulating the grounds in a way that made them seem to have belonged to the Tiergarten in the first place.[33] By blending the buildings into her open space designs through irregularly shaped groups of trees and ground modulations, Hammerbacher tried to counteract what she had by this time come to criticize in many designs: the disconnection between slab buildings and their surrounding green open space.

While Hammerbacher's ideas gained a new impulse through her visit to Japan on the occasion of the 1964 IFLA conference held in Tokyo, she also saw her existing garden and urban design ideas confirmed. In Japan, she wrote after the conference, new urban plans were based on regional and local landscape features, and garden designs formed a unity

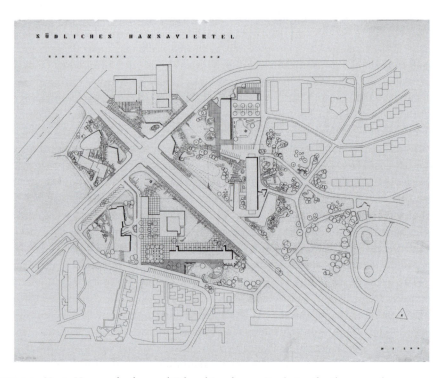

FIGURE 1.4 Herta Hammerbacher and Edvard Jacobson, site design for the areas along Altonaerstraße and Hansaplatz, Hansaviertel in Berlin, 1957. Ink on trace paper. Courtesy Architekturmuseum TU Berlin.

FIGURE 1.5 Paving pattern of path between the library and Altonaerstraße, Hansaviertel in Berlin, 1957. Design by Herta Hammerbacher. Courtesy Architekturmuseum TU Berlin.

with adjacent buildings. She was impressed by the work of the metabolists, a group of architects led by Kenzo Tange, who devised plans for dense vertical urban landscapes.[34] Still under this impression in 1966, she participated together with a group of young architects – among them her daughter Merete Mattern – in the competition for an urban design for Ratingen-West, 50 kilometers north of Cologne (Figure 1.6).[35] Drawn and sketched by her daughter Merete, the design merged Hammerbacher's old ideas regarding the city landscape with visionary ones exemplified by the work of the metabolists: a central green open space was surrounded by vertical terraced housing blocks that tapered down toward areas of single-family houses on the outskirts of the neighborhood. Fittingly, Hammerbacher described the design as both "built landscape" and "landscape as built form." With this she acknowledged, for the first time, that the city landscape could also be determined by architectural built form instead of only by open space. As Jeong-Hi Go has noted, the Japanese experience therefore induced Hammerbacher to distance herself from the "structured and dispersed city" concept that was based on the dispersal of low-density housing and that was supported by many postwar architects and planners. It also made her realize that technology did not only harm the environment but could also be used to benefit an environmentally conscious society.[36]

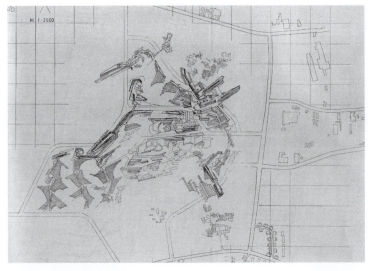

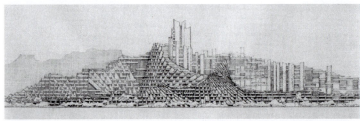

FIGURE 1.6   Herta Hammerbacher with her daughter Merete Mattern and a group of young
architects, plan, section and perspective for an urban design for Ratingen-West, 1966.
("Wettbewerb Ratingen-West/IV," *Der Architekt* 16, 1 [1967]: 12–23 [14–15].)

Sylvia Crowe: landscapes of power and Harlow New Town

In a general climate of anxiety revolving around uncontrolled urban growth and the pro-
liferation of new technologies, Sylvia Crowe became one of the leading landscape architects in Britain dealing with roads and what she called the "landscapes of power." How to
insert roads and buildings of modern industry – the results of technological advancement like
nuclear power plants, transformer stations, power lines, wires, reservoirs and airfields – into the

landscape was one of the concerns that guided her postwar work. Born in 1901 and educated at Swanley Horticultural College from 1920 to 1922, Crowe (Figure 1.7), like Hammerbacher and Parpagliolo, first worked for a tree nursery. Immediately after World War Two, she opened her own practice in London, profiting from office space given to her by Brenda Colvin and commissions handed on to her by Geoffrey Jellicoe, two colleagues who were part of the closely knit network of pioneering landscape architects in Britain involved in work for the Institute of Landscape Architects.

Crowe embarked rapidly on a national and international career. In 1948, she became the first honorary secretary of the newly founded IFLA; she was elected vice president in 1953 and the first woman president of IFLA in 1969. In 1988, she received the American Society of Landscape Architects' medal. She was also the most prolific writer of the three women discussed here. In the four years between 1956 and 1960 alone, she published four books, among them *The Landscape of Power* and *The Landscape of Roads*, as well as a number of articles that influenced the work of her peers, ministerial officials and industrialists in Britain. The realization that new technologies and industries directly or indirectly determined the function

FIGURE 1.7 Sylvia Crowe at the time when she became president of the Landscape Institute in 1957. (*Journal of the Institute of Landscape Architects* no. 40 [November 1957]: 2.)

and visual appearance of the national landscape and the livelihood of the entire nation led her to embrace national planning issues, including large industrial and infrastructure projects. She began to tackle the "problem of absorbing the machine-scale into the human-scale land-scape,"[37] and of finding "the synthesis between" the technological and the organic natural worlds.[38] Crowe believed that the landscape had to "reflect the growing mechanization of the economy . . . and the increased mobility of the population,"[39] but that it also had to be designed and planned to protect human and environmental health. Her agenda was deter-mined by the idea that the buildings and structures of new industries like nuclear power, communication and transportation – fascinating "cosmic shapes"[40] – needed to be assimilated into the landscape by preserving and redesigning, where necessary, "the entire surface-cover of the land into one flowing comprehensive pattern."[41] Several of her drawings illustrate how power and transformer stations, gasometers, telegraph poles and the masts of power lines could unobtrusively be integrated into the existing landscape pattern. Crowe compared the patterns of the "landscapes of power" and "roads" with abstract modern art and, in particular, with Paul Klee's composition of arrows and interpenetrating lines. The interlocking shapes and lines of abstract art had so far only been translated into garden designs, for instance by Thomas Church in California. Crowe aimed at using "patterns of interlocking shape" to transform entire landscapes.[42]

Besides the patterns seen from the air and from elevated positions on hill and moun-tainsides, building masses and forms also had to blend into the landscape from the ground view, and the new roads needed to offer drivers attractive views.[43] For example, the careful positioning of plantings could hide masts and overland transmission lines (Figure 1.8); siting and excavating could be used to screen transformer stations and make them appear as if they "sprung from the earth."[44] True to the British landscape, Crowe promoted the adoption of the eighteenth-century ha-ha to blend buildings with the landscape contours: "This is," she argued, "a useful device when the building requires the appearance of rising cleanly from the open ground, with the landscape sweeping up to it, without planting or walls."[45] The Central Electricity Generating Board subsequently adopted this principle in their landscape guidelines. Among the design principles Crowe embraced in her postwar work were the disruption and breaking-up of clear edges, forms and silhouettes of large buildings through plantings and landforms, the use of colors that matched buildings to their surroundings,[46] and roads and fences running parallel to contour lines. According to Crowe the "organic pattern" of the rural surroundings should impose itself on the industrial plant.[47]

Trawsfynydd, the fourth nuclear power station of Britain's 1955 nuclear power program, whose construction was begun in 1959 in Welsh Snowdonia, was one of the sites where Crowe, employed as landscape consultant, strove to achieve "a direct union between the main buildings and the surrounding Welsh mountain landscape" by carrying the "wild land-scape . . . right up to the structures."[48] There, she could also use design principles she would later use in road and forestry projects. The station's pump house was sunk below ground level, the approach road was unlit, uncurbed and laid out along the contours, the substation was sited on low ground and its surface partly sown with dwarf clover "to break up the great expanse of hard surface as seen from higher viewpoints."[49] Ground modeling was used to merge the buildings with the surrounding landforms, e.g. the ground between the turbine house and the substation was modeled so as to appear as a spur of the surrounding hills. She enlarged small existing woods on hillsides by forestry plantings that could screen and absorb the buildings. At the northeast corner of the substation tree-planted mounds were built to conceal parts of the power station from the road.[50]

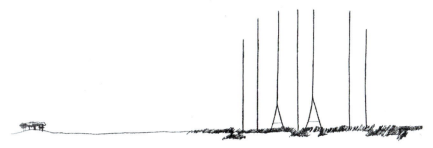

Fig. 16. Pine clumps on the left, once a dominant feature in the landscape, are reduced to the stature of shrubs.

Fig. 17. Where trees and masts are equi-distant from the eye, the trees are dwarfed. But trees near the viewpoint merge the masts into the pattern of their trunks.

FIGURE 1.8   Michael Laurie for Sylvia Crowe, illustrations of methods to merge telegraph and electricity masts with the landscape. (Sylvia Crowe, *The Landscape of Power* [London: Architectural Press, 1958].)

Crowe's concerns for the proper dimensions and locations of the forestry plantings were the basis of more detailed studies and reports for the Forestry Commission, to which she was appointed as landscape consultant in 1963. Her guidelines addressed the scale of plantings, their shape, the choice of tree species and the ways and patterns of felling trees. While her concern was always based on the visual effect of the plantings, she also took into account wildlife habitat and "the health of the landscape"[51] besides the economic aspects that she was presented with by the foresters. Hedgerows characteristic of agricultural land in a valley could, for example, be connected to coniferous hillsides, "if broadleaves also feather up the gullies on the hillside and thereby unite it to the valley." This treatment was not only visually accept-able, she argued, but it also provided an ideal wildlife habitat.[52] The shape of forestry plant-ings along roadsides to evoke visual interest was another topic that also tied into her interest in the landscape of roads, a topic investigated at the time from varying perspectives. While Crowe was exploring what could be learned from the landscape treatment of the early motor-ways in Germany and from the North American parkways, her American colleagues Donald Appleyard, Kevin Lynch and Lawrence Halprin were studying human perception, affect and behavior as it related to the new urban environment of high-speed mobility in the United States.[53] Crowe established guidelines for best practices of how to embed the new national road network into the British landscape on the basis of case studies from various countries. Grounded in Britain's landscape design tradition, she approached "the problem from a land-scape point of view"[54] which first and foremost was the visual point of view both of the driver and the onlooker. According to Crowe, this meant not only to consider the "damage [that] has been done to the countryside by new road works" but also to "exploit their potential value as a new element of design."[55]

Roads were central to the designs of the new towns that were built in Britain in the postwar years. Not surprisingly, for the time, the urban designs were based on private auto-mobile traffic, the concept of the neighborhood unit and the separation of different modes of movement and transportation. Like many of her British colleagues, Crowe profited from the opportunity that Lord Reith, chairman of the New Towns Committee in 1945–1946, had created by determining that each of the postwar new towns had to have a landscape architect on the design team from the outset. In 1947, she was appointed to develop the landscape proposals for Harlow New Town, Essex, collaborating with the town's planner Frederick Gibbert. She was a consultant until 1973.[56] At Harlow, Crowe was also engaged in projects that involved integrating human habitation with landscape and designed green open space. Like her German colleague Hammerbacher, Crowe followed an urban paradigm that was based on the idea of landscape and green open space as structuring elements (Figure 1.9). In Harlow, existing natural features like valleys, brooks, woods and clumps of trees that could forge identity were preserved and used as "'pegs' on which the design is hung." As stated in the 1952 Planning Proposals Report, the town design was to have "its own existence as landscape," and was to weld landscape and building groups "into a coherent whole."[57] The countryside, in the form of green wedges of forest, meadows and streams running along the valleys that intersected the area, was both physically and visually to "flow" through the town, providing both boundaries and connectors between the different neighborhoods and their surroundings and space for paths as well as for recreational amenities and schools in the neighborhood centers.[58] Crowe envisioned that inhabitants could, in this way, be drawn to enjoy nature and the countryside more easily.[59] Her work at Harlow also involved detailed open-space designs for industry and neighborhoods, including play spaces and other recreational areas. She supported the idea of separated traffic systems that had been experi-mented with in the North American garden suburbs Radburn, New Jersey, and Greenbelt, Maryland, in the 1920s and 1930s. At Harlow, the idea led to the conversion of old lanes into pedestrian and bicycle paths connecting neighborhoods designed by different architects for individual character.[60]

Maria Teresa Parpagliolo: the Festival of Britain and Casalpalocco

The British New Towns were influential in urban planning in a number of countries, includ-ing Italy. Maria Teresa Parpagliolo (Figure 1.10), who had begun her career as a landscape architect in the 1930s in Rome, had already worked on urban planning schemes during the Fascist period. In 1940, she had been appointed head of the Planning Department for Parks and Gardens of the World Exhibition site south of the city, planned by Mussolini to open in 1942. Serving the Fascist regime, she adhered to its political vision with her theoretical state-ments and design work for the exhibition.[61] And yet, she showed no regret and no lack of self-confidence when reflecting, in 1971, on her work within the male-dominated planning team: "It was such an enormous job that I learned the profession doing one job and teaching all the architects to see the site in a different way."[62] Although she was hired for the job because of

FIGURE 1.9 Aerial view of Harlow showing Mark Hall South in the foreground and Mark Hall North and the industrial estate beyond. (Frederick Gibberd, "Harlow New Town," *Architectural Review* 117 (May 1955): 311–329 [313].)

her excellent botanical know-how and her ability to design planting plans and flower beds,[63] Parpagliolo realized the new opportunities it offered for becoming involved in urban design and planning.

After her marriage to the Englishman Ronald Shephard in 1946, she began to work in England. There, acting as Frank Clark's deputy when, in 1948, he started to work as landscape consultant to the Festival Office of the Festival of Britain, Parpagliolo again ventured into the realms of urban design and planning. Celebrating the centenary of the first World Exhibition and the nation's recovery after the war, the Festival was also supposed to promote modern design in all fields. In contrast to the world's exhibition grounds of the previous one hundred years that had been organized around central axes, the festival grounds were to be experienced along a meandering pathway. The grounds had, in fact, been conceived as a model for a modern townscape grounded in the nation's honorable past by realizing "in urban terms . . . the principles of the Picturesque." This was believed to be achieved through "The skillful incorporation of already existing buildings into the scene, the use of water to provide an invisible but effective barrier, carefully contrived alternations of concealment and disclosure, studied changes of level and of surface, contrasts between apparent enclosure and sudden glimpses of far distance . . . ."[64] In addition to the preparation, organization and oversight of

FIGURE 1.10 Maria Teresa Parpagliolo's portrait on her death card. Courtesy Pier Luigi Nicolini.

the plantings, Parpagliolo was responsible for the design of several plant containers and open spaces on the exhibition grounds on London's South Bank. In her and Clark's design for the Regatta Restaurant garden they adopted the design language influenced by molecular science and crystallography that – in keeping with the exhibition's theme, the fusion of art and science – had guided Misha Black and Alexander Gibson's architecture of the building.[65] The Regatta Restaurant garden featured amoeba-shaped planting beds that formed an island in a rectangular water basin surrounded by the café terraces. On the island, profuse plantings of perennials surrounded a mature Zelkova serrata and a spiky abstract metal sculpture by the British artist Lynn Chadwick.[66]

In 1954, Parpagliolo accepted a position as landscape architect for one of the leading Italian real estate and building companies, the Società Generale Immobiliare (SGI), to provide the company with open space and garden designs as well as planting plans for its new housing developments and residential developments in and outside Rome. Thus, while Hammerbacher and Crowe were producing plans and designs for the Hansaviertel and Harlow respectively, Parpagliolo worked on the landscape plans for new residential neighborhoods in and around Rome.[67] Her international experience and familiarity with Anglo-American and North European landscapes, including parkways and community gardens, made her a suitable candidate for the company's projects. At the Roman garden suburb Casalpalocco (1954–1960), located 10 kilometers southwest of Rome, Parpagliolo produced the designs for the parkway, public and communal open spaces besides a number of private gardens. The plan, drawn up for Casalpalocco during the postwar reconstruction period by the architects Emilio Pifferi, Alberto Ressa, Adalberto Libera, Ugo Luccichenti, Mario Paniconi, Giulio Pediconi and

Giuseppe Vaccaro, was inspired by American suburbs that some SGI executives had visited during a trip to the United States (Figure 1.11). The plan envisioned a settlement for 15,000 middle-class inhabitants that provided ample green open space, including sports grounds and a social community fostered by a commercial, religious and community center. Casalpalocco was to provide a healthy alternative to living in what was then considered to be the congested, polluted and anonymous city of Rome and new opportunities for homeownership for the young middle-class aspiring to an "American way of life" that emphasized leisure, relaxation and freedom from conventions. The suburban plan was structured into subdivisions, made accessible by a curved ring road designed as a parkway. Throughout the suburb, described by Bruno Bonomo as an "'American' model of modernity,"[68] Parpagliolo used vegetation that was typical of the region and in particular of the Mediterranean macchia. She chose different tree and shrub species for each neighborhood: specific species like orange and olive trees and laurel acted as signifiers providing the subdivisions with a name and identity. Planting beds incorporated into sidewalks ran alongside the roads, and properties were divided by hedges instead of by fences and walls to substantiate the "green effect" of the new town. Parpagliolo tried to increase the naturalistic effect by loose and informal shrub and tree plantings, by scattered planting of narcissus and by letting pathways develop along desire lines in the central strip of the parkway (Figure 1.12). She also designed communal gardens within individual subdivisions that provided spaces for different structured and unstructured play, sports and leisure activities (Figure 1.13).

Parpagliolo, Crowe and Hammerbacher sought to shape cities through landscape architecture at a time when the associate editor of the American journal *Landscape Architecture*, Grady Clay, disregarded women entirely. Clay observed in his 1958 editorial

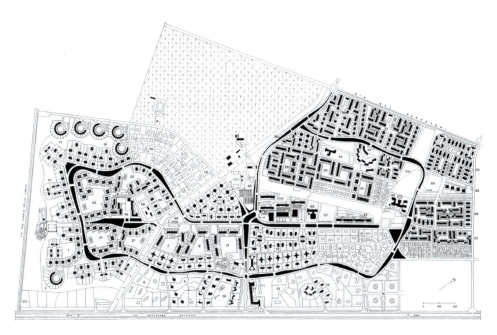

FIGURE 1.11 Plan of Casalpalocco south of Rome showing the urban development in 1973. Parkway marked in black. (Societa generale immobiliare, *SGI Realizzazioni e studi nel settore edilizio* [Rome, 1973].)

FIGURE 1.12 Parkway with central pathway, Casalpalocco, 1999. (Photo: author.)

titled "Shapely Women and Cities: what's the urban equivalent of '38-24-34'?" that "more men . . . than ever before are working to shape our urban landscape according to principles of design." Comparing the formal and aesthetic qualities of the city to the customary figures used to describe the beauty of the ideal female body, he noted that "few influences more subtly repel our advances or more surely arouse us than the spatial qualities of our cities."[69]

The classical ideal of the *dulce utili* – the combination of the beautiful and useful – in turn underlay the work by Hammerbacher, Crowe and Parpagliolo. They were humanists at heart,[70] trying with their designs to achieve both beautiful and functional landscapes, or, as Crowe put it, an "aesthetic expression of practical land-use."[71] They sought to produce what their slightly older peer Brenda Colvin described as designs that were "contemporary, individual and true to the needs of humanity,"[72] thereby negating the modernist notion of the separation of functions and, instead, embracing synthesis as a design principle (for example, in their concepts to merge city and landscape and in their ideas to connect technology and nature). Based on the different inflections of their respective countries' intellectual ideas and cultures, the three women aspired to base their designs on a holistic and synthetic understanding of the world. Seeking to explore the relationship between different landscape elements and scales, between different professions and points of view, they tried in their work to "see the picture as a whole."[73] Firmly grounded in the history and craft of their profession, the women embraced the future. Their designs responded to the new opportunities, requirements and conditions in the postwar years. The use of new plant cultivars, abstract forms and shapes, the attention to creating "flowing" space accessible and enjoyable to the greatest possible number of people determined many of their designs. They challenged themselves and their profession

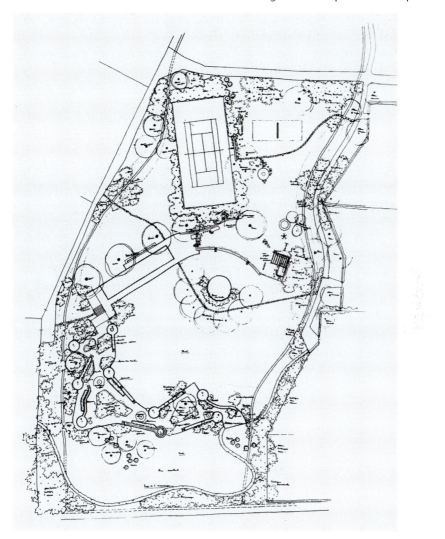

FIGURE 1.13   Maria Teresa Parpagliolo, design for communal park area adjacent to the properties of ten family homes, Casalpalocco, ca. 1959. (R. W. Rose, "Engineers, Planners and the Institute of Landscape Architects," *Journal of the Institute of Landscape Architects* 43 [1959]: 6–9 [8].)

to address questions about humankind's future on earth. "How can we explore the moon, yet not destroy the wild flowers, travel faster than sound, yet still hear the birds sing?" Crowe asked in 1960.[74] Parpagliolo developed similar concerns, particularly after her visit to Japan in 1964. She appealed for a spiritual understanding and a sensitive use of the land, paying attention to environmental resources, including flora and fauna.[75] All three women, having broken out of the domestic sphere and working in the public realm with the ability to master micro and macro scales, assumed responsibility both for the appearance and the function of the land in their countries, often arguing vehemently for environmental protection. This interest, along with their concerns for landscape planning on regional and national levels, is expressive of their times and shows they did not stand in their male colleagues' shadows. More than their male colleagues, however, the women had to assume strategies to stand and hold their ground, and they also made sacrifices in their private lives. Both Crowe and Parpagliolo never had children; Crowe never married, and Parpagliolo married late in life. Divorced with one daughter, Hammerbacher kept her second husband at a distance, keeping her maiden name and never moving in with him.[76]

All three women also played an important role in the establishment and recognition of landscape architectural practice in their home countries, in particular after World War Two. They held various top positions in the field, ranging from a professorship to various presidencies in national and international associations and, in the case of Parpagliolo, undertook the first attempt at establishing education in landscape architecture in Italy. Their expertise led them to become nationally known and sought-after figures, in the cases of Hammerbacher and Parpagliolo, and a person of international renown, in the case of Crowe.

The realization that landscape architecture was both an art and a science, and therefore suitable to bridge the gap between the two, was perceived particularly strongly again in the postwar years, and guided the women in much of their work.[77] Thus, it was only a logical consequence that all three – like many of their male and female colleagues – would play mediating roles. As Crowe put it in her Presidential Address to the British Institute of Landscape Architects in 1957, landscape architecture's function was to "translate all the diverse and sectional interests of different land-users, into one complete and healthy landscape."[78] In Hammerbacher, Crowe and Parpagliolo's idealist vision, the "healthy landscape" consisted of functional natural systems and integrated social communities, and it provided the cultural meanings to support human life. Landscape architecture for them was a work of synthesis.

Notes

1 Russell H. Butler and Loutrel W. Briggs, "The International Conference with the Institute of Landscape Architects as Hosts," *Landscape Architecture* 39 (1949): 72–75.

2 Thaïsa Way, "Women as Force in Landscape Architecture, 1893–1942," Ph.D. dissertation, Cornell University, 2005, 1. Also see Thaïsa Way, *Unbounded Practice: Women and Landscape Architecture in the Early Twentieth Century* (Charlottesville and London: University of Virginia Press, 2009).

3 Karen Madsen and John F. Furlong, "Introduction: Women Land Design: Considering Connections," *Landscape Journal* 13, no. 2 (1994): 88–101.

4 See Geoffrey Jellicoe, "War and Peace," *Landscape Design* 2 (1979): 10. Already in the 1930s, Brenda Colvin had discussed the founding of an international federation with a small group of landscape architects on the continent. See Sylvia Crowe, "International Scene," *Landscape Design* 2 (1979): 14. Also see Trish Gibson, *Brenda Colvin: A Career in Landscape* (London: Frances Lincoln, 2011), 124.

5 For Lady Allen of Hurtwood see Marjory Allen and Mary Nicholson, *Memoirs of an Uneducated Lady* (London: Thames and Hudson, 1975).

6 Four years Sylvia Crowe's senior, Brenda Colvin (1897–1981) was a model for many of the women who followed her into the profession of landscape architecture in Britain. As a well-respected pioneering professional, Colvin served as the first female president of the British Institute of Landscape Architects from 1951 until 1953. She worked on similar projects as her pioneering colleagues Jellicoe and Crowe, broadening the profession's scope to include, among other tasks, the treatment of roads and industrial sites. In fact, she was often the one to forge the necessary contacts in the first place. In the postwar years, she shared her office space, and finally also an assistant and secretary, with Crowe, although they always maintained independent practices. The two women also went on trips together and, despite their different character and temperament, held each other in high esteem. Although Brenda Colvin played an important role in the development of the profession in Britain, this essay focuses on her slightly younger peer, Sylvia Crowe, who stood in more direct contact with one of the other figures treated in this essay, Maria Teresa Parpagliolo. For Brenda Colvin's work and career, see Trish Gibson, *Brenda Colvin: A Career in Landscape* (London: Frances Lincoln, 2011).

7 For a short account of the similarities and parallels in their early careers, see Sonja Dümpelmann, "Breaking Ground: Women Pioneers in Landscape Architecture. An International Perspective," in *CELA 2006 Shifting Grounds Proceedings*, ed. Patrick Mooney (Vancouver, 2006), 45–50.

8 Jeong-Hi Ri, "Herta Hammerbacher (1900–1985): Virtuosin einer Neuen Landschaftlichkeit-Der Garten als Paradigma," Ph.D. thesis, Technische Universität Berlin, 2004, 23.

9 See Arminius, *Die Grosstädte in ihrer Wohnungsnoth und die Grundlagen einer durchgreifenden Abhilfe* (Duncker & Humblot: Leipzig, 1874). For the occupations of royal gardeners in Europe, pre-dominantly in the German states, see *Preussisch Grün. Hofgärtner in Brandenburg-Preussen*, ed. Stiftung Preussische Schlösser und Gärten Berlin-Brandenburg (Berlin: Henschel Verlag, 2004); Iris Lauterbach, "Gärtner, virtuoso, Gartenkünstler – Zum Berufsbild des Gartenarchitekten in der Frühen Neuzeit," in *Der Architekt. Geschichte und Gegenwart eines Berufsstandes*, vol 2, ed. Winfried Nerdinger (München, London, New York: Prestel, 2013), 727–743; Clemens Alexander Wimmer, "Der Garten- und Landschaftsarchitekt in Deutschland ab 1800," in *Der Architekt. Geschichte und Gegenwart eines Berufsstandes*, vol 2, ed. Winfried Nerdinger (München, London, New York: Prestel, 2013), 745–751; *Die Preussischen Hofgärtner*, ed. Stiftung Preussische Schlösser and Gärten Berlin-Brandenburg (Berlin: Hentrich, 1996).

10 Herta Hammerbacher-Mattern, "Neues Bauen und Neues Gartenwesen: Der Garten Poelzig," *Gartenschönheit*, 12, no. 2 (1931): 26–30.

11 Catherine M. Howett, "Careers in Landscape Architecture: Recovering for Women What the 'Ladies' Won and Lost," *Feminist Visions*, eds. Diane L. Fowlkes and Charlotte S. McClure (Tuscaloosa: University of Alabama Press, 1984), 139–148 (144).

12 Brenda Colvin, "Beginnings," *Landscape Design* 2 (1979): 8; Alan Powers, "Landscape in Britain," in *The Architecture of Landscape, 1940–1960*, ed. Marc Treib (Philadelphia: University of Pennsylvania Press, 2002), 65; Trish Gibson, *Brenda Colvin: A Career in Landscape* (London: Frances Lincoln, 2011), 124.

13 See Ri, "Herta Hammerbacher," 78.

14 Ibid., 30–33, 132–137.

15 Ibid., 10, 39.

16 For the "city landscape" and "settlement cells," see Jörn Düwel and Niels Gutschow, *Städtebau in Deutschland im 20. Jahrhundert* (Stuttgart, Leipzig, Wiesbaden: Teubner, 1965), 90–136; Werner Durth and Niels Gutschow, *Träume in Trümmern*, Bd. 1 (Braunschweig, Wiesbaden: Friedrich Viehweg & Sohn, 1988), 174–196; David Kuchenbuch, "Circles within circles: Visions and Visualizations of the City of Tomorrow," in *A Blessing in Disguise: War and Town Planning in Europe 1940–1945*, eds. Jörn Düwel and Niels Gutschow (Berlin: Dom Publishers, 2013), 52–65 (57–59).

17 For the concept of the settlement cells in Hamburg, see Jörn Düwel, "Hamburg: Two Catastrophies in 1842 and 1943," in *A Blessing in Disguise: War and Town Planning in Europe 1940–1945*, eds. Jörn Düwel and Niels Gutschow (Berlin: Dom Publishers, 2013), 194–261.

18 See for example Gert Gröning, "Teutonic Myth, Rubble, and Recovery: Landscape Architecture in Germany," in *The Architecture of Landscape 1940–1960*, ed. Marc Treib (Philadelphia: University of Pennsylvania Press, 2002), 120–153 (127–129).

19 Reinhold Lingner, "Die Stadtlandschaft," *Neue Bauwelt* 3, no. 6 (1948): 83–86. For the paradigm of "city landscape" and the Berlin Kollektivplan, also see Elke Sohn, *Zum Begriff der Natur in Stadtkonzepten* (Lit Verlag: Hamburg, 2008), 80–95.

20 See Ri, "Herta Hammerbacher," 110.

21 Herta Hammerbacher, "Über landschaftsbezogene Bauplanung," *Garten und Landschaft* 1 (1967): 12–14 (12).

22 See Alexander von Humboldt and Aimé Bonpland, *Essay on the Geography of Plants*, ed. Stephen T. Jackson, transl. Sylvie Romanowski (Chicago and London: University of Chicago Press, 2009).

23 See Josef Schmithüsen, "Was ist eine Landschaft?" *Erdkundliches Wissen* 9 (1964): 7–24.

24 See Hammerbacher's quote of Schmithüsen in her article "landschaftsbezogene Bauplanung," 12.

25 Hammerbacher, "landschaftsbezogene Bauplanung," 12–14.

26 Ri, "Herta Hammerbacher," 113.

27 On Hansaviertel see Stefanie Schulz and Carl-Georg Schulz, *Das Hansaviertel. Ikone der Moderne* (Berlin: Verlagshaus Braun, 2007).

28 See Walter Rossow, "Städtebau und Landschaft," in *Interbau Berlin 1957. Amtlicher Katalog der Internatinalen Bauausstellung Berlin 1957* (Berlin: Graphische Gesellschaft Grunewald, 1957), 332–334.

29 See minutes of "Sitzung des Ausschusses zur Auswahl der Architekten für das Hansa-Viertel am 27.8.54." Landesarchiv Berlin, B Rep. 009, Acc. 2427, Nr. 0037.

30 See minutes of "Sitzung des 'Leitenden Ausschusses' vom 28–30 März 1955." Landesarchiv Berlin, B Rep. 009, Acc. 2427, Nr. 0037.

31 See Ri, "Herta Hammerbacher," 45.

32 For the program of Interbau see *Interbau Berlin 1957. Amtlicher Katalog der Internationalen Bauausstellung Berlin 1957* (Berlin: Graphische Gesellschaft Grunewald, 1957).

33 See Herta Hammerbacher, "Gartenarchitekten planen im Hansaviertel," *Garten und Landschaft* 10 (1957): 263–265. Gabi Dolff-Bonekämper and Franziska Schmidt, *Das Hansaviertel. Internationale Nachkriegsmoderne in Berlin* (Berlin: Verlag Bauwesen, 1999), 37–38.

34 Herta Hammerbacher, "Japanische Städte-heute und morgen," *Garten und Landschaft* 74, no. 10 (October 1964): 326–335 (329).

35 See Ri, "Herta Hammerbacher," 60.

36 Ibid., 115. Also see Hammerbacher, "landschaftsbezogene Bauplanung," 12–14.

37 Sylvia Crowe, "Landscape USA: Impressions of an English Visitor," *Landscape Architecture* 49, no. 2 (1958–1959): 120, 122.

38 Sylvia Crowe, *The Landscape of Roads* (London: The Architectural Press, 1960), 13.

39 Sylvia Crowe, "The Landscape of Power," *Landscape Architecture* 49, no. 2 (1958–1959): 106–109 (107).

40 Ibid., 109.

41 Sylvia Crowe, *The Landscape of Power* (London: The Architectural Press, 1958), 110.

42 Ibid., 24. Also see Sylvia Crowe, *The Landscape of Roads* (London: The Architectural Press, 1960), 34. See Sonja Dümpelmann, "The Art and Science of Invisible Landscapes: Camouflage for War and Peace," in *Ordnance: War + Architecture and Space*, eds. Gary Boyd and Denis Linehan (Farnham: Ashgate, 2013), 117–135; Sonja Dümpelmann, *Flights of Imagination: Aviation, Landscape, Design* (Charlottesville and London: UVA Press, 2014), 199–207.

43 Crowe, *Landscape of Roads*, 34, 113.

44 Crowe, *Landscape of Power*, 87–88.

45 Ibid., 50–51.

46 Ibid., 36; Sylvia Crowe, "Power and the Landscape," *Journal of the Institute of Landscape Architects* 52 (Nov. 1960): 3–7 (6).

47 Crowe, "Power and the Landscape," 4.

48 Sylvia Crowe & Associates, "Trawsfynydd Nuclear Power Station," 2. (Sylvia Crowe Collection, Landscape Institute).

49 Ibid.

50 Ibid. For Crowe's work on Trawsfynydd Nuclear Power Station see Dümpelmann, *Flights of Imagination*, 199–207; Dümpelmann, "Invisible Landscapes."

51 Sylvia Crowe, *Forestry in the Landscape* (London: Her Majesty's Stationery Office, 1966), 27.

52 Ibid., 13.

53 Donald Appleyard, Kevin Lynch and John R. Meyer, *The View from the Road* (Cambridge, published for the Joint Center for Urban Studies of the Massachusetts Institute of Technology and Harvard University by the M.I.T. Press, Massachusetts Institute of Technology, 1964); Lawrence Halprin, *Freeways* (New York, Reinhold Pub. Corp., 1966).

54 Crowe, *Landscape of Roads*, 12.

55 Ibid., 28. For Crowe's work on roads in Britain also see Peter Merriman, ""Beautified" is a Vile Phrase': The Politics and Aesthetics of Landscaping Roads in Pre- and Postwar Britain," in *The World Beyond the Windshield*, eds. Christoph Mauch and Thomas Zeller (Athens: Ohio University Press, 2008), 168–186.

56 David Scott, "New Towns," in *Sylvia Crowe*, eds. Geoffrey Collens and Wendy Powell (Woking: Landscape Design Trust, 1999), 47–67 (50).

57 Jeremy Spark and Peter Gawn, "Reassessment 2. Harlow New Town," *Journal of the Institute of Landscape Architects*, 86 (May 1969): 22–23.

58 Sylvia Crowe, "Recreational Landscape in England," *Landscape Architecture* 49, 1 (1958): 32–35 (33).

59 Sylvia Crowe, "Landscape Architecture in the New Towns," *Journal of the Institute of Landscape Architects* 18 (July 1950): 4–6 (5); David Scott, "New Towns," 58.

60 Powers, "Landscape in Britain," 63. Also see Crowe, *Landscape of Roads*, 26; Sir Frederick Gibberd, "Harlow New Town," *Architectural Review* 117 (May 1955): 311–329.

61 For the life and work of Parpagliolo, see Sonja Dümpelmann, *Maria Teresa Parpagliolo Shephard (1903–1974): Ein Beitrag zur Geschichte der Gartenkultur in Italien im 20. Jahrhundert* (Weimar: VDG, 2004); Sonja Dümpelmann, "Maria Teresa Parpagliolo Shephard (1903–1974): Her Development as a Landscape Architect between Tradition and Modernism," *Garden History* 30, no. 1 (2002): 49–73; Sonja Dümpelmann, "The Landscape Architect Maria Teresa Parpagliolo Shephard in

Britain: Her International Career 1946–1974," *Studies in the History of Gardens and Designed Landscapes* 30, no. 1 (2010): 94–113.

62 Parpagliolo cit. in "Maria Shephard talks to Tony Southard, On design No. 6," *Landscape Design* 11 (1971): 11–14 (11).

63 Massimo De Vico Fallani, *Parchi e Giardini dell'EUR. Genesi e sviluppo delle aree verdi dell' E42* (Rome: Nuova Editrice Spada, 1988), 48.

64 *The Architectural Review*, 110, 656 (August 1951), first page, without number.

65 Becky E. Conekin, *"Autobiography of a Nation": The 1951 Festival of Britain* (Manchester and New York: Manchester University Press, 2003), 57.

66 For Parpagliolo's work in Britain, see Dümpelmann, "The Landscape Architect Maria Teresa Parpagliolo Shephard in Britain."

67 For Parpagliolo's work in Casalpalocco and other Roman suburbs, see Dümpelmann, *Maria Teresa Parpagliolo Shephard (1903–1974). Ein Beitrag*, 248–266.

68 Bruno Bonomo, "'On Holidays 365 Days a Year' On the Outskirts of Rome," in *Urban Planning and the Pursuit of Happiness: European Variations on a Universal Theme (18th–21st Centuries)*, eds. Arnold Bartetzky and Marc Schalenberg (Berlin: Jovis, 2009), 194.

69 Grady Clay, "Shapely Women and Cities. An Editorial: What's the Urban Equivalent of '38-24-34'?" *Landscape Architecture* 49, no. 1 (1958–1959): 7.

70 See, for example, Crowe, "Recreational Landscape," 32.

71 Sylvia Crowe, "Presidential Address," *Journal of the Institute of Landscape Architects* 40 (Nov. 1957): 3–5, 20 (3).

72 Powers, "Landscape in Britain," 69.

73 Crowe, *Landscape of Roads*, 14.

74 Ibid., 13.

75 Maria Teresa Parpagliolo-Shephard, "Eindrücke beim IFLA-Kongress in Japan," *Garten und Landschaft* 74, no. 10 (October 1964): 343–344 (344).

76 See Ri, "Herta Hammerbacher," 33–34.

77 Ri, "Herta Hammerbacher," 60. Also see Sylvia Crowe, "The Landscape of Power," *Landscape Architecture* 49, no. 2 (1958–1959): 106–109 (108).

78 Crowe, "Presidential Address," 3.

2

INTERNATIONAL TRAINING AND NATIONAL AMBITIONS

Female landscape architects in Sweden, 1900–1950

Catharina Nolin

When the Swedish landscape architect Ester Claesson died in 1931, obituaries were published not only in Sweden, but also in Germany and Denmark. She was presented as a very talented landscape architect and an authority in Sweden who had achieved professional stature in a short time, and who had contributed to leading the profession to high esteem (Figure 2.1).[1] Her position was in many ways unique. She was one of the first female landscape architects in Sweden, the designer of many gardens and parks, and the author of numerous articles and books. Her artistic ability earned her an international reputation. Yet, within only a few decades after her death, she was almost forgotten. Not until around 2000 did researchers pay attention to her life and work. Unfortunately, this is rather typical of many professional women's careers in landscape architecture in Northern Europe.

Most female landscape architects in Sweden were well known during their active years and made significant contributions to designing parks and gardens. They wrote essays and books, took part in public debates and participated in professional organizations. However, in the historiography of landscape architecture and in public awareness, they hardly exist.[2] Some careers are fairly well known, yet a more comprehensive picture is missing. There are several reasons for this. One is that, for a long period, the history of gardens and landscape architecture occupied a marginal realm, both in academic disciplines like art and architectural history and in popular literature. In Sweden, not even landscape architects themselves were interested in writing their own history. Once garden history had come into focus, beginning around 1990, attention was paid either to originators of royal and manor gardens from the seventeenth and eighteenth centuries, like Nicodemus Tessin the Younger and Carl Hårleman, or to landscape architects active in the interwar and postwar periods, like Holger Blom and Sven A. Hermelin. Women were excluded from the narrative, both as originators and users.

My aim in this essay is to contribute to a revision of this narrative of Swedish landscape architecture. In what follows, I will present selected individual careers of female landscape architects who practiced in the first half of the twentieth century. This is a topic with enormous potential, as women in the overall history of garden design and landscape architecture were very important, but they have not been discussed very thoroughly thus far. Without doubt, conducting research on female landscape architects presents many challenges. Records from the women's practices have not been transferred into official archives, thus making it

FIGURE 2.1 The Swedish landscape architect Ester Claesson spent two years at Joseph Maria Olbrich's studio at Mathildenhöhe, in Darmstadt. The photograph shows Olbrich (in the middle) with a group of architects in his studio, ca. 1905. Ester Claesson, sitting to the left, was the only woman working with Olbrich. Photo credit: Institut Mathildenhöhe, Darmstadt, Germany.

difficult to track drawings and other original material. Determining what their gardens and landscapes looked like is even harder, as few of them are kept in an original state of design, if indeed they survive at all. On the other hand, many of the women's various publications have survived, and they are, today, together with contemporary photographs, important sources in reconstructing their careers. As a result of these circumstances, this historical narrative draws from numerous sources, not only in Sweden but also in Germany, Great Britain and Denmark, which in itself is an expression of the fact that many landscape architects had international contacts and experiences.

A woman's profession?

The prevailing idea holds that landscape architecture in the early twentieth century became a women's profession in Sweden, in the sense that many women were practicing it. To the contrary, I would like to underline that, although Swedish women established themselves earlier within this field than in the field of architecture, and earlier than in the other Scandinavian countries, they clearly were a minority.[3] The first generation of female landscape architects consisted of only a few individuals. Between 1900 and 1950, about fifteen women established themselves within the field. Although most of them were based in Stockholm, it is difficult to talk about them as a group. If, or how well, they knew each other is still a question to be answered. However, sources indicate that some of them inspired each other or worked together. Most of them had an upper-middle-class background. Their fathers were physicians, businessmen or teachers, which might have been an advantage in obtaining commissions from their middle-class clients. With some rare exceptions, they stayed unmarried and had no children, living on their own, or perhaps sharing a home with a sister. Not getting married was often a necessary decision if the goal was to work professionally and to have a practice of one's own.

The most important issue for the Women's Movement in Sweden at the turn of the twentieth century was, without a doubt, women's suffrage, which was obtained in 1921. Other important issues on the agenda were the right to participate in municipal commissions, the right to inherit and to come of age, in accordance with legal conventions. Several early women's organisations in Sweden that lobbied for women's rights and equality also aimed at encouraging women to choose between a wider range of professions that went beyond the usual choices of maid, nurse and teacher. One of the most important women's organisations in Sweden at the time was the Fredrika Bremer Association, founded in 1884 and named after the novelist and feminist activist Fredrika Bremer (1801–1865).[4] Through meetings, committees and publications, the association pursued the advancement and emancipation of women. Gardening and even landscape architecture were among the professions the association found suitable for women, which they promoted by distributing grants to individual women for training at schools abroad or for field trips. The association also founded a gardening school for women and tried to persuade landowners to accept female trainees. Several years of practical experience of working in a garden was necessary for entering higher gardening schools, but women often had problems obtaining this training as landowners were reluctant to accept them. It was not considered appropriate to accommodate both young female and male workers on a farm or an estate, and some landowners also preferred male trainees as they could work harder. The Fredrika Bremer Association's way of pursuing gender politics through encouraging higher education, special training and professional careers for women echoes the emancipatory activities of German female political activists, social reformers, journalists and artists, who encouraged women to establish a new relationship with the city in spatial and architectural terms, as has been investigated by Despina Stratigakos in *A Women's Berlin*.[5] The leading women in the Fredrika Bremer Association initiated, for example in 1914, a Women's House with reading room etc., to be built in Stockholm, with inspiration from the Women's House in Copenhagen.[6] These Houses gave women access to a safe and stimulating public meeting place to exchange knowledge, ideas and intellectual thought. The same year, just before the outbreak of World War I, the association participated with a Women's House in honour of Fredrika Bremer at the Baltic Exhibition in Malmö, the largest town in the south of Sweden.

Many lively discussions and public debates about women as gardeners and landscape architects took place in several contexts around 1900. Both men and women declared that gardening was a suitable profession for women because of its close connection to the home and because of its nurturing character, while others thought that gardening required the aesthetic sensibility that was more often attributed to women in this period. Skeptics existed too, and some of these, mainly men, believed that working in a garden was too much physical work for women. The public debate about women and gardening was most intense in the first decades of the twentieth century and until around 1930.

As Despina Stratigakos has shown, the first female architects working in Germany around 1900 had to adjust to existing views and attitudes. Much of the public debate revolved around the body. As Stratigakos has noted, "The body became a central site where the gendered construction of the architect was played out. Whether arguing for or against women's inclusion, German writers agreed that the architect needed a healthy, strong and athletic body."[7] The situation in Sweden was similar. Women who applied to gardening schools had to attach a health certificate to their applications and, in some cases, even a photograph. According to the landscape architect Inger Wedborn (1911–1969), female gardeners and landscape architects had to overcome a wide range of difficulties. She opposed the notions that, for women, gardening was only an innocent pastime, and that women's work in a garden was different from men's gardening. Instead, she emphasized the variety of work that women were conducting. She also strongly advocated for women's rights to adequate training, believing that, otherwise, they would never be able to compete or cooperate with men.[8] The public debate also included women's physical appearance and clothes, and numerous articles were published on which clothes to wear and which to avoid.

Training for professional activities

Although Swedish women were allowed to apply to the established gardening schools, they did not go there. A main reason for this was, without doubt, their difficulties in obtaining the necessary apprenticeship, as discussed above. Without this experience they would not be accepted at the schools. As a consequence of this, and because of ideas about the type of skills women needed, special gardening schools for women opened beginning in the 1890s. These were often owned and led by female educators who had acquired a gardener's training. However, for ambitious women who intended to work professionally as landscape architects, this was not a suitable option because the main aim of these schools was to train women in taking care of their own gardens or in teaching gardening to school children.[9] Going abroad for training, usually to Denmark, England or Germany, was often the best solution. This step required money, supportive parents, funding or all of this together.

Sweden's first female landscape architects: Ester Claesson and Ruth Brandberg

Ester Claesson (1884–1931) and Ruth Brandberg (1878–1944) were pioneering professionals in Sweden, as they were already well established by around 1910. Ester Claesson's way of finding herself an education is in many ways a very good illustration of Sweden's education system during this period, especially in relation to the consequences it had for women. After working in a garden in the south of Sweden, Claesson entered the most-renowned gardening school in Denmark at the age of sixteen. She graduated three years later in 1903 as the second best of her class. This opened an opportunity for her to continue her education at a polytechnic school in Vienna. Her stay in Vienna, and later in Germany, was possible due to the funding that she received from the Fredrika Bremer Association, intended for studies in landscape architecture.

In 1905, Ester Claesson joined the Austrian architect Joseph Maria Olbrich's artists' colony at Mathildenhöhe, in Darmstadt, Germany, founded in 1899.[10] She had made inquiries into whether he would accept her as his assistant in laying out his now famous *Farbengärten*, the radical monochrome gardens in red, blue and yellow, for the gardening exhibition he had initiated in the Orangeriegarten, in Darmstadt.[11] However, when Claesson's letter reached Olbrich, the gardens had already been laid out for the exhibition. Instead, he invited her to come and take on the artistic maintenance of the gardens during the exhibition period. Something in her letter must have caught his interest, some drawings perhaps, or other samples of her work showing her artistic abilities. Claesson's intention was to stay at Mathildenhöhe for a couple of weeks and then return to Vienna; but Olbrich was eager to support her development, and so she stayed for two years. Besides learning about garden history and design, she took classes in drawing and landscape painting. She was the only woman working with Olbrich, and probably also the only person at the office specializing in gardens. After an initial training period, she worked closely with Olbrich, assisting him, not only in designing and making drawings for gardens, but also in drawing furniture and interior decorations. From time to time he even left her in charge of the regular work in the studio.[12]

One of her first projects at Mathildenhöhe was a splendid rose garden, followed by the so-called Frauen-Rosenhof for the German Art exhibition in the Flora garden in Cologne, in 1906. Claesson also participated in planning the garden city, *Am hohlen Weg*, in Darmstadt. Some drawings of this project have survived, showing house and garden as a synthesis, withdrawn from the street and well protected by surrounding hedges (Figure 2.2). This was a very productive period for her and she was able to develop her skills in many different directions. In Darmstadt, Claesson also made friends with important figures in modern German intellectual culture, above all the German literary scholar and poet Friedrich Gundolf, one of the members of the influential literary and academic circle around the poet Stefan George. What impact Claesson's and Gundolf's relationship had on their professional work is difficult to assess, but letters to and between some of Gundolf's friends reveal its importance for the latter.[13]

In 1907, Ester Claesson was featured at length in the important German journal *Deutsche Kunst und Dekoration*, with a variety of drawings, some of which belonged to projects she had been working on in Olbrich's office. Comparing these drawings with Olbrich's reveals how much she learned from him, but also that she contributed to a high artistic standard in the office. In her elegant and colourful perspectival drawings, the gardens are presented as works of art, both as representations and as three-dimensional settings. Some drawings with monochrome plantations are obviously inspired by Olbrich's *Farbengärten* (Plate 2.1). Others in black and white are full of nuances, light and shade, and often show a very detailed way of representing different types of foliage, so detailed that you can determine the individual plant or tree (Plate 2.2). Drawings and photographs show how walls, stairs and other built structures are used to create spatiality on different levels and to underline the perspectival views through the gardens. Trees, bushes and flowers are chosen to harmonize with the buildings, to underline their structures and to create representative settings, although on a modest scale.

When Claesson participated the following year in *Die Woche*'s well-known competition for a house garden, she was not only one of very few women competing; she was also

FIGURE 2.2 Design proposal for a villa and a garden for the garden city, Am hohlen Weg, in Darmstadt, Germany 1906–1907. The drawing was made in Joseph Maria Olbrich's studio, very likely by Ester Claesson. Photo credit: Institut Mathildenhöhe, Darmstadt, Germany.

awarded a prize for one of her entries. It is obvious that her supporters in Sweden closely followed her development in Germany and had great expectations of her. Already in 1907, she was introduced in the Swedish press as the country's first woman in the field. The Swedish women's magazine *Idun* noted with regret that her talent was spent on Germany, but added hopefully that her return to Sweden was forthcoming.[14] When she was introduced some years later, in 1912, to an international audience in *The Studio*, the author underlined that "Miss Claesson's perspectives testify to a considerable talent for drawing, and the well-thought-out treatment of detail which we find in her designs shows that she has made a serious study of this department of architecture, to which of late years much attention has been paid in Germany" (Figure 2.3).[15]

Claesson left Olbrich's office in 1907, probably returning to Vienna. In 1909, she joined the architect Paul Schultze-Naumburg at his Saalecker Werkstätte in Saaleck, Germany, where she stayed until 1913. Working with Schultze-Naumburg was in many ways different from what Claesson had experienced at Mathildenhöhe. Schultze-Naumburg's office was divided into three departments – architecture, landscape architecture and interior decoration – and he was in need of specialists who could work with a variety of commissions. Schultze-Naumburg was, like Olbrich, a founding member of the Deutscher Werkbund in 1907, a fact that is also revealed in how he organized his practice. With the three departments at Saaleck and with branches in Berlin, Cologne and Essen, Schultze-Naumburg was able to present his work and products, as well as his intellectual approach

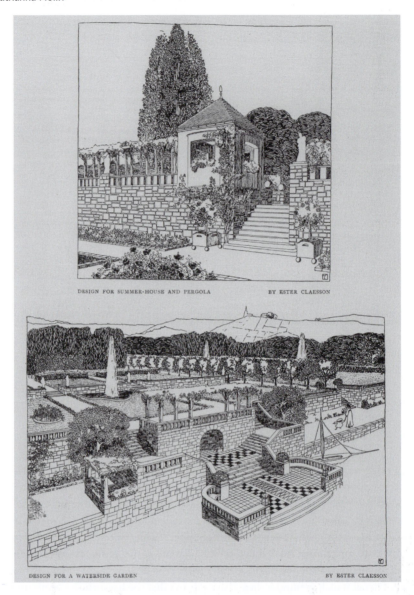

DESIGN FOR SUMMER-HOUSE AND PERGOLA   BY ESTER CLAESSON

DESIGN FOR A WATERSIDE GARDEN   BY ESTER CLAESSON

FIGURE 2.3 Ester Claesson, design proposal for two gardens published in *The Studio*, in 1912. The drawings were probably made around 1907, when she was working in Germany. They show the influence of German garden design. The top drawing was also published in *Deutsche Kunst und Dekoration*, in 1907. Photo credit: National Library of Sweden.

to German culture to prospective clients. His branch in Berlin was especially important as a showcase for promoting his arts and crafts products to his circle of customers.[16] Ester Claesson was also introduced to *Heimatschutz*, the growing conservation movement in Germany, for which old towns, gardens and structures were of particular interest. In short, the work in Schultze-Naumburg's Saalecker Werkstätte was characterized by historical references and continuity as well as modern bourgeois culture. Because documentary sources are lacking, it is today almost impossible to say exactly which commissions Claesson was engaged in at Schultze-Naumburg's office; it is only possible to say that her work included garden, interior and furniture design and that it ranged from first design sketches to construction drawings.[17]

After returning to Sweden in 1913, Claesson initially worked with the renowned and innovative Swedish architect Isak Gustaf Clason and as a landscape architect for Theodor Adelswärd, Minister of Finances and a wealthy and progressive landowner. But after around a year, in 1914, she set up her own office in Stockholm. One of her first independent achievements was her participation with the architect Harald Wadsjö in the international competition for the Woodland Cemetery in Stockholm in 1914–1915. Their award of third prize in the competition received attention in Swedish and German journals.[18] During her first years back in Sweden, Claesson worked hard to establish her practice not only as a landscape architect, but also as a writer, and she published several essays on gardens and gardening in leading Swedish journals. She travelled widely and used her camera for documentation and for illustrating her writings. Among her clients were private bankers, nobility and wealthy landowners, as well as famous people, such as the poet and Nobel Prize laureate Erik Axel Karlfeldt and the film director and actor Mauritz Stiller.[19]

That Ester Claesson's German experience was of continuing importance to her after returning to Sweden is shown in her writings, in which she introduced German garden culture to a Swedish audience. A frequent topic was old Swedish and European garden culture and modern German landscape architecture. She introduced her Swedish audience to the work of Joseph Maria Olbrich and Paul Schultze-Naumburg, but without revealing that she had been working closely with them. She also contributed essays to *Die Gartenkunst* and *Die Gartenschönheit*. Claesson received international attention throughout her career. She participated in several international garden exhibitions, for example, in London in 1928. She was the only female landscape architect to be included in *Modern Gardens, British and Foreign*, Special Winter Number of *The Studio* (1926/1927) and in Hugo Koch's book *Der Garten. Wege zu seiner Gestaltung* (1927).[20] Some of her gardens were also highlighted in *Die Gartenkunst* (1928).[21]

Today, Ester Claesson's work is often understood to have been influenced by the British Arts and Crafts Movement. It is true that she kept well-informed about developments in the field of gardens and landscape architecture in Britain, probably through British journals, but also by a study trip in 1913. However, I would like to stress that her work reveals even more strongly her experiences studying and working in Austria and Germany during ten very formative years. She referred to this experience not only visually in her drawings and layouts, but also in her writing. My standpoint is also based on the fact that Ester Claesson, in an essay written in 1918 on landscape architecture as a female profession, clearly stressed that the best education would be obtained in Germany and Austria.[22] It is well known that much inspiration for the German reform garden around 1900 came from the British Arts and Crafts Movement. Looking at British and German gardens from a Swedish perspective reveals differences such as that the latter gardens were even more formal than the former, with more built structures and gravel and less use of grass. When it comes to Claesson, the German influence can be seen in her visual representations of gardens. Besides the inspiration from Olbrich and Schultze-Naumburg, whom Ester Claesson introduced to Swedish readers together with Hugo Koch, her drawings have much in common with those by the Austrian landscape architects Frantz Lebisch and Adolf Holub, whose work was featured in the same issue of *Deutsche Kunst und Dekoration* as hers.

Ester Claesson's contemporary Ruth Brandberg (1878–1944) took another path into the profession. She entered the Women's Teacher Academy in Stockholm, but changed her plans after her father's death. Between 1907 and 1909, she trained at the English Horticultural College for Women, in Swanley, Kent. From a Swedish perspective, this was the most popular school, and from the 1890s until around 1940, about fifteen Swedish women were trained there. The training consisted of a combination of practical work under skilled supervision and theoretical instruction.[23] As a schoolgirl, Ruth Brandberg had been a pupil of the novelist Selma Lagerlöf, who, after receiving her Nobel Prize in literature in 1909, was able to buy back her treasured childhood home Mårbacka (Figure 2.4). After Brandberg had finished her training and received her diploma in 1909, Lagerlöf invited her to come to Mårbacka to work as her gardener. The two women complemented each other. Lagerlöf supported Brandberg in her work, and Brandberg renewed the kitchen garden and the fruit tree plantation, thanks to practical experience from the British gardening school. Although Brandberg was capable of modernizing the garden according to prevailing British gardening ideas, she seems to have had problems introducing them. Lagerlöf was eager to keep her father's garden, which reminded her of her childhood. However, Brandberg managed to add a new herbaceous border and standard roses, which could be problematic to maintain because of the harsh climate. At Mårbacka, Brandberg also was in charge of all other garden workers, mainly men, which was an invaluable experience for her future career.

After a period at Mårbacka, Brandberg and her friend and colleague Gertrude Bråkenhielm decided to open their own market garden, but this project did not last very long, perhaps

FIGURE 2.4 Ruth Brandberg and Selma Lagerlöf in the garden at Lagerlöf's Mårbacka in Sweden, ca. 1910. Ruth Brandberg (right) is wearing a female gardener's uniform, resembling the British uniforms at the time. Photo credit: Mårbackastiftelsen, Sweden.

because running a market garden in those days was hard work and Ruth Brandberg lacked the necessary physical strength. However, the two women were not afraid of launching big projects. From 1911 onwards, Brandberg worked as a landscape architect with her own office located near Stockholm. She called herself a consultant gardener, but her work was more qualified than this title suggests. Most of her first private clients belonged to the nobility, and she mainly obtained these commissions on a word-of-mouth basis, grounded on the family relations between her clients. Her former employer Selma Lagerlöf was probably instrumental in establishing the first contacts as she had provided Brandberg with a letter of introduction.

However, Brandberg's most important commissions were hospital parks, which she designed during the third phase of her career (Figure 2.5).[24] These projects were carried out mainly between 1920 and 1940, in collaboration with the architect Gustaf Birch-Lindgren, who specialized in hospital architecture. Her full capacity is shown in these big civic commissions, which usually took several years to carry out. Today, only parts of these environments are kept in their original state of design, which makes it difficult to evaluate them in detail; but contemporary photographs and some drawings give invaluable information. The hospital parks were often designed to provide both a representative setting and an outdoor open space for the staff and patients. Established hierarchies between physicians and nurses, staff and patients, children and adults, were maintained in the design, so that these different groups

FIGURE 2.5 Ruth Brandberg, roof garden at the Serafimer Hospital in Stockolm, ca. 1930. The garden was made for the nurses and included seating furniture as well as a small conservatory. Photo credit: The Swedish Centre for Architecture and Design.

would meet only occasionally during breaks. Brandberg was especially eager to create outdoor space for children in direct connection with their wards, if possible. This interest in outdoor space for children at hospitals was new in Sweden in the 1920s.

A second generation: Inger Wedborn and Ulla Bodorff

Despite fast societal changes and development between 1900 and 1930, there were hardly any more or any easier opportunities for women to become landscape architects or gardeners, and the number of women entering the profession did not increase much. While in other countries, like Denmark, England and Germany, more women (and men) began to receive academic training in landscape architecture, beginning in the 1930s, this was still not the case in Sweden.[25] However, the type of commissions changed in Sweden, as it did in many other countries. New housing estates, projects for developing industries and for different types of institutions became more and more frequent. Inger Wedborn and Ulla Bodorff are in many ways representative of the generation that began its practice in the 1930s.

Inger Wedborn (1911–1969) was trained at the Horticultural College for Women at Swanley. She was inspired in her career and school choice by Ruth Brandberg. When Wedborn came to Swanley in 1929, she had basic gardening skills, which made it possible for her to enter a two-year-long course that resulted in a British Beekeepers Association's Examination and a Junior Craftsman's Certificate in 1931.[26] During her stay at Swanley, she published an article in which she presented the school and its training (Figure 2.6). The article introduced young Swedish women in search of a suitable education to the training, accommodation, clothes, fees and costs at the British Horticultural College.[27]

After working with her future and, today, more well-known partner Sven A. Hermelin, Wedborn continued her training in Germany between 1935 and 1936. She studied at the Institut für Gartengestaltung in Berlin-Dahlem, that was led by Heinrich Friedrich Wiepking-Jürgensmann.[28] Although only minor details are known about Wedborn's time at the school, it must have been a very formative period. Her time in Germany was concluded with an internship in the office of landscape architect Alwin Seifert in Munich, in 1936. Seifert was responsible for designing the vegetation along the new Reichsautobahnen, the big German motorway project largely carried out during the Nazi period.[29] The main purpose of this propaganda project was, of course, to encourage motorization. The project stressed landscape beauty, and the motorways were supposed to be embedded into the landscape following the ideals of the *Heimatschutz* movement (movement for the protection of the homeland). Through the use of native plants the motorways were also supposed to be turned into landscapes that could foster a German identity. Seifert used the vegetation to contribute to the creation of scenic beauty along the motorways. Another important part of the work was to restore the landscape that had been disturbed during construction work. Besides Wiepking-Jürgensmann, Seifert was the leading national socialist landscape architect in Germany, and Wedborn's work with him was probably facilitated by Wiepking-Jürgensmann.

After her period in Germany, Wedborn published an article on her experience of working with Seifert.[30] Together with some of her other writings, this article shows that she and her partner Sven A. Hermelin were interested in addressing questions concerning the construction of roads and the conservation of landscape. Building new roads through the old Swedish countryside inevitably led to changes in the landscape. Wedborn and Hermelin's writings echo the German *Heimatschutz* movement. Although Wedborn was interested in *Heimatschutz*, she did not continue with conservation work. Hermelin, on the other hand, became one of

Rosenpergolan får nya stolpar.

Foto: Förf.

FIGURE 2.6 Photo by Inger Wedborn, showing some of her fellow students working in the garden at the Horticultural College for Women, Swanley, Kent, UK. Originally published by Wedborn in *Allmän svensk trädgårdstidning*, in 1932. Photo credit: National Library of Sweden.

the leading national authorities with regards to road construction and landscape conservation. However, it appears that Wedborn acted in the background, as she had the connection with Seifert, whom Hermelin regarded as a key figure for his work.

The topics of some of Wedborn's early writings also show her interest in vernacular German gardens, including old farm gardens that she had visited on a field trip with Wiepking-Jürgensmann. When she wrote an article about this field trip some years after the war, she recalled it as one of the happiest moments of her life, highlighting how it had brought Wiepking-Jürgensmann's students together. She recalled, "I am sure that those friends of mine who still are alive hold the memories of this journey as dear as I do."[31] She was more concerned about what had happened to her former fellow-students than reflecting on Wiepking-Jürgensmann's political role. It is difficult to assess what impression Seifert and Wiepking-Jürgensmann's ideology made on Wedborn, and how World War II affected their relationship. According to Sven Hermelin, Wedborn and Wiepking-Jürgensmann developed a lifelong friendship.[32]

After returning to Sweden, Wedborn continued to work with Sven A. Hermelin and, in 1941, they founded the company Sven A. Hermelin and Inger Wedborn Trädgårdsarkitekter, which would become one of the most important offices in Sweden in the postwar period. Several generations of Swedish landscape architects passed through the office, being nurtured and trained in their early careers by Wedborn and Hermelin. The office worked on a wide range of commissions: housing estates, churchyards, private gardens, and open-space designs for companies and institutions (Figure 2.7). The Marabou Park for the chocolate company Marabou laid out from 1937 is often considered one of the office's most important commissions. The philanthropic Norwegian owner, Henning Throne-Holst, wanted to provide his employees with a park-like area that they could use during their breaks and that could be used by the general public during weekends. Throne-Holst also collected art, and sculptures adorn the five acres of park. As a result of its dynamic contours, Marabou Park is divided into two designed gardens in a dramatic setting: a formal, closed garden relates to the factory building; an open and informal garden space is located on a lower level, and is dominated by a generous lawn sprinkled with large trees.

FIGURE 2.7 View of a villa garden, designed by Inger Wedborn and Sven A. Hermelin, published in the journal *Hem i Sverige*, in 1949. Note the connection between the house and the garden for easy garden access. Photo credit: National Library of Sweden.

Inger Wedborn had a leading position in the company, both distributing and supervising work in the office and taking an active role in shaping the design process of gardens and landscapes. Like most other female landscape architects, she also contributed polemical articles, project presentations, essays and book reviews to professional journals and books. After her death in 1969, the joint venture was renamed Sven A. Hermelin AB. As a result, many of the office's projects have been attributed only to him, while Wedborn has become almost forgotten or has been referred to as dealing mainly with smaller projects, like color schemes for herbaceous borders. Only recently, scholars have begun to pay more attention to her, and mainly to her extensive writings, in which she discussed the landscape architect's roles and duties.[33]

Inger Wedborn's contemporary Ulla Bodorff (1913–1982) arrived in England in 1933 for studies in landscape architecture at the University College in Reading. Bodorff came from a family that was well established in the social and cultural life of Stockholm. She was one of the first Swedish women to receive a university degree in landscape architecture. The training involved subjects such as horticulture, garden design, building construction, art and chemistry. The exams consisted of theory papers, practical and oral tests and designs for different types of gardens. After receiving her diploma in landscape architecture in 1935, Bodorff returned to Sweden, where she worked for some time at the Stockholm City parks department before opening her own office in 1937. This coincided with the development of the Swedish welfare state and immense building projects, initially in the major towns. In a remarkably short time period she managed to obtain commissions from some very important entities, such as The Swedish Co-operative Union (Figure 2.8), leading building companies and the National Federation of People's Parks. People's Parks were arranged from around 1890 onwards all over Sweden, originally as places for social democratic political agitation and meeting places for workers. During the 1940s and 1950s, many of these parks were modernised with new theatre buildings, concert halls, cafés, etc. Bodorff was involved with projects at around 100 of these parks.

In her 1948 article "The Swedish Society of Landscape Architects: Brief Statement on Professional Practice in Sweden," in the American journal *Landscape Architecture*, Bodorff gave a general introduction to the profession in Sweden and to the landscape architects' different commissions and assignments. The most interesting aspect of the article is her reflection on her own practice:

> However, I think the social side of landscape making is the one that the man in the street – the taxpayer, you know – will enjoy most; and as it decidedly and very rightly is the taste of the common ordinary Swede whom we have to please, the landscape architect has to follow the style called Swedish Modern. It is a friendly social style, made for man, not superman. As a matter of fact, I would like to add: for the Swedish woman. Whether it concerns building architecture, indoor decoration, or landscape and garden layout, Swedish Modern is planned for mother and child perhaps more than for man.[34]

In taking this gendered perspective, stating that the modern housing areas were designed mainly for women and children, she was unique in Sweden at this time and it shows that, to a high degree, she was aware of societal changes and conflicts, although she herself belonged to the upper middle class (Figure 2.9). All illustrations for the article came from one of her most renowned commissions, the housing area Reimersholme, in Stockholm. This project was also

FIGURE 2.8 Ulla Bodorff, roof garden at the head office of the Swedish Co-operative Union, Stockholm, ca. 1940. The garden was divided into separate rooms for different functions. Shown here is the sunbathing area. Photo from *Trädgårdskonst. Den moderna trädgårdens och parkens form* (1948). Photo credit: Department of Art History, Stockholm University, Sweden.

exhibited at the Landscape of Work and Leisure Exhibition in London, in 1948. According to her colleague, the Italian landscape architect Maria Teresa Parpagliolo Shephard, Sweden was one of the countries setting the agenda for the exhibition: "Out of the Exhibition there can be clearly seen a modern trend that ultimately will mark the style of our age. The most typical examples shown are those from Denmark, Sweden, Switzerland, Norway, Poland."[35] This was a valuable recognition for Ulla Bodorff and her colleagues.

Ulla Bodorff was also working as a landscape planner on a large scale. An interesting example is her involvement in the drawing up of the city plan for the suburb Fröslunda by Eskilstuna in the late 1940s, a rapidly growing industrial town affected by the industrialisation and the influx of foreign labour after World War II. Bodorff worked with different landscape and vegetation types, concentrating pine trees in some areas, for example, and deciduous trees in others, but all the time in harmony with the houses.[36] This was a method that she would continue to develop during her long career. Another project from the same period is Stora Vika, an industrial landscape and a small village for the leading cement company, about 70 kilometres south of Stockholm (Figure 2.10).[37] The project included gardens for a wide range of inhabitants, from the managing director's representative villa garden to the workers' small garden plots near their terraced houses, as

FIGURE 2.9 Ulla Bodorff, housing estate at Gärdet, Stockholm, for the cooperative housing company HSB (the Tenants' Savings Bank and Building Society). Published in an article on the estate's landscape design, by Ulla Bodorff, in *Allmän svensk trädgårdstidning*, 1940. Photo credit: National Library of Sweden.

well as a sports ground, a small community center, and recreational areas near the office buildings. The construction of the industry had an immense effect on the landscape. To become nostalgic was not a solution. It was Bodorff's conviction that the landscape planner had no possibility of repairing the enormous damage to the landscape; instead, she should give the destroyed landscape a new face. This metaphorical way of describing landscape planning in terms of surgical operations echoes an international discourse, as seen in much of Sylvia Crowe's writings, and in Peter Shepheard's essay, "The Setting for Industry in the Landscape" (1966).[38] This grand-scale operational project, which today is difficult to grasp, both visually and emotionally, because the industry has closed and the vegetation has not been tended to according to the original ideas, was, without doubt, one of Bodorff's greatest achievements.

By the time Bodorff chose to close her office, around 1970, she had been a leader in the profession for more than thirty years, working on hundreds of commissions. Her experience in designing private gardens, housing areas and urban parks, church yards and institutional parks, as well as conducting landscape planning on a grand scale during this long and sometimes turbulent period of enormous changes and challenges, gives her a very special position within

En industrianläggning av Vikas mått skapar s:n egen landskapstyp med eget skönhetsvärde. Den har sin speciella dynamik. Landskapsplaneraren läker inte sår i berget — han ger berget ett annat ansikte. Man sätter inte buskar och planterar inte träd, utan modellerar terrängen i slänter och åsar i samspel med skogskonturerna i landskapets horizontbild. Vegetationen, som inplanteras, understryker landskapets egenvärde, men följer även geografiska betingelser, d. v. s. slån och nypon på torrslänter, poppel och pil i dalsänkor och fur och gran samt björk i övergång till skogsmarken.

FIGURE 2.10 Ulla Bodorff, sketch showing the landscape design for the cement company Skånska Cement at Stora Vika. The drawing shows the enormous industrial group of buildings integrated into the landscape. Published in *Hem i Sverige*, 1951. Photo credit: National Library of Sweden.

Swedish landscape architecture. A characteristic in many of her projects was their sensitivity towards the place, and a wish to incorporate existing structures such as trees, plants and rocks into the composition, both for economic and artistic reasons. The lack of original drawings, photographs and correspondence, due to her decision to destroy the office's archives, makes it difficult to examine many of her projects in detail. However, this circumstance is richly compensated by her extensive writing, covering project presentations as well as theoretical discussions of landscape architecture.

Running a practice: collaboration and exchange

In the first half of the twentieth century, most female landscape architects in Sweden owned their own offices, but the office locations and layouts varied. For the first generation, the physical location of the office was usually a separate room in the home. Most likely, they were working on their own or with a very limited staff. Leading their offices without a permanent staff does not necessarily mean that they were isolated. On the contrary, contacts and discussions with architects, construction companies, gardeners and other professionals were frequent. Moreover, the women usually both hired and directed workmen during the construction phase.

Many female landscape architects were regularly collaborating with architects. Although some of these collaborations are well known, it is difficult to stipulate the exact relationships. The collaborative work of the landscape architect Helfrid Löfquist (1895–1972) and the architect Cyrillus Johansson (1884–1959) is a case in point. His office was big and well established, hers was small and she usually worked by herself. He needed her skill; she needed the commissions. While he made sketches with detailed instructions, she turned these into drawings, including plant lists and working instructions that could be used by a gardener during the construction phases. Sometimes they worked so closely together that it is almost impossible to identify their individual contributions (Figure 2.11 and Plate 2.3). They both published their projects in different journals, and he never failed to give her credit for contributing to the overall design.[39]

Ulla Bodorff and Inger Wedborn (together with Sven A. Hermelin) led bigger offices with several employees, which made it possible for them to be engaged in more and bigger projects.

2. Around the southern part of the almost level courtyard the green cubes of maple and poplar hedges to the south form high walls. Within these walls the vegetation becomes lower and lower as it approaches the lawn.

Entourant la partie Sud du jardin, des carrés verts d'érables et des rangées de peupliers forment une sorte de haute fortification. A l'intérieur de celle-ci, la végétation se fait de plus en plus basse, jusqu'au au gazon.

FIGURE 2.11   Helfrid Löfquist and Cyrillus Johansson, photo showing the garden they designed together for the Armed Forces, Stockholm. Photo from an article by Helfrid Löfquist, published in *Havekunst*, 1952. Photo credit: National Library of Sweden.

These offices were mainly engaged with the design and planning processes and were not involved in the construction work. They followed and documented their commissions with photographs, drawings and other types of media and they published essays about them. As most women were trained abroad, they did not have natural platforms for contacts with former teachers or colleagues in Sweden. They had to build networks on their own. Advertising in journals, newspapers and telephone directories and contributing to professional journals became an overarching aim for most women, and an important part of the professionalization process. Ulla Bodorff's office had big windows facing a busy shopping street in Stockholm, which enabled passers-by to observe office life and the ongoing work. Of course, this was the best advertisement for her company.

Communication and networks

Swedish women represented their country at international exhibitions and landscape architecture congresses from around 1930. Dorothée Imbert has pointed out Ulla Bodorff's instrumental role in drafting the International Federation of Landscape Architects' constitution in Paris, in 1949. René Pechère had suggested her election as a member of the executive committee representing the Scandinavian countries.[40] By then, she had about fifteen years of experience at international meetings, starting with the meeting of the Association des Architectes de Jardins at the World's Fair Exhibition in Brussels, in 1935. She was 22 at the time and wrote a skillful and confident report on the meeting that was published in the Scandinavian journal *Havekunst*.[41] In 1938, she was among several other renowned landscape architects who participated in the second International Congress of Garden Architects, held in Berlin and Essen. Unlike C. Th. Sørensen and Christopher Tunnard, she did not avoid the Germans at this time.[42]

Bodorff became the editor of IFLA's publication, *International Landscape*, in 1959, a problematic task as it turned out to be difficult to publish. As the federation's honorary secretary, she was involved in organizing the Stockholm Congress, in 1952, with the theme "An idea and its realisation," including excursions and meetings around Sweden. At the Vienna Congress, in 1954, she represented the Scandinavian landscape architects and, during the meeting, she was elected IFLA's honorary treasurer, an assignment she carried out until 1964.[43] Bodorff's professional network was widespread, and it is obvious that she was a key figure in IFLA, with contacts in Scandinavia, Europe, the United States and Japan. Her international engagement was increased even further in 1953, when she was elected a corresponding member of the American Society of Landscape Architects. However, in a national context, Bodorff's appearance and clothes were highlighted as much as her professional attitude and her success. The women's magazine, *Idun*, introduced her in 1944 as "a highly efficient professional woman, well-looked-after and perfect as a flowerbed."[44] Here, the ambition was to present her as a model for other women and the play on words was a comment on her occupation. After her death in 1982, her colleague Sven A. Hermelin emphasized in his obituary how colourful she had been and that "she combined female beauty with ungovernable willpower."[45] This focus on her appearance parallels comments in a 1988 monograph on her, in which she was introduced as a vain extravagant sociable person, self-confident, rich and arrogant; a woman who knew how to enter a meeting room too late, elegantly dressed with a broad-brimmed hat and a cigarette holder in her hand. Although she received much attention and recognition from her IFLA colleagues, her work within the federation was played down in these publications.[46]

Ulla Bodorff was not the only Swedish woman working for IFLA during the 1950s and 1960s. Her contemporary, Sylvia Gibson (1919–1974) had a similar position. Gibson was born in Sweden but had spent part of her childhood and youth abroad, mainly in Brussels. She started her training at the Horticultural College for Women in Swanley, Kent, England in 1936, at seventeen, and received her certificate in 1939. After working for some years in Sweden, she continued her education at the Swedish Agricultural University, where she graduated in 1947. She came to Hermelin & Wedborn that year, working for a number of years on a wide range of projects until she opened her own practice in 1954. She received many private and public commissions, including designs for urban parks, infrastructure and city plans. At the time she was engaged in questions concerning legislation, education and training for landscape architects.

As Sweden's delegate to IFLA between 1954 and 1966, Gibson participated in several congresses and Grand Council meetings.[47] She was a member of the Education Committee and played an instrumental role in developing the federation's constitution, and in discussing the elections of new member countries, often from a political point of view. Her political interests are also expressed in her many articles, for example on the British Institute of Landscape Architects and its reports and on IFLA and its committees.[48] That Sweden, at this time generally seen as one of the most progressive and prosperous countries of the world, despite its peripheral European location, was represented by two women deeply involved in the federation's work during its crucial early development, raises questions about positions, gender and professionalization. Only a handful of women participated in the IFLA working committees at that time, among them Brenda Colvin, Sylvia Crowe and Gerda Gollwitzer. Bodorff's and Gibson's service in IFLA shows that they, and other women, were much more involved in processes concerning the professionalization of, and education in, landscape architecture than has so far been recognized, at least in Scandinavia. While they did not accept these positions because they were women, they proved that they were capable of taking on leading positions in developing the profession.

Concluding remarks

Swedish women managed to establish themselves as landscape architects from the beginning of the twentieth century onwards, not because of the Swedish education system, but in spite of it, usually leaving the country to obtain the appropriate training. Their travels provided them with opportunities to take part in discussions about landscape architecture with their peers and to study gardens and designed landscapes across Europe. They also invited colleagues to visit Sweden and, in various ways, therefore, facilitated the exchange of ideas. It has often been stated that female landscape architects were mainly occupied with private commissions. From the 1930s onward, however, their commissions became more varied, and included public projects, infrastructure and city planning. In many ways, the development in Sweden mirrors that of the United States, as presented by Thaïsa Way in *Unbounded Practice: Women and Landscape Architecture in the Early Twentieth Century* (2009), but on a smaller scale. However, this is not true for the establishment of educational institutions for landscape architecture, which took longer to develop than in the United States. No matter how well known and recognized the Swedish female landscape architects were during their lifetime, almost all of them are forgotten today. The women stand in the shadows of their male colleagues, who have been turned into icons by other male professionals and historians. We can only hope that ongoing research and a growing interest in gender questions as well as in questions related to gardens, parks and landscapes as cultural heritage will give women their due in the history of gardens and designed landscapes.

Notes

1 At least three obituaries were published in Swedish journals and papers, one in the Scandinavian joint journal *Havekunst* and two in Germany, in *Die Gartenkunst* and *Die Gartenschönheit*.
2 The role of women in landscape architecture and the lack of gender studies in Sweden in many ways parallels the situation in the US, as analyzed by David C. Streatfield in the essay "Gender and the History of Landscape Architecture, 1875–1975," in *Women in Landscape Architecture: Essays on History and Practice*, eds. Louise A. Mozingo and Linda Jewell (North Carolina and London: McFarland & Company, 2012), 5–31.

3 Bengt Persson, Eivor Bucht and Peder Melin, *Svenska landskapsarkitekter. Glimtar från branschen 1920–1960* (Stockholm: Arkus, 1991), 13.

4 Fredrika Bremer was a friend of Andrew Jackson Downing, whom she met during her stay in the US in 1849–1854. Several of her books were translated into English, among them *The Homes of the New World*, in which she wrote on her stay in the US (1853).

5 Despina Stratigakos, *A Women's Berlin: Building the Modern City* (Minneapolis and London: University of Minnesota Press 2008), ix–xvii.

6 The house was presented at length in *Idun* 27 (1914): 425–426.

7 Despina Stratigakos, "The good architect and the bad parent: on the formation and disruption of a canonical image," *The Journal of Architecture* 13, 3 (2008): 285.

8 Inger Wedborn, "Anna Weber: Kvinden som Gartner og Havebruger," *Lustgården* 14 (1933): 168.

9 Gardening classes were taught in Swedish schools.

10 For a thorough presentation of Joseph Maria Olbrich and Mathildenhöhe, see Ralf Beil and Regina Stephan, eds. *Joseph Maria Olbrich 1867–1908: Architekt und Gestalter der frühen Moderne* (Ostfildern: Hatje Cantz Verlag, 2010).

11 Catharina Nolin, "Ester Claesson und die deutsch-schwedischen Beziehungen am Anfang des zwanzigsten Jahrhunderts," *Die Gartenkunst* 21, no. 2 (2009): 260. See also Christiane Geelhaar, "Ein Stück lebendiger Kunst. Olbrichs Gartengestaltungen," in *Joseph Maria Olbrich. 1867–1908. Architekt und Gestalter der frühen Moderne*, eds. Ralf Beil and Regina Stephan (Ostfildern: Hatje Cantz Verlag, 2010), 313–319.

12 Östersund Municipal Archives, letter of introduction from Joseph Maria Olbrich to Ester Claesson (1907).

13 Nolin, "Ester Claesson und die deutsch-schwedischen Beziehungen am Anfang des zwanzigsten Jahrhunderts," 268.

14 "Vår första kvinnliga trädgårdsarkitekt," *Idun* 20 (1907): 522.

15 "Recent Designs in Domestic Architecture," *The Studio* 55 (1912): 132.

16 Norbert Borrmann, *Paul Schultze-Naumburg. Maler, Publizist, Architekt 1869–1949. Vom Kulturreformer der Jahrhundertwende zum Kulturpolitiker im Dritten Reich* (Essen: Bacht, 1989), 104–106.

17 Östersund Municipal Archives, letter of introduction from Paul Schultze-Naumburg to Ester Claesson (1913).

18 See Georg Hannig, "Der Wettbewerb für Erweiterung des Südlichen Friedhofes zu Stockholm," *Die Gartenkunst* 28, 9 (1915): 118–119. The competition was won by the architects Erik Asplund and Sigurd Lewerentz. This progressive and much-appreciated cemetery has been listed as World Heritage since 1994.

19 Stiller came to Hollywood together with the more famous actress Greta Garbo in 1925, but he returned to Sweden in 1927.

20 Percy S. Cane, *Modern Gardens, British and Foreign*. Special Winter Number of *The Studio* (1926–1927): 139, 151.

21 Ilse Tromm, "Beispiele schwedischer Gartenkunst," *Die Gartenkunst* 41, no. 3 (1928): 35–37.

22 Ester Claesson, "Trädgårdsanläggningskonst som kvinnligt verksamhetsfält," *Stockholms Dagblad*, 24 June 1918.

23 *The Horticultural College, Swanley, Kent. Syllabus of Work* (April 1907), 5.

24 A large number of Ruth Brandberg's drawings are kept in a public collection, The Swedish Centre for Architecture and Design, which is unusual for the work of female landscape architects. However, one of the most important sources for understanding Brandberg's ideas is her correspondence with Selma Lagerlöf. In these letters, we get to know some of Brandberg's commissions, her thoughts about them and her own abilities, as well as Selma Lagerlöf's view of her former pupil and protégée, which is tremendously important, both in understanding a profession in development and the individual woman in practice.

25 A Swedish university degree in landscape architecture was first possible in the 1960s.

26 *Swanley Horticultural College Magazine*, May (1933).

27 Inger Wedborn, "Från en engelsk trädgårdsskola," *Allmän Svensk Trädgårdstidning* 4 (1932): 12–14, 43–45.

28 Gert Gröning, "Teutonic Myth, Rubble, and Recovery: Landscape Architecture in Germany," in *The Architecture of Landscape, 1940–1960*, ed. Marc Treib (Philadelphia: University of Pennsylvania Press, 2002), 120–123.

29 For a thorough investigation of the Autobahn project, see Thomas Zeller, *Driving Germany: The Landscape of the German Autobahn, 1930–1970* (New York/Oxford: Berghahn Books, 2007).

30 Inger Wedborn, "Tysk väg- och landskapsvård," *Lustgården* 18–19 (1937–1938): 51–59.

31 Inger Wedborn, "Mitt bästa trädgårdsminne," *Hem i Sverige* 49 (1949): 208.

32 Sven A. Hermelin, "Inger Wedborn," *Landskap* 50 (1969): 41. Perhaps future research can specify how Wedborn dealt with these ideological and politically difficult processes.

33 Catharina Nolin, "Publicering och professionalisering. Om kvinnliga trädgårdsarkitekters författarskap som en väg till etablering och legitimering," *Bebyggelsehistorisk tidskrift* 60 (2010): 7–21.

34 Ulla Bodorff, "The Swedish Society of Landscape Architects: Brief Statement on Professional Practice in Sweden," *Landscape Architecture*, 38, no. 3 (April 1948): 91–94.

35 Maria Teresa Parpagliolo Shephard, "Landscape of Work and Leisure," *Building*, 1948, 271–274. Other Swedes participating in the exhibition were Hermelin and Wedborn.

36 Ulla Bodorff, "Landskapsplaneringen," *Byggmästaren* 26 (1947): 269–270.

37 Catharina Nolin, "Ulla Bodorff, landskapet och industrin," in *Berättelser från markerna. En antologi om järnet, skogen och kulturarvet. En vänbok till Gert Magnusson*, ed. Ing-Marie Pettersson Jensen et al. (Norberg: Skrifter från Bergslagens medeltidsmuseum 1, 2013), 297–306.

38 See, for example, Sylvia Crowe, *The Landscape of Power* (London: Architectural Press, 1958). Peter Shepheard, "The Setting for Industry in the Landscape," in *Landscape and Human Life: The Impact of Landscape Architecture upon Human Activities*, ed. Clifford R.V. Tandy (Amsterdam: Djambatan, 1966), 91–95.

39 Drawings and documents showing their cooperation and collegial work are kept in his collection in the Swedish Centre for Architecture and Design. From her practice nothing has survived.

40 Dorothée Imbert, "Landscape Architects of the World Unite! Professional Organizations, Practice, and Politics, 1935–1948," *Journal of Landscape Architecture* 3 (spring 2007): 17.

41 Ulla Bodorff, "Från den internationella trädgårdsarkitektkonferensen i Bryssel," *Havekunst*, 1935, 134–136.

42 Dorothée Imbert, *Between Garden and City: Jean Canneel-Claes and Landscape Modernism* (Pittsburg: University of Pittsburg Press, 2009), 121.

43 "IFLA News," *Anthos: Zeitschrift für Landschaftsarchitektur* 3 (1964): 33.

44 "En blomma åt en dam," *Idun* 42 (1944): 22.

45 Sven A. Hermelin, "Ulla Bodorff Gyllenhaal död." Similar wordings appear in other obituaries also.

46 Claus Nowotny and Bengt Persson, *Ulla Bodorff: Landskapsarkitekt 1913–1982* (Stockholm: Arkus, 1988), 6–8.

47 She participated in the congresses in Madrid 1950, Vienna 1954, Washington 1958 and Israel 1962, and in the Grand Council meeting in Lisbon in 1965.

48 Gibson's report on the Institute of Landscape Architects and its committees was published in *Havekunst* 29 (1948): 57–59, her reports on IFLA in *Havekunst* 48 (1967): 22 and *Havekunst* 49 (1968): 126–127.

3

URBANIST LANDSCAPE

Militsa Prokhorova, Liubov' Zalesskaia, and the emergence of Soviet landscape architecture

Alla G. Vronskaya

Summarizing the tendencies of contemporary urbanism in 2006, Charles Waldheim argued that, "Over the past decade, landscape has emerged as a model for contemporary urbanism, one uniquely capable of describing the conditions for radically decentralized urbanization, especially in the context of complex natural environments."[1] Waldheim connected the emergence of "landscape urbanism" to the postmodernist cultural turn, which prioritized indeterminacy, open-endedness and change that modernist town planning had lacked. However, the rigidity of modernist urbanism and the flexibility of landscape architecture appeared side by side long before the emergence of postmodernism. This essay will consider an early example of their dialog, an example that occurred at the apex of early modernism, in late-1920s Moscow. As it will demonstrate, there, landscape architecture was subjugated to the methods and principles of modernist urbanism, but, nevertheless, due to an association of landscape with nature and nurturing, preserved a traditional fascination with change and diversity and aimed at granting the beholder an experience of aesthetic gratification. In early-modernist masculine culture, this association and the values that it brought were, first and foremost, perceived as feminine – and indeed, in a contrast to the architectural profession that was dominated by men, women played key roles in early Soviet landscape design.

The first Soviet landscape architects were trained in the workshop of Nikolai Ladovskii (1881–1941) at VKhUTEMAS (Higher Art and Technical Studios, since 1927, VKhUTEIN, Higher Art and Technical Institute) and Ladovskii's architectural group ASNOVA (Association of New Architects), which united his students and co-thinkers. Subsequently, ASNOVA members formed the core of the Office of Design and Planning [Proektno-planirovochnyi otdel] of the Central Park of Culture and Leisure [Tsentral'nyi park kul'tury i otdykha, or TsPKiO] in Moscow, the biggest public park of the Soviet era, which was opened in 1928 as the testing ground for developing design principles for socialist public landscapes. Among the key employees of the Office, which became the intellectual center of the new discipline, were Ladovskii's students and members of ASNOVA, Mikhail Korzhev, Vitalii Dolganov, and their female colleagues, Liubov' Zalesskaia and Militsa Prokhorova. Prokhorova had worked in the Office since its first days in 1928, under the directorship of the famous avant-garde architect Konstantin Mel'nikov, himself a member of ASNOVA. The following year, Mel'nikov was replaced by another avant-garde luminary and a close collaborator of Ladovskii, El Lissitzky, who introduced Zalesskaia to the team. As both Mel'nikov and Lissitzky were simultaneously engaged with other commissions and were not able to devote themselves fully to the work at the TsPKiO, the elaboration of the practical solutions for the park was left to their subordinates at the Office, who worked in close contact with the TsPKiO director Betti Glan. It was through this collaboration between Ladovskii's former students, who were eager to put to practice novel modernist architectural principles they had just learned, and the park's director, savvy in the latest turns of Soviet ideology and responsible for using the park for mass propaganda, that the principles and methods of the architecture of Soviet public parks were laid out.

First women in Soviet architecture

Prokhorova and Zalesskaia were among the first women who entered the architectural profession, which in tsarist Russia remained closed to them in spite of a continuous pressure of the leftists. Only in the 1900s were women officially allowed to pursue university degrees in two disciplines – medicine and education. Although they were admitted to several art schools,[2] becoming an architect was harder because it required higher education. Since the early 1900s, "higher female architectural courses" existed in St. Petersburg and Moscow, providing an education that was practically equal to the one at an architectural institute but not granting its graduates professional degrees. Finally, the economic needs during World War I forced the government to confer on those courses the status of higher-education institutions, thus establishing the two polytechnic institutes for women. Their first graduates, however, appeared only after the 1917 Revolution.

The Revolution introduced co-education, and the first female students entered the First and Second Free Art Studios (Svomas, since 1920, VKhUTEMAS) in Moscow, although the percentage of women in VKhUTEMAS remained much lower than in the Moscow Polytechnic Institute – the former Moscow Polytechnic Institute for Women – where they comprised nearly half of the graduates.[3] Only in 1927 did the first women graduate from the Architecture Department of VKhUTEIN (as VKhUTEMAS was by then renamed), and later, with an increase in student numbers, the percentage of women among the graduates declined from 11 percent in 1928 to 6 percent in 1930.[4] Nevertheless, the female presence at VKhUTEMAS/VKhUTEIN was noticeable, in particular in the avant-garde, so-called "left," workshop of Nikolai Ladovskii. Five out of thirteen student members of ASNOVA were female (Prokhorova, Zalesskaia, Nadezhda Bykova, Maria Kruglova, and Irina Tikhomirova).[5] One can only speculate why Ladovskii's workshop was so popular among women. Perhaps, breaking free from traditional social roles, they considered themselves agents of historic progress and were inclined to follow most radical theories. Or perhaps Ladovskii's attention to subjective perception of architectural forms, which differentiated his design methodology from the functionalist approach of the constructivists, his major rivals among Soviet architectural modernists, seemed to conform better to a perceived female humanism. In any case, as a result of his popularity, Ladovskii's vision of architecture as an organization of dynamic perception defined the thinking of his students, including Prokhorova and Zalesskaia, thereby playing an important role in Soviet landscape architecture in its formative years.

Militsa Ivanovna Prokhorova (1907–1959; Figure 3.1) was born into the family of a machine engineer in Novogireevo, today within the boundaries of Moscow. At home, she learned two foreign languages – a rather uncommon ability among the first generation of Soviet intelligentsia, which explains her noted knowledge of garden history. In 1924, Prokhorova enrolled in the Architecture Department of VKhUTEMAS, where she studied

FIGURE 3.1 Militsa Prokhorova at her workplace at the Moscow TsPKiO. 1930. Courtesy of A.
V. Shchusev State Museum of Architecture (MUAR).

under Mel'nikov and Ladovskii. Shortly thereafter, she joined ASNOVA and in 1928
completed her education. As was common during this period of an acute shortage of specialists needed for the industrialization of the economy (in particular, during the so-called
First Five-Year Plan, 1928–1932), Prokhorova left school without graduating, moving on
to work in Mel'nikov's TsPKiO Office of Design and Planning; she graduated in 1930. An
outsider to the Moscow architectural establishment, Prokhorova remained timid in both her
work and personal life. She always wore her hair short, and neither married nor had children.
"At first glance it might seem that Militsa Ivanovna Prokhorova was not a 'hero' of . . . the
battles on the front line," began her obituary by Mikhail Korzhev. "A seemingly austere
person, who rarely spoke at meetings, modest and, as it were, secluded and unsociable, in the
inner circle of her friends Militsa Ivanovna changed into a person of a big soul and a tender
heart," who "sharply saw the world, perceived its beauty, keenly reacted to everything ugly
and foul."[6]

Coming from a well-connected family, Liubov' Sergeevna Zalesskaia (1906–1979;
Figure 3.2) was the only child of Moscow architect Sergei Zalesskii, in whose workshop
she received early exposure to the nuts and bolts of the architectural profession.[7] Zalesskaia
could read and write in English, French, and German.[8] She entered VKhUTEMAS in 1923
and graduated in 1929, defending an architectural plan for the TsPKiO as her thesis project

FIGURE 3.2   Liubov' Zalesskaia with her son. 1935. Courtesy of Russian State Archive for Literature and Arts (RGALI).

under Ladovskii. Immediately after, she took the position at the TsPKiO Office of Design and Planning and, like Prokhorova, devoted the rest of her professional career exclusively to landscape architecture. Unlike Prokhorova, however, Zalesskaia comfortably performed her social and family roles. The wife of the composer Nikolai Anosov and the mother of their two children, she remained active as a landscape designer and, from 1939, as a professor of urbanism and the history of landscape architecture at the Moscow Architectural Institute.[9]

A socialist park

Prokhorova and Zalesskaia entered Soviet architecture at a pivotal moment when its direction, principles, and forms were actively debated by both architects and state bureaucrats. One of the major new tasks that the architects faced in the late-1920s was the elaboration of the program for a socialist public park, the so-called "park of culture and leisure." The initial guidelines were given by the chairman of the Moscow Soviet (Council) Konstantin Ukhanov, who defined it as a place for "meaningful leisure" of the working class.[10] According to Ukhanov's concept, published in the Party newspaper *Pravda* in March of 1921, the park was conceived as an entertainment complex where workers could find everything for a day outside of the factory:

> The park has to have a cinema and a theater, both outside and inside, a radio, music, and a circus. The park has to [offer] all kinds of sports: football, shooting, running, athletics, water and rowing sports, bathing, swimming, boating . . . In the park, playgrounds and special children events have to be organized, as well as a switchback. Various exhibitions have to be demonstrated within specially constructed buildings in the park. Book and newspaper kiosks, dining rooms, cafes, milk and grocery stands will be open in the park.[11]

At Ukhanov's request, the concept was further elaborated by the minister of education and culture, Anatolii Lunacharskii, who shifted its emphasis from function to form and method. In 1929, Lunacharskii offered the directorship of the park to his protégé Betti Nikolaevna Glan (1904–1992), a twenty-five-year-old woman who had previously led one of the largest Moscow workers' clubs and participated in the executive committee of the Young Communist International. Young, energetic, and enthusiastic, "a person of a Komsomol training, who could inspire people and rally them for a big work," Glan herself seemed to embody the new Soviet woman.[12] "The foremost task of the park is a mobilization of the creative forces of the working class for the construction of socialism," announced Glan. Like Lunacharskii, she prioritized not individual, but collective forms of entertainment, such as grandiose performances and mass processions.[13] This program could only be implemented, Glan believed, in a park that was extraordinarily large. "The giants of industry demand the giants of culture," she declared, citing Marxist dialectical law of the transformation of quantity into quality.[14] The park had to possess "giant alleys, suitable for the movement of demonstrations of workers . . . giant squares or stadiums for political meetings, mass actions, and competitions, drawing dozens and hundreds of thousands of people together."[15]

It was arguably this giant scale of Moscow's TsPKiO, paralleled by equally grand territories allocated for parks of culture and leisure (PKiOs) in other Soviet cities, that substantiated the necessity of employing town-planning strategies for their design – a practice widely used by Prokhorova and Zalesskaia in their work at the Office of Design and Planning. The methods of landscape architecture were informed by four key principles of Soviet modernist town planning: Ladovskii's notion of a dynamic subject of urban design; a redefinition of this subject as an organized rally; Ladovskii's principle of the organic growth of cities; and functionalist zoning. As will be demonstrated below, once contextualized within the realm of landscape architecture, these principles were significantly modified, and their modernism mitigated and enriched by an aesthetic of the picturesque.

Kinetic subject

Ladovskii based his architectural theory on psycho-physiological aesthetics, which appeared in Europe in the 1870s in response to the emergence of experimental psychology (psycho-physiology). The question of perception, central to psycho-physiological research, formed the core of the new aesthetics, codified by such writers as Theodor Lipps and Adolf Hildebrand. Aesthetic thinkers found kinaesthesia, or muscle sense, particularly pertinent to architecture, which, unlike other arts, was perceived by a moving subject. The concept of space as a function of movement originated within this German-language discourse of "kinesthetics."[16] Space and movement also became central notions for Ladovskii and the members of ASNOVA, who made kinesthetics the basis of their architectural theory.[17] As a result, they focused their attention on "spatial" disciplines, such as landscape architecture and urbanism. The goal of architecture, for Ladovskii, was to direct the movement of spectators through space, allowing them to evaluate its formal qualities and thus to orientate themselves.

At the time when architecture, landscape design, and urbanism were not yet differentiated in Russia, Ladovskii not only saw the three fields as one discipline, defined as the arrangement of space; he also believed that landscape architecture and urbanism, working with space rather than solid mass, presented architecture *par excellence*. As the German psychologist Carl Stumpf put it, "What we perceive originally and directly is the visual field, the whole visual field . . . . If this continually changes through movement, we retain the disappearing parts in our minds and unite them with the newly perceived spaces into a whole. Thus, out of many spaces arises one space; this is explained by the continuity of space."[18] This principle dominated the approach of Ladovskii's second organization, ARU (Association of Architects-Urbanists, founded in 1928), which was exclusively concerned with urban planning. The task of ARU urbanism was to unite separate buildings into a unified and coherent whole: Ladovskii claimed in the ARU declaration that "Architecture, understood as a unified spatial whole, not only has to solve the problem of the design of separate structures, but also has to unite a group of structures into a unified spatial system, in which separate structures are only parts of the general architectural unity."[19]

This urbanist paradigm formed the framework for Ladovskii's interpretation of the TsPKiO. He responded to this task with great enthusiasm, assigning the design of the park as the topic of diploma projects to his students graduating in 1929 – Zalesskaia, Dolganov, Mikael Mazmonian, Karo Alabian, Ivan Bolbashevskii, Oganes Bal'ian, and Sergei Matorin. Following the method of her teacher, Zalesskaia organized the TsPKiO as a system of routes and perspectives (Figures 3.3 and 3.4). A 100-meter-wide alley led demonstrating columns of people toward the Rally Field, the compositional center of the park. A carefully planned arrangement of a series of "large spectacular points" [*krupnykh zrelishchnykh punktov*], which superseded each other as views in a picturesque garden or stills in a film, directed the movement of people through the landscape.[20] These spectacular points were regulated by a series of parallel diagonal alleys, which hit the main alley at acute angles: the latter, according to psycho-physiologists, seemed "occupied" compared to "empty" obtuse angles and thus provoked in a visitor an unconscious desire to move forward and discover.[21] Zalesskaia used the same principle of acute angles to design the area of the main tram route, which, passing along the edge of the Children's Village, led from the main entrance into the park. The Children's Village was located near the main entrance at the north-east corner of the TsPKiO, so that the parents, having left their children in this "live cloakroom," could start their journey through the park.[22] It was structured by a zigzag alley, in which each segment terminated with an architectural monument (Figure 3.5).[23] The tram route then passed along a spectacular hilly bank of the Moscow River, as if responding to the suggestion of Ukhanov that "even a ride on this tram alone along the beautiful bank of the Moscow River can give a great pleasure."[24] Elaborating this idea for the 1931 competition for the design of the TsPKiO, Prokhorova, Zalesskaia, and Innokentii Kychakov, working together as "The TSPKiO Brigade," supplemented their entry with a "Scheme of Transportation," which included both the means of connection between the park and the city and the transportation within the park (Figure 3.6). Metro, railway, and water transport were designed to bring visitors to the main entrances in the

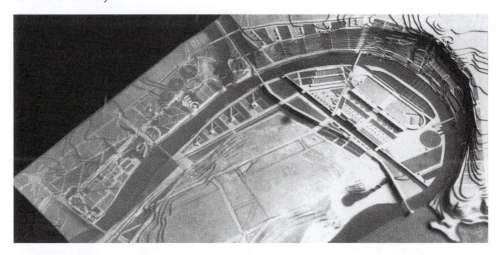

FIGURE 3.3   Liubov' Zalesskaia. Moscow TsPKiO. Diploma project at VKhUTEIN, 1929.
Model. Published in: *Stroitel'stvo Moskvy*, no. 10 (1929): 14.

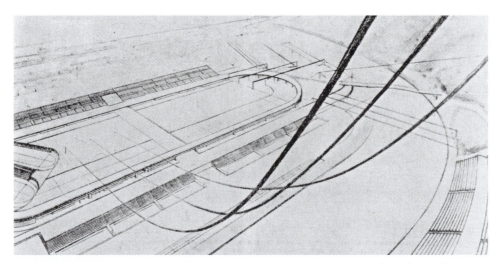

FIGURE 3.4   Liubov' Zalesskaia. Moscow TsPKiO. Diploma project at VKhUTEIN, 1929.
Perspective. Published in: *Stroitel'stvo Moskvy*, no. 10 (1929): 16.

north-east corner and the center of the TsPKiO; trams and buses were to run along the upper
bank of the river; and a "hanging railroad" (another idea borrowed from Zalesskaia's diploma
project) united the two banks.

Scenic perspectives offered by buses, trams, and, especially, the hanging railroad, whose sole
purpose seemed to have been sightseeing, made the approach of the TSPKiO Brigade very
different from the modernist functionalist attitude to transportation. Rather, the spectacle of
nature that the TsPKiO Brigade hoped to stage with the help of modern means of transport
connected it to an old tradition of landscape architecture, the experience of parks by horse
riders.[25] In other words, making their design dependent upon transportation, the architects

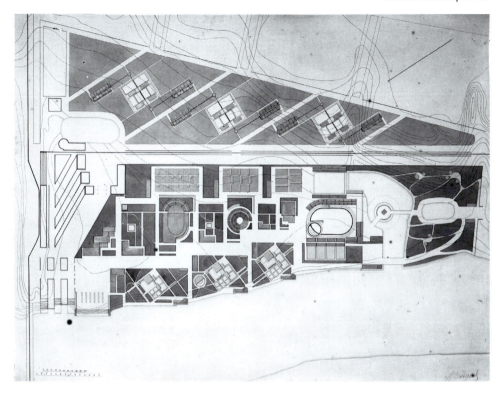

FIGURE 3.5   Liubov' Zalesskaia. Children's Village in the TsPKiO. Part of Diploma Project (?),
ca. 1929. Courtesy of A. V. Shchusev State Museum of Architecture (MUAR).

achieved not an economy of time or movement, but an efficiency of beholding a faster and
easier change of viewpoints and, ultimately, a deeper and more dramatic emotional effect.
Zalesskaia, Prokhorova, and Kychakov reinterpreted the functionalist preoccupation with
modern transport within Ladovskii's theory of a unified spatial field, making trams and buses
unite not only places, but also impressions.

Activation of visitors

Glan adapted the picturesque vision of nature as spectacle for the political and social realities of
the time. According to the principle of the activation of visitors [*printsip aktivizatsii posetitelei*],
which she developed as one of the park's defining postulates, the visitors to the park were
not passive spectators; on the contrary, they were co-workers who participated in the park's
perpetual creation through collective performative actions, a particular area of Glan's professional specialization.[26] Moreover, she claimed credit for creating a novel form of mass action,
a combination of political rally and theater performance, which destroyed the boundaries
between actors and spectators, and in which people, objects, and machines took equal part.[27]
Unlike individual (and thus rational) processes of reading and learning, also widely offered by
the park, these collective celebrations provided a nonrational aesthetic experience, aiming to
convince the visitors of the advantages of socialism not by logical reasoning, but by a "cheerful
and joyful organization of pastime" – a collective emotional experience.[28]

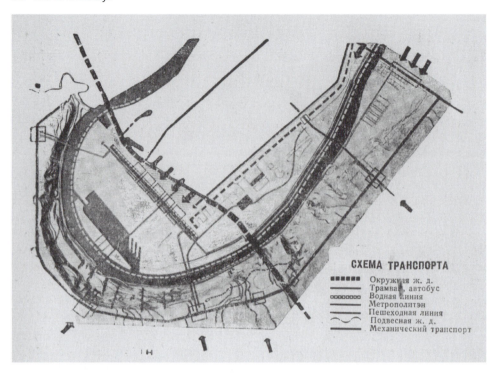

СХЕМА ТРАНСПОРТА

- Окружная ж. д.
- Трамвай, автобус
- Водная линия
- Метрополитэн
- Пешеходная линия
- Подвесная ж. д.
- Механический транспорт

FIGURE 3.6 TsPKiO Brigade (I. Kychakov, M. Prokhorova, L. Zalesskaia). Moscow TsPKiO (Competition Entry). Transportation Scheme. 1931. Published in: Betti Glan, *Za sotsialisticheskii park*. Moskva: Izdatel'stvo Mosoblispolkoma, 1932.

Glan's point of departure in elaborating on this concept was the practice of political rallies and theatrical processions staged on the streets of Soviet cities in the first post-revolutionary years under the patronage of Narkompros. Already in 1920, the minister Lunacharkii defined "organized masses" as the collective subject of the new art. It was organized masses that the park both served and fabricated, creating the space for its co-production by participating people:

> In order for the masses to make themselves felt, they must outwardly manifest themselves, and this is possible only when, to use Robespierre's phrase, they are their own spectacle. If organized masses march to music, sing in unison or perform some extensive gymnastic manoeuvres or dances, in other words, organize a kind of parade, then those other, unorganized masses clustering round on all sides of the streets and squares where the festival takes place, will merge with the organized masses, and thus, one can say: the whole people manifests its soul to itself.[29]

The idea of demonstration as spectacle (which realized both meanings of the word "demonstration," referring to the act of movement as well as to that of showing), together with Lunacharkii's concept of organized masses, informed Ladovskii's students' vision of a kinesthetic subject of architecture. In 1931, these ideas formed the core of several projects for the competition for the Palace of the Soviets, in particular of those submitted by the two groups most directly affected by Ladovskii's teaching – ASNOVA and ARU.[30] The ASNOVA Brigade, which united Prokhorova, Viktor Balikhin, Mikhail Turkus, P. V. Budo, Romual'd Iodko, and Flora Sevortian, proposed "not . . . a static monument, but . . . a live, acting organism, living the same life as the demonstrations and revolutionary-political mass celebrations" (Figure 3.7).[31] Moreover, Prokhorova and her colleagues planned the Palace of the Soviets not as an independent ensemble, but as part of a grandiose project to transform Moscow into a space of mass spectacle, in which the Palace occupied a central place in the processional route between Red Square and the TsPKiO. The ASNOVA Brigade presented a scheme for mass processions moving through the city rather than a project for a building. Coming from Moscow's ten districts, organized rows (referred to as columns, as in military marches) of demonstrators would enter Red Square through a complex system of ramps, which allowed the flows to bypass each other and go in opposite directions, just like clover-leaf formations of today's highways. Exiting Red Square, the demonstration would divide into three streams – one flowing into Il'ich Alley,[32] a broad ceremonial avenue between Red Square and the Palace of the Soviets; another moving along the Kremlin; while the third occupied both banks of the Moscow River. All three finally reunited at the Palace of the Soviets. As a sign of greatest distinction, awarded for revolutionary achievements and for exceeding production requirements, the columns that were to go through the Kremlin would ascend two wide ramps to the spacious Lenin Hall of the Palace of the Soviets; two flows would then encircle the amphitheater of the presidium, greet the delegates sitting in the Hall, then exit the palace through a 40-meter high Bridge of Shock Workers, and on two gentle ramps descend to the bank of the river to reunite with the flow of other demonstrating columns. Finally, all columns would surround the Palace of the Soviets and then head along both banks of the Moscow River to the TsPKiO, where the celebration would culminate.[33]

Prepared by the TsPKiO Brigade the same year, the plan for the park was based on ASNOVA's vision of mass processions within Moscow. Appended to the general plan were "The Scheme of Demonstrations" and "The Scheme of the Formation of a Mass Action" (*Schema postroenia massovogo deistviia*; Figures 3.8, 3.9, 3.10). Just as in the ASNOVA project for the Palace of the Soviets, Il'ich Alley connected the Palace with the TsPKiO, passing through the park as an avenue on two levels, culminating at the Field of Mass Actions

FIGURE 3.7 ASNOVA Brigade (V. Balikhin, P. Budo, R. Iodko, M. Prokhorova, F. Sevortian, M. Turkus). Palace of the Soviets (Competition Entry). 1931. Published in: *Sovetskaia Arkhitektura*, no. 4 (1931): 53.

FIGURE 3.8   TsPKiO Brigade (I. Kychakov, M. Prokhorova, L. Zalesskaia). Moscow TsPKiO
(Competition Entry). General Plan. 1931. Courtesy of A. V. Shchusev State Museum
of Architecture (MUAR).

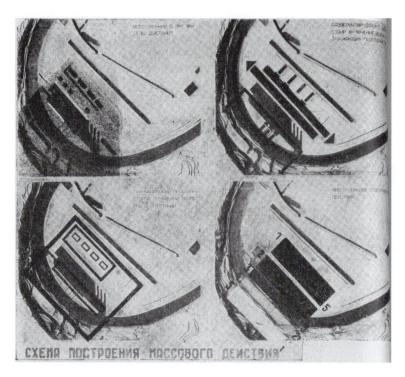

FIGURE 3.9   TsPKiO Brigade (I. Kychakov, M. Prokhorova, L. Zalesskaia). Moscow TsPKiO
(Competition Entry). The Scheme of Mass Action Formation. 1931. Published in:
Betti Glan, *Za sotsialisticheskii park*. Moskva: Izdatel'stvo Mosoblispolkoma, 1932.

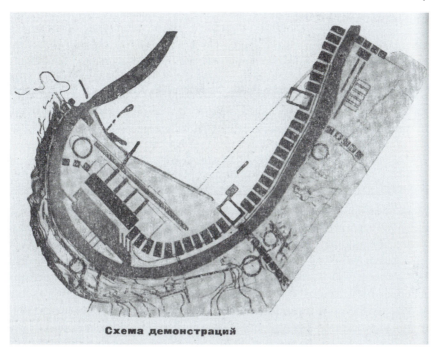

Схема демонстраций

FIGURE 3.10 TsPKiO Brigade (I. Kychakov, M. Prokhorova, L. Zalesskaia). Moscow TsPKiO (Competition Entry). The Scheme of Demonstrations. 1931. Published in: Betti Glan, *Za sotsialisticheskii park*. Moskva: Izdatel'stvo Mosoblispolkoma, 1932.

that was described by the authors as "the basis of the design of the TsPKiO."[34] Entering through side gates, smaller demonstrating columns would merge with the major one, which moved through Il'ich Alley. The spectacle continued on the water, in the Moscow River, in the Water Basin that stretched parallel to the Field and on the beach. On the slopes of the Vorob'evy Hills, one could enjoy the complexity of the mass action, creating a novel spatial unity that transformed the scale and shape of the landscape.[35]

"The organization of the masses" of city dwellers through mass spectacles and celebrations was a common practice during the first post-revolutionary years. Responding to the attempts to revive this practice in the late 1920s, Glan's principle of the activation of visitors through their participation in collective performance and the subsequent use of this principle by the TsPKiO Brigade was an attempt to integrate the park into Moscow's system of mass procession routes. As the masses were the object of their own spectacle, the old notion of a park was dramatically redefined. It was no longer understood as the natural surroundings or the architectural framework for mass movement; the park was the visitors who inhabited it. In other words, the visitors were the ultimate object of the park's architectural design and the focus of Glan's attention as the director. Despite this de-architecturalization of the Soviet park, the aesthetic experience that it offered remained surprisingly similar to the one produced by the parks of nineteenth-century Europe: by erasing the boundary between the subject and the object, the TsPKiO transferred the source of its psychological effect – the emotional experience of the sublime – from the natural scenery to the collective, returning to the Soviet park the nineteenth-century romantic aesthetic.

Organic growth

In 1930, when different projects and approaches to the planning of Soviet parks competed with each other, Ladovskii took part in another important debate – the discussion of the future of the city of Moscow, to which he contributed his major urbanist project, a parabolic scheme for Moscow's "organic" growth. Ladovskii claimed that the other projects understood Moscow mechanistically, as a static object. Suggesting a rational plan that organized the city at a given moment, they would necessarily break apart as soon as the city changed, Ladovskii believed. Unlike these projects, he wanted to approach the city as a living organism. The architect analyzed the city's various "organs" (functional zones) and provided each of them with space for independent "natural" growth, at the same time preserving the mechanisms that allowed these organs to collaborate. As a result, the traditional circular plan of the city had to be "torn open" into a horseshoe shape that would enable its further growth, while the city center acquired a fan-like shape that expanded towards the periphery.[36]

However, the hallmark of the ARU urbanist approach, the idea of organic urban development, first appeared three years before Ladovskii's parabola. It can be discerned in a collaborative student project of Prokorova and Georgii Kliunkov, titled "A Collective Farm" [*kolkhoz*] and submitted in 1927 (Figure 3.11). The project, which was Prokhorova's major success as a student, attracted the attention of the entire VKhUTEIN due to a novel method of clay skeleton construction and to the growth algorithm embedded in the *kolkhoz*'s plan.[37] Analyzing growth models of a Russian village, Prokhorova and Kliunkov suggested replacing its typical linear pattern of growth with other more rational ones, which they generated by subjugating the village to the process of "evolutionary development."[38] According to the authors, its linear growth evolved into an angular one when a second axis, perpendicular to the first, emerged from the same center. It was then transformed into a diagonal growth pattern that occupied the median space between them. Subsequently, tree-like branches extended outwards from the diagonal axis, expanding the settlement horizontally. Finally, other axes appeared and were interconnected by traversing perpendicular lines, creating a fan-shaped urban plan that possessed a potential for circular development. It was a circle that Prokhorova and Kliunkov considered the most appropriate form for the plan of *kolkhoz*, as "in the conditions of a contemporary village the major element is the administrative center, which replaces old individual service wings, and around which public and residential zones are grouped."[39]

Whether it was Prokhorova and Kliunkov's solution for a *kolkhoz* that influenced Ladovskii, or Ladovskii's gestating approach to urbanism that influenced his students is not an issue here; important is Prokhorova's early interest in the theories of organic urban growth, an interest that prompted her to apply these theories on a scale smaller than that of an entire city. It seemed to be a particularly appropriate solution for the design of "park-giants," such as the Moscow TsPKiO, which occupied 573 hectares (5.73 square kilometers), and whose construction had to be incremental by necessity.

Surpassing even the TsPKiO in Moscow, the PKiO in Cheliabinsk (an industrial city in the Ural Mountains), was to stretch over 1,800 hectares (18 square kilometers). When, in 1934, Prokhorova and Zalesskaia were asked to develop the strategy for the park's design, they presented the project as a diagram of growth patterns, a scheme for a long-term gradual expansion of the park, which could be opened to the public almost immediately.[40] The project became, in fact, an illustration of their universal method of park design, in which the scale of required architectural intervention was far greater than the resources of the local municipalities, a problem that was faced even in the case of Moscow TsPKiO.

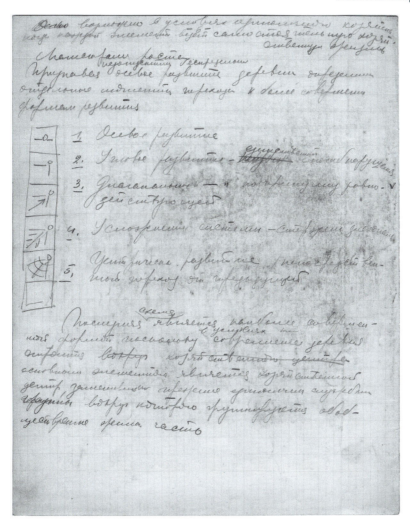

FIGURE 3.11 Militsa Prokhorova. List from her notes illustrating her student project (collaboratively with Georgii Kliunkov) "Collective Farm." 1927. Image courtesy of A. V. Shchusev State Museum of Architecture (MUAR).

The project for Cheliabinsk PKiO discussed several possible models of park growth and offered an example of applying them to local conditions (Figure 3.12). The first of these models, "central development," stipulated the expansion of the park "as one massif," which, just like Ladovskii's parabola, created a wedge that grew wider towards the park's periphery. It allowed for the shortest distances between various zones of the park and the city, and created a compact zone where emotional and ideological triggers were condensed. However, this model limited the directions of the park's development and meant that most of the park territory was beyond the reach of its visitors. The second model, the development of the land as "separate elements," established several centrically growing cores. It allowed for an equal growth of all zones and for access to most of the landscape, but dissipated the psychological impact of the park and made the distances between the park and the city too long. The third, "linear," model of the park's growth concentrated all zones along a strip that could expand outwards in both directions. According to Prokhorova and Zalesskaia, this was a palliative measure, which did not allow for the fulfillment of any of the requirements, but, at the same time, did not completely contradict any of them. The last model, "a secondary development," suggested a gradual creation in various parts of the park of smaller "park-combinats," each providing the basics of all functional zones. It enabled access to the park's various parts and simplified its construction, but made a comprehensive development of each zone difficult. As neither of these models was ideal in Cheliabinsk, Prokhorova and Zalesskaia suggested combining all of them (Figure 3.13). The northern part of the PKiO, adjacent to the city, was to be first developed as a "micropark" that possessed a minimum of the required features. Taking it as a starting point, the development then was to acquire an axial form and to spread in both directions parallel to the river, facilitating access to the water. The southern part of the park, assigned for health, was to be developed as separate clusters of sports facilities. All the sectors and the major objects of the park were located along the PKiO's major thoroughfare, the "automobile alley" (a park drive), which tied different segments of the park together.

Developed as a method of urban design, the incorporation of a model for growth into a city plan was, for Ladovskii and ARU, a critique that questioned modernist functionalism without dismantling its basic premises. Whereas, in town planning, the principle of organic growth was understood as an intrinsic tendency of urban form towards infinite expansion,

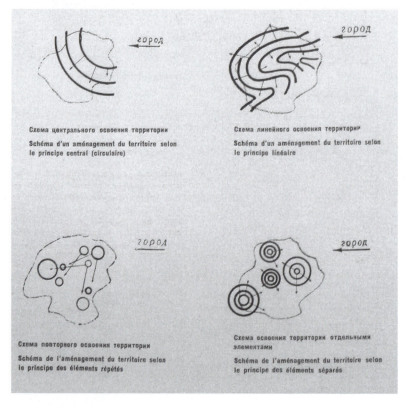

FIGURE 3.12 L. Zalesskaia and M. Prokhorova. Four models of a growth of a park. Published in: *Arkhitektura SSSR*, no. 5 (1934): 29.

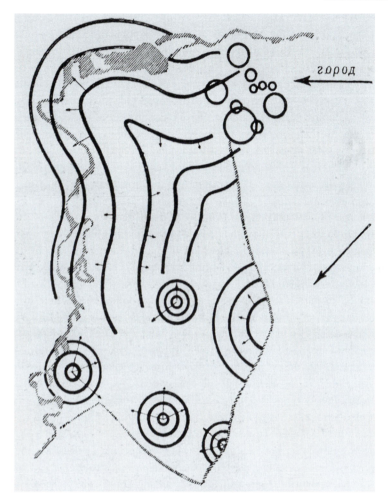

FIGURE 3.13 L. Zalesskaia and M. Prokhorova. Scheme of prospective development of
Cheliabinsk PKiO. Published in *Arkhitektura SSSR*, no. 5 (1934): 29.

it was applied to landscape architecture in a search for practical solutions to the dilemma
of building for the future with the limited resources of the time. The park, like a tree, was
to grow and mature slowly, reaching its ideal shape only years after it was planned and
opened.

The principle of switching

By 1928, when the seminal modernist town-planning initiative, Congrès International
d'Architecture Moderne (CIAM) had been founded, functional zoning had become one of the
acknowledged cornerstones of modernist urbanism. In the words of historian Eric Mumford,
it was "the most significant theoretical approach of CIAM," which dominated its discourse
from 1930 onwards.[41] Functional zoning was the topic of CIAM's fourth meeting, initially
scheduled to take place in Moscow in 1933.[42] Never questioned by modernist architects, functional zoning was also accepted by all Soviet modernist architects, regardless of their political

affiliations. After the Soviet delegate to CIAM, Moisei Ginzburg, and the first director of the Office of Design and Planning, Mel'nikov, had made zoning the guiding principle of their entries to the Moscow TsPKiO competition, zoning became a necessary principle of planning of Soviet public parks.

Glan, too, welcomed zoning in the Moscow TsPKiO: structuring the park according to the interests of the visitors, zoning allowed them to develop their individuality. However, while she asserted zoning as the principle of park design, Glan also asked the architects to devote special attention to borders and the spaces between different zones to ensure "a correct transition of the worker from one activity to another."[43] Thus, the principle of zoning was supplemented with – to use a term introduced by El Lissitzky – "the principle of switching." According to Lissitzky, who assumed the position of the director of the Department of Design and Planning of Moscow TsPKiO at the same time as Glan became the director of the entire park, the principle of switching guaranteed the correct ideological effect of the park, as it tacitly prompted the visitors to move between zones, exploring all of them rather than only one. Starting their movement through the park in the zone of their particular interest, the visitors then found themselves in a neighboring area, from which they moved further, being thus subjected to a "combined effect [*kompleksnoe vozdeistvie*] of all forms of work of a park."[44]

The employees of the Office of Design and Planning adopted the method of their superiors. Arranging the zones and providing transitions between them became Prokhorova's main concern in her largest independent project of these years, the TsPKiO in Tula (1934), an old industrial city south of Moscow (Figure 3.14).[45] Prokhorova's scheme significantly enlarged the preexisting park, which was now to occupy 1.5 square kilometers. To use Prokhorova's expression, the park had "to suck in" 10 percent of the city's population (twenty to thirty thousand people) on weekends and holidays.[46] Whereas zoning allowed an even distribution of the masses throughout the park, the circulation of visitors between the zones was made possible by their carefully arranged sequence and the creation of transitional spaces between them.

The key to the effective functioning of the zoning of the Tula TsPKiO was the "switching zone [*zona perekliuchenia*]" that was located at the main entrance to the park. There, the visitors received initial information about the park's plan and could develop their route through it and their personal program of pastime. As planned and partially built, the zones for various activities or different groups of visitors formed segments of a circle around the central square, similar to Mel'nikov's solution for the Moscow TsPKiO. An external circular alley ran along the park's periphery, allowing for a fast transition between different zones, however, the main way of connection between zones remained direct trespassing. To facilitate this connection, zones with similar functions were planned adjacent to each other. Lacking defined boundaries, they gradually merged together. The Children's Village, where the youngest could swim and waddle in pools and play in playgrounds while their mothers rested in the shade of trellises and tents, bordered the sector for school-age children, a miniature of the adult park with its own main house, stadium, theater, libraries, and sport- and playgrounds. The Children's Theater was to be located on the border with the adult zone in order to be accessible to those children who visited the park with their parents. Older children could also use the Popular-Scientific Sector, which hosted grounds for mass gatherings and processions, exhibition pavilions, and "scientific-technical attractions." A demonstration of military technology continued the exhibition program in the largest zone – the Military Sector. It occupied the space to the west of the Popular-Scientific Sector and was connected both to it and to the stadium, with which it shared the training agenda. Stretching out nearby was a row of military playgrounds that subsequently merged with the grounds of the abutting Sport Zone. An outdoor swimming

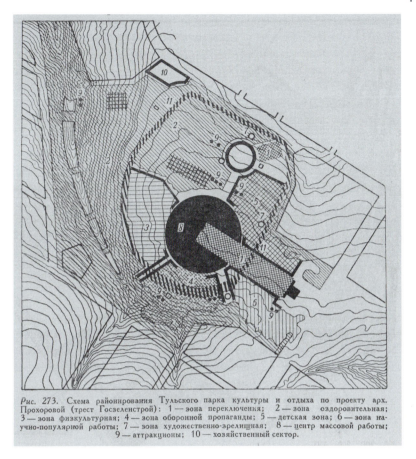

Рис. 273. Схема районирования Тульского парка культуры и отдыха по проекту арх. Прохоровой (трест Госзеленстрой): 1 — зона переключения;   2 — зона оздоровительная; 3 — зона физкультурная; 4 — зона оборонной пропаганды; 5 — детская зона; 6 — зона научно-популярной работы; 7 — зона художественно-зрелищная; 8 — центр массовой работы; 9 — аттракционы; 10 — хозяйственный сектор.

FIGURE 3.14   Militsa Prokhorova. Tula PKiO. Zoning scheme. Published in: L. B. Lunts, *Parki kul'tury i otdykha*. Moskva: Gosstroiizdat, 1934. P. 310 (fig. 273). Courtesy Dumbarton Oaks Research Library and Collection.

pool surrounded by green walls divided the Sport Zone from the Zone of Health, with its grounds for individual exercise. Next to it were a dancing ground and a stage for amateur performances, which bordered with the area of quiet rest on the western side of the park. There, a network of narrow paths connected occasional benches, gazebos, and reading huts.[47]

The principle of switching, developed by Glan and Lissitzky and adopted by Prokhorova for her Tula project, appeared as a reaction against the confining and segregating approach of functionalist zoning, which proved even harder to follow in landscape architecture than in urban design. If modernist town planning disentangled different types of activity, aspiring to make them more efficient, the park simultaneously separated them and brought them together to encourage visitors to diversify their activities in order to contribute to their full and multi-faceted personal development as well as to a more comprehensive absorption of state propaganda.

The urbanist landscape of Prokhorova and Zalesskaia employed and simultaneously subverted the strategies of modernist urbanism in the emerging field of landscape architecture. It prioritized movement and dynamism, progress and expansion; it facilitated the formation of an obedient and suggestible organized collective subject; it relied on transportation and functional zoning. At the same time, the very medium of landscape, its ephemeral characteristics and its association with aesthetic contemplation, seemed to defy a strictly urbanist program, and the projects of Prokhorova and Zalesskaia returned to landscape architecture some of its traditional qualities rejected by modernism. Introducing modern means of transportation into the park became an opportunity for creating picturesque effects, while the new collective subject transformed into the object of its own aesthetic contemplation and created a new sublime; growth and expansion demanded open-endedness and changeability; and even the boundaries between the different functional zones of a park were reinterpreted as liminal, transitory spaces.

Although it was soon replaced by other approaches, the program of urbanist landscape developed at the Office of Design and Planning of Moscow TsPKiO between the late 1920s and the early 1930s became the first Soviet methodology of landscape design, which influenced the subsequent development of the discipline in the USSR. Some of its characteristic traits, such as the production of spectacles and the functional specialization of various park zones, persisted throughout the years. It informed the methodology of landscape architecture in the late-Soviet era in the context of Khrushchev's return to modernism in the 1960s when, after Prokhorova's death, Zalesskaia revived, promoted, and headed the discipline.[48]

Acknowledgment

This research was made possible through the generous support of a Dumbarton Oaks Research Library fellowship in Garden and Landscape Studies in the fall of 2011. I am particularly indebted to John Beardsley, Michael G. Lee, Robin Veder, and Michael Herchenbach. I am also thankful to my dissertation committee: Mark Jarzombek, Caroline Jones, and Danilo Udovički-Selb.

Notes

1 Charles Waldheim, "Landscape as urbanism," in *The Landscape Urbanism Reader*, ed. Charles Waldheim (New York: Princeton Architectural Press, 2006), 37.

2 Many women, indeed, enjoyed successful artistic careers: Zinaida Serebriakova, Olga Rozanova, Varvara Stepanova, and Liubov' Popova, to name just a few highly successful female artists.

3 Moscow Women Polytechnic Institute was formed in 1916 on the basis of Women Building Courses (est. 1902). In 1918, it was transformed into Moscow Polytechnic Institute, but the first men appeared there only in 1920. See Selim Khan-Magomedov, *Pervye vypuski molodykh storonnikov arkhitekturnogo avangarda: MPI-MIGI (1920–1924 gg.)* [*First graduates of young supporters of architectural avant-garde: MPI-MIGI (1920–1924)*] (Moskva: Architectura, 1997).

4 Khan-Magomedov, *Pervye vypuski molodykh storonnikov arkhitekturnogo avangarda*, 29, 193.

5 Vladimir Krinskii, "*Vozniknovenie i zhizn' ASNOVA*" ["The emergence and life of ASNOVA"], *Sovetskaia arkhitektura* [*Soviet architecture*], 18 (1969): 27.

6 Mikhail Korzhev, "*Doklad o tvorcheskom puti parkovogo arkhitektora, chlena SSA i chlena sektsii ozelenenia goroda Moskvy Prokhorovoi Militsy Ivanovny*" ["Report on the professional path of landscape architect, member of Soviet Union of Architects and member of the Section of Greening of the City of Moscow Militsa Ivanovna Prokhorova"], March 1960: 2, 24. Unpublished manuscript. Archive of A.V. Shchusev State Museum of Architecture, Moscow.

7 Zalesskaia personal profile at VKhUTEMAS. Russian State Archive for Literature and Arts (RGALI). VKhUTEMAS collection.

8 Zalesskaia's personal profile at Moscow Architectural Institute (MARHI). MARHI Archive.

9 Moscow Architectural Institute was formed in 1933 as a result of a series of reorganizations of VKhUTEMAS, inheriting its Architecture Department. For more on Zalesskaia's later career, see "Liubov' Sergeevna Zalesskaia," *Arkhitektura SSSR* [*Architecture of the USSR*], 3 (1968): 43.

10 Konstantin Ukhanov, "*V bor'be za kul'turu (K organizatsii v Moskve 'Parka kul'tury i otdykha')*" ["In a fight for culture (On the opening of 'Park of culture and leisure' in Moscow"], *Pravda* [*Truth*], March 21, 1928. The program was subsequently developed in a resolution of the Moscow Committee of the

Party, in a special decree of Narkompros, and in the materials of the All-Union Meeting on Parks of Culture and Leisure held by the Central Soviet of Trade Unions (VTsSPS) in 1933.

11 Ukhanov, "*V bor'be za kul'turu.*"

12 Mikhail Korzhev, "*Doklad o tvorcheskom puti . . . Prokhorovoi Militsy Ivanovny,*" 8. Betty Glan was born into the family of a small factory manager in Kiev, where she attended the French Department of Higher Courses of Foreign Languages. At Lunacharkii's invitation, she moved to Moscow, where she subsequently became the head of Krasnopresnenskii Youth Club. In 1925, she graduated from the Department of Social Sciences of Moscow State University and became the executive secretary of the Russian section in the Executive Committee of The Young Communist International. She became the director of TsPKiO in 1929. In 1937, Glan's husband, the head of the Central Committee of the Communist Party of Yugoslavia between 1932 and 1937, Milan Gorkić was executed, while she was subjected to repression. Rehabilitated after the death of Stalin, in 1955 she returned to work at the Union of Composers of the USSR, All-Russian Theatrical Society, and the Union of Theatrical Workers of the RSFSR. In 1988, Glan published her memoirs, *Celebration is always with us* (B.N. Glan, *Prazdnik vsegda s nami.* Moskva: Soiuz teatral'nykh deiatelei, 1988).

13 Slogan in *Park kul'tury i otdykha* [*Park of Culture and Leisure*], August 12, 1931, 3.

14 Betti Glan, "Tri goda raboty parka" ["Three years of the park's work"], *Park kul'tury i otdykha,* August 12, 1931, 1.

15 Betti Glan, "Za sotsialisticheskii park" ["For a socialist park"], in *Za sotsialisticheskii park. Obzor proektov general'nogo plana Tsentral'nogo parka kul'tury i otdykha Mossoveta* [For a socialist park. A review of projects for the general layout of the Central Park of Culture and Leisure of Mossovet], ed. Betti Glan (Moskva: Izd. Mosoblispolkoma, 1932), 14.

16 Zeynep Çelik, "Kinaestheisa," in *Sensorium: Embodied Experience, Technology, and Contemporary Art,* ed. Caroline Jones (Cambridge, MA: MIT Press, 2006), 159–162; Zeynep Çelik, "Kinaesthetic Impulses: Aesthetic Experience, Bodily Knowledge, and Pedagogical Practices in Germany, 1871–1918" (PhD diss., Massachusetts Institute of Technology, 2007).

17 See, for instance, Nikolai Dokuchaev, "Arkhitektura i tekhnika" ["Architecture and technology"], *Sovetskoe iskusstvo* [*Soviet art*], 8–9 (1926): 3–9.

18 Carl Stumpf, *Über den psychologischen Ursprung der Raumvorstellung* (Leipzig: S. Hirzel, 1873), 278. Translated into English in Harry Francis Mallgrave and Eleftherios Ikonomou, "Introduction," in *Empathy, Form and Space: Problems in German Aesthetics, 1873–1893,* eds. Harry Francis Mallgrave and Eleftherios Ikonomou (Los Angeles, CA: Getty Research Institute, 1994), 60. Stumpf's 1907 book *Erscheinungen und Funktionen* [*Phenomena and [psychic] functions*] was translated into Russian in 1913 (Karl Stumpf, "Iavlenia i psikhicheskie funktsii," in *Novye idei v filosofii* [*New ideas in philosophy*], vol. 4. St. Petersburg: Obrazovanie, 1913).

19 "Ob'edinenie arkhtitektorov-urbanistov" ["Association of architects-urbanists"], *Arkhitektura i VKhUTEIN* [*Architecture and VKhUTEIN*] 1 (January 1929), 8.

20 Vitalii Lavrov, "Park ku'tury i otdykha v Moskve po proektam diplomnikov VKhUTEINa" ["Park of Culture and Leisure in Moscow in the projects of VKhUTEIN graduating students"], *Stroitel'stvo Moskvy* [*The construction of Moscow*], 10 (1929): 18.

21 Georgii Chelpanov, "Glazomer i illiuzii zrenia" ["Eye-balling and visual illusions"], *Voprosy filosofii i psikhologii* [*Issues of Philosophy and Psychology*] 17 (1893): 53; 18 (1893): 1–13.

22 Lavrov, "Park ku'tury i otdykha v Moskve po proektam diplomnikov VKhUTEINa," 18.

23 Lavrov, "Park ku'tury i otdykha v Moskve po proektam diplomnikov VKhUTEINa," 17.

24 Ukhanov, "V bor'be za kul'turu."

25 Originating in the Renaissance, in the nineteenth century this tradition was continued by an exploration of the scenic possibilities of railroads and, later still, parkways.

26 Glan, "Za sotsialisticheskii park," 10.

27 Glan, "Tri goda raboty parka," 1.

28 Glan, "Za sotsialisticheskii park," 14.

29 Anatolii Lunacharskii, "O narodnykh prazdenstvakh" ["On popular festivals"], *Vestnik teatra* [*Theater Courier*], 62 (27 April–2 May 1920); 13. English translation: *Street Art of the Revolution: Festivals and Celebrations in Russia, 1918–1933,* eds. Vladimir Tolstoy, Irina Bibikova, and Catherine Cooke (London: The Vendome Press, 1990), 124.

30 This was the infamous competition that commemorated the turn to historicism in Soviet architecture.

31 Brigada ASNOVA [Viktor Balikhin, Militsa Prokhorova, Mikhail Turkus, P.V. Budo, Romual'd Iodko, Flora Sevortian], "ASNOVA. Drovets Sovetov" ["ASNOVA. The Palace of the Soviets"], *Sovetskaia Arkhitektura* [*Soviet architecture*], 4 (1931): 52.

32 Il'ich, Lenin's patronymic, was often used by Soviet propaganda.

33 Brigada ASNOVA, "ASNOVA. Drovets Sovetov," 62–65.

34 Leonid Lunts, "Opisanie proektov general'nogo plana Tsentral'nogo parka kul'tury i otdykha Mossoveta" ["Description of the projects of the general layout of the Central Park of Culture and Leisure of Mossovet"] in *Za sotsialisticheskii park*, 24.

35 While these grandiose demonstrations were to happen only on major holidays, smaller performances were to become a part of the TsPKiO's everyday life. They were to be staged near the entrance to the park, transforming a flower parterre designed by Mel'nikov into a "living newspaper" – constantly changing *tableaux vivants*, exhibitions, and performances that illustrated issues of international, national, city, district, and, finally, park significance. Leonid Lunts, *Parki kul'tury i otdykha* [*Parks of Culture and Leisure*] (Moskva: Gosstroiizdat, 1934), 215–218.

36 Nikolai Ladovskii, "Moskva istoricheskaia i sotsialisticheskaia" ["Historic and socialist Moscow"], *Stroitel'stvo Moskvy* [*The construction of Moscow*], 1 (1930): 20.

37 Militsa Prokhorova and Georgii Kliunkov, "Ob'iasnitel'naia zapiska k proektnoi kontrol'noi rabote studentov 5go kursa VKhTI Prokhorovoi M. I. i Kliunkova G. I. 'Proekt – kollektivnoe krest'ianskoe khoziaistvo i obsluzhivaiushchii ego kombinat" ["Explanatory note to the design project of fifth-year students of VKhTI M. I. Prokhorova and G. I. Kliunkov Project: collective farm with a service complex"], s.a. Unpublished manuscript. Archive of A.V. Shchusev State Museum of Architecture.

38 Prokhorova and Kliunkov, "Ob'iasnitel'naia zapiska . . ."

39 Prokhorova and Kliunkov, "Ob'iasnitel'naia zapiska . . ."

40 Leonid Lunts, "Parki kul'tury i otdykha gorodov-novostroek" ["Parks of culture and leisure of new cities"], *Arkhitektura SSSR* [*Architecture of the USSR*], 5 (1934): 24–27, 29.

41 Eric Mumford, *The CIAM Discourse on Urbanism, 1928–1960* (Cambridge, MA: MIT Press, 2000), 59.

42 The congress in Moscow was cancelled; it later took place aboard the ship *Partris II*, sailing from Marseille to Athens, where the famous "Athens Charter" was drafted.

43 Glan, "Za sotsialisticheskii park," 18.

44 Lunts, *Parki kul'tury i otdykha*, 265.

45 The implementation of the project was interrupted by World War Two and was never carried out completely; however, the realized parts (mostly the general layout) can still be seen today.

46 Militsa Prokhorova, "Eskiznyi proekt planirovki parka kul'tury i otdykha v gorode Tule, i poiasnitel'naia zapiska k nemu" ["Preliminary project of planning of the park of culture and leisure in Tula, with an explanatory note"]. April 1934. Unpublished manuscript. Archive of A.V. Shchusev State Museum of Architecture.

47 At the same time, Prokhorova's project for the Tula TsPKiO followed the principle of organic growth. The core of the initial stage of the park's construction, the neighboring territory of the old Petrovskii Park, was to be developed and used as a multi-functional small-scale park, with its own stages, dancing grounds, and spaces for manifestations and exhibitions.

48 See, Liubov' Zalesskaia, ed. *Landshaftnaia arkhitektura: sbornik statei po materialam soveshchania, posviashchennogo voprosam landshaftnoi arkhitektury* [*Landscape architecture: a collection of articles based on the meeting devoted to the issues of landscape architecture*] (Moskva: Gosizdat lit-ry po stroitel'stvy, arkhitekture i stroitel'nym materialam), 1963.

4

ANNA PLISCHKE AND HELENE WOLF

Designing gardens in early twentieth-century Austria

Ulrike Krippner and Iris Meder

In early twentieth-century Austria, creating private gardens was the main task of garden design. Inspired by the new ideas in architecture and the arts and influenced by a new understanding of bourgeois living, more and more landowners had new homes constructed and their gardens adapted or designed as outdoor living spaces. Thus, the interwar period was a prosperous time for garden architects. In Vienna, the lively capital of a shrunken empire after the collapse of the Austro-Hungarian monarchy, an increasing number of professionals opened their own businesses. Men outnumbered women, but, nevertheless, a few middle-class women achieved advanced training and professional independence. Among them were Anna Plischke (Figure 4.1) and Helene Wolf (Figure 4.2), who started their careers as gardeners and garden architects in the 1920s. Although their professional backgrounds and their biographies vary in many respects, a precise look at their narratives and projects provides an insight into the maturation of landscape architecture in Austria and allows for conclusions about the changing role of women in the profession.

Most challenging for today's research is the fact that Anna Plischke and Helene Wolf, who came from Jewish families, were expelled during National Socialism and, as a consequence, their estates were scattered or destroyed. Some of Anna Plischke's projects survived within the estate of her husband, the architect Ernst A. Plischke, at the *Kupferstichkabinett* of the *Akademie der Bildenden Künste Wien* (Academy of Fine Arts Vienna). As for Helene Wolf, we have no primary documents of her work; a few articles in historic journals are the only evidence of her career. Owing to the fragmentary nature of the primary sources, a comprehensive analysis of the professional careers of Plischke and Wolf and of their design projects is difficult. However, we want to reveal their contribution to modern garden architecture in the 1920s and 1930s, which appears almost unknown today when compared to the better-known achievements of their male colleagues. This imbalance or ignorance is not only a question of gender but can also be attributed to the fact that Plischke and Wolf were Jewish – persecuted, exiled, and not remembered after 1945. Thus, our aim is to present some of their garden projects that exemplify the *Wohngarten* style of the 1920s and 1930s, the most popular garden style at that time, and to analyze the projects' spatial concepts and the relationship between garden and house. Owing to the fragmented condition of project-related evidence, conclusions about

FIGURE 4.1 Portait of Anna Lang, 1930. (Courtesy of Anna M. Lang)

details like the use of materials and plants remain vague. As a consequence, this examination will focus on the question of how these women organized their professional careers in terms of cooperation and partnership. After all, striving for professional independence was still a challenging enterprise for women in the early twentieth century.

The modern house and its garden

Around 1910, rejecting the Otto Wagner School[1] and the aestheticism of the Vienna Secession and Wiener Werkstätte, the architects Oskar Strnad, Josef Frank, and Oskar Wlach developed the Wiener Schule (Viennese School) of modernism. Predominantly working on private housing, they followed the relaxed style of Anglo-American country houses and were sceptical of the radical and often dogmatic functionalism of the German Werkbund, and later the Bauhaus. A circle of like-minded students, mainly from the liberal, assimilated Jewish bourgeoisie, followed them.[2] The next generation of Wiener Schule architects came from the

FIGURE 4.2 Helena Wolf in February 1949 in the backyard of her home in Hayward. (Archive of the Hayward Area Historical Society. Foto: Lester Kent, Kent Studio, Hayward, California, 1949)

Vienna Kunstgewerbeschule, where Frank and Strnad taught after World War I. Among them was Ernst Plischke, who had studied in Strnad's master class and then worked in Frank's office.

At that time in "Red Vienna" – the city was now governed by the social democrats – architects such as Frank, Strnad, Adolf Loos, and Margarete Schütte-Lihotzky worked together with garden architects like Albert Esch to design allotment gardens and courtyards of communal housing projects inspired by Leberecht Migge and Camillo Sitte. Unlike the Vienna Secession's aestheticist approach, the Wiener Schule essentially followed an ideal of cultivated nonchalance and strove for a close relationship of house and garden in the tradition of the English country house. The house was supposed to become an integral part of its surroundings.[3]

In 1925, Josef Frank and Oskar Wlach established a home-furnishing business named Haus und Garten that offered not only interior design and furniture, but also garden design. An example of the company's Wiener Schule garden architecture is Frank's Vienna house for the rubber manufacturers Julius and Margarete Beer, which was built in 1930. In his programmatic article *Das Haus als Weg und Platz* (The house as path and place), Frank described his concept of a heterogeneous layout of living room and garden that could only be fully appreciated by moving in them. The multiple shapes of open and closed spaces correspond to the diversity of spatial relations and dimensions inside the building. Strnad's and Frank's open systems do not claim conclusiveness, but deal with their own contradiction. In ambivalent surroundings, the architects provided *offene Welten* (open worlds).[4] The design of the house was not to be understood from a single standpoint, but only as one moved through it and perceived how the different parts related to one another. Frank applied Camillo Sitte's urbanistic concept of path and place[5] to the layout of the house and its garden, following Leon Battista Alberti's notion of *domus minima civitas* (the house as a small town).[6] The duality of the notions of path and place with its implication of rest and movement, statics, and dynamics, is essential in Frank's work.

The unity of house and garden remained the most important task for garden architects as well, even though a new garden style – the *Wohngarten* – had emerged out of the architectural garden of the 1900s and 1910s. The garden architect Paula Fürth, who had studied natural sciences at the University of Vienna and then founded a nursery and a private horticultural school for women in Vienna, gave a succinct description of this new design: "The modern garden corresponds to the modern house: functionality, comfort, simplicity and maintenance are its ultimate aims."[7] The aim to structure the garden functionally in analogy to the house was certainly not avant-garde, but derived from the architectural garden, whereas the *Wohngarten* – in terms of form – replaced the architectural garden's radical and rigid program with a more relaxed design. Paths were still laid out orthogonally next to the house, yet, a less-strict geometry was employed in more distant garden areas, where stepping stones were positioned in a looser manner. Plants were no longer clipped and planted in homogenous groups, but arranged in curved forms and varied combinations. Flowerbeds became key features, as well as seating areas, sports grounds, water basins, and outdoor showers.

The *Wohngarten* offered ease and comfort and served as a nature-like enclave in a city that steadily grew denser and more functionalized. This understanding corresponded to the modern needs of the urban population, where physical outdoor activities and relaxation gained importance. The Viennese garden architect Willi Vietsch, who was a supporter of the Wiener Schule's settlement concept based on Camillo Sitte's urbanistic theories, propagated the idea of the *Wohngarten* as being destined to serve the comfort of its user: "At times when sports and hygiene have become important topics, the garden also has to be accorded great significance. It does not only serve representational purposes (as it used to do) but especially habitation."[8] Light, sun, and air were the slogans of modern living, for the garden as well as the house and the urban structure. "In our garden, we want to live, play and do sports – we want to use it like our house, which it should complement," concluded the German garden architect Otto Valentien.[9] The *Wohngarten* – sometimes rather small in size – was the garden of the urban middle class, of owners who wanted to use their garden actively.

The new garden design encouraged a closer exchange between architects and garden architects. A discussion in publications and educational institutions ensued on how to improve the cooperation between the professions. This development paralleled the increasing professionalization of garden architecture in Austria. Thus, Fürth indicated that "today, through the cooperation of architect and garden architect, the house and garden form an organic union."[10] Vietsch shared Fürth's notion of the contemporary garden design and – distinctive to Vienna modernism – searched for a close unity of house and garden, which leads to a harmony between the two spaces and "turns the garden owner into a garden lover."[11]

The role of women in garden and landscape architecture in Austria

At the beginning of the twentieth century, the role of women in garden and landscape architecture, as in professional life in general, changed greatly in response to new political, social, and cultural conditions. As in most professions, advanced training became essential for women starting a career in design. Traditional horticultural schools like the Höhere Gartenbaulehranstalt Dahlem (Berlin) and Höhere Gartenbaulehranstalt Eisgrub (Lednice, Czech Republic) accepted women from the 1900s onward, but asked for an apprenticeship in gardening prior to enrollment, which was difficult for women to obtain, as they were often rejected as trainees. Thus, many women chose private horticultural schools that accepted only female students. The first of these schools had been founded in the second half of the nineteenth century in England and Germany.[12] Following these examples, Yella Hertzka established a horticultural school for women in Vienna in 1912. Like horticultural schools for women in Germany, Hertzka's school aimed at offering a solid horticultural and business education. Garden design was an important component within the school's curriculum; time devoted to the subject amounted to 80 hours each year, which equaled nearly 10 percent of the total class time. The subject included drawing and designing gardens, public spaces, and nurseries. Landscape construction courses entailed 18 hours in the second year.[13] In the mid-1920s, the well-known Viennese garden architect Albert Esch taught garden design at the Viennese gardening school for women.[14] The school's final degree at the end of the second year equalled a full apprenticeship and allowed for admission to a horticultural training school such as the Höhere Gartenbaulehranstalt Eisgrub.

However, it took another decade until a handful of women became gardeners and garden architects. Of the thirty garden architects practicing in the 1920s and 1930s in Austria, only five were women – Anna Plischke, Paula Fürth, Grete Salzer, Hanny Strauß, and Helene Wolf. All of them, except for Plischke, began their careers by founding a plant nursery. Later, as their businesses were well established, they became involved in designing gardens – a career development common among their male colleagues as well, but not as frequent.[15] Twenty years later, the gender ratio in garden and landscape architecture in Austria had deteriorated. In 1950, only one woman was among the twenty-one landscape architects in the professional association. Gaining ground in a male-dominated field remained a challenge for female garden architects throughout the early twentieth century. Katharina Homann and Maria Spitthöver show that in Germany, up to the 1940s, women were strongly cautioned against starting an independent professional career as a garden architect. The authors conclude that, back then, a woman garden architect was more successful when she was able to enter a family business or work together with her husband.[16] We want to look closer at these working partnerships, because Anna Plischke and Helene Wolf both cooperated with their husbands: Anna Plischke with the architect Ernst A. Plischke and Helene Wolf with the garden architect Willy Wolf.

The best-known couples in garden architecture in Germany were Herta Hammerbacher (see Chapter 1 in this volume), who started her career with her husband Hermann Mattern, Ruth and Georg Bela Pniower, Liddy and Harry Maasz, and Rose and Gustav Wörner. Little is known about the private and professional relationships of these couples, their mutual influence, job-sharing, and performance in public and professional circles. As a young woman, Herta Hammerbacher dreamed of a professional life closely interwoven with a private partnership, like that of Marie and Pierre Curie. She strove to realize this ideal through her marriage with Hermann Mattern and the working group the couple established with Karl Foerster.[17] Seven years later, in 1935, when Hammerbacher and Mattern were divorced, she experienced the failure of this business and partnership model. Nevertheless they continued working together until 1948.

Georg Bela Pniower founded his garden design studio and construction business in 1925. In the same year, he married Ruth Hartmann, who, like her husband, was trained as a garden architect. Although an extensive archive exists, Ruth Pniower's specific contribution to the couple's professional work cannot be determined.[18] This is quite similar to the case of Rose and Gustav Wörner, who started their careers in the 1960s. Frank Schalaster indicates that plans preserved in the Wörners' archive do not give any indication of the quality and amount of the individual contributions made by Rose, Gustav, or the members of their team.[19] Compared to the extensive archives of the Pniowers' and Wörners' work, only fragmentary evidence has survived for Anna Plischke, and especially for Helene Wolf, which makes a comprehensive analysis of their oeuvres even more challenging.

Anna Plischke, trained as a gardener

As far as we know, Anna Plischke designed about twenty private gardens throughout her career in Austria and New Zealand. Born into a liberal, cultivated Viennese middle-class family on July 20, 1895, Anna Schwitzer graduated from the Lyceum and attended Rosalia Rothansl's textile class at the Vienna Kunstgewerbeschule, from 1913 to 1914. She then received horticultural training at the Rothschild's gardens in Vienna. These English landscape gardens were famous for their enormous collections of orchids, cacti, exotic trees, and flowers cultivated in ninety greenhouses. Their reputation as a place to work and train attracted gardeners from as far away as England.

At the Rothschild's gardens, Anna Schwitzer obtained a solid training in plant cultivation and garden maintenance. Her professional books that are kept in Ernst A. Plischke's estate allow for some assumptions about how she acquired her design skills. Among the early books which she must have consulted when she started her career as a garden architect in the 1920s, only one book focuses on garden design: Willy Lange's *Gartengestaltung der Neuzeit*; a book she took along when moving from Vienna to Wellington, New Zealand, and back again.[20] We also know of another Jewish garden architect, Hanka Huppert-Kurz, who relied on Willy Lange's theory of the *Naturgarten* (nature garden) that was imbued with nationalist ideologies.[21] Huppert-Kurz graduated from Hertzka's horticultural school and immigrated to Palestine in 1929, where she started a successful career as a garden architect. In 1951, she was the only woman among the nineteen professionals who founded the Israeli Association of Landscape Architects (ISALA).[22] Huppert-Kurz adopted Lange's theory for conserving and using the local native vegetation in her designs.[23] It is idle speculation if Plischke and Huppert-Kurz, despite Lange's nationalistic attitude, favored his idea because of its ample nature-like combinations and arrangements of shrubs and perennials.

In her garden projects, Anna Plischke closely cooperated with the architect Ernst A. Plischke. Ernst Plischke worked in Josef Frank's studio when Anna and her first husband, Robert Lang, owner of a metalware factory, commissioned Frank to design a winter garden for their Vienna family house in 1927. This occasion, when Anna Lang met her later second husband Plischke, was the beginning of a fruitful partnership that lasted for forty years.

One of the first joint projects by Ernst Plischke and Anna Lang was the Vienna house for the bronzeware manufacturers Konrad and Therese Mühlbauer (Figures 4.3 and 4.4). The house, designed in 1929 and built in 1932, is a cube with cut-out corner loggias on the first and second floors. They are framed by concrete beams and additionally characterized as rudimentary indoor rooms by sunshade grids. Plischke described his design concept for the house as follows: "What seemed essential to me while designing was to insert the house as an abstract body into the landscape and allowing its structure to decompose. This would occur through the massive building's disaggregation into a fragmented architectural sculpture with the help of geometric elements like terraces, loggia and pergola."[24] Corresponding to Ernst Plischke's design philosophy, Anna Lang followed her concept of interpreting gardens as enlarged living spaces, closely connected to the house. To handle the sloping terrain of the elongated plot, she replaced the traditional turf slope with orthogonal terraces and dry stone walls. These architectural structures formed a link between house and garden and created small outdoor areas. While the top terrace was paved and served as a sitting area, the following levels were planted, the lowest containing a square swimming pool. Perennials, evergreens, and small shrubs covered these terraces, criss-crossed by paths of large stepping stones. In contrast to these dense plantings, Anna Lang designed the garden part most distant from the house as an open lawn with fruit trees.

In the 1930s, orthogonal terraces and dry stone walls were a common feature in garden designs of Viennese modern single-family houses on sloping terrain. They can be found in Albert Esch's dos Santos garden (architects Hofmann & Augenfeld) and Rezek garden

FIGURE 4.3 Mühlbauer garden designed by Anna Lang, house and attached terraces in 1931. (Kupferstichkabinett der Akademie der bildenden Künste, Vienna, Sign. 6_7)

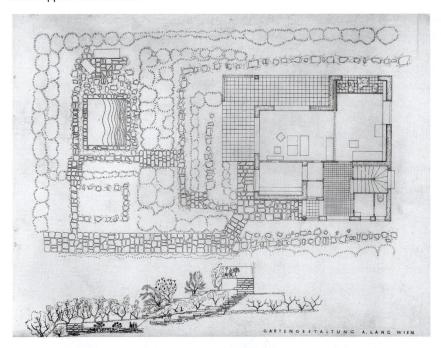

FIGURE 4.4 Mühlbauer garden, ground plan, and section. (Kupferstichkabinett der Akademie der bildenden Künste, Vienna, Sign. 6_7)

(architect Hans Glas), both located in Vienna; in his Haas garden in Brno (architect Ernst Wiesner); and in Josef Oskar Wladar's Luser garden in Kritzendorf near Vienna (architect Walter Loos). There, the houses – all of them designed by architects from the circles around Adolf Loos and Josef Frank – opened to the garden via vast terraces, the garden being an outdoor succession of the inner rooms. They were equipped with transparent, lightweight, and moveable furniture. The gardens' materiality and design, with single stepping stones and exuberant plantings, were visibly closer to nature than the houses' interiors. Thus, the *Wohngarten* functioned as an in-between zone of house and nature.

In 1932, Anna Lang, together with the architects Franz Singer and Friedl Dicker, was commissioned to redesign and plant the garden of Hans and Anny Moller (Figure 4.5). Anny Moller, née Wottitz, in particular seemed not to be satisfied with the garden that Adolf Loos had created along with the house four years earlier. In 1932, Anny Moller asked her former fellow students at Johannes Itten's private art school in Vienna, Friedl Dicker and Franz Singer, to redesign parts of the garden. Singer and Dicker created a small guesthouse, a paved seating area, and new garden paths, while Anna Lang was commissioned to redesign and plant the garden. She designed lush flowerbeds alongside the paths and arranged fruit trees and stepping stone paths on the lawn in order to loosen the rigidly orthogonally organized plot.

A new career in New Zealand

In 1935, when the Austrian democracy had already been shattered and a totalitarian Austrofascist regime had been installed, Jewish Anna Lang, now divorced, married Ernst

FIGURE 4.5 Moller garden designed by Anna Lang. (*profil* 2, no. 4 (1934): 116)

Plischke and converted to Catholicism. This was only a fragile protection, however, that became meaningless after the *Anschluss* in March 1938. Finally, in December 1938, the family obtained immigration permits to New Zealand through Ernst Plischke's connection. In Wellington, Anna Plischke started to earn her living as a gardener. The family rented an old house with a huge garden, which Anna gradually redesigned and where she grew fruits, vegetables, perennials, and shrubs. A shaded path led up the hill toward the house, allowing for a view onto slopes with azaleas and magnolias. In an article about her own garden, she described her approach to designing gardens as follows: "In the matter of design good gardens have very little in common: they depend so much on peculiarities of site and on the preferences of their owners. That, of course, is a virtue, for standardization of gardens becomes much less tempting than it is with houses."[25] Flowers played a prominent role in her garden designs. As she emphasized, "With every plant I always try to find a place where it looks its best; of course, the growing conditions that a plant wants also have to be taken into consideration. [. . .] In other words, I make the utmost use of the space devoted to flowers."[26] Based on her profound knowledge of European plants, she explored New Zealand's flora and arranged perennials and shrubs in exuberant colourful compositions, blooming in all seasons.

In the mid-twentieth century, the modern concept of a *Wohngarten* was unknown in New Zealand, where traditional gardens were still divided into a representative Victorian garden in front of the house and a kitchen garden behind the house. Encouraged by Wellington's mild climate, Anna Plischke tried to follow her ideas of composing gardens as enlarged living spaces. Only in 1948 did she gain her first commission to design a garden, for the sisters Katherine and Moira Todd, a psychiatrist and a paediatrician (Figures 4.6 and 4.7). While Ernst Plischke attached lightweight, transparent sunrooms to the small Edwardian-style building to have more air and sun inside the house, Anna Plischke was commissioned to redesign the garden. She arranged several terraces and garden rooms around the house, which "[. . .] gives shelter and sun space for outdoor living even in the winds of Wellington. The sunroom forms the core of the layout, and its proportions are related and interlocked with the courtyard, the steps and terraces."[27] Sliding glass doors separated the living room from the terraces. Next to the paved seating area, Anna Plischke structured the sloping terrain with a sequence of dry stonewalls and terraces, abundantly planted with flowering perennials and shrubs, such as roses, azaleas, heather, and camellias, Katherine Todd's favourite plants. Five wide steps led past a rose terrace and a second, higher terrace to a sunken lawn, bordered by native trees.

In Katherine Todd, Anna Plischke found a like-minded passionate gardener. Asked about what she especially liked about gardening, Plischke declared, "I like the various kinds and varieties of plants individually. I like to handle them, to plant them to their best advantage, to multiply them, even to weed them; in short, to be in their company as much as possible."[28] Within her designs, she always tried to put blooming plants as close to the house as possible in order to interweave the inner rooms with nature.

During her time in New Zealand, Anna Plischke designed about fifteen gardens, some of which are still well preserved. She felt well integrated in her new homeland, both professionally

FIGURE 4.6 Todd garden designed by Anna Plischke, terraces in front of the new sunroom. (Kupferstichkabinett der Akademie der bildenden Künste, Vienna, Sign. 6_26)

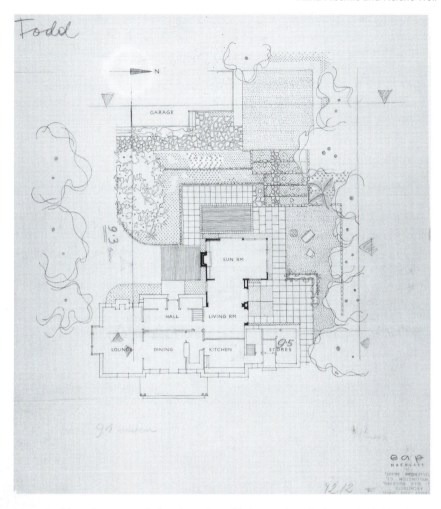

FIGURE 4.7 Todd garden, ground plan. (Kupferstichkabinett der Akademie der bildenden
Künste, Vienna, Sign. HZ_31.040)

and privately. Nevertheless, she and her husband returned to Vienna in 1962 when he was
appointed head of the architectural master course at the Academy of Fine Arts. They continued working together, for example when Ernst A. Plischke designed a house for his relatives,
the Frey family in Graz in 1970–1973. Similar to Adolf Loos' *Raumplan*, he arranged cubes
of different heights and on different elevations on both sides of a straight path that connected
the entrance with the terrace. The rooms could be united or separated by sliding walls. The
reference to Josef Frank's designs of the 1930s becomes evident in Plischke's theoretical texts:
"The path, the room, the opening to the outside, the outside and the inside, rooms on different levels, enclosed patios and open terraces with a view, and not least clearly legible forms
are essential means for me. [. . .] However, the utilitarian fulfilment of the construction program has to remain the premise."[29] The house's garden façade is characterized by variations
of protrusions and setbacks, sliding glass walls, translucent balcony railings, and massive walls.
Similar to the Todd house, this garden façade forms two different outer rooms, directly connected to the house, but of different character and use: in front of the dining room is a larger,

patio-like sitting area, shadowed by a brise-soleil pergola and ornamented with a flowerbed planted with bulbs and perennials; a smaller terrace faces the living room (Figure 4.8). Again, Anna Plischke structured the sloping terrain with orthogonal flowerbeds, planted with roses and perennials, and crowned by a row of standard roses on the lowest level. This colourful scene could be viewed from the living room and the terrace. The Frey garden was one of Anna Plischke's last projects. She died in Vienna on April 8, 1983, at the age of 87. Ernst A. Plischke died on May 23, 1992.

Helene Wolf and Helenium: on the clarity of authorship

Helene Pollak was born in Vienna on September 24, 1899, as the daughter of a textile manufacturer. Following grammar school, Pollak, a keen gardener since childhood, attended the Höhere Gartenbauschule für Frauen in Vienna from 1915 to 1917. In 1921, she established a nursery for perennial plants, called Helenium, in Hadersdorf-Weidlingau, today part of Vienna. She began to exhibit her perennials at flower shows in 1924, later also showing garden designs. After her marriage to Willy Wolf, in 1926, she operated the business together with her husband. Willy Wolf, originally from Northern Germany, had been a gardener at the Allotment Garden Department of the City of Vienna from 1923 to 1926. At that time, the housing program of Red Vienna had already curtailed the active allotment movement of the early 1920s, and the Allotment Garden Department had lost influence and expertise.[30] Being a professional and a

FIGURE 4.8 Frey garden designed by Anna Plischke, ca. 1972. (Kupferstichkabinett der Akademie der bildenden Künste, Vienna, Sign. 5_21)

businesswoman was evidently part of Helene Wolf's self-conception, even when married. She sometimes used her maiden name, Pollak, as an appendix when publishing articles, mainly on plants and plantings. Later, she always stressed that she had established her business five years before meeting Willy Wolf and that she remained a co-manager throughout her married life.[31]

As the nursery developed well over the years, Helene and Willy added a construction business and a garden design studio. It is likely that customers who consulted Helenium for plants started to ask for both maintenance and construction work as well as garden design. Journals of the period show that the firm designed fifteen private gardens in and around Vienna, between 1927 and 1939, as well as the gardens of two housing estates in Vienna, the Starchant settlement (1929) and a housing complex for the Phönix insurance company (1930).[32] It is most likely that Helenium was also responsible for the garden of the new Jewish ceremonial hall at the Vienna central cemetery, on which Willy Wolf published an article illustrated with an unsigned plan in 1930.[33]

In 1939, Helene Wolf had to emigrate to escape the Nazi terror, and she left her business in Vienna including her papers and works. Today, her estate and documents of the pre-war period are lost. Thus, analysis of her firm and projects can be based only on articles illustrated with rough plans and poor photos. As most of the articles indicate no address, we have been unable to localize the projects and find on-site evidence. It is also impossible to identify any individual project authorship and determine the amount and quality of Helene and Willy's respective contributions to the various design projects of their working partnership. We have no evidence whether Helene and Willy Wolf had designed any gardens before or after their joint commitment at Helenium, and we can only speculate concerning their skills in garden design.[34] Both were trained at horticultural schools: Helene Wolf was a student at Hertzka's horticultural school for women in Vienna where garden design was part of the curriculum; Willy Wolf, who was born in Melle near Hanover in 1896, was trained at the Gärtnerlehranstalt Köstritz in Germany. No research on this horticultural school, founded in 1887, exists, so it is impossible to draw any conclusions about his training in garden design. However, we know that eleven graduates from Köstritz worked in Austria as gardeners and garden architects in the early twentieth century. Among them was Willi Vietsch, who, together with Wilhelm Hartwich, established a garden business with a design studio named Hartwich & Vietsch in Vienna in 1927.

We draw most evidence of Helenium's projects from three articles Imre Ormos published in 1930 and 1931. Ormos, born in Budapest in 1903 and a graduate of the Königliche Gartenbaulehranstalt in Budapest, joined Helenium at the end of 1929 to improve his skills in garden design. The fact that he chose Helenium and stayed there for two and a half years until he was called back to Budapest in early March 1932, later establishing a program in garden architecture at the Königliche Gartenbaulehranstalt in Budapest, shows that Helenium was already well established as a garden design studio at that time. Many of the projects Ormos referred to in his articles had been commissioned and realized before his time at Helenium. He illustrated the articles with perspective sketches, marked with his initials IO. The attached plans show the firm name and date but are not signed. Thus, the authorship of the projects remains unclear.

Helenium's *Wohngärten* of the late 1920s and the 1930s

In 1927, Helenium designed a garden for the textile manufacturer Max Delfiner (Figures 4.9 and 4.10). The strictly symmetrical layout of the small garden referred to the axial structure of

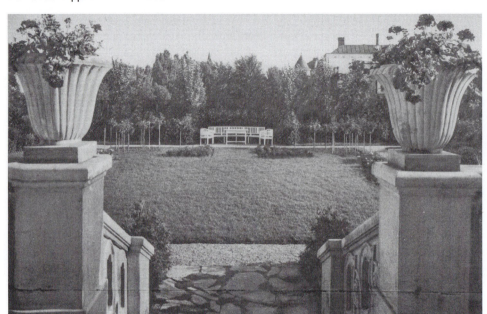

FIGURE 4.9 Delfiner garden designed by Helenium, view from the villa to the seating area. (*Die Bühne*, no. 285 (1930): 29)

the neo-baroque house, designed by Ernst Epstein.[35] In the central axis, five steps led down from the villa to a large lawn, flanked by flowerbeds of polyanthus and standard roses, the form of the beds taking up the curved corners of the house. A semi-circular seating area formed the end of this axis. Next to the ornamental garden area in an angled part of the L-shaped plot was a fruit tree garden slightly elevated and framed by a dry stone wall. Helene Wolf frequently used this architectural element to form garden areas: "Initially a mere utilitarian architectural structure, we do believe that walls and steps cannot tell us anything – until when steadily walking down, stone by stone, plant by plant start to speak for themselves."[36] Planted with perennials and dwarf shrubs, these walls formed a colorful arrangement, based on the contrast of colorful live plant material and the hard surface and greyish tones of the stones.

Quite similar and of the same period, the garden of Villa Paula,[37] also referred to as the garden of Kommerzialrat P., featured a central lawn, flanked by perennial beds and two solitary trees at the back of an older, symmetrical house (Figures 4.11 and 4.12). There, the central axis was highlighted by a sculpture-like composition of garden facilities – a terrace paved with irregularly shaped stones, a corner bench in expressive art deco forms, a small pool with two fountains, and an outdoor shower whose design resembled Erich Leischner's 1926 lighting masts for the entrance of the Kongressbad, a municipal open-air swimming pool in Vienna. The shower as well as the furniture was painted white, following the demand of "light, air, and sun" in modern architecture and garden architecture. The need to use the garden actively for leisure and daily life set the principles for designing modern *Wohngärten*, as Willy Wolf indicates: "Merely representative gardens are not the ultimate ambition for people who are happy to have fled the mass of houses and want to use their spare time to relax. The garden is not only supposed to be beautiful but it should in every respect also account for our practical needs and wishes."[38]

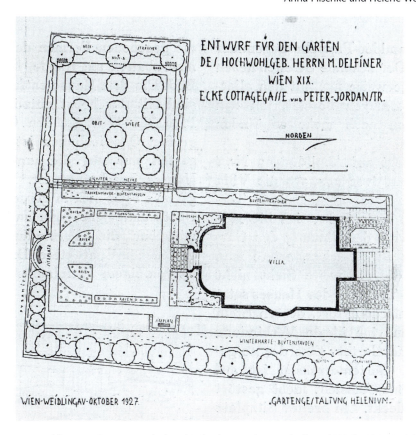

FIGURE 4.10 Delfiner garden, ground plan (*Architektur und Bautechnik* 17 (1930): 101–112 [103])

Thus, several garden rooms for social and physical use were arranged around the central, neo-classical lawn – a seating area for outdoor meals under an old lime tree, a gymnastic and playing field as well as a kitchen garden with fruit trees. "Through the transformation of the representative formal garden with its unalterable rigidity, we have approached the personal garden; and it is not least the modern material that, with its kaleidoscope-like diversion, closely connects the human to the garden and mesmerizes him continually anew,"[39] explained Helene Wolf. Modern material in this context was not glass and concrete but perennials. Wolf loved arranging shrubs and annuals in flush compositions to give the architectural structure of the garden a natural and scenic character.

Redesigning the large garden of the country house of Prague-based glass manufacturer Fritz Heller in Gresten, Lower Austria, Helenium kept a part of the former garden in the nineteenth-century landscape style, but redesigned the vicinity of the house in a modern, strictly orthogonal pattern. Wooden trellises, painted white, were introduced to structure the new garden rooms, to frame a sheltered seating area next to the house and to connect the house with the garden (Figure 4.13). Perennial beds were laid out close to the house. These architectural and plant features functioned as a link between architecture, formal garden, and the old landscape garden. A circular white bench around an old walnut tree, designed by Helenium like all the garden furniture, was the viewpoint to be seen from the main garden path.

FIGURE 4.11 Villa Paula garden designed by Helenium, seating area with pool and shower. (*Architektur und Bautechnik* 17 (1930): 106)

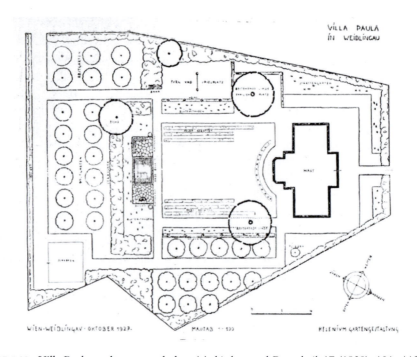

FIGURE 4.12 Villa Paula garden, ground plan. (*Architektur und Bautechnik* 17 (1930): 101–112 [106])

FIGURE 4.13 Heller garden designed by Helenium, point de vue with bench and walnut tree. (*Architektur und Bautechnik* 17 (1930): 101-112 [110])

In designing a garden, Helenium reacted to the form and character of the building. In contrast to the Delfiner, Paula, and Heller houses, with their historicist, symmetrical structures, the projected house for the composer Aladár Nagypál, was cuboid, flat-roofed, and modern. A loggia cut into the corner on the ground floor linked the house to the garden.[40] Helenium picked up the clear architectural lines and structured the sloping terrain with simple walls and a steep turf slope in three orthogonal terraces (Figure 4.14). Most striking were climbing trellises, a popular feature at that time, which stretched from the upper terrace to the second one and softened the architectural layout. A water basin and rose beds were situated in close proximity to the house, whereas the kitchen garden with fruit trees was at the back of the plot. This architectural garden design of 1930 that resembled Esch's dos Santos garden of the same year was never realized.

Exile and the post-war years

Up to the late 1930s, Helenium was well known for its garden design and for its perennials presented at flower shows. However, the *Anschluss* in March 1938 marked a break in its work. On September 30, 1938, when Helene and Willy divorced as a consequence of an affair that he had, Helene Wolf lost the fragile protection of a marriage with a non-Jewish man. In December 1938, due to the impending "Aryanization," she handed her estate to her former husband. Both agreed that she would restart her business once political circumstances changed. Helene Wolf left Vienna on July 21, 1939. She settled in the San Francisco Bay Area as a teacher at the California School of Gardening for Women at Stanford. Founded in 1924, this school was the third horticultural school for women in the USA, besides the Lowthorpe School of

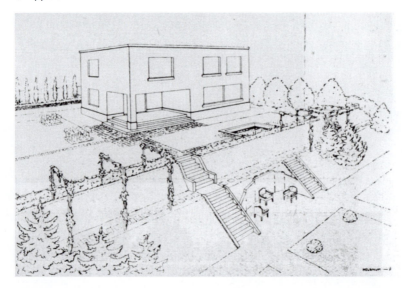

FIGURE 4.14 Nagypál garden designed by Helenium, perspective of the garden design by Imre Ormos. (*Architektur und Bautechnik* 17 (1930): 101–112: 104)

Landscape Architecture, Gardening, and Horticulture for Women in Groton, Massachusetts, and the Pennsylvania School of Horticulture for Women in Ambler, Pennsylvania. It was the only one on the West coast.

Helene (then Helena) Wolf was affiliated with the California School of Gardening for Women, from 1939 to 1942. Most likely, from 1942 on, she earned her money at Friden Calculating Machine Company in San Leandro but, besides her day job, she continued to teach garden classes at evening schools. Garden design was among her subjects, but, so far, we have no evidence that she designed any gardens after 1938/1939. Deprived of her firm and her professional network in Vienna, it seemed to be nearly impossible to reestablish a garden business at a time when the demand for private garden design was decreasing. However, Helena Wolf quickly became involved in a network of San Francisco Bay Area gardeners, among them Frank Reinelt, of Czech origin, who had immigrated to California in 1926 and who was particularly famous for his begonias. In 1948, Wolf had her Viennese property refunded and in 1962 she sold it to a housing company. She died in Hayward on May 2, 1975.

Back in Vienna in 1940, Willy Wolf rented Helenium out to two gardeners – Felix Martschitsch and Hermann Kujal – and moved to Styria, where he worked as a garden manager for Baron Franz Mayr-Melnhof at Neupfannberg Castle, until 1949. Willy Wolf never rejoined Helenium. He retired in 1949, at the age of 53, perhaps after falling seriously ill. His 1954 obituary says that "All the sorrows of the latest years had shattered his health."[41] In 1950, Willy Wolf indicated that, due to political reasons, he had resigned from the Reichskammer der bildenden Künste in 1941, although a membership had been essential for working as a garden architect. He said he had felt professionally oppressed as he objected to the Nazi party.[42] It might be possible that his leaving Vienna in 1940 and moving to a rural manor had been an attempt to escape the National Socialist government in Vienna.

Conclusion

At first glance, an oeuvre of about 25 design projects – plus perhaps a few more examples undetected so far, due to the fragmented nature of archival sources – may seem little evidence for an active and important practice. By comparison, Albert Esch, Willi Vietsch, and Josef Oskar Wladar, all located in Vienna, each designed 70 to 200 gardens. Nevertheless, Plischke and Wolf reached an important objective as women by establishing a professional business at a time when the profession was still male-dominated. In the early twentieth century, the majority of Austrian garden architects, like Anna Plischke and Helene Wolf, ran a small garden design business, sometimes with an attached nursery or a construction firm.

The training situation for women improved from 1900 onward, but it only really changed in 1912, when Yella Hertzka, a Viennese feminist and promoter of female education and economic independence, opened a horticultural school for women in Vienna. Within its first fifteen years of existence, the school trained 180 women as gardeners, among them Helene Wolf. Yet, in Austria, we only know of a handful of women who successfully started their own professional business at that time. While others relied on horticulture, Plischke and Wolf regarded garden architecture as an integral part of their business. For both, the close professional cooperation with their husbands influenced their careers and projects and, in both cases, the influence was reciprocal. Today, however, we may only surmise the extent of this influence, as it is almost impossible to judge the respective partners' contributions.

In their garden design, Plischke and Wolf drew on the principles of the *Wohngarten* and – together with Esch, Vietsch, and Wladar – consolidated this style in the 1920s and 1930s in Austria. Plischke and Wolf's fundamental knowledge of plants, especially of perennials, was exceptional among this group of garden architects. This knowledge proved a valuable skill as plantings became central features in the *Wohngarten*. Plischke and Wolf employed architectural principles as a means of arranging gardens into a series of outdoor living rooms, each one providing a different character and addressing different needs. Moreover, in using a great variety of plants, they implemented vivid and richly composed schemes. Promoting perennials in Austrian gardens was their specific contribution to the garden design of the 1920s and 1930s.

Plischke and Wolf were able to maintain their fervor for gardens and garden architecture throughout the great breaks of persecution and exile in 1938/1939. However, their violent expulsion and the destruction of their work and their archives are an incalculable loss to the history of women and design. The *Wohngarten* style was revived in the 1950s and 1960s; but it took more than 30 years until new generations of women began to work as garden and landscape architects in Austria.

Acknowledgments

This essay is the result of a two-year research project focusing on women in Austrian garden and landscape architecture, financed by the Austrian Science Fund (FWF) [P 24421-G21].[43] Additionally, a summer fellowship at Dumbarton Oaks, Washington D.C. granted Ulrike Krippner the opportunity to explore the professional framework for women landscape architects in America in the 1940s and 1950s.

We are grateful to Anna Lang, of Australia, and Erica Lang, of New Zealand, for sharing their memories of their grandmother Anna Plischke with us. We also thank Eva B. Ottillinger, of the Hofmobiliendepot Vienna; Ilona Balogh-Ormos, of the Corvinus University of Budapest; as well as Charles Birnbaum and Nancy Slade, of the Cultural Landscape Foundation. Special thanks to Marlea A. Graham, of the California Garden & Landscape History Society, who has been providing us with much information on Helena Wolf's life and career in California, and to Diane Curry of the Hayward Area Historical Society.

Notes

1 Around the fin de siècle, Otto Wagner was the dominant figure in Viennese architecture. However, Jewish students avoided his master class at the Academy of Fine Arts, as it was considered anti-Semitic.

2 See Iris Meder, *Offene Welten – Die Wiener Schule im Einfamilienhausbau 1910–1938* (PhD diss., Stuttgart University, 2004).

3 See Iris Meder, "Natur und Architektur werden hier ineinandergeschoben – Haus und Garten in der Werkbundsiedlung," in *Ein Manifest des Neuen Wohnens. Werkbundsiedlung Wien 1932*, eds. Andreas Nierhaus and Eva Orosz (Salzburg: müry salzmann, 2012), 96–101.

4 Oskar Strnad, "Neue Wege in der Wohnraum-Einrichtung," *Innendekoration* 33, no. 9 (1922): 323–328 (323).

5 This principle of articulating the path in curved or broken lines, only tangentially touching rooms or areas regarded as closed spaces, resembles the urbanistic principles of Camillo Sitte. In his book, *City Planning According to Artistic Principles* (*Der Städtebau nach seinen künstlerischen Grundsätzen*), published in 1889, Sitte promoted asymmetrical, irregular squares and streets following the examples of medieval cities. Sitte's writings were fundamental, both for the housing projects of Red Vienna and for the Wiener Schule.

6 In 1910, Frank had written his dissertation about Alberti.

7 "Der moderne Garten entspricht dem modernen Hause: Zweckmäßigkeit, Wohnlichkeit, Einfachheit und Instandhaltung sind seine obersten Gesetze." Paula Fürth, "Gärtnerinnen sprechen über ihre Gärten," *Österreichische Kunst* 3, no. 7 (1932): 29–30.

8 "In der Zeit des Sports und der Hygiene kommt auch dem Garten eine erhöhte Bedeutung zu. Er dient nicht mehr in gleichem Maß wie früher der Repräsentation, sondern vor allem auch den Zwecken des Wohnens." Gartenarchitekten Hartwich und Vietsch, *Wie gestalte ich meinen Garten?* (Vienna: authors' publishing, ca. 1930), n. p.

9 "Wir wollen in unserem Garten leben, spielen, turnen – wollen ihn benutzen wie unsere Wohnung, die er ergänzen soll." Otto Valentin, *Zeitgemässe Wohn-Gärten* (München: F. Bruckmann, 1932), 6.

10 "heute, wo Haus und Garten durch das gemeinsame Schaffen von Bau und Gartenarchitekt als eine organische Einheit entstehen." Paula Fürth, "Stein und Beton als Gartenwerkstoffe," *Innendekoration* 48, no. 5 (1937): 176–182 (178).

11 "Der verständnisvolle Gartengestalter wird sich bei der Formgebung des Gartens immer bemühen, einen Einklang zwischen Haus und Garten herzustellen. Gelingt diese Absicht, dann hat sie von allein die Harmonie zwischen Haus und Garten zur Folge, die den Gartenbesitzer auch zum Gartenfreund werden läßt." Willi Vietsch, "Der Weg zum schönen Garten," *Das Wüstenroter Eigenheim* 7, no. 7/8 (1937): 250.

12 On the impact of horticultural schools for women in England, see Anne Meredith, "Horticultural Education in England, 1900–40: Middle-Class Women and Private Gardening Schools," *Garden History* 31, no. 1 (2003): 67–79. For Germany, see Anke Schekahn, *Spurensuche 1700–1933. Frauen in der Disziplingeschichte der Freiraum- und Landschaftsplanung* (Kassel: Universität Gesamthochschule Kassel, 2000), 77.

13 Stadtschulrat für Wien to Österreichische Gartenbaugesellschaft, Feb. 2, 1929, box 20, file Höhere Schule, Österreichische Gartenbau-Gesellschaft, Vienna, Archives Department.

14 VIII. Land- und forstwirtschaftliches Schulwesen, box 20, file Höhere Schule, Österreichische Gartenbau-Gesellschaft, Vienna, Archives Department: 170.

15 Ulrike Krippner and Iris Meder, "Cultivating, Designing, and Teaching: Jewish Women in Modern Viennese Garden Architecture," *Landscape Research* 36, no. 6 (2011): 657–668.

16 Katharina Homann and Maria Spitthöver, "Freiraum- und Landschaftsplanerinnen. Ein Beitrag zur Disziplingeschichte von 1900 bis 1945," *Stadt+Grün* 56, no. 12 (2007): 26–33 (31).

17 Jeong-Hi Go, "Herta Hammerbacher (1900–1985). Garten als Kleinuniversum" (paper presented at the Stralsunder Akademie für Garten- und Landschaftskultur, Stralsund, Germany, June 4, 2012), http://herta-hammerbacher.blogspot.co.at, accessed December 2, 2013.

18 Joachim Wolschke-Bulmahn and Peter Fibich, *Vom Sonnenrund zur Beispiellandschaft. Entwicklungslinien der Landschaftsarchitektur in Deutschland, dargestellt am Werk von Georg Pniower (1896–1960)* (Hannover: Institut für Grünplanung und Gartenarchitektur, 2004), 16.

19 Frank Schalaster, "Zum Zusammenwirken der Landschaftsarchitekten Gustav und Rose Wörner im Büroalltag: Was verraten Akten und Pläne?" *Die Gartenkunst* 21, no. 2 (2009): 171–186 (174).

20 Anna Plischke's set includes forty-nine books of which only eight were published in the 1910s and 1920s. Willy Lange's *Gartengestaltung der Neuzeit* is the only publication extensively discussing garden design; the others focus on plants, horticulture, and gardening, like the 5th edition of *Hampels Gartenbuch für Gärtner und Gartenliebhaber* of 1920. The majority of the books were purchased after 1945 in Wellington.

21 See Joachim Wolschke-Bulmahn, "The Nationalization of Nature and the Naturalization of the German Nation: 'Teutonic' Trends in Early Twentieth-Century Landscape Design," in *Nature and Ideology*, ed. Joachim Wolschke-Bulmahn (Washington, D.C.: Dumbarton Oaks, 1997).

22 Kenneth I. Helphand, *Dreaming Gardens* (Santa Fe, NM: Center for American Places, 2002).

23 Shmuel Burmil and Ruth Enis, *The Changing Landscape of a Utopia: The Landscape and Gardens of the Kibbutz, Past and Present* (Worms: Wernersche Verlagsgesellschaft, 2011), 260, and Ruth Enis, "Zionist Pioneer Women and their Contribution to Garden Culture in Palestine 1908–1948," in *Frauen und Hortikultur*, eds. Heide Inhetveen and Mathilde Schmitt (Hamburg: LIT-Verlag, 2006), 101.

24 "Was mir beim Entwerfen wesentlich erschien, war das Einfügen des Baus als abstrakter Körperform in die Landschaft und das Ausklingenlassen in ihr. Es geschah dies durch seine Auflockerung vom massiven Baukörper zur durchbrochenen Bauplastik mit Hilfe geometrischer Elemente wie Terrassen, Loggia und Pergola." Cited in Eva Ottillinger and August Sarnitz, *Ernst Plischke. Das Neue Bauen und die Neue Welt. Das Gesamtwerk* (Munich/Berlin/London/New York: Prestel, 2003), 234.

25 Anna Plishke, "A Garden for Pleasure," *Design Review* 3, no. 6 (1951): 139–143 (139).

26 Plishke, "A Garden for Pleasure," 140.

27 Ernst A. and Anna Plischke, "Sunrooms and a Garden," *Design Review* 4, no. 4 (1952): 82–85 (83).

28 Ibid.

29 "Der Weg, der Raum, das Öffnen nach außen, Außen und Innen, Räume auf verschiedenen Niveaus, umschlossene Wohnhöfe und offene Terrassen mit Aussicht und nicht zuletzt klar lesbare Formen sind für mich wesentliche Mittel. [. . .] Die utilitaristische Erfüllung des Bauprogramms muß hierbei Voraussetzung bleiben." Ernst A. Plischke, "Gegen Vereinfachungen," *Die Furche* 23, no. 51/52 (1967): 12.

30 We await more conclusions on the impact of the Vienna Allotment Garden Department from Sophie Hochhäusl's dissertation *Modern by Nature: Architecture, Politics, and Socio-Technical Systems in Austrian Settlements and Allotment Gardens between Reform and the Welfare State, 1903–1953*, at Cornell University.

31 Helena Wolf to Major Weaver, May 14, 1946, Records of the Property Control Branch of the U.S. Allied Commission for Austria (USACA), 1945–1950, Correspondence and Related Records Regarding Pending Claims, file P-672 Helena Wolf, USA National Archives, http://www.fold3.com/document/306815790, accessed Oct. 22, 2013.

32 Emmerich Ormos, "Von den Arbeiten des modernen Gartengestalters, Zu den Arbeiten der Firma Helenium, Abteilung Gartengestaltung," *Architektur und Bautechnik* 17, no. 7 (1930): 101–112 (112); Emmerich Ormos, "Ein Miethausgarten," *Architektur und Bautechnik* 17, no. 26 (1930): 426–429.

33 Willy Wolf, "Friedhofsgestaltung," *Architektur und Bautechnik* 17, no. 5 (1930): 66–70.

34 A special edition of *Architektur und Bautechnik*, discussing the exhibition of garden architecture at the Vienna Spring Fair of 1933 shows several private gardens, with the remark "designed by Helenium" (*Architektur und Bautechnik* 20, no. 5/6 [1933]). The index attributes them to Wilhelm Wolf, which has been the only hint so far that he was responsible for garden design, besides the fact that he called himself garden architect in the 1940s.

35 Epstein cooperated with Helenium at least one more time when Helenium designed the gardens of a housing structure for the Phönix insurance company.

36 "Zuerst nur ein Zweckgebilde des architektonischen Aufbaues, glauben wir, daß uns Mauern und Stufen nichts sagen könnten, bis dann bei ruhigem Abschreiten Stein um Stein, Pflanze um Pflanze, selbst für sich zu sprechen beginnen." Helene Wolf, "Blühende Stufen," *Der getreue Eckart* 7, no. 2, appendix Heim und Geselligkeit (1929/1930): 54–55 (54).

37 The Villa Paula was on a plot next to Helene Wolf's property. The commissioners' identity could not be clarified, yet.

38 "Rein repräsentativ gestaltete Gärten sind nicht mehr das höchste Ziel für Menschen, die froh sind, dem Stein- und Häusermeer entflohen zu sein, die ihre freien Stunden der Erholung widmen wollen. Der Garten soll nicht nur schön sein, er soll auch unseren praktischen Bedürfnissen und Wünschen in jeder Hinsicht Rechnung tragen." Willy Wolf, "Schöne Zweckgärten," *Der getreue Eckart* 6, no. 2, appendix Heim und Geselligkeit (1928/1929): 52–54 (52).

39 "Durch die Wandlung des repräsentativen Stilgartens mit seiner unverrückbaren Starrheit sind wir einen großen Schritt dem persönlichen Garten näher gekommen und nicht zuletzt ist es der neuzeitliche Werkstoff, der es mit seiner kaleidoskopartigen Abwechslung zuwege bringt, den Menschen innig dem Garten zu verbinden und ihn stets von Neuem zu fesseln." Helene Wolf-Pollak, "Von Steingärten und ihrer Bepflanzung," *Architektur und Bautechnik* 17, no. 5 (1930): 71–77 (77).

40 The author of the house in Helenium's garden project is unknown. The house was realized differently, following a design by Walter Loos.

41 "Gartenarchitekt Wilhelm Wolf," *Gärtner-Kurier* 9, no. 12 (1954): 3.

42 Fragebogen für die Aufnahme in die Berufsvereinigung der bildenden Künstler Österreichs, June 21, 1950, folder 243, Berufsvereinigung der Bildenden Künstler Österreichs, Archives Department.

43 Project management: Lilli Lička; research: Ulrike Krippner, Iris Meder, and Nicole Theresa Raab.

5

CREATIVE MARGINS

Three women in post-war French landscape architecture

Bernadette Blanchon

Introduction

Why focus on the role of women in the building of the profession of landscape architecture in France? Hidden by the practice of their male colleagues, women nevertheless made significant contributions to the profession, which we owe in some part to their cultural experience and personalities. But their contributions are insufficiently recognized and deserve proper representation, analysis and critical assessment. Without seeking a hagiographic or feminist account, appreciating female practitioners' slightly different approaches and ideas makes it possible to widen the historical understanding of this continuously evolving profession. Exploring what first appear as the margins of professional practice offers relevant new perspectives into the recent history of landscape architecture.

In France today, more than 60 percent of the students in landscape architecture are women.[1] Almost half of the 130 landscape architects listed as consultants to the State, are women. This number is evidence of the progress made since the creation of the first training program for landscape architects in 1945 at the École d'Horticulture de Versailles. It was only in the sixth year (1951–1953) of the Department of Landscape Architecture and Garden Arts (Section du Paysage et de l'Art des Jardins) that a woman was listed in the alumni directory. Beginning in the 1970s, the number of women increased to finally make up half of the twenty admitted students;[2] yet, few of these students went on to practice as landscape architects. In most cases they were perceived as gardeners or were made fun of for supposedly seeking an occupation and a husband, and were referred to as *cuscutes* (dodders or parasites).[3]

Nevertheless, the women presented here have been forces in the profession and bear witness to significant changes in its general evolution. Ingrid Bourne (b. 1933) played a key role in introducing ideas based upon the Northern European cultural landscape and German landscape architecture into a rather conservative profession in France. Isabelle Auricoste (b. 1941) provided an atypical example of political engagement and literary passion that informed her practice. She was the first woman to be awarded the Grand Prix du Paysage. Marguerite Mercier (b. 1946) was implicated very early on in advising commissioning authorities on land-use planning. Her career provides evidence of an early diversification in the profession, which is gradually being confirmed today.

These three women experienced changes in the profession, along with its old constraints and a new freedom that were characteristic for women of their period. This essay follows the women's careers and their training at Versailles, which, for a long time, offered the only training available in France. At Versailles, they experienced key moments in the renewal of the teaching programs.[4]

Contexts and challenges

The need for specialized training and a diploma

The Section du Paysage et de l'Art des Jardins,[5] located in the Potager du Roi, was founded in 1945 to train professionals to assist in the reconstruction of France after the war. The Section du Paysage was the foundation of what later, in 1976, became the École Nationale Supérieure du Paysage, which has since gained worldwide recognition. It offered "a dual set of required skills. That of the art and expertise of the architect and that of the horticulturist."[6] It included the training in art and design which had been lacking in the establishments existing to date; the Jardin-École municipal Du Breuil (1867), which trained the maintenance personnel of the Parisian parks and gardens; and the École d'Horticulture de Versailles (1874), which trained engineers, some of whom practiced as landscape architects.

The major challenge for the new curriculum was to dissociate landscape architecture from garden contracting and to ensure the recognition of a scholarly profession. From 1940 onwards, the Order of Architects prohibited these designers from using their favored title of "architecte-paysagiste." The landscape architects' aim at the time was to distinguish themselves from architects and demonstrate their mastery of specific skills.

Shortly before World War Two, these young professionals saw their disciplinary heritage both in urban design, embodied in the figure of J.-C. N. Forestier (1861–1930), and in the long-standing horticultural tradition carried by the heirs of Édouard André (1840–1911). They were reacting to the modernist movement in architecture that they considered cold and sterile and to the architects' appropriation of garden architecture in the interwar years. Added to this was the effect of the slogans of the Vichy government extolling the virtues of a return to the land, which generated a very conservative relationship with the existing landscape and a difficult position for a profession searching to adapt to the changes resulting from the war.

Large housing projects: a vast experimental field for the landscape architect

The transformations of society and new public commissions brought with them a radical change in the scale of projects. During the years of the Section du Paysage, big housing projects were realized in response to the housing crisis during the post-war boom (1945–1975), offering many citizens access to modernity and comfort. The industrialization of construction and the study of residential housing involved engineers and architects, but they did not know how to deal with the vast spaces surrounding the housing blocks that were built according to the principles of the Athens Charter. This "bible" that was to shape postwar modernism did not provide any detailed instructions for the design of open space.

Bourne, Auricoste, and Mercier began their careers with a lot of confidence in the future, a sentiment common at the time. It was their ambition to transform the profession of landscape architecture, turning it into a discipline that could contribute to building a new urban society.

Ingrid Bourne: the creation of the profession of landscape architecture *au féminin*

For Ingrid Bourne, née Cloppenburg, "these years, were a time when people were sub-jected to pressures and living and working conditions which forged their character and made them very creative."[7] Bourne was born in 1933 into a wealthy Dutch immigrant family in Germany. She grew up in Berlin and Kiel, the child of a businessman and shop owner (her father), and of a patron of the arts (her mother). The war, reversals of fortune, repeated moves, and her parents' divorce were compensated for by her close-knit relations with her many siblings. Ingrid had always had a keen interest in plants and, after studying at a horti-cultural school in England, she obtained a degree from the Royal Horticultural Society. In 1954, she audited courses at the Section du Paysage in Versailles, where she met her future husband, Michel Bourne, with whom she later ran the Bourne family business in the region of Lyon. While Michel ran the gardening firm, Ingrid ran the design agency and had four children. Initially working on social housing programs in the region where their pioneer-ing approach earned them recognition, from 1967 onwards they developed the Atelier de Paysage in St Marcellin and widened the scope of their design activities. They worked on campus, new town, and public space designs. At the same time, Ingrid continued to design private and public gardens. Both taught at the School of Architecture in Grenoble and were active members of professional associations. In the 1990s, they obtained various prestigious commissions, including the Place Antonin Poncet project in Lyon. They then moved their firm to Germany, where they are still living in retirement today.

Versailles: revelation and composition

After graduating from high school in 1953, a world of opportunity awaited Ingrid Cloppenburg, a resourceful young woman. When she enrolled in the Section du Paysage as an auditor, in 1954, she had already acquired an extensive knowledge of plants and soils during her year at the Somerset Farm Institute in Cannington. Her intention in France was simply to learn French. However, her arrival in Versailles was a revelation: the town and its layout fascinated her even before she visited the gardens, and so did her first assignments (installing a bench in a small garden). Her composition teacher, Théodore Leveau (1876–1971) realized the potentials of this young woman who had a different background from most other students. An architect, urban planner, and landscape architect who had studied under J.-C. N. Forestier, Leveau taught design that was inspired by the Grand Siècle Français and the École des Beaux Arts. In her designs, Ingrid also drew from her childhood experiences of dyked landscapes in the area of Kiel (Plate 5.1). She also evoked the vast English lawns dotted with trees, that she had cycled across during her stay in Britain. In her work, the horizon and the vastness of an open sky have always played an important role.

New inspiration from Northern Europe

Her summer internships in Germany shaped her experiences at the Section du Paysage and her later practice. In 1955, Bourne started an internship with Karl Plomin who in 1935 under the Nazi regime had designed the first garden exhibition grounds Planten un Blomen[8] in the cen-ter of Hamburg. After completing the new grounds in 1953, he was also put in charge of the exhibitions of 1963 and 1973. His main objectives, to which Ingrid remained loyal throughout her practice, were to ensure balanced ecological plant combinations and a sense of well-being

FIGURE 5.1 Ingrid Bourne visiting Planten un Blomen, Hamburg, 1956. Photo credit: Ingrid and Michel Bourne.

in his gardens. To design the plant compositions, he used hardy species, "indigenous" plants he had specially grown in local nurseries. As reported by Bourne, "He derived the greatest satisfaction from seeing people admire the plants, and he did not consider plants . . . in the French manner, as loud colors and in masses; they were the subtle association of a graphic design, a texture, a pastel color . . . , combined with odorous plants and insects . . . He was a sort of 'aesthetic ecologist' ahead of his time."[9] The plant was not considered as a material but as a living being, deserving respect; this basic principle also was to lie at the heart of Ingrid Bourne's work (Figure 5.1).

In addition to the use of plants as structural material, she noted the importance of the earthworks "which created private spaces while generating green axes, . . . , with these small valleys he created fluid spaces . . . " (Plate 5.2). It was only later that she noted the limits of Plomin's work:[10] a lack of interest in composition and complicated clusters of plants difficult to maintain. In her own projects, Ingrid addressed the issue of maintenance. How to combine structure and plants – "Le Nôtre and Plomin" – was the question Ingrid explored in her second year at Versailles where she acquired the right – usually denied auditors – to pass her degree in 1966.

Plomin also introduced her to Alwin Seifert (1890–1972),[11] who had been in charge of landscape designs along the German motorways built during the Nazi dictatorship, and who had adopted the principle of "stitching the landscape back together once the motorway has passed through it." Whereas in France motorway embankments were draped in rose bushes and ornamental plants, in Germany, species characteristic of the regional landscape were planted. Building upon the idea that designs should relate to a landscape's past and to the existing cultural and natural landscape patterns, Ingrid and Michel developed a similar approach for their practice in France. Together, they conducted a series of studies of existing sites to understand planting patterns and plant communities and to develop ideas for how these could be used in new projects. Finally, the "simple masterful" designs by the Swiss Willi Neukom (1917–1983)[12] who published in the review *Anthos*, was another opus they referred to. Like Neukom, they would stress the importance of site analysis and of a thorough understanding of scale and landform, as well as of fitting planting designs.

First professional challenges: pragmatism and inventiveness

Once Michel had taken over the family business, he and Ingrid were running a gardening firm and a design agency. This enabled them to realize what they had learnt abroad: the garden contracting firm worked on motorway projects and many private gardens. Ingrid's work in the design office was for housing projects. In spite of keeping these two activities separate, their practice attracted criticism. "At the time," they explained, "in the provinces, we wouldn't have been credible without our own gardening firm; the profession of landscape architecture was unheard of. Often, landscape architects were paid by the gardening firm for their design work."[13]

Immediately after graduating, they received a commission for the design of the open spaces of a public housing development, a new type of project at the time. Ingrid, who first dealt with the project, worked in the architect's office on site. The Bron-Parilly neighborhood[14] was designed with the enthusiasm associated with the experimental projects of the Reconstruction. The landscape architects were asked to deal with the height differences of several meters between roads and buildings. There were no measured drawings, no budget for survey plans, and a small budget for the project altogether. Ingrid used plant alignments at the foot of the buildings and tree copses, "like in the drawings of le Corbusier"[15] to protect the inhabitants from traffic noise and pollution. Using these elements of an intermediate scale, she created spaces for different uses (Figure 5.2). The new scale of the landscape required new construction techniques. As Ingrid explained, "This had never been done before. We had to invent and execute as we went along: first of all we had to learn how to direct road workers with their bulldozers and guide them to greater precision."[16] Hectares of lawns were sown using agricultural seed drills. Local, hardy trees, including plane trees, poplars, linden trees, and a few pine trees that were adapted to sterile soils, were planted using forestry techniques. "It required courage to wait four to five years for it to become attractive."[17] A few large trees structured the space providing some shade and spatial organization in the meantime. Gradually, the nurseries adapted the plants on offer to the new types of projects: stool shoots, saplings, untrained forms, and hardier species of trees that replaced many usual exotic species.

These innovations were the subject of many exchanges with colleagues who faced similar challenges, such as Jacques Simon (b. 1929), another pioneer working on large housing projects. A leading figure in the profession, Simon was also a graduate of the Section du Paysage at Versailles. The Bournes never subscribed to transforming rubble into hillocks like Simon did, which, according to them, broke up the space. Instead, they used the rubble to model the terrain into subtle shapes, thus still avoiding the cost of having to dispose of it off site.

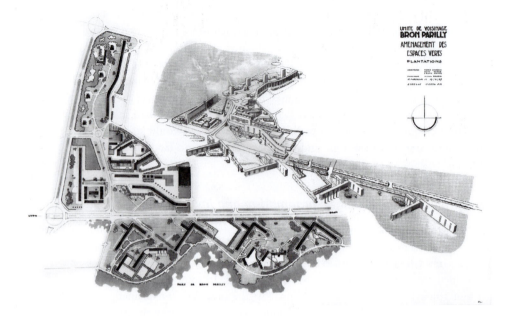

FIGURE 5.2 Bron-Parilly mixed-use neighborhood, OPHLM du Rhône, 1951–1963. Plan of the green spaces and plantations, 1957. Axonometric projection completed after realization, according to the architects' model. The plantations establish a link between the human scale and that of the buildings. Photo credit: Ingrid and Michel Bourne.

Consolidation of practice: acknowledgments and partnership

Working for famous architects opened the door to many other commissions on the sites of large housing projects. For Ingrid, each project enabled her to shoulder more responsibilities, and the couple were soon able to pass on the gardening business to their employees and focus on the Atelier de Paysage which they opened in 1967 in St Marcellin. In the new firm, Ingrid had her own clients and worked on designing and implementing her own projects. She developed a more flexible approach, less inspired by classic French gardens. She sought a balance between architectural lines and plants, between geometric shapes and the irregular forms of live plants.

Her projects for the Parc Paul Mistral (1966–1971)[18] in Grenoble opened in preparation for the Winter Olympics of 1968; she also designed park areas in the new town of Echirolles, located west of Grenoble.[19] She was involved in this latter project from the beginning through the consultation process and its implementation. In each project, Ingrid built upon her international experience. In Grenoble, the public was given access to the lawns, and a lighting specialist was consulted to ensure their security at night (Figure 5.3). In Echirolles, the outlying areas were treated with extensive plantings and by leveling the ground between the park and the housing units. During these same years, Ingrid was frequently called upon to design private gardens. She helped clients design their garden projects in accordance with their tastes, budgets and the time they were able to dedicate to maintenance.

Ingrid's professional convictions and sense of responsibility enabled her to assert herself in many situations, including when people showed reluctance in receiving instructions from a young woman. She recalled, "When you're sure of your project, you've designed it yourself

FIGURE 5.3 Parc Paul Mistral, Grenoble, 1968. The project builds upon Ingrid Bourne's international experience. The park links neighborhoods, institutions and leisure areas. Photo credit: Ingrid and Michel Bourne.

and it's a part of you, no one can weaken your resolve."[20] She has claimed that the partnership with her husband facilitated her work in the provinces of France after World War Two. According to her, it enabled her collaboration in a variety of fascinating commissions closely linked to the social issues of the day. During twenty years of designing large housing projects, the Bournes invented techniques and contributed to adapting landscape architecture to a new scale of intervention. Building upon their experience in garden contracting work, the couple also benefited from the resources their family heritage provided them with. They referred to themselves as "planters,"[21] and their practice was based on the craftsman's understanding of the plant as both a building material and a living being with its own agency. In contrast, others like Jacques Sgard (b. 1929) referred to the landscape architect as a "mediator" between man and nature.[22] Sgard had done an internship in the Netherlands before obtaining a Ph.D. in urban planning (1958) and introducing into France the idea of landscape planning and management and the notion of "le grand paysage." In 1960, Sgard opened an office near Paris together with two colleagues that resembled the Bournes' Atelier de Paysage. These new landscape design firms were places where interns from different countries met and exchanged ideas, references, and experiences. Sgard also became a teacher at the Section du Paysage, where he came to teach Isabelle Auricoste.

Isabelle Auricoste: the landscape, a lever for societal change

Isabelle Auricoste (b. 1941) spent her childhood in the Beauce region, in the shared custody of artistic parents. She attended evening classes in architecture at the City of Paris, while attending a course in urban planning at the Institut d'Urbanisme de Paris (IUP).[23] She then began to study for a master's in art history at the École Pratique des Hautes Études (EPHE)[24], where she developed a keen interest in sociology and anthropology, and enrolled in the Section du Paysage in 1961. At the time Auricoste joined the Section du Paysage, the section was renewing its teaching methods. The former graduates Sgard and J.-C. Saint Maurice (1928–2001) introduced new teaching methods. In 1963, they hired the artist Bernard Lassus (b. 1929), a student of Fernand Léger, whom Sgard had met while working on the experimental project of La Maurelette.[25] In 1967, they introduced a course in ecology and phytogeography by Jacques Montégut (1925–2007),[26] who had taught similar content to horticultural engineers since 1958. "He introduced an interpretation of the landscape based on plant structures from which it is possible to deduce the local characteristics of the site (climate and soil) which provide information on the present, the past and the future of the site."[27] His lectures transmitted some of the ideas these young graduates had sought in the countries of Northern Europe, much like those Ingrid Bourne had introduced into her practice earlier.

Despite this new training in art and ecology, Auricoste also remained in close contact with the worlds of architecture and political activism throughout her career. Together with her husband Hubert Tonka, she continued to explore ideas initially developed at EPHE in the review *Utopie* (1967 to 1978). From 1966 onwards she practiced as a landscape architect, working on big housing projects in the Parisian suburbs. Between 1980 and 1987, she shifted her attention to translation, publishing, and writing in English, and to teaching. She taught at ENSP in Versailles and in 1991 joined the founding team of the École de Paysage de Bordeaux. She collaborated with many talented landscape architects, including the young Yves Brunier (1962–1991). Since 1991, she has been actively engaged in many rural landscape-management initiatives with her Mandragore Workshop in Charente. In 2000, she was awarded the Grand Prix du Paysage.

Human sciences and political engagement

For Auricoste, the post-war boom was a period of liberation but also of alienation brought about by consumerism and capitalist development. "My artistic background," she claims, "provided the cultural references and implicit keys to understanding situations, which I feel I have used all my life."[28] It enabled her to play an active role in the "intellectual ferment" of the period.

At the EPHE, she started to study the teachings of the anthropologist Claude Lévi-Strauss and the sociologist Henri Lefevbre under the supervision of the art historian Pierre Francastel. This was to be the foundation of her future work that was based on both political activism and humanist thought. As she later recalled, "Lefebvre was very interested in urbanism and everyday life (*la vie quotidienne*)[29], which was quite unusual, and also architecture. He thought that life could be changed, in a way through architecture and urbanism."[30] At the IUP, under the guidance of Robert Auzelle, training in social geography and design history were at the heart of discussions about the plans for the new housing projects. The famous urban historian Pierre Lavedan was teaching both at IUP and at the Section du Paysage where Auricoste completed her studies.

At Versailles, she greatly appreciated the advanced courses shared with horticultural engineers and the practice assignments at the Potager du Roi, but she was disappointed by the musty first-year training focused on the design of rose gardens and the decoration of swimming pools. The second year provided her with a welcome reprieve, thanks to the arrival of the young teachers Sgard and Saint Maurice, who raised new issues and initiated large-scale projects, including the new business district of Mériadeck, in Bordeaux, and various housing developments. During this time, Auricoste kept her distance from conservative circles who criticized her participation in a pro Algerian National Liberation Front (FLN) demonstration by forbidding her to pass her diploma and get the degree. She never sought to obtain government certification.

Urban utopias

Instead, Auricoste remained closer to the world of architecture and pursued her sociological approach initiated at EPHE through the founding of a "council" Marxist group and of the review *Utopie*, with a group of Henri Lefevbre's students, including Hubert Tonka, Jean Baudrillard, René Lourau, and Catherine Cot. However, *Utopie* had little to do with landscape, and it was her activist involvement that motivated her in her practice. She later recalled, "We really had the idea that we could change something and that's why we took classes on urbanism, to acquire the knowledge that would have allowed us to act. But, in the *Utopie* group, I think we all very quickly realized that this great urban planning was an instrument of capitalism that could not change anything."[31]

The entire technical process of producing the review, including its layout and typography – the cover was designed by Auricoste – was at the heart of the issues they addressed: "the idea of erasing or blurring the boundaries between the different categories of expression. Between literary practices and art, architecture . . . " (Plate 5.3). Beyond the expression of dissent that culminated in France in May 1968, the review, which was also distributed abroad, established the group within international critical currents of thought on architecture and social issues. Auricoste's commitment extended to living in a commune organized around a cooperative printing press in Fontenay sous Bois, where she set up her landscape design office. She would argue later that "since I was . . . in a new profession that was in the process of inventing itself, I had less of a feeling of collaborating with the system."[32]

Green spaces: from the blank page to everyday living spaces

The large housing projects enabled her to finance her studies by working on competitions for architects who needed the skillful efforts of young landscape architects to enhance the open spaces surrounding the buildings. For twelve years Auricoste worked on such projects in the Parisian suburbs of Sartrouville and Bobigny.[33] At the time, large housing projects were put forward as the consensual solution to the housing crisis, but no one had any idea of what would fill the "white blanks between the buildings and the roads . . . We hadn't had the training but we did it! . . . lawns, trees." As everywhere else, the excavated earth from the buildings was simply deposited in the empty spaces and was used in the shaping of ground surfaces between the facades by working with contour lines, as taught by Sgard (Figure 5.4). She reported: "In Sartrouville, the site plan was comprised of housing blocks which formed inner courtyards . . . with obtuse angles – and I tried to create reliefs conferring a different identity to each courtyard . . . We were also fascinated by the plasticity of concrete! So I had designed a system of modules with a straight bar and at least two different curves making it possible to build planters on which people could sit, with an included bench from time to time . . . and I planted local species of trees, the least exotic possible out of a refusal to bow to horticultural gardening conventions" (Figure 5.5).[34]

Auricoste gradually sought to practice in accordance with her "theoretical" ideas by creating spaces adapted to the needs of the immigrant populations who lived there (garages, places to do handiwork, etc.) before denouncing these urban development programs and ceasing to

FIGURE 5.4 Bobigny, town center, 1975. Landforms "taming" the space between roads and buildings. Photo 1988. Photo credit: Isabelle Auricoste.

FIGURE 5.5 Bobigny, area surrounding the housing units: pre-fab modules for planters and concrete seats, 1972. Photo credit: Isabelle Auricoste.

participate in them for reasons discussed below. She stopped practicing and became involved in publishing and writing instead. She copyedited French texts for *Time Life* to earn a living and translated Irish literature, thereby developing a taste for the English language and culture.

Auricoste was pregnant when she started her first project; and the first issue of *Utopie* was published in 1967 when her daughter was born. She managed the review, a child, a design practice, and teaching classes at the same time, without, as she has said, "encountering any particular problems as a woman . . . One is tested of course, but in the construction world, people are judged on their competence."[35] At *Utopie*, the gender issue was addressed like any other issue. "Everyone was talking about that. At the time it was a banality. We were reasonably feminist, but not militant."[36] Today, she considers what often are thought to be feminine qualities like listening and collaborating a regular way to work for anybody that should not involve any power struggles.

The 1970s: a period of transition between criticism and redefinition

Le Droit à la ville (1968), by Henri Lefebvre, was instrumental in calling into question the large housing projects. It was published the same year the Bournes, working on the Minguettes[37] project, obtained the right to contribute to the site plan rather than just play the role of accompanying the construction process. "The large housing projects took landscape architects out of their role as gardeners"[38] and gradually helped them to develop a role for themselves that went beyond the design of house gardens and parks. In a few years these large housing projects came to embody what ailed urban society. They were heavily criticized by a ministry torn between anxiety and confidence during a construction boom, and by the press that reported on the "new town blues" experienced by the tenants.

The creation of the Ministry of the Environment, in 1971, responded to an increasing ecological awareness driven by the opponents of capitalism such as the editors and authors of *Utopie*. The creation of the Délégation à l'Aménagement du Territoire et à l'Action Régionale (DATAR) in 1963 and of the new towns in 1965, heightened expectations in terms of the quality of the landscape and of the living environment. Landscape architects occupied positions in the new agencies for research in urban planning, namely the Organisations d'Etudes d'Aménagement d'Aires Métropolitaines (OREAM) created in 1967, and those for the promotion of tourism, such as the Racine agency (1963–1983) for the southern coastal area, and the Mission Interministérielle d'Aménagement de la Côte Aquitaine (MIACA, 1967–1989) for the southwest coast.

In spite of the increased demand for landscape architects, the Section du Paysage was closed in 1974. It was partly replaced by the National Center for Landscape Research (CNERP), founded in 1972 in Trappes, near Versailles, which began to respond to the need for landscape managers by training agronomists, architects, and landscape architects with a teaching team from the former Section du Paysage.[39] Once the new École Nationale Supérieure du Paysage had been founded in 1976, from 1978 onwards landscape design was taught there by the painter Bernard Lassus and the designer Michel Corajoud (1937–2014).[40] The latter offered a teaching approach inspired by architecture, as in the Atelier Le Nôtre, where Auricoste taught from 1981 to 1990.

Diversification of teaching contents and methods, and professional recognition

Like Alexandre Chemetoff (b. 1950),[41] who acknowledged the profession's recent history, Isabelle Auricoste re-appropriated knowledge from the past and began to teach the history of garden art for ENSP and the neighboring School of Architecture.[42] For her, historical knowledge was indispensible to ensuring the quality and legitimacy of the contemporary landscape architect's work, and to avoiding an excessive architectural influence. It was always a question, as she has said, "of not separating praxis from poesis."[43] At ENSP, she tutored the talented Yves Brunier[44] (1962–1991), whose work using collages and edible mock-ups she welcomed. In partnership with him she designed public spaces such as the square in front of the Tours high-speed train station (1991–1992) (Plate 5.4). In 1991, she joined the team that founded the École de Paysage de Bordeaux, where she spent seventeen years developing a teaching curriculum that combined practice and theory (Figure 5.6).

During these years of instability, landscape architects gained public recognition as the young profession came to maturity and the fragmented professional associations united. Ingrid and Michel Bourne took part in the founding of the Chambre des Paysagistes Conseils, which defended the status of the *libéral-planteur*.[45] In 1982, they supported, along with Isabelle Auricoste and Marguerite Mercier, the creation of the current Fédération Française du Paysage. In 1984, Ingrid Bourne represented France at the International Federation of Landscape Architects congress and organized the 1987 event in France. There Auricoste facilitated and managed a workshop on the theme "Jardins Historiques, Continuité et Création" hosting an international panel of experts who discussed the possibility of developing projects within a historical framework, inspired by the 1981 Charter of Florence.

Integration of the landscape in regional dynamics

While Ingrid Bourne was designing urban gardens (Le Verger) on the Colline de Fourvières, the main hillside in Lyon, Auricoste moved to the region of Charente, where she now lives in retirement – at least from teaching.[46] She is deputy mayor of her municipality, the president of the committee for the coordination of regional development, and vice president of the Syndicat

FIGURE 5.6 "Fagus Hug." Isabelle Auricoste hugging a beech tree, study trip in England, Petworth, 2007. Photo credit: Serge Briffaud.

du Pays Ruffecois (representing ninety municipalities). She is continuing her active engagement with landscape-related issues in rural areas through the development of new models for land-use planning and management. In October 2007, she successfully conducted a mediation project concerning the cliff landscape and prehistoric dwellings in the Vallée de la Vézère, in Dordogne, helping to resolve a stalemate between local authorities and UNESCO. The political dimension of her profession has always seemed obvious to her. She has commented, "When you work for people, you automatically fall within the scope of a social project."[47] Though essential, form is only a means, never an end in itself. Landscape architects are trained to interpret sites and their dynamics and they are also trained to anticipate future scenarios. In the face of energy, environmental, and social crises they are able to invent alternative models of development. According to Auricoste, "This ability to think systemically is insufficiently put to use in decision making and project development by landscape architects themselves."[48] A similar involvement in institutional projects can also be seen in Marguerite Mercier's career. Her personality and profile bear witness to a form of commitment that is complementary to those of the two previous figures.

Marguerite Mercier: supporting public landscape policy

Born in 1946, Marguerite Mercier studied at the Section du Paysage from 1965 to 1967. She gradually learned about the subtleties of her profession, which "was to be a guiding element in (her) life." According to her, it was to be more than simply a professional experience, it was "the adventure of a lifetime."[49] Mercier benefitted from the new courses already appreciated by Auricoste; ecology taught by Jacques Montégut and "the living perception of the site"[50] taught by Bernard Lassus (Figure 5.7). She then enrolled at the IUP, where she studied the history of urban development and sociology. In 1968, the sociologists at IUP, inspired by Henri Lefebvre, "provoked heated debates concerning a new, free and generous utopian society!"[51] Although these two programs provided the foundation for her practice, it was her involvement in the field that made her evolve constantly.

After working with architects on a large housing project, she decided to work freelance and actively canvassed potential public clients (regional authorities dealing with agriculture and public utilities, national parks, urban planning agencies, and the forestry department). She developed elaborate arguments in favor of addressing public issues through landscape architecture. Her approach was inspired by ideas expounded in the journals *Anthos* and *Urbanisme* that were also cited by her female colleagues. For five years (1972–1976) Mercier worked for the planning authority of the new town of Saint-Quentin-en-Yvelines (Etablissement Public de la ville nouvelle de Saint-Quentin-en-Yvelines; EPASQ), near Versailles, where she contributed to the development of the town's public space infrastructure. She ensured that the initial urban and landscape development concepts were adhered to despite the administrative division between design and implementation.

In 1976, in search of a life in a more natural environment, open to the sky and near the ocean, she joined the regional development agency for the coast of Aquitaine (MIACA) where she conducted intensive research for twelve years (Figure 5.8, Plate 5.5). Mercier approached all her activities embracing landscape architecture, ecology, and forest management.[52] While having been directly involved in urban planning and design at EPASQ, her role at MIACA was to delegate. She defined the landscape programs and the specifications for the interventions of landscape architects in private practice. Her work required establishing a multidisciplinary approach involving designers, urban planners, and experts from a variety of fields. In the process, she had to maintain a balance between contributing her

FIGURE 5.7 Graduation dinner in a restaurant in Versailles with the teachers and students, 1967. Section du Paysage et de l'Art des Jardins, ENH. Six out of eleven students were women. From left to right: (a student, A. Belin), Jacques Sgard, (a student, F. Trebucq), Professor Montégut, Marguerite Mercier, Jean-Claude St Maurice. Photo credit: Marguerite Mercier.

knowledge and professional expertise and respecting the role of the designer in charge of the project.

For seventeen years, Mercier worked for the regional public works department (DDE, Direction Départementale de l'Équipement) in Gironde. Working within this large entity covering several constantly changing areas (urban planning and development policies, utilities, infrastructures, and housing), she collaborated with other government departments and local authorities, helping to build a local landscape policy. While teaching at the School of Architecture in Bordeaux (ENSAB), she proposed a new school to train landscape architects with Caroline Stefulesco, then the president of the Fédération Française du Paysage (FFP), and participated in its initial definition.[53] However, when the project was finally launched, her job at the DDE of Bordeaux prevented her from actively participating in its implementation.

Today, Marguerite Mercier says she "was fortunate in having taken part in initiatives of exceptional scale which would no longer be possible today in the context of decentralization."[54] It was also a lesson in humility, serving the public interest. In Aquitaine she "learnt to acknowledge nature, its strength and its fragility"; she "discovered the importance of time for allowing natural environments to regenerate as well as the importance of the management

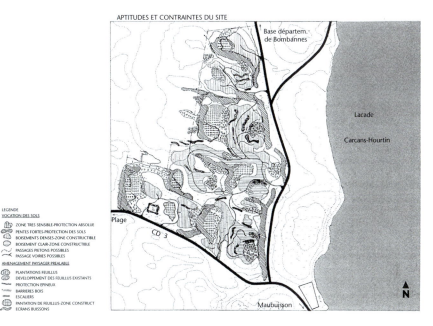

Base départem.·
de Bombannes

Lacade

Carcans-Hourtin

Plage

CD 3

Maubuisson

LEGENDE
VOCATION DES SOLS

ZONE TRES SENSIBLE-PROTECTION ABSOLUE
PENTES FORTES-PROTECTION DES SOLS
BOISEMENTS DENSES-ZONE CONSTRUCTIBLE
BOISEMENT CLAIR-ZONE CONSTRUCTIBLE
PASSAGES PIETONS POSSIBLES
PASSAGE VOIRIES POSSIBLES

AMENAGEMENT PAYSAGER PREALABLE

PLANTATIONS FEUILLUS
DEVELOPPEMENT DES FEUILLUS EXISTANTS
PROTECTION EPINEUX
BARRIERES BOIS
ESCALIERS
PANTATION DE FEUILLUS-ZONE CONSTRUCT
ECRANS BUISSONS

N

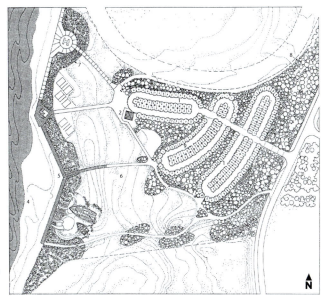

LEGENDE

1 - PARKING
2 - COMMERCES/SANITAIRES
3 - POSTE SECOURS/DOUCHES
4 - PLAGE
5 - PROMENOIR FRONT DE MER
6 - PELOUSE SOLARIUM
7 - ARBUSTES
8 - ARBUSTES/BALIVEAUX
9 - ARBRES TIGES

N

FIGURE 5.8 Landscape and site plan for new holiday resorts. From: Marguerite Mercier, *Aménagement et Paysage, 11 réalisations*, MIACA, December 1988. Top: Development plan by the Bureau Ecologie et Paysage Santucci-Pruvost/Eco Projet for the Carcans Maubuisson joint development zone based on an environmental impact assessment for the development of a holiday center with 6600 beds in the dune woodland area set back from the western shore of Hourtin Lake (1979); Bottom: Landscape plan for the Basque coastal area by Bureau de Paysage API. Development of the Chiberta beaches, including a promenade along the foredune with beach lookout, a solarium, play area, a parking lot with 500 spaces, and plantations resistant to the spray from the sea (1981). Photo credit: Marguerite Mercier.

of natural and planted environments."[55] This knowledge was put to use in many regional projects, but little was done to capitalize on the lessons learned. They are often still ignored by the teams developing these sites today (Figure 5.9).[56] Mercier describes herself as "a trail-blazing plant, the one which crosses fire and prepares the ground for the species that will follow."[57] According to her, women introduced a "fresh approach . . . open to the multiple dimensions underlying a situation,"[58] a posture seemingly well adapted to addressing constantly evolving landscape problems.

Three committed women

This female genealogy contributes to the history of recent landscape architecture in France. These three creative individuals trod original paths that no other women in France had traveled before. The freedom with which they contributed to changing the practice of landscape design bears witness to their determination, flexibility, and openness. Ingrid Bourne may be considered a European pioneer in the type of ecological thinking that many landscape architects still share today. Isabelle Auricoste, who was heavily invested in education, can be seen as a political radical, advocating an artistic and humanistic sociopolitical approach to landscape design. Marguerite Mercier's contribution has been as a pioneer in serving the state and creating frameworks for the involvement of landscape architects on a regional scale.

These areas of interest can also be found in the work of their more famous male colleagues. The work by Gilles Clément in the realm of gardens and the environment is internationally

FIGURE 5.9 Marguerite Mercier on the coastal dune between the ocean and the dune woodland. February 16, 2014, sketching a coastal protection scheme after the heavy storms at the beginning of the year. The dunes in the background were planted with beach grass and stabilized by forest plantations in the nineteenth century. Photo credit: Marguerite Mercier.

PLATE 0.1 Joane Pim in collaboration with Anglo American Corporation architecture and planning section, amphitheater at the male mine workers' compound, Western Deep Levels, South Africa, 1960s. Photograph by Jeremy Foster, 2012.

FÖRSLAG·TILL·EN·LITEN·TRÄDGÅRD·PÅ·SLUTTNING·MOT·SJÖ·

PLATE 0.2 Ester Claesson, design proposal for a villa garden, ca. 1905. The drawing shows Ester Claesson's artistic abilities, and that she developed a drawing technique very close to Joseph Maria Olbrich's. Private collection.

PLATE 1.1 Herta Hammerbacher, Open Space Plan for Wirsitz (Wyrzysk), Poland, 1940. Color pencil on diazotype. Courtesy Architekturmuseum TU Berlin.

PLATE 2.1 Joseph Maria Olbrich's monochrome gardens "Rot, gelb und blau" (Red, yellow, and blue) on a postcard from the garden exhibition held in Darmstadt in 1905. Photo credit: Institut Mathildenhöhe, Darmstadt.

PLATE 2.2 Ester Claesson, design proposal for a garden, c. 1907. Hand-colored drawing, later published in black and white, in *Deutsche Kunst und Dekoration*, 1907, and in *The Studio*, 1912. Private collection.

PLATE 2.3 Cyrillus Johansson, design proposal for a garden for the Swedish Armed Forces, Stockholm, c. 1945. Photo credit: Matti Östling, The Swedish Centre for Architecture and Design.

PLATE 5.1 Near the Baltic sea, Schönberg. Vast open spaces in the North of Germany, open to the sky and horizon, were a source of inspiration for Ingrid Bourne. Watercolor, Michel Bourne, 1975.

PLATE 5.2 Planten un Blomen, Hamburg, 1956, Karl Plomin, landscape architect. Plant associations surrounding a pathway: "dotted everywhere there were clusters of tall trees and under the trees, there were these flowers and shrubs." Photo credit: Ingrid and Michel Bourne.

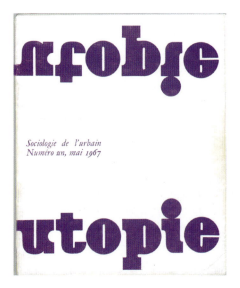

PLATE 5.3 *Utopie.* Cover of first issue, May 1967. The cover and its typographical design is by Isabelle Auricoste. The idea was to abolish the boundaries between different modes of expression. Photo credit: Hubert Tonka.

PLATE 5.4 The public square at the high-speed train station in Tours. Stool shoots of Lagerstroemia indica, and a fountain providing light for the parking lot underneath. Isabelle Auricoste and Yves Brunier, landscape architects, 1991. Photo credit: Isabelle Auricoste.

PLATE 5.5 Proposed landscape development presented by the Bureau Santucci Paysage at the end of 1977 for the Carcans Maubuisson joint development zone for a holiday resort. The plan defines land use depending on the topographical and vegetation characteristics. Land for potential development appears light, the protected zones colored, and the projected plantations as dotted areas. Photo credit: Marguerite Mercier.

PLATE 6.1 St. Helena Park, Welkom, 1960s. Joane Pim in collaboration with Anglo American Corporation architecture and planning section. (*Welkom* [Johannesburg, Keartland Press, 1968])

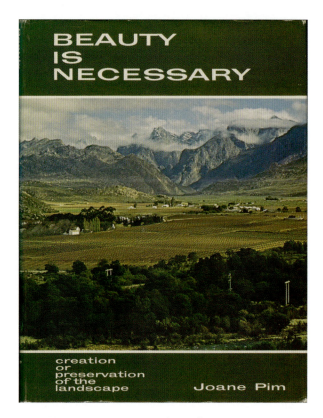

PLATE 6.2   Cover, Joane Pim, *Beauty Is Necessary* (Purnell, Cape Town, 1971).

PLATE 6.3   View of Orange Free State mining area from top of spoil heap. (MuseumAfrica, ref. PH2013_140)

PLATE 6.4 Mature landscape, municipal park, Welkom, 1960s. (Anglo American Photographic Library; ref. GT60_14_40930)

PLATE 6.5 Mine managers house showing *in situ* stonework and topographic modulation, Western Deep Levels, 2012. (Photo: author)

PLATE 6.6 Joane Pim in front of mature honey locust trees, Klippan Nursery, Welkom. (*Welkom* [Johannesburg, Keartland Press, 1968])

PLATE 6.7   Planted parade, black single mine workers' compound, Western Deep Levels, 2012. (Photo: author)

PLATE 7.1   Postcard for Pepperdine College in Los Angeles, CA. Students socializing around the central fountain, c.1946, Katherine Bashford and Fred Barlow Jr, landscape architects, 1937. Courtesy of Pepperdine University Archives.

PLATE 7.2   *Landscape Architecture Magazine* cover, January 1967: Salishan Lodge and Resort, Lincoln, Oregon, Barbara Fealy, landscape architect, John Storrs, architect, 1964.

PLATE 7.3 View from Spa of Oregon coastal landscape as designed, Salishan Lodge and Resort, Lincoln, Oregon. Barbara Fealy, landscape architect, John Storrs, architect. 1964. Courtesy of Salishan Lodge.

PLATE 7.4 Wessinger garden in Portland, Oregon. Barbara Fealy, landscape architect, begun in 1976. Photograph: Joseph Wessinger.

PLATE 7.5 Freeway Park, designed by landscape architect Lawrence Halprin with Jean Walton and others, Seattle, WA. Photograph: Iain Robertson.

PLATE 7.6 For the once-polluted Mystic Reservation, Carol R. Johnson worked with consultants who developed new soil mixes and drainage techniques to solve problems posed by toxic soils. Carol R. Johnson, landscape architect, 1979.

PLATE 8.1 Ruth Shellhorn and Walt Disney, Train Station, Disneyland, 1955. Photo: Harry Kueser. Author's collection.

PLATE 8.2 Pedestrian bridge over arroyo, University of California, Riverside, 2011. Ruth Shellhorn, landscape architect. Photo: Ruth Taylor Kilday. Author's collection.

PLATE 9.1 Aerial view of Library Square rooftop design. Landscape architect: Cornelia Hahn Oberlander (Photo credit: Stuart McCall/North Light).

PLATE 9.2   Skeena Terrace gingko trees. Landscape architect: Cornelia Hahn Oberlander. Architects: Erwin Cleve with Underwood, McKinley, Cameron (Photo credit: Turner Wigginton).

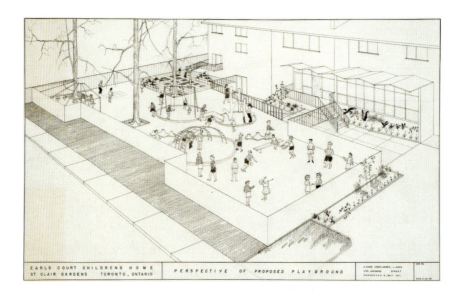

PLATE 9.3   Earl's Court Children's home in Toronto, 1958. Landscape architect: Cornelia Hahn Oberlander (Centre Canadien d'Architecture/Canadian Centre for Architecture).

PLATE 9.4   Robson Square and Provincial Law Courts "stramps," Vancouver, circa 1978. Architect: Arthur Erickson. Landscape architect: Cornelia Hahn Oberlander (Photo credit: Stuart McCall/North Light).

PLATE 9.5   Oberlander's grass mix reestablished at the UBC Museum of Anthropology landscape, Vancouver, 2011. Landscape architect: Cornelia Hahn Oberlander (Photo credit: author).

PLATE 10.1 Flamengo Landfill Park, conceived by a multidisciplinary design team, led by Lota Macedo Soares, Rio de Janeiro. Photo by Alicia Nijman, Wiki Commons.

PLATE 10.2 Rosa Kliass, João Carlos Cauduro and Ludovico Martino, Paulista Avenue comprehensive streetscape project, São Paulo, City of São Paulo, 1973. Rosa Kliass Collection.

PLATE 10.3 Rosa Kliass, Heron's Mangrove Park on Guamá River in Belém, state of Pará, 1999. Rosa Kliass Collection.

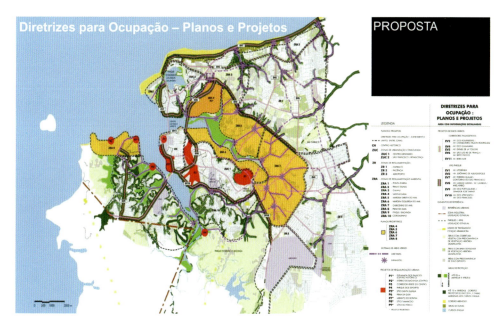

PLATE 10.4 Rosa Kliass, Urban landscape project for São Luís, capital of Maranhão, 2003. Rosa Kliass Collection.

PLATE 10.5 Rosa Kliass, Fortress Park in Macapá, capital of the state of Amapá, 2004. Rosa Kliass Collection.

PLATE 10.6 Rosa Kliass, Youth Park, detail of incorporation of preexisting structures. São Paulo, state of São Paulo, 2006. Rosa Kliass Collection.

PLATE 10.7 Rosa Kliass, Youth Park, preservation areas, sports facilities, and connecting internal street. São Paulo, state of São Paulo, 2006. Rosa Kliass Collection.

renowned; in the fields of teaching and politics, Michel Corajoud has earned recognition, and Alexandre Chemetoff has received acclaim by attempting to "train" commissioning authorities. In a more institutional context, Pierre Dauvergne[59] has been involved in regional services since their beginning, although he is less well known outside of France.

In their own individual ways the three women redefined commissions that were initially limited and unclear by developing what might be termed "program design" within the landscape project: they first invented and then challenged commissions for large housing units. They sought to better define the public commission and render its bureaucratic processes more transparent for planning and teaching purposes. Together with their trail-blazing male and female colleagues, they indirectly contributed to changing institutions and public policies. However, despite these activities, there are few references to the women in architectural, planning, and landscape histories. This is partly due to special circumstances: Bourne was the spouse of a more vocal and visible associate; Auricoste focused more on rural than on urban issues; and, as a planner, Mercier was less visible and less likely than a designer to attract media coverage of her commissions for public institutions. The women shied away from media coverage and its resulting simplistic images, while sharing a conviction that the practice of landscape architecture could help improve society.

Inspired by landscapes that they felt emotionally attached to, such as the Baltic Sea, the English countryside, the Aquitaine shoreline, and the region of Charente, they committed their lives to their professional practice. They experienced practice, in Mercier's words, as "a privilege enabling them to acquire an exceptional view of the world, progressively wider and attentive to details, . . . providing them with the ability to foresee the potential development of sites." One can only rejoice in the knowledge that more and more women are following in their footsteps.

Notes

1 Statistics of the competitive exam for the government-certified training of landscape architects of the schools of Versailles, Lille, and Bordeaux; from 2006 to 2012 (secretariat for the competitive exam, ENSP Versailles).

2 "Section du Paysage 1946−1972," *Annuaire des anciens élèves de l'ENSH et de l'ENSP, 1994* (Versailles: Association des ingénieurs horticoles et anciens élèves de l'Ecole Nationale Supérieure d'Horticulture et de l'Ecole Nationale Supérieure du Paysage, 1994), 96.

3 *Cuscute*, French for dodder, a parasite of alfalfa, a nickname the engineering students at the School of Horticulture gave to the students in landscape architecture and which the latter gave to the free auditors and young women.

4 We may also note that the literature sketching the history of the discipline of landscape architecture and of its instruction in France mentions few female figures. See Dorothée Imbert, "On site and time: French Landscape architecture in the twentieth century," in *Het landschap/The Landscape*, 53−75 (Antwerp: De Singel, 1995) and Pierre Donadieu and Moez Bouraoui, "La formation des cadres paysagistes en France par le ministère de l'Agriculture, 1874−2000" (Research report, Ministère de l'Écologie et du Développement Durable/CEMAGREF Bordeaux, 2003). Increased female presence in the profession is only explicitly referred to by sociologists. See Chantal Cicé and Françoise Dubost, "La profession de paysagiste" (research report, Centre de Sociologie des Arts, EHESS, Mission de la recherche urbaine, 1986), 79−83.

5 Henceforth, I will refer to this department as the Section du Paysage. The training program lasted one year, then two years from 1950, after a preparatory year for those who were not already horticultural engineers. It was followed by a competitive exam validating the sketch of a project to be presented after a minimum of a one-year internship, resulting in a total of five years of training.

6 "Décret du 5 décembre 1945 relatif à l'institution d'un diplôme de paysagiste de l'École Nationale d'Horticulture. Exposé des motifs," in Bernard Barraqué, "Le paysage et l'administration" (Research report, Ministère de l'Urbanisme, du Logement et des Transports, Mission de la Recherche Urbaine, Paris, 1985), 169−170.

7 Ingrid Bourne, in discussion with the author, Strasburg, October 15, 2013.

8 See Heino Grunert, "75 Jahre Planten un Blomen, Hamburgs Niederdeutsche Gartenschau von 1935," *Stadt+Grün*, November 2010, 51–59.

9 Bourne, Strasburg, 2013.

10 It should be noted that the major projects designed earlier by the landscape architect Leberecht Migge and the architect Fritz Schumacher in Hamburg seemed unknown to Plomin and to his young student. The reference to discussions on landscape architecture in Germany after the war goes beyond the scope of this article.

11 See Gert Gröning and Joachim Wolschke-Bulmahn, *Grüne Biographien, Biographisches Handbuch zur Landschaftsarchitektur des 20. Jahrhunderts in Deutschland* (Berlin: Patzer Verlag, 1997), 361–363.

12 See Udo Weilacher, "Entre naturalisme et minimalisme, évolution de l'architecture paysagère suisse du 20ᵉ au 21ᵉ siècles," in *Guide suisse de l'architecture du Paysage*, eds. Udo Weilacher and Peter Wullschleger (Genève: Presses Polytechniques et universitaires romandes, 2005), 26–55.

13 Ingrid and Michel Bourne, in discussion with the author, Lyon, October 23, 2013.

14 Bron-Parilly mixed-use neighborhood, "Secteur Industrialisé," OPHLM du Rhône, architects: Bourdeix, Gagès, and Grimal, 30 hectares, 2607 housing units, 1951–1963.

15 Michel Bourne in discussion with the author, Lyon, November 20, 1995.

16 Bourne, Strasburg, 2013.

17 Ibid.

18 For this park see Alexandre Chemetoff, *Visits* (Basel: Birkhäuser, 2009), 296–365.

19 Echirolles, La Ville Neuve, SADI (Société d'Aménagement de l'Isère), 5000 housing units, 1967–1985.

20 Bourne, Strasburg, 2013.

21 See Françoise Dubost, "Les paysagistes et l'invention du Paysage," *Sociologie du travail* 25, no. 4 (1983): 439.

22 See Michel Racine, ed. *Créateurs de jardins et de paysages en France du XIXe siècle au XXIe siècle* (Arles: Actes Sud/Ecole Nationale Supérieure du Paysage, 2002), 266–268.

23 Les "Cours du soir de la Ville de Paris" offered two separate trainings at the time, for graphic designers and for architect's assistants, as still does today the EPSAA (École Professionnelle Supérieure d'Arts graphiques et d'Architecture de la Ville de Paris).

24 Section 4 of EPHE (École Pratique des Hautes Études), Sciences Économiques et Sociales, which achieved independence in 1975, leading to the creation of the EHESS (École des Hautes Etudes en Sciences Sociales).

25 See Bernadette Blanchon, "Public Housing Landscapes," *Landscape Research* 36, no. 6 (December 2011): 689–693.

26 Among others, he trained Pierre Donadieu and Marc Rumelhart (who both headed the department of ecology at ENSP from 1977 to 1987 and from 1987 to 2013 respectively), as well as the landscape architect Gilles Clément.

27 Pierre Donadieu in conversation with the author, Versailles, January 2014. See Marc Rumelhart, "Éco-logiques pour les projets de paysage. Autobiographie d'un héritage," *Les Carnets du Paysage* 20 (November 2010): 196–197.

28 Isabelle Auricoste in discussion with the author, Poitiers, October 25, 2013.

29 Henri Lefebvre, *La vie quotidienne* (Paris: L'Arche, 1947); *La vie quotidienne II, Fondements sociologiques de la quotidienneté* (Paris: L'Arche, 1961); *La vie quotidienne III, De la modernité au modernisme* (Paris: L'Arche, 1981); *La vie quotidienne dans le monde moderne* (Paris: Gallimard, 1968).

30 Interview with Isabelle Auricoste, "Utopie: Sociologie de l'Urbain, Editor, 1967–78." Interview by Craig Buckley, Poitiers, October 7, 2007, in *CLIP/STAMP/FOLD, The radical architecture of little magazines, 196X to 197X*, eds. Beatriz Colomina and Craig Buckley (Barcelona: Actar, 2010), 197–200.

31 Ibid., 197.

32 Ibid., 197.

33 Cité des Indes, ZUP (Zone à Urbaniser en Priorité – priority urban development zone) de Sartrouville, architect: Roland Dubrulle, 3000 housing units, 1967–1981; and Cités Karl Marx et Paul Eluard, ZAC (Zone d'Aménagement Concerté- joint development zone) de Bobigny, architect: Michel Holley, 1971–1976.

34 Auricoste, Poitiers, 2013.

35 Isabelle Auricoste in discussion with the author, Paris, March 1, 2009.

36 Buckley, 200.

37 ZUP des Minguettes, Vénissieux, Société d'Équipement de la Région Lyonnaise, architects: Beaudouin, Bornarel, and Grimal, 2nd stage, 1966–1972.

38 Auricoste, Poitiers, 2013.

39 In parallel to the CNERP, it was intended at the time to develop a training for landscape engineers in Angers École Nationale d'Ingénieur des Techniques Horticoles (ENITH), which was finally created in 1987 (ENITHP – École Nationale d'Ingénieur des Travaux d'Horticulture et de Paysage).

40 See Jean-Pierre, *Le Dantec, Le Sauvage et le régulier, Art des jardins et paysagisme en France au XXe siècle* (Paris: Le Moniteur, 2002), 208–215.

41 Alexandre Chemetoff, "The landscape after the battle" (lecture, Symposium Modern Landscape Architecture [Re]Evaluated, University of California, Berkeley, 1989).

42 The current master program Jardins Historiques, Patrimoine, Paysage (Historical Gardens, Heritage, Landscape) started in 1992 with the architect Janine Christiany and the garden art historian, Monique Mosser.

43 Buckley, 200.

44 A collaborator of Rem Koolhas and Jean Nouvel. See *Yves Brunier, Landscape Architect* (Bordeaux: Arc en rêve, Birkhauser, 2001).

45 Cicé and Dubost, "La profession de paysagiste," 32. Applicants had to be "free-lance" (*libéral*) and "skilled in planting techniques" (*planteur*) to be able to join the Chambre des Paysagistes Conseils.

46 In Parc des Hauteurs, Lyon, 1993.

47 Auricoste, Poitiers, 2013.

48 Ibid.

49 Marguerite Mercier, "Une aventure de vie," unpublished manuscript, September 2007, Microsoft Word file.

50 Ibid.

51 Ibid.

52 For details, see Frédéric Pousin, "Projeter la grande échelle. L'aménagement du littoral aquitain (1967–88)," In *L'emprise du vol*, eds. Nathalie Roseau and Marie Thébaud-Sorger (Genève: MetisPresses, 2013), 147–160; and *Urbanism* 41, no. 130 (1972). Special Issue "Aménagement de la côte Aquitaine."

53 A landscape architect trained at the Section du Paysage in 1961–1963.

54 Marguerite Mercier, in telephone conversation with the author, January 4, 2014.

55 Mercier, "Une aventure de vie."

56 Marguerite Mercier, lecture, "La Miaca qu'est-ce? L'aménagement de la côte Aquitaine, quels résultats?" Cycle *Expériences de Paysage*, Fédération Française du Paysage (FFP), Pavillon de l'Arsenal 30 April 2011, http://www.f-f-p.org/fr/experiences-de-paysage/?id=4&max=8&st=16 (accessed December 23, 2013).

57 Mercier, "Une aventure de vie."

58 Mercier, telephone conversation, January 4, 2014.

59 Born in 1943. See Racine, *Créateurs de jardins et de paysages*, 302–304 and Barraqué, "Le paysage et l'administration," 81–89.

6

MODERNITY, MINING AND IMPROVEMENT

Joane Pim and the practice(s) of "landscape culture" in mid-twentieth-century South Africa

Jeremy Foster

> Landscape is a dialectical image, an ambiguous synthesis whose redemptive and manipulative aspects cannot finally be disentangled, which can be neither completely reified as an authentic object in the world, nor thoroughly dissolved as an ideological mirage.
>
> Stephen Daniels, *"Marxism, Culture, and the Duplicity of Landscape"*[1]

Introduction

In 1948, the same political watershed year in which Afrikaner Nationalists replaced South Africa's pro-British Smuts government, one of the country's oldest, most powerful mining houses, Anglo American, embarked on the exploitation of massive new gold deposits recently discovered in the Orange Free State. Revealed by a new technique that made it possible to find new deposits without costly exploratory drilling, these mines presented quite different developmental opportunities compared to the original Vaal Reef mines around Johannesburg, some of which were then nearing the end of their productive life. Because they were deeper, potentially richer and longer lasting, it was believed these new reefs would justify significant upfront investment. Located in remote areas, they were also considered an opportunity to avoid the impacted, chaotic character of the earlier mines. Anglo American chairman, Sir Ernest Oppenheimer, argued that the creation of these new industrial-scale complexes in empty landscapes without existing municipalities should not occur through ad hoc alterations and additions; instead, their construction needed to reflect the latest ideas about town and landscape planning.[2]

Much of the work of shaping this vision was assigned to a then-unknown designer, Joane Pim. In 1950, Anglo American made her responsible for shaping all the parks and open spaces of an area of the northern Free State, twenty-four square miles in extent, including fourteen mines and mine villages that would eventually become the city of Welkom.[3] In many ways, this commission was extraordinary. The project was vast and complex, and Pim had no formal training as a landscape architect or town planner, and only a few years' experience in garden design. She was also an independent-minded, single woman, living in a male-dominated society, and working in a city renowned for its utilitarian, engineering-driven approach to the built environment. Born and raised in Johannesburg, Pim only discovered

FIGURE 6.1 Early published town plan showing proposed parks in Welkom, Orange Free State. (*Optima*, March 1956, 30)

landscape architecture when she was 30 years old. While in Britain, in 1933, she worked with Brenda Colvin for six months, and subsequently made an extended study tour of gardens in the United States. Pim began "doing gardens" in 1937, but during the war, she pursued other interests, and she only began practicing seriously again in 1947, designing residential gardens in Johannesburg's well-to-do northern suburbs, and for clients like the Johannesburg Country Club and Anglo American's headquarters.

The Welkom commission (Plate 6.1), which occupied Pim until 1960, would transform her from a gifted amateur into an authoritative professional, and led to similar commissions for other large mining companies, as well as other Anglo projects. She also became the garden consultant for the Oppenheimer's sprawling Johannesburg estate, Brenthurst, and their stud farm in the semi-desert Karoo near Kimberley, Mauritzfontein. Pim used these prestigious projects to lever similar work in South Africa as well as Rhodesia, Swaziland and even Tunisia. Although she also worked on private estates, embassy grounds, urban parks, natural reserves and commercial and residential developments, the bulk of her work involved the improvement of mining properties. She worked closely with the mining corporations' own architects, planners and engineers to lay out what were effectively new company towns, landscapes of unprecedented scale that eventually included housing, recreational facilities, playing fields, administrative quarters and hospitals.[4] The mid-1960s – when Pim was entering her sixth decade – was a particularly busy period; in addition to domestic and urban consulting, she was working on projects at President Brand, President Steyn, Lorraine, Harmony, Western Deep Levels and Vaal Reefs mines. For most of her career, she oversaw a commercial nursery outside Johannesburg, which she established to supply the kinds and numbers of plants she needed for her projects.[5] At the end of her career, she seldom took on domestic work, and only favored large-scale projects.[6]

Today, Pim is usually remembered as the founder of landscape architecture in South Africa. Her large projects made her an advocate for the psychological, social and economic benefits of landscape design. She was a firm believer in landscape's power to create "a settled attitude of mind" and be a "civilizing influence"[7] and, unusual for the period, she was distinguished by her interest in the environmental aspects of landscape transformation. Although she mostly took up and popularized others' strategies, she is often credited with bringing indigenous South African plants into common garden use. Pim felt that, even though they lived outdoors a great deal, white South Africans were paradoxically apathetic towards their national landscape.[8] She blamed this on a "pioneer psychology" that manifested itself in a love of game reserves, and the obsession with the private house, but little in between. Pim was critical of the country's so-called town and country planning, and local planners' obliviousness towards landscape features, natural or manmade, that could help give urban development identity, and lamented the lack of trees in the new African townships, where barren pieces of veld were expected to serve as "parks." She supported the preservation of indigenous flora and fauna, but also criticized the lack of common lands and protected river corridors accessible from urban areas – in other words, dedicated public open-space networks.

A forceful speaker, Pim lectured to mining companies, property developers, farmers, municipalities, surveyors, engineers, architects, planners, students and anyone else who would invite her to speak. She promoted landscape as the "missing link" between the architectural, engineering, town planning and surveying professions, capable of redeeming urban development. Pim also saw landscape architecture as a potential agent of reform in a young country with a thorny social and political inheritance. Her illustrated public lectures, radio talks and journal articles became the core of her 1971 book, *Beauty Is Necessary*, the first publication to discuss landscape design and conservation in a South African context, and whose underlying message was captured by its subtitle: "*creation or preservation of the landscape*" (see Plate 6.2). This book made her the person anyone with an interest in landscape issues contacted for information and guidance, and she helped launch the careers of many of the country's first generation of professional landscape architects. A founder of a local landscape institute in 1961, and instrumental in inviting a distinguished array of international visitors to South Africa in 1971,[9] Pim helped broker the funding and shape the curriculum of the first landscape architecture department in Africa, at the University of Pretoria, in 1972. During the last decade of her life, her international reputation grew, thanks to her study and lecture trips abroad and the publication of articles on her work in British and American journals.[10] She died in 1974 at the age of sixty-nine.

Despite her importance in establishing the profession in South Africa, Pim is little known outside South Africa today, perhaps because she doesn't fit comfortably into histories of landscape architecture that turn on lineages of influence and design expression. Although she was a dedicated and forceful practitioner, who, once she discovered landscape architecture, had "no other thought for a profession,"[11] she was neither a trained landscape designer nor a gardener. Pim corresponded with Geoffrey and Susan Jellicoe, Sylvia Crowe and Brenda Colvin and was familiar with work being done in the United States, Israel, Australia and Germany through journals as well as travel. She attained her British Institute of Landscape Architects licentiate via correspondence in 1954, but the Institute initially refused to grant her full membership. In part, this difficulty reflected the unsettled state of the profession immediately after World War Two. Outside North America, only a few practicing landscape architects had academic training and, except in Northern Europe, the modernist idea that the built environment would be the agent of a better society had still not had much impact on the profession. In

Museum Africa, Johannesburg. PH2007-17659

FIGURE 6.2 Joane Pim working at her drawing table, The Mews, Parktown. (MuseumAfrica; ref. PH2007_17659)

Europe, landscape design was concerned either with garden aesthetics or with making public landscapes and regional infrastructures – a division that also tended to be gendered.[12] The challenges of post-war reconstruction and urban expansion, as well as new technologies and scales of work, encouraged the belief that the best way to manage the effects of industrialization was objective technical and scientific knowledge.[13] Aesthetic experimentation was confined to the work of a few creative practitioners like Jellicoe, Daniel Kiley and Roberto Burle Marx.[14] While some architects had begun thinking about calibrating the city's form to the regional landscape, the less-radical garden city formula of green belts and neighbourhood units was becoming the default mode of urban development in most parts of the world.

Still, as Burle Marx's career demonstrated, modern design sometimes had unexpected valencies on the global periphery, where local elites often sought cultural legitimacy by "jumping into modernity," and rapidly growing cities provided opportunities for design experiments that were hard to implement in the metropole. The substitution of design modernity for social and political modernity that this led to – for example in cities like Bombay and São Paulo – was stronger on the Witwatersrand than in the rest of South Africa, which remained fundamentally conservative until the 1970s. Johannesburg's white population embraced modernity in many

FIGURE 6.3 Aerial view of the shopping center and civic area of Welkom with the main
gardens as initially planted, 1950s. (Anglo American Photographic Library; ref.
Welkom60_689_200705.jpg)

different forms, because it allowed them to justify their existence as Europeans in Africa, and
because mining capitalism was so bound up with technological progress and cosmopolitan
networks. Although the city acquired some outstanding modernist buildings, thanks to local
architects' links to their contemporaries in Europe, the overall cityscape received little attention, and perceptions of urban disorder were channelled into the repetitive rebuilding of its
fabric.[15] This utilitarian, short-term and profit-driven approach to urban development extended
beyond the commercial center and adjacent mining lands into the city's suburbs.[16] After 1950,
however, apartheid planners adopted modernist planning, and the garden–city paradigm came
to dominate urban development in both European and African parts of the city.[17]

Pim embraced many forms of modern technology,[18] and the importance of comprehensive design, but she was ambivalent about modernist ideas that moved the city out into the
landscape. While she saw the solution to the city as more greenery and less density, she
also criticized garden suburbs for their bland, anonymous character and hated the effects of
sprawl. Although Pim did attempt some Burle Marx-like fusion of indigenous iconogra-
phy and industrial materiality,[19] she seldom referred in her lectures or writing to aesthetic
creativity, and she doesn't appear to have had close ties with Johannesburg's vibrant art
community. That her work at its best copied the modernist-Picturesque design vocabulary, then current in Britain, is hardly surprising.[20] She had little formal design education
and limited graphic skills and, as Christopher Tunnard observed, the "English Picturesque
tradition" had a tenacious hold throughout the world during the first half of the twentieth
century.[21] Over the course of her career, Pim's work became as much about planning and
implementation as about design, and the people with whom she had the closest working

relations were usually experts on technical and environmental problems rather than artists and designers. In any case, local social, economic and environmental circumstances made it hard to borrow ideas directly from abroad, and, like most autodidacts and people working in isolation, Pim needed to be a jack of all trades. She worked in a bricoleur-like way, attuned to the job at hand.

In trying to understand Pim's relation to design modernism, we also need to remember she was nearly fifty when she took on the Welkom commission, and belonged to a section of white settler society that was both privileged and embattled at this time. The daughter of an Irish-Quaker accountant brought to South Africa by the mining magnate Cecil John Rhodes, Pim grew up just after the South African War. She spent her childhood and teenage years in Parktown, a residential enclave that was the home to an administrative, political and entrepreneurial Anglophone elite who maintained close social and cultural ties to their counterparts in Britain. As friends and neighbours of the Oppenheimers (major shareholders in Anglo American), the Pims were an integral part of this elite. Like the Oppenheimers, they lived in a Herbert Baker house on the edge of the city.[22] Its Gertrude Jekyll-inspired garden, also designed by Baker, enjoyed a northward, continent-raking view – a landscape setting that, quite physically, embodied the belief that enlightened governance would transform a backward region into a modern "Europe in Africa."[23] By the 1960s, when Pim still lived on the same property, and Parktown's privileged relationship with the African landscape had long since been eroded by suburbanization, nevertheless she maintained the colonial-era relationship to the landscape through active participation in the Rand Hunt Club's various equestrian activities in the still-open countryside north of Johannesburg.[24]

It is easy to see, then, how Pim's subjectivity as a landscape designer might have been shaped by an equivocal attitude towards the effects of modernity. While design discourse

FIGURE 6.4 Joane Pim riding in peri-urban landscape north of Johannesburg, 1960s. (William Cullen Library, University of Witwatersrand)

tends to focus on modernity as a matter of aesthetic and intellectual rupture and innovation, modernity can also be thought of as ceaseless or rapid sociopolitical, economic and technological change, usually due to the increased circulation of capital, facilitated by practices of optimization, standardization and reproduction. The latter condition creates the tension between what Holston calls the two "experiences of modernity" – the enthusiastic embrace of new technologies for the reshaping of the world and anxiety about technical rationality and uniformity's intrusion into all aspects of society. In colonial societies like South Africa, where Western modernity and premodern ways of life regularly collide, the tension between embracing modern techniques as a salvation to the social and environmental consequences of industrial capitalism, and fearing the social and aesthetic effects of these techniques, can be especially acute. This ambivalent attitude towards modernity probably describes Pim's situation best, and accounts for her frequent description of landscape as a vital "missing link" in mid-century South Africa.

Visual versus practical regimes of landscape modernity

Contradictions between the redemptive and destructive aspects of capitalist modernity haunt the very idea of landscape. Although it is accepted that the "landscape idea" is integral to occupying and investing a given territory with meaning, there is less agreement about how this "production of landscape" occurs; that is, whether landscape is a primarily visual and spatial projection or image (i.e. *landskip*), or a realm of social and material practices, customs and negotiations (i.e. *landschaft*). Recently, cultural geographers have challenged theorizations of landscape as the manifestation of an empowered, Western "way of seeing," which objectifies the terrain and thereby overlooks the work of creating and maintaining it, arguing that such projections are often far from hegemonic and fractured by ambivalence. Increasingly, emphasis is placed on the narratives, beliefs and attitudes that become embedded in landscapes through social *praxis*. "Landscape" is seen as a realm of practical engagement where meaning is constructed, and identity is formed, through *acts of doing, using and making* that leave traces of varying degree of solidity, opacity or permanence. Landscape thus becomes implicated in processes of social reproduction as material culture rather than cultural-symbolic representation. This shift from thinking *about* landscape, to thinking *with* it brings to the fore connections between materiality, consciousness and action.[25] It also introduces a strand of Foucauldian discourse that describes both the governance of the conduct of social groups, as well as the manner in which individuals and groups *fashion* themselves, through codes of practice that emanate from without and within.[26]

Cultural geographers propose a variety of ways such "governmentality" plays out in landscape production. One is Don Mitchell's Marxist/materialist reading of how capitalism utilizes labor to transform raw materials in order to generate profits. For Mitchell, the creation of a landscape like a mining town has to be understood primarily in terms of the struggles between capital and labor; "the production of landscape is an essential moment in the production of surplus value"; consequently, to "understand the forms we see in any (landscape) scene, we have to refer to the systems of capital production and reproduction (that generated it)."[27] By contrast, John Wylie's interpretation of landscape "governmentality" emphasizes bodily practices and habits; thus, a "discourse of landscape" is not a set of things said or reproduced regarding a terrain, but something that creates that landscape as a particular *set of meaningful beliefs, attitudes* and *everyday practices*. Sometimes related to livelihoods, such "cultures *of landscape*" often help groups navigate significant sociopolitical change.[28] David Matless, in turn, links landscapes' "governmentality" to larger moral geographies. Usually associated with analyses of landscapes as visible manifestations of particular social formations, moral geographies also mediate normative relationships between space and behavior. "[Modern] distinctions of citizenship and anti-citizenship turn on questions of *appropriate conduct and aesthetic ability*"; they work through "a mutual constitution of the aesthetic and the social . . . teaching people how to see and appreciate landscape is tempered by a desire to control potentially disruptive affects. The education of the eyes is accompanied by the control in and of the body."[29]

Most landscape architects subscribe to the notion that the physical transformation of landscape brings about the moral and social transformation of those who inhabit it. The role of landscape as a governmental "vehicle of social (re)production" becomes more complex and elusive, however, when one considers the values and meanings mediated by landscape's *materiality*, rather than its *appearance* or *use*,[30] and the hermeneutic affects of "procedures of a technical nature whose emphasis on action . . . supports a mode of significance found in the activity of relating."[31] As Anita Berrizbeitia and Linda Pollak argue, such material operations create different kinds of knowledge about natural and cultural worlds "through the displacement of elements in their native contexts"; instead of being a mute standing reserve at the *service of form*, matter contributes to the *content of the work*.[32] This local reworking of the site's native materiality is usually combined with the importation of matter from elsewhere, as part of complex, historic and enduring connections between people, places and technologies.[33] Materiality is also imbricated in another fundamental of landscape-making, what James Corner calls "measure" – "the exercise of good propriety and the practice of ethical judgment" in making everyday determinations that "conjoin appearance and apportionment with utility and strategy."[34] "Measure" is bound up with practical factors involved in the realization of the designed project, not only available materials and technologies, but also modes and rhythms of working (or "labor").[35] Thus, the *spacing* and *means* of realization cannot be entirely separated from ideology and ethics or the affordances and resistances offered by the local physical environment.

This overview of the landscape medium's different modalities of "governmentality" invites an account of Pim's career that focuses as much on the practices through which she produced her work as on what she produced. This might be justified by a postcolonial concern with how peripheral societies engage metropolitan discourse, and a desire to explore a more social-constructive analysis of landscape design.[36] But, it also raises broader questions about how landscape design enacts and performs as part of an expanded, less-disciplinary "culture of landscape"[37] – an important consideration in mid-twentieth-century South Africa, where many whites still found the local physical environment illegible and inhospitable. Especially on the raw, treeless Highveld, where Pim mostly worked, modernity was unthinkingly equated with the built environment's "progress" towards a green, planted European landscape.[38]

Focusing on the material rather than design practices involved in producing landscape recognizes the importance of Pim's ongoing struggle to counter the dismissal of a little-known skill at the time ("large-scale landscaping and beautification")[39] and of prejudices against white women being involved in any kind of environmental work.[40] It also foregrounds issues of expertise and authority; in mid-twentieth-century South Africa, the handful of landscape designers were foreign-trained, and what constituted their legitimate work, and where their responsibility ended in relation to other professions, was unclear.[41] There was no professional organization recognizing landscape design in South Africa or the rest of Africa,[42] no established protocols for the contractual use of drawings and documentation and no standardized procedures for supplying and installing material or sources for manufactured landscape components. In addition, neither the kinds nor the quantities of plant material required for the projects that

Pim worked on were available. A practice-focused approach also recognizes the impact of Pim's interactions with "landscape agents" usually overlooked in design histories – botanists, engineers, architects, horticulturalists, mine managers, "above-ground operations managers" and conservationists – on what she actually produced. Finally, a practice-focused approach helps navigate the fact that, although she had an acute eye for landscape – Pim was an excellent photographer – she apparently had little interest in design experimentation, which makes a conventional design-historical analysis of her work difficult.[43] Arguably, as her book's subtitle suggests, she was ultimately more interested in promoting public debate about the character- istics and conservation of South Africa's broader cultural landscape than she was in design.

I therefore propose that Pim's contribution to landscape modernity was mediated through the range of practices – not only documentational, technological and managerial (i.e. "pro- fessional"), but also travelling, imaging, writing and speaking (i.e. "cultural") – involved in producing her projects. Because these practices blurred the personal and the sociopolitical, as well as the appreciation and making of landscape, they blurred the distinction between landscape architecture and landscape thinking in general.[44] As a result, I would argue, her professional career modelled a material and aesthetic disposition – a "culture of landscape" that rehearsed a particular form of citizenship in response to the political situation of apartheid South Africa. However, my focus here is on how the various kinds of obvious and unobvious work Pim used to transform the mining landscapes tested what it meant to be "modern" in mid-twentieth-century South Africa.

Mining capital, the moral geography of "improvement" and garden making

Pim's landscape practice(s) reflected the landscape values of her race, class and culture. There is little doubt that this background underpinned both her professional success and her advo- cacy for landscape thinking. As we have seen, Pim grew up among a liberal, Anglophone elite with social and economic ties to the mining industry. After World War Two, this urban elite's conviction that political reform was linked to industrial and economic pro- gress placed it in a charged position in national politics. Modern South Africa was built by mining. Beginning in the last quarter of the nineteenth century the subcontinent had been transformed from a pastoral to an urban society, and integrated into the global economic system, by the discovery of diamonds and gold. Most of the capital required to extract these minerals came from abroad and led to the concentration of economic power in a few large corporations controlled by wealthy families like the Oppenheimers. By the 1940s, the min- ing industry had become the engine of the national economy,[45] and had begun to alter the face of the broader national landscape (Plate 6.3).[46] This was especially true on the Highveld, where many new urban developments were dominated by the massive site works and infra- structures required by the adjacent gold mines. Rapid expansion in the 1950s increased the mines' economic importance, but created tensions between their Anglophone owners and the new Afrikaner government who needed mining revenues to underwrite the moderniza- tion of South Africa's cities and infrastructure.

Invariably, these tensions played out in terms of labor. The mines had always depended on unskilled non-European labor to be profitable, and much legislation passed by the white parliament was directly or indirectly designed to ensure this supply. This legislation eventu- ally had massive repercussions on African education, housing, influx control, tribal authori- ties and agricultural production. By siphoning large numbers of able-bodied men away from tribal areas, employment in the mines promoted the uneven development of urban and rural areas,[47] and over time, the mines helped transform Africans from a population with land-based livelihoods to one dependent on wage labor provided by white industry. This created a dehumanizing triangulation between race, employment and "rights to the land" that was heightened by laws requiring mines to house workers on their own property,[48] and further entrenched by formal apartheid, when the link between the right to reside in urban areas and employment reduced Africans to "worker-citizens" (i.e. "citizenship" was contingent on having work).[49] As a result, when mining expansion led to labor shortages in the 1950s, housing became one way mining companies could encourage both white and black workers' loyalty. Anglo American, which prided itself in its beneficial treatment of its workers,[50] lobbied the government to allow them to provide married quarters for African mine workers rather than the usual barrack like single-sex compounds.[51] This shift would have dramatically altered the landscape of the mining areas if it had been implemented.[52]

Attempts like this to address broader national issues on the mines exemplify how the Anglophone mercantile class sought to use its still-considerable economic power to resist Afrikaners' political policies during the 1950s. Less obviously, they also exemplify how much in South Africa, as in most settler societies, political discourse remained rooted in imaginaries that linked citizenship to a specific relationship to the land. Like their counterparts elsewhere during decolonization, South Africa's Anglophone whites felt increasingly abandoned by Britain, and as a result developed a sense of trusteeship towards aesthetic and cultural principles perceived to be innately liberal and English.[53] One of these was over a century of English landscape discourse, which projected two complementary versions of the pastoral onto South Africa's national territory; first, the subcontinent as an idyllic retreat, a scenic escape from the ills of civilization; and second, the region as a *garden awaiting the hand of man in order to bloom*.[54] Both were underwritten by a way of seeing in which the pleasure of picturesque, "unbidden effects" coexisted with, and mediated, strong moral undercurrents of "improvement." After the Union of South Africa was founded in 1910, this imaginary geography underpinned the rhetoric of nation-building, in which physical "land" was transformed into cultural-symbolic "Land." The setting that most succinctly expressed this landscape subjectivity was the white farm, with its tidy dwelling enjoying a prospect over a fertile, expertly tilled valley, surrounded by African wilderness.[55] The aesthetics of improvement, like those of modernity, often depended on the co-presence of its opposite (Plate 6.4).

Given its origins during the time of the enclosures, when landscape aesthetics became intertwined with political and philosophical discourse, it is no surprise that this *imaginaire* developed complicated aesthetic and moral resonances in twentieth-century South Africa. In Britain, the picturesque had served historically to elide the tensions between economic liberalism and parliamentary democracy.[56] It favored pragmatic thinking and knowledge arrived at through trial and error rather than through rationalism or idealism. An "improved landscape" was also one in which a responsible landlord husbanded the land's resources, planted trees for future generations and cared for his tenants. The picturesque also mediated the ideology that those best able *to make the land productive* had the strongest right to it (an idea that complicates notions that picturesque visions of landscape obliterate all signs of associated labor). That prudent husbandry and a general sense of paternalistic responsibility were an integral part of Anglophone landscape subjectivity is suggested by how many of the mining elite maintained unprofitable farms in remote scenic parts of the interior. In nineteenth-century Britain, such values had been deemed to be lacking in newer landlords who regarded their estates as commercial enterprises and exploited their tenants; in twentieth-century South Africa, similar accusations could be leveled at the Afrikaner bourgeoisie, then gaining political and economic power, in part through harsher treatment of the African population. Pim grew up immersed in this liberal Anglocentric ethos of improvement, in which profit-making and innovation was balanced by a moral sense of trusteeship and the "natural" aesthetics of pragmatism. She frequently visited Britain, and in her lectures and writing on the origins of landscape design and on how South Africa's national landscape might be shaped, she often referred to English landscape history, and specifically the work of Lancelot Brown and Humphrey Repton.

It is hard to overestimate the symbolic role of garden-making in mediating this ideology of improvement. The garden has long been used to domesticate new and untamed worlds, both in a physical and a metaphorical sense.[57] Europeans had been making gardens in South Africa since the seventeenth century,[58] but the influx in the nineteenth century of settlers from Britain, a nation with "a tradition of gardening in their blood," who moreover construed the subcontinent as a "garden awaiting the hand of man," raised the moral charge of doing so, and led to the emergence of a garden culture that was, initially at least, strongly Anglocentric.[59] It is no surprise that the first books to explore this link were written by female garden writers. In South Africa, as elsewhere in the British Empire, women were responsible for implanting and domesticating European "civilization." The ideal imperial homemaker was one who devoted time and energy to activities *outside the home*. Perceptions of gardens as places of craft, creativity and renewal, and the gardener as someone who develops and passes on horticultural knowledge through continuous engagement with local nature, chimed perfectly with this gendered role. All of South Africa's first garden writers – Dorothea Fairbridge and Ruby Boddam Whetham before World War Two, Sima Eliovson and Una van de Spuy after it – were women who, in their own way, saw gardening as a form of "proto-citizenship."[60] However, their books also perpetuated notions that landscape-making was a sentimental, unpaid activity, "women's work," peripheral to the more pressing, profitable and implicitly masculine concerns of business and administration. In twentieth-century South Africa, this marginalization of landscape-making was reinforced by the fact that the physical work involved was invariably performed by Africans.

Practicing/producing: documentation, labor and citizenship

We can see, then, that Pim had to navigate a complex set of values, attitudes and beliefs in transforming herself from a garden designer into a landscape architect. Coming from the same social and cultural milieu as her patrons made her sympathetic to their vision of landscape improvement as an integral part of development projects,[61] and probably also to the idea that to do so was to thwart the growth of the apartheid state. But Pim also knew that her patron's unreflective cultural vision of landscape required significant translation when applied to industrial-scale projects, and that, to realize these projects, she had to engage their profit-centered, instrumental ways of organizing and recognizing knowledge.[62] In this, she was both empowered and limited by her gender. As a woman, she was intensely aware of the scrutiny to which she was subjected by her male employers and the mining officials to whom she had to give directions on site.[63] Although only a consultant, Pim frequently found herself acting as the mining company's agent, demanding action from managerial-level employees who in every other respect had significant power.[64] Like other women in situations where patriarchal structures are weakening, Pim constructed a role for herself by simultaneously exploiting mainstream beliefs and subverting their restrictions.[65]

A classic tactic for navigating situations of uncertain agency and authority is to adopt the language of the interlocutor, itself a kind of "self-disciplining." Pim was also strongly influenced by her accountant father, who was a renowned Johannesburg philanthropist.[66] As a Quaker, Howard Pim taught his children to eschew unfair or nefarious practices, and be sympathetic towards the disadvantaged. However, he also told them that "It is no use pursuing [a] policy unless we are convinced it will pay," and inculcated in them the belief that investment in employees' well-being led to a financial return for the employer.[67] This helps explain Pim's scrupulous precision in matters of money and time. Documentation, accountability and record keeping (along with the avoidance of any "aesthetic," subjective expression) are, of course, a signature of the modern, self-disciplined, managerial culture. Nevertheless, the size of Pim's archive – over 13,000 documents[68] – is striking, given that she only ever had one or two assistants, and she clearly maintained a punishing schedule.[69] There is little doubt that this comprehensive self-documentation helped Pim establish her credentials as she struggled for recognition by formal professional bodies. At the same time, meticulous records of her work also helped her build a body of specialized knowledge and expertise, a form of cultural capital that could be profitably deployed in the future as a practitioner of an unknown profession.

Pim's papers reveal the extraordinary diversity of her practice, not only in terms of kind, but also type and scale. She was not only responsible for the layout and design of projects, but also for monitoring the actual work (in other words, she functioned like a contractor). Her papers trace the management of the sourcing, supply, distribution and use of labor, skills, soil, manure, plants, water and equipment as well as payment for services, and all site visits and hours spent were thoroughly documented. She maintained detailed correspondence with

FIGURE 6.5 Bird's-eye view of Western Deep Levels – "An artist's impression of the initial development of Western Deep Levels – the deepest mine in the world but one of the most aesthetically pleasing." (Anglo American Photographic Library; ref. WDL61_140)

mine managers and Anglo American headquarters about techniques for the upkeep of the mining landscapes and the reclamation of slime dams and toxic wastelands. Pim's archives also reveal that she was interested in all aspects of landscape production, from soil preparation to highway design. She was also constantly trading seeds and plant material with nurseries around the country and abroad, thereby acquiring substantial knowledge of South Africa's native flora.[70] In all these arenas, Pim worked pragmatically, uncertain what methods, techniques and materials would work the best. The records also reveal that a significant proportion of Pim's "design" occurred through *in situ* discussions with work crews as well as architects, town planners, surveyors and engineers.

Work practices characterized by thoroughness, consistency, pragmatism and on-site decision making not only helped Pim construct her sense of professional agency *vis-à-vis* her employers, they also informed her relations with her employees. Pim clearly had a far more engaged relationship with the Africans she employed than most white South Africans[71] – a significant fact, given the then-common perception that white women "could not handle African labor."[72] On urban projects, she depended on site crews she selected and trained herself, based on their aptitude for specific tasks like site-clearing, grading, planting, step and wall construction and site maintenance. Taking them with her from project to project allowed her to minimize the use of working drawings, and provided valuable semi-skilled employment for African men in cities at a time when government policies of work reservation were in force.[73] In her letters to wealthy clients, she stressed the merits and importance of using trained permanent employees. Following contemporary practice, she sometimes called them "boys," but she also used their individual full names and kept careful records of their work. Even when working with mine crews, Pim's weekly site reports meticulously record the labor involved, listing names, hours, skills and pay. She also negotiated on her workers' behalf with employers for medical leave, and with the Department of Native Affairs concerning renewal of their passes. Unsurprisingly, many of her workers remained loyal to her for years.[74]

At one level, Pim's interest in her workers was logical. She belonged to a liberal elite, came from a philanthropic family and was personally involved in running several charities that sought to expand educational and recreational opportunities to Johannesburg's African population. Pim also took a keen interest in African music and dance, even though she did not speak Sotho or Zulu. Still, at this time of rapid industrialization in South Africa, ideas of race were also bound up with questions of labor and "rights to the land." Pim's concern for labor relations co-existed with a belief that the mines were broadly beneficial enterprises and that such enterprises required expertise, long-term commitment and capital investment.[75] She also argued that the mines provided Africans with a significant source of employment, and helped nurture a culture of interdependence and loyalty between white employers and black labor. When presenting her work in transforming the mining landscapes, Pim often mentioned those who worked *on the mines* – their origins, the conditions under which they worked and their physical and psychological transformation as a result of this work.[76] She herself records her father's maxim that "educated, contented, healthy workers – well housed, [and] encouraged to live up to high standards of behavior – were not only a credit to themselves and their employers, but . . . more productive and orderly."[77]

Today, of course, such arguments sound paternalistic and self-serving. To be sure, the industrial-scale production of landscape required by the mines relied on the constant supply of semi-skilled, migrant male African workers, and reinforced existing social regimes which linked uneven development and labor-intensive practices to the division between genders based on skills and bodily strength. But, as pursued by Pim, this landscape production also challenged dominant equations of race, labor and citizenship. Unmechanized, labor-intensive landscape production not only provided a form of employment that was a significant alternative to working underground, it developed transferrable skills that could be used at other sites and in other positions. Favoring artisanal techniques, and the relatively simple recombination of locally available materials,[78] this work allowed laborers to retain agency in the making of the landscape and deploy their own experience about the region's stone, soils, water and plants into what was built. Handling and learning about landscape through cultivating a "practical intelligence" that went beyond repetition was a subtle form of governmentality that enabled workers to make independent judgements about and work with other materials and sites.[79] At the same time, this "practical intelligence" helped Pim develop a design vocabulary that could be reliably produced by manual labor (rather than technology), and wherever possible made use of indigenous materials (Plate 6.5).

Pragmatic forms of governmentality not only permeated Pim's relationships with her employers and workers, but also her landscaping methods and techniques. As we have seen, the Anglophone ideology of improvement was underpinned by the notion that the "right to the land" was contingent on the investment of capital and labor. Being fundamentally urban and intellectual, this ideology was easily haunted by its own detachment from the land, and preoccupied with practices that enriched the soil. Consequently, as Isabel Hofmeyer has observed, twentieth-century white South African agriculture sought to distance itself from the practices of indigenous African pastoralists. European settlers saw their work as "thickening" the soil through frequent, intensive cultivation and fertilization, in contrast to the Africans' thin, bodiless "scratching."[80] Echoes of this mentalité can be found in early local gardening books' emphasis on the importance of material operations in which the difference between the *horticultural* and the *agricultural* were blurred.[81] Pim herself became famous for the thoroughness and specificity of the site operations she used on every project. These encompassed the meticulous preparation of below-grade conditions and soil, including deep trenching and importing massive amounts of manure, sludge and organic matter; establishing a reliable source of locally grown, site-compatible plants; developing proper planting procedures to ensure survival; making the best use of limited water and topsoil; and finally setting up a system of ongoing monitoring and maintenance.

This was partly because most of Pim's projects were desert-like wastelands to begin with. At Welkom, she found soil depleted by droughts and years of maize farming, and dust storms that would rip leaves off newly established trees three times in one year. Many projects required the invention of an entirely new topography.[82] Either there were no natural features or environmental niches a designer might capitalize on, or the "site" was buried by excavated subsoil or mining waste. Pim became famous for her expertise in the storage, movement, placement and regeneration of soil and subsoil – arguing that it "cost no more" to do this in a planned than an unplanned way.[83] Showing a learned familiarity with local circumstances as well as successional theory, she favored progressive (or "staged") planting schemes, using tougher, more vigorous nonnative species initially to promote growing conditions that would allow longer-lasting indigenous plants to take hold. She started most large projects by creating a full-scale site nursery to provide acclimatized plants required for the property (Plate 6.6).[84] Over the years, she used experimentation and record keeping to develop a palette of indigenous and non-native plant material that was easy to grow and could survive throughout the Highveld. Her attention to planting operations became increasingly ambitious as the core areas of the mines began to mature, and she could turn her attention to the bio-remediation of the slime dams and waste dumps that surrounded all gold mines.[85] Working with horticulturalists and mining engineers, Pim developed innovative planting strategies and restoration techniques for these "man-made deserts," some of which she used later when creating the picturesque "garden in a desert" at Mauritzfontein. Some of these techniques, methods and strategies were adopted by municipalities and contractors less able to afford this large-scale, long-term experimentation, and became standard practice in sites across the region. In multiple ways, then, Pim's landscape practice transcended design trends, and developed "governmental" as well as environmental agency and relevance.

A more recognizably modernist – and behavorial – entanglement of the ideological and the aesthetic can be found in Pim's preoccupation with the psychological effect that her landscape projects had on both European and African mine inhabitants. She liked to recount how skeptical white workers, drawn from poor, rural communities, were transformed into firm advocates of modern landscaping after living on the new mines for a few years.[86] She also quoted one mine manager saying that the behavior of black workers on the landscaped mines was better, because they took pride in and identified with the mine.[87] When she revisited Harmony Mine to assess mineworkers' opinions on the gardens she had established there, she was pleased to find that some of the men picked flowers for their rooms.[88] On another mine, the manager argued that the orderliness of the landscape above ground translated into similar conditions below, an important consideration, given the mines' need to develop some

FIGURE 6.6 Western Deep Levels white mine managers village – "A management team house complemented by the Joane Pim gardens." (Anglo American Photographic Library; ref. WDL64_120_200689.jpg)

FIGURE 6.7   Western Deep Levels black married workers housing – "The tidy miners homes with indigenous vegetation and natural stone walling." (Anglo American Photographic Library; ref. WDL61_48)

form of *esprit de corps* (or dependency) between European and African miners in what were often dangerous underground working conditions. The ideological and aesthetic aspects of improvement were deemed to converge in other ways, too. At some mines, workers were provided with free plants from the mine nursery to encourage them to take responsibility for beautifying their own environment; at others, new, frequently malnourished recruits from rural areas were employed in landscape work for several months to make them sufficiently fit to go underground.

Conclusion: landscape duplicity, and a "landscape culture" of practice

In hindsight, it would be easy to argue that Pim, despite her relatively powerful position as a member of the privileged elite, had limited effects as a maker of landscape, at both the site and national scales. Competent, even pioneering though her work was, it neither altered the economic and political inequities of South Africa nor addressed the broader environmental impacts of mining, which have only become clearer over time.[89] Although some of her projects matured into distinctive landscapes and succeeded in stemming the "wastage" of trained white managers, others failed to evolve into the layered places she had hoped for. Despite her concern for her African workers, her practices did not alleviate their political and psychological deprivation. Pim's lectures and publications also had relatively little impact on the broader cultural landscape of South Africa, including the segregated African townships,[90] nor did they lead to the creation of a local cultural landscape preservation organization like Britain's National Trust, as she had hoped. If a "landscape consciousness" exists in South Africa today, it manifests itself as a preoccupation with environmental conservation, and the sustenance of traditional livelihoods, rather than as a concern for a "man-induced heritage."[91] Perhaps this is why many of the worst effects of unplanned growth Pim predicted have occurred, particularly around Johannesburg.

Consulting for mining companies gave Pim scope and agency, but the nature of the work and her inability to put her visions on paper limited the influence of her design practice, both during her lifetime and afterwards.[92] It is also questionable if she ever managed to transcend Anglocentric mining capitalism's picturesque and "improving" way of seeing, and find a design vocabulary able to address the actual character of either wilderness or post-industrial landscapes.[93] On the other hand, Pim was hardly in a position to dismantle the dominant economic and political structures of the day. And, as a self-taught woman working in an unknown field, she was effective at realizing projects of great scale, complexity and duration by exploiting her relationship to an elite which controlled vast tracts of land, and which, unlike the government, aspired to "improve" the environment and society. In the process, she brought home the reality that such massive, long-term improvement required *continuous* research, expertise and management and this in turn demanded capital investment.

In fact, Pim's work embodies the profound moral ambiguity that underlies most landscape improvement, which, because it derives agency from *and* ameliorates the effects of dominant economic and political regimes, often helps perpetuate them.[94] It was precisely as a practitioner that Pim was caught up in the "duplicity of landscape," an expression Stephen Daniels coined to capture how the ameliorative aesthetics of beautified landscape often mask socially unjust relations and conflict (Plate 6.7). However, this duplicity can be levelled at most forms of landscape improvement and, as we have seen, Pim partly subverted it, using a picturesque aesthetic to nurture rather than erase the skills involved in creating and maintaining the landscape. In this sense at least, her work challenged the "aesthetics of superfluity" – the contrapuntal devaluation of bodies and reification of material forms – that cultural theorists have come to associate with the built environment of the Witwatersrand.[95]

Pim's landscape work not only contributed to industrial modernity, however, it also *naturalized*, in "traces of varying degrees of solidity, opacity or permanence" (to quote Wylie again), a locally meaningful set of landscape attitudes. While modernism and improvement share a Western belief in enlightened progress, guided by knowledge and expertise, beyond this, they diverge. Modernism places its faith in detached idealism and supposed universals like objectivity and theoretical abstraction that, in the guise of science, technology and economics, can transcend cultures, nations or regions. Improvement, by contrast, brackets such "universals" with *local* considerations of technical pragmatism, social continuity and material contingency. Sometimes the two play off each other; pragmatic traditions acquire heightened value when challenged by new theories. Thus, some have argued, true "modernity" is not mediated through recognizable aesthetic forms (i.e. design) but rather through local convergences of the material and the governmental (i.e. practices) that challenge what forms of knowledge count as "modern"; also, that such "local improvements" are moments in the making of larger modernities rather than matters of their transfer or imposition.[96]

It is perhaps in this light that we can best understand Pim's contribution to "landscape modernity." Her age, Anglo-Quaker upbringing, Reptonian subjectivity and lack of formal training encouraged her to subscribe to a culture of improvement that unproblematically aligned the social and the aesthetic with good business practice, landscape *design* with practical *technique*. In an era that increasingly favored technocratic instrumentality, her approach retained something of older, colonial models of development that emphasized social welfare and collaboration between insiders using knowledge acquired in the field rather than the enthusiasms of outside theorists. At the same time, she linked local material traditions and understandings to contemporary techniques, technologies and methods by participating in, and occasionally contributing to, global professional networks of environmental knowledge. Paradoxically, it was precisely because she was culturally empowered but *not* a mainstream professional – a gifted amateur – that Pim was able to navigate entrenched ideas about gender, race and labor, and promote previously unconsidered landscape practices.

Ultimately, Pim was a pioneer not so much in her aesthetic vision, as in the landscape practice she helped develop, legitimize and establish. Her role as a generator and disseminator of "landscape modernity" derived from the kinds of knowledge and skills her projects inaugurated and legitimized. Her modernity lay in the pragmatic, managerial means she developed to displace, configure and maintain plants, soils, stone and water, and how this unspoken code of practice constructed a distinct "neo-nature" out of the human and nonhuman systems of the mid-twentieth-century Highveld. Developed on the mines and then reproduced in countless urban landscapes and private gardens of the region, as well as the nation's first landscape architecture curriculum, these taken-for-granted material, operative and environmental intelligences defined what was possible using "exercise of good propriety, and the practice of ethical judgment" (to quote Corner again). Less obviously, Pim's landscape-making also gestured towards a pragmatic, non-racial environmental citizenship in which care for nature and redemptive labor were reconciled with techno-aesthetic modernity and capital accumulation. In this way, Pim's work rehearsed a moral geography that articulated the region's natural and (post)colonial histories as part of knowledgeable, regulated and ongoing landscape cultivation.

Acknowledgments

My sincere thanks to Tim Payne, Wim Tijmens and Strilli Oppenheimer for generously sharing with me their personal recollections of working with Joane Pim in different contexts. I am also indebted to Gabriele Mohale, Zofia Sulej, Diana Wall, Pamela Hutchinson, Phillip Baum and Danielle Mericle for their help in tracing and preparing images of Pim's work; to Carolize Jansen for her comments on an earlier version of this paper; and to Melinda Silverman for her introduction to the forgotten corners of the Highveld.

Notes

1 Stephen Daniels, "Marxism, Culture, and the Duplicity of Landscape," in *New Models in Geography Vol. 2*, eds. Richard Peet and Nigel Thrift (London: Unwin Hyman, 1989), 206.

2 Anglo American was worried about attracting and retaining white managerial staff, whose wives hated the barren, monotonous rural environs of the mining areas.

3 Welkom's overall layout seems to have already been completed when Pim was hired. Its wide boulevards, traffic circles, extensive lawns and expansive open spaces epitomized the modernist town planning of the period and were considered extremely advanced for South Africa. See William Backhouse, "Welkom – a Town Planned to Serve the New Gold Mines," *Optima*, March 1952, 12–17.

4 See, for instance, Christopher Herbst, "Architecture and Town Planning of Western Deep Levels Village: Integrating Landscape and Buildings to Construct a Sense of Home," in *Carletonville: Explorations of a Small South African Mining Town*, ed. M. Silverman (Johannesburg: University of Witwatersrand, 2010), 77–83.

5 Although Pim provided the land, operating capital and overall direction, a Mr. L. Liebenberg ran the nursery. Its first large order was from Anglo American. Pim's ownership of the nursery caused problems when she applied to upgrade her ILA membership from Licentiate to Fellowship in 1957–1958.

6 Esmé Moseley Wiesmeyer (ed. P. Widdas), *Joane Pim: South Africa's Landscape Pioneer* (Pinegowrie Natal: South African Horticultural Society, 2007).

7 Carolize Jansen, "Joane Pim," accessed October 31, 2014, http://www.carolizejansen/Joane-Pim.

8 As she wrote: "we are neglecting this lovely country: we are not preserving it, we are not making it more beautiful, nor are we taking sufficient precautions to ensure that the rising generations will be able to enjoy what is our heritage today." Joane Pim, *Beauty Is Necessary: Creation or Preservation of the Landscape* (Purnell: Cape Town, 1971), 34.

9 Before the 1971 International Federation of Landscape Architects conference in Paris. Pim's overtures to hold the main meeting in South Africa were rejected for political reasons.

10 See Dudley Dewes, "Coaxing a Garden from the Veld," *Country Life*, June 20, 1963, 1480–1482 and Joane Pim, "African Gold: The New Mining Landscape," *Landscape Architecture*, April 1968, 192–195.

11 Wiesmeyer, *Joane Pim*, 10.

12 Dorothée Imbert, "Landscape Architects of the World Unite," *Journal of Landscape Architecture* 2, no. 1 (2007): 12.

13 For a global overview of the profession during this period, see Lance Neckar, "Conference Review: Recovery into Prosperity," *Landscape Journal* 16, no. 2 (1997): 211–218.

14 See, for instance, Anita Berrizbeitia, *Roberto Burle Marx in Caracas: Parque del Este, 1956–1961* (Philadelphia: University of Pennsylvania Press, 2005).

15 See Martin Murray, *Taming the Disorderly City: The Spatial Landscape of Johannesburg After Apartheid* (Ithaca, NY: Cornell University Press, 2008), 160–161.

16 On the cityscape of 1950s Johannesburg, see Nikolaus Pevsner, "Johannesburg," *Architectural Review*, July 1953, 361–364, 381.

17 See Jeremy Foster, "From Socio-nature to Spectral Presence: Re-imagining the Once and Future Landscape of Johannesburg," *Safundi: Journal of South African and American Studies* 10, no. 2 (April 2009): 175–213, and "The Wilds and the Township: Articulating Modernity, Capital and Socio-nature in the Cityscape of Pre-apartheid Johannesburg," *Journal of the Society of Architectural Historians* 71, 1 (March 2012): 45–59.

18 She was, for instance, a keen motorist, and always drove an imported Citroën. These icons of modern design sometimes appeared in the foreground of her project photographs.

19 For instance, the use of mining drill cores and assay cupels to create representations of native South African flowers in the paving of the patios at Brenthurst. See Alan Huw Smith, *The Brenthurst Gardens* (Houghton, SA: Brenthurst Press, 1988), 18–19.

20 For a discussion of the relationship between the Picturesque and modernism, see Jonathan Hill, *Weather Architecture* (Abingdon: Routledge, 2012), 224–226, which also notes Nikolaus Pevsner's argument in the 1950s that the picturesque was "tied up with English outdoor life, and ultimately even the general British philosophy of liberalism and liberty."

21 See W. H. Adams, *Grounds for Change: Major Gardens of the Twentieth Century* (Boston: Little Brown, 1993), 41.

22 Timewell was built by South Africa's future "architect laureate," shortly after he arrived in Johannesburg in 1902. Even in a neighbourhood renowned for its gardens, Timewell's was admired.

23 See for instance Jeremy Foster, *Washed with Sun: Landscape and the Making of White South Africa* (Pittsburgh: University of Pittsburgh Press, 2008), 144–177.

24 Pim not only kept her own horses and rode twice a week at the Club, she orchestrated the purchase of its Kyalami estate, laid out courses for its annual hunts and negotiated with landowners for the access rights this required. She also lobbied local government to create dedicated bridleways through this peri-urban area. Her favorite forms of holiday were week-long pony treks in the roadless highlands of neighbouring Basutholand. See Wiesmeyer, *Joane Pim*, 54–74; Historical Papers Archive, William Cullen Library, University of Witwatersrand (hereafter Cullen Archives) Boxes Ad4, Ad5 & Ad10.

25 See Tim Cresswell, "Landscape and the Obliteration of Practice," in *Handbook of Cultural Geography*, eds. Kay Anderson, Mona Domosh, Steve Pile and Nigel Thrift (London: Sage, 2003), 269–281.

26 "Governmentality" encompasses practices across a wide range of scales that regulate and improve behaviour through both formal and official codes, through action taken by subjects themselves in relation to particular techniques and technologies. See John Wylie, "Cultures of Landscape," in *Landscape* (London: Routledge, 2007), 94–138.

27 Wylie, "Cultures of Landscape," 106.

28 See, for instance, Melissa Caldwell, *Dacha Idylls: Living Organically in Russia's Countryside* (Berkeley: University of California Press, 2011), and Louise Green, "Changing Nature: Working Lives on Table Mountain, 1980–2000," in *Imagining the City: Memories and Cultures in Cape Town*, eds. Sean Field, Renate Meyer and Felicity Swanson (Cape Town: HSRC Press, 2007), 173–190.

29 David Matless, "Action and Noise Over a Hundred Years: The Making of a Nature Region," *Body & Society* 6, no. 3/4 (2000): 141–165. Matless argues that in modernizing, increasingly democratic, inter-war Britain, "an array of landscape practices lead to the creation and preservation of a certain *worked view*, and the British landscape as a whole was brought into being as an objectified form through place-based social praxis." See David Matless, *Landscape and Englishness* (London: Reaktion, 2000).

30 For an account of how landscape production, landscape consciousness and citizenship might be linked, see Anita Berrizbeitia, "Amsterdam Bos: Modern Public Park and the Construction of Collective Experience," in *Recovering Landscape: Essays in Contemporary Landscape Architecture*, ed. James Corner (New York: Princeton University Press, 1999), 186–203.

31 Anita Berrizbeitia and Linda Pollak, *Inside/Outside: Between Architecture and Landscape* (Gloucester, MA: Greenwood Press, 1999), 48.

32 See, for instance, David Leatherbarrow, *The Roots of Architectural Invention: Site, Enclosure, Materials* (Cambridge: Cambridge University Press, 1993), 145–177; David Leatherbarrow, "Leveling the Land," in *Recovering Landscape: Essays in Contemporary Landscape Architecture*, ed. James Corner (New York: Princeton University Press, 1999), 170–184.

33 Tim Edensor, "Entangled Agencies, Material Networks and Repair in a Building Assemblage: The Mutable Stone of St Ann's Church, Manchester," *Transactions of the Institute of British Geographers* N.S. 36 no. 2 (2011): 244.

34 James Corner, "Paradoxical Measures: the American landscape," *Architectural Design Profile* 124 (1999): 49.

35 For contrasting accounts of the effects of "landscape work," see Caitlin DeSilvey, "Cultivated Histories in a Scottish Allotment Garden," *Cultural Geographies* 10 (2003): 442–468; Michel Conan, "The Hortillonages: Reflections on a Vanishing Gardener's Culture," in *The Vernacular Garden*, eds. John Dixon Hunt and Joachim Wolschke-Buhlmahn (Washington, D.C.: Dumbarton Oaks Research Library, 1993), 19–46; John Stilgoe, *Alongshore* (New Haven: Yale University Press, 1994), 101–130.

36 As Stephen Daniels observes, "The task (of landscape history today) is to situate historical sites and spaces not just in terms of wider material changes in the physical environment, but in terms of how those changes are seen and understood by those who live through them." Related to this is the challenge of "countering histories that over-emphasize the structural agency of power regimes as well as the individual agency of designers and patrons." See "Landscape History: Material and Metaphorical Regimes," *Journal of the Society of Architectural Historians* 65, no. 1 (2006): 16.

37 Such a "turn to practice" frees social action from the over-determining "grasp of objectified social structures and systems," and has, "to varying degrees, animated things and technologies in new ways, showing how activity is embodied and that nexuses of practices are mediated by artifacts, hybrids, and 'natural objects.'" See Jane M. Jacobs and Peter Merriman, "Practising Architectures," *Social & Cultural Geography* 12, no. 3 (2011): 211–222.

38 See Foster, "From Socio-nature to Spectral Presence," 198.

39 During the early years at Welkom, a local population hostile to her work regularly destroyed new plantings.

40 In her correspondence with prospective landscape architects, Pim wrote that horticulture and garden design was a particularly difficult field for women to qualify in, because neither local authorities nor the national botanical garden would take female trainees. Thus, a woman wanting to become a landscape architect would "have to make [openings] for herself, as I did, through the medium of private clients." Letter, April 10, 1963, Cullen Archives.

41 Bannie Britz, "Reflections on Being a Young Architect in South Africa: 1965–70," Unpublished paper, www.artefacts.co.za/main/Buildings/archframes.php?archid=2123.

42 When Pim attended the 1956 IFLA conference in Zurich, she was the only delegate from Africa.

43 Pim seems to have made rough sketches and given them to more skilled designers and drafts-people to draw up (personal communication, Wim Tijmens, June 2012).

44 For a similar analysis, see Stephen Daniels, *Humphrey Repton: Landscape Gardening and the Geography of Georgian Britain* (New Haven: Yale University Press, 1999).

45 The mines' importance can be gauged by the fact that in the 1980s, more than three-quarters of all gold mined in human history had been extracted from the Vaal Reef since its discovery in 1886. See

John Oxley, *Down Where No Lion Walked: The Story of Western Deep Levels* (Johannesburg: Southern Book Publishers, 1989).

46 See A. J. Christopher, "Mining Landscapes," *South Africa: The World's Landscapes* (London: Longmans, 1982), 119–133. In the 1970s, around 200,000 ha (500,000 acres) of rotation plantings were required to meet annual demand for timber mine props. See *Our Green Heritage: The South African Book of Trees*, eds. W. F. E. Immelman, C.L. Wicht and D. P. Ackerman (Cape Town: Tafelberg, 1973).

47 The usual contract period on the mine was 6 to 8 months.

48 The gold mines, which operated 24 hours a day, depended on round-the-clock, on-site access to large numbers of workers.

49 See Anne-Maria Makhulu, "The Conditions for after Work: Financialization and Informalization in Post-transition South Africa," *PMLA* 127, no. 4 (October 2012): 782–799.

50 *Optima*, Anglo American's prestigious quarterly magazine, started in the 1950s, regularly published scholarly articles on the challenges of African urbanization.

51 When launching operations at the Welkom mine in 1947, Sir Ernest Oppenheimer said Anglo American aimed to "have the best possible housing conditions for white staff and materially to improve the conditions in the housing of black workers." He felt the corporation should "create . . . modern native villages that would attract workers from all over Southern Africa." See Oxley, *Where No Lion Walked*, 166.

52 This would have been a radical departure, both in terms of employer–worker relations, and in terms of a political system which only admitted Africans as temporary residents to white areas. Although the concept of "married housing" was a complete anomaly to Nationalist policy, Anglo American continued to argue this point until influx control, a pillar of apartheid, was scrapped in 1986. See Jonathan Crush, "The Compound in Post-apartheid South Africa," *Geographical Review* 82, no. 4 (1992): 388–400.

53 See, for instance, Jonathan Hyslop, "An Anglo-African Intellectual, the Second World War and the Coming of Apartheid: Guy Butler in the 1940s," in *South Africa's 1940s*, eds. Saul Dubow and Alan Jeeves (Cape Town: Juta & Company, 2005), 212–226; and Peter Merrington, "Cape Dutch Tongaat: A Case Study in Heritage," *Journal of Southern African Studies* 32, no. 4 (2006): 683–699.

54 By contrast, that is, with the "Georgic" imaginary of the garden degenerating into wilderness. See J. M. Coetzee, *White Writing: On the Culture of Letters in South* Africa (New Haven: Yale University Press 1988), 4.

55 See, for instance, Foster, *Washed with Sun*, chs. 3 and 9.

56 This elision stemmed from the fact that locating the origins of aesthetic effects of nature in human experience and subjectivity rather than metaphysical, divinely ordained rules, upheld *the right to private exploitation of nature*.

57 Denis Cosgrove, *Geography & Vision: Seeing, Imagining and Representing the World* (London: I.B. Tauris, 2008), 51–67.

58 As Anglophone colonial nationalist activists anxious to emphasize white South Africans' common Protestant heritage liked to argue, the founding act of European settlement was the creation of the VOC Garden at the Cape in the 1660s.

59 As Sima Eliovson wrote: "Gardens within a natural garden, created by people who have a tradition of gardening in their blood – these are the components that have made average South African gardens among the most beautiful in the world." Sima Eliovson, *Garden Beauty in South Africa* (Johannesburg: Macmillan South Africa, 1979), 27.

60 See Dorothea Fairbridge, *Gardens of South Africa* (London: A & C Black, 1924); Ruby Boddam Whetham, *A Garden in the Veld* (Wynberg Cape: Speciality Press, 1933); Sima Eliovson, *The Complete Gardening Book for South Africa* (Cape Town: Howard Timmins, 1962) and *South African Flowers for the Garden* (Cape Town: Howard Timmins, 1955); and Una Van der Spuy, *Ornamental Shrubs and Trees for Gardens in Southern Africa* (Cape Town: Juta, 1954). Fairbridge once wrote that making gardens was tantamount to "holding the land for civilization."

61 Harry Oppenheimer, Ernest's son and successor, with whom Pim worked for many years, was known for his philanthropy and support for the arts.

62 I.e. "The Chairman and directors of a gold mining company are perforce hardheaded and practical individuals. Dependent in the development stage on capital from other countries, . . . their duty is to produce gold and uranium, and reassure the shareholder that all monies spent in development can be justified in terms of L.s.d." – Joane Pim. Typescript of paper delivered at International Federation of Landscape Architects conference, 1962, Cullen Archives.

63 Wiesmeyer, *Joane Pim*, 32.

64 Within their own domains, mine managers had extraordinary power, combining the roles of CEO, town mayor and local squire. See Jonathan Crush, "Power and Surveillance on the South African Gold Mines," *Journal of Southern African Studies* 18, no. 4 (1992): 825–844. Most did not consider landscape improvement should be taken seriously, especially as the actual work was performed by Africans (personal communication, Wim Tijmens, July 2012).

65 For many years, her engraved letterhead, in addition to "Joane Pim L.I.L.A," read "Landscape and Garden Consultant to the Anglo American Corporation."

66 Pimville, one of Johannesburg's earliest purpose-built African locations is named after Howard Pim, who was renowned in the city as someone who was unafraid of criticizing accepted policies or exposing malpractices (Wiesmeyer, *Joane Pim*, 3).

67 Pim, *Beauty Is Necessary*, 145.

68 I.e., letters to clients, collaborators and contractors; site visit reports, order for materials, orders for and on behalf of clients, registers of letters received, as well as innumerable lectures, talks articles and position pieces.

69 Most days Pim started work at 7 a.m.; when not travelling, she worked on site visits in the morning and on plans and correspondence in the afternoon. She also went riding two mornings a week. Weekends were the only time she had for writing.

70 She received many indigenous seeds from Wim Tijmens at Stellenbosch University, with whom she collaborated for years.

71 Personal communication, Wim Tijmens, July 2012.

72 Letter, Joane Pim to Hazel Short, April 10, 1963; Cullen Archives.

73 These men came from rural areas where land-related work was done by women. In cities, they had to take on menial jobs, because their education did not prepare them for anything else, and government policies reserved most artisanal employment for whites. For Pim's own account of how this kind of landscape production affected the nature of her practice, see, for instance, her letter to the British Institute of Landscape Architects, June 3, 1953; Cullen Archives.

74 Wiesmeyer, *Joane Pim*, 19

75 Pim often referred to Bos Park, outside Amsterdam, which she visited in 1956 and which had taken decades to reclaim from an old polder.

76 She argued that "tribute must be paid to the vast contribution the South African gold and other mines . . . have made to the fitness of young Africans from Angola and Tanzania southwards." Joane Pim, "The Deepest Gold Mine in the World: Life on the Surface." Typed draft of future article submitted to Anglo American for review, May 1967, Cullen Archives, 4.

77 Pim, *Beauty Is Necessary*, 145.

78 Pim was proud of the wall construction method she developed, which combined concrete and local field stone. See Pim, "African Gold."

79 These comparisons were meant to include those between the mine compound and the worker's home environment of the "kraal." See Pim, *Beauty Is Necessary*, 18.

80 See Isabel Hofmeyr, *"We Spend Our Years as a Tale That Is Told": Oral Historic Narrative in a South African Chiefdom* (Portsmouth NH/Johannesburg: Heinemann/Witwatersrand University Press, 1993), 72.

81 Boddam Whetham, for instance, devotes entire chapters to soil preparation, shading, watering (amount and timing), depth and movement of water table and the effects of drought and frost on plant growth, none of which would have been found in English garden books.

82 Joane Pim, "Creating a Landscape for a Mining Town," *Optima*, March 1956, 26–31.

83 Typically, she backed this up with financial figures obtained from one sympathetic mine manager.

84 These supplied plant material for large-scale operations as well as white mine workers' own gardens and the African workers' compounds, usually free of charge.

85 During the late 1950s, as part of a South African Chamber of Mines initiative, Pim experimented with different combinations of manuring, seed mixes and planting schedules, and eventually covered 1,000 acres of abandoned slime dams and sand dumps with grasslands capable of attracting bird and animal life. See Joane Pim, "Industrial Landscape: The South African Mines," in *Shaping Tomorrow's Landscape, Vol 2: The Landscape Architects Role in the Changing Landscape*, eds. S. Crowe and Z. Miller (Amsterdam: Djambatan, 1964), 90–94; also "Laying the Dust on Mine Dumps and Slime Dams," *Optima* 16, no. 3 (1966): 159–160 (no identified author, but probably Pim).

86 See Pim, "Creating a Landscape for a Mining Town," *Optima*, March 1956, 31.

87 The underlying tensions of mine compound life are hinted at in Pim's account of Western Deep Levels: "Who wants to fight when one can relax under shady trees on a pleasing lawn or where one

can natter to one's friends in the beer garden, or take part with enthusiasm and energy in games and athletics, or compete in tribal dancing – again in planned and planted surroundings?" Pim, "The Deepest Gold Mine in the World," 5.

88 http://www.carolizejansen/Joane-Pim; accessed May 2012.

89 Apart from huge dust storms and many square kilometers of semi-toxic waste dumps, the mines left a larger legacy of restricted land use, due to the constant danger of subsidence on dolomitic land and hundreds of kilometres of underground passages containing polluted groundwater that have to be constantly pumped. Dorothy Tang and Andrew Watkins, "Ecologies of Gold: The Past and Future Mining Landscapes of Johannesburg," in *Places Journal*, accessed October 31, 2014, http://placesjournal.org/article/ecologies-of-gold-mining-landscapes-of-johannesburg.

90 Though beautification of a black township would also have been, as Steve Biko put it, "a soporific to the blacks while salving the consciences of the guilt-stricken white." See http://www.carolizejansen/Joane-Pim; accessed 2012.

91 See William Beinart and Peter Coates, *Environment and History: The Taming of Nature in the USA and South Africa* (London: Routledge, 1995), 108.

92 Indicative of a limited "landscape culture" is the fact that most of the thousands of landscape photographs Pim bequeathed to the University of the Witwatersrand were discarded in the 1990s because they "lacked documentary value."

93 If fixing a boundary between the wild and the cultivated is the primary act of gardening, then the garden metaphor's ability to address the large-scale effects of industrial modernity, including man-made wilds, is limited.

94 "By becoming part of the everyday, the taken-for-granted, the objective and the natural, the landscape masks the artificial and the ideological nature of its form and content. . . . It is therefore, as unwittingly read as it is unwittingly written." James Duncan, *The City as Text: The Politics of Landscape Interpretation in the Kandyan Kingdom* (Cambridge: Cambridge University Press, 1990), 19.

95 See Achille Mbembe, "The Aesthetics of Superfluity," in *Johannesburg: Elusive Metropolis*, eds. Sarah Nuttall and Achille Mbembe (Durham, NC: Duke University Press, 2008), 37–67.

96 See Miles Ogborn, "Spaces of Modernity," in *Spaces of Modernity: London's Geographies 1680–1780* (London, Guilford, 1998), 1–22.

7

AMERICAN LANDSCAPE ARCHITECTURE AT MID-CENTURY

Modernism, science, and art

Thaïsa Way

As Catherine Howett has suggested, ecological values have been a part of landscape design practice since the "primitive fence" defined a zone of human control.[1] They are evident in the early work of landscape architect Frederick Law Olmsted, who sought to make natural systems visible within existing social and cultural contexts, as argued so persuasively by Anne Whiston Spirn in her essay "Constructing Nature: the Legacy of Frederick Law Olmsted."[2] Olmsted's design for the Emerald Necklace and the Backbay Fens with Charles Eliot addressed both environmental processes and natural systems. Nevertheless, narratives of landscape architecture in the late nineteenth and early twentieth centuries, as it emerged as a profession, have focused on the art of design, often neglecting the agency of nature.[3] Such histories have not considered how landscape architecture was informed by the simultaneous rise of the nascent disciplines of both environmental science and ecology. The overlapping discourse of these fields is evident in the early issues of *Landscape Architecture Magazine* (LAM) that included articles by Catherine E. Koch on wetland marsh plants and by Elma Loines on garden plants, both in issues published in 1916.[4] In 1931, Frank Waugh's essays in *LAM*, including "Ecology of the Roadside," testified to continued ecological thinking among designers.[5] In 1933, Elsa Rehmann published her article, titled "An Ecological Approach."[6] Clearly ecology, understood as a science, was considered relevant to the profession of landscape architecture.

Among the growing community of landscape architects interested in ecology as well as the science of horticulture were a significant number of women. In the first half of the twentieth century, the public could read books such as Edith Adelaide Roberts and Elsa Rehmann's *American Plants for American Gardens: Plant Ecology – the Study of Plants in Relation to Their Environment* (1929) and Marian Cruger Coffin's *Trees and Shrubs for Landscape Effect* (1940), as well as those by Ruth Dean, Louise Carter Bush-Brown, Martha Brookes Hutcheson, and Louise Beebe Wilder, each engaging ecology, horticulture, and environmental science in a variety of ways.[7] In fact, a more careful investigation of the design practices of women reveals that ecology played an important role in practice, suggesting that the use of scientific paradigms was a critical, if not unique, contribution of women to the profession.

But what happened at mid-century? How did these interests in the first half of the century inform landscape architecture, particularly as practiced by women, in the midst of the modern movement? Was modernism really anti- or pre-ecological? The answer is no. In fact, there were many who sustained an interest in ecology and in modernism. Women, in particular, contributed to this merging of the two domains as they often came to the profession of landscape architecture through their interest in the natural world and the environment.

Compounding the complexity of the narrative, as historian Dorothée Imbert has noted, was the fact that "[l]andscape architecture did not present a unified front in its pursuit of modernism."[8] Modernism in landscape architecture was, in fact, a messy practice, aimed both at disrupting historic assumptions of style and reshaping design for a modern world. It was a practice that grappled with the increasing challenges of environmental health as well as social well-being. It was at this professional nexus that many women contributed as they brought to practice knowledge of plants and horticulture, along with environmental concerns as they impacted the well-being of families and communities.

From the late nineteenth century through the mid-twentieth century, women were attracted to landscape architecture, in part because it engaged the knowledge of horticulture, botany, gardening, and the fine arts, all considered appropriately feminine areas of study.[9] As noted in a description of Martha Brookes Hutcheson on the occasion of her election as a fellow of the American Society of Landscape Architects (ASLA), "Furthermore, for all these women, the conviction to pursue the subject came from a deep love of plants. When this horticultural interest was combined with a sense of design and good living, the gardens that were made were distinguished."[10] And yet, despite these contributions, the profession of landscape architecture in the 1930s through the 1960s sought to distinguish the profession from the craft of gardening and anything that might associate landscape architects with gardeners, nurserymen, or florists. In the late 1930s, Jens Jensen, after resigning from the ASLA, wrote a friend that there was a "strong tendency by the American Landscaper to get away from gardening, as if that word smelled of cabbage. He has a fear of being classed with the craftsman instead of the professional, and today the art is practically killed, because of his efforts to make a profession of it."[11] For many in the ASLA and the profession, an emphasis on plants was overtly feminine, and thus ran the risk of diminishing the professional nature of landscape architecture. Women who applied their knowledge of ecology, environmental science, and plants as designers were classified as merely planting designers, garden designers, or as consultants to landscape architects. In this way, women were doubly marginalized, first as women and second as gardeners and garden designers. In fact, their ecologically oriented contributions would come to define a legitimate approach to landscape architecture, but only once men such as Ian McHarg and, later, Michael Van Valkenburgh became advocates.

History of the profession in the United States

Landscape architecture in the United States became an official profession in 1899, when the American Society of Landscape Architects (ASLA) was founded. The profession was not confined to one typical practice, rather it was shaped by practitioners from distinct backgrounds, including women: Beatrix Jones (later Farrand) was a founding member and Elizabeth Bullard was elected as one of the first fellows, along with Frederick Olmsted, Jr.[12] Women rose as leaders and mentors, including Florence Yoch, Annette Hoyt Flanders, Ellen Shipman, Helen Jones, Katherine Bashford, and Mabel Parsons (Plate 7.1).

The influence of women was strengthened as more women entered the profession. By 1940, 19 percent of ASLA members were women, which provided evidence of an expanding female presence.[13] The practice of women reflected the broad range of projects typical for

FIGURE 7.1   The United States Pavilion at the Montreal Expo 1967, geodesic-dome designed by Buckminster Fuller and Cambridge Seven Architects, with landscape architecture by Carol R. Johnson (AIA honor award). Courtesy of Carol R. Johnson & Associates.

contemporary professionals from the small domestic garden to the city plan, from the intimate neighborhood park to industrial parks, from the bog to hydrological infrastructure. Similar to their male colleagues, women explored a variety of styles and design approaches.

Modernism at school

Modernism in landscape architecture did not arrive with a big splash. It was an incremental change in approach, intention, and composition. While histories of modernism locate the genesis of interest circa 1940 at Harvard, with the publication of essays by Garrett Eckbo, Daniel Kiley, and James Rose,[14] explorations into what modernism might offer were evident earlier in the curriculum of a number of schools. The Cambridge School of Architecture and Landscape Architecture for Women prepared graduates to design livable communities for the future, as it was the "duty of the schools to lead in progressive thought in design and construction." In 1930, the school sponsored lectures by Fletcher Steele, who had visited the 1925 International Exhibition of Modern Decorative and Industrial Arts in Paris, and by Jean Jacques Haffner, the recently appointed head of the Harvard School of Architecture, titled "Modern Trends in Architecture, Decoration, and Garden Design." The school celebrated its twenty-fifth anniversary in 1939, with lectures at the Museum of Modern Art by alumna Cynthia Wiley and Ilse Frank Gropius. Titled "Experiences in Modern Architecture" and "Modern Trends in Landscape Architecture," they were part of the opening of the exhibition Houses and Housing: Industrial Arts in New York City. The exhibition included projects by students and faculty demonstrating the application of modern ideas in architecture and landscape architecture. While students explored the ideas of modernism, they continued to take courses in ecology, plant science, and horticulture. They learned geology as well as landscape surveying. Their education was firmly grounded in a long tradition of teaching women the craft of gardening and the sciences of horticulture and botany.[15]

A similar approach was evident at the Lowthorpe School of Landscape Architecture and Horticulture for Women in Groton, Massachusetts, where courses in horticulture, botany, and planting design were part of the core of the program. Moreover, at many of the universities and colleges, courses in the plant sciences and planting design were frequently taught by female faculty. These women have been recognized for their substantial contributions to plant knowledge in design and their work is, in turn, reflected in the practices of their numerous students, who today practice across the nation.

Geraldine Knight Scott (1904–1989) graduated from the University of California, Berkeley's College of Agriculture in 1922 and received a degree in landscape architecture in 1926. Scott's first design position was in the office of A. E. Hanson, in Los Angeles, which she left in 1930 to travel to Europe. In 1933, she returned to California, working in partnership with Helen Van Pelt in Marin County for three years, and then sharing an office with her while working independently for another three years. In 1939, on her return from a second extensive trip that included attending the 18th Congress of the International Federation for Housing and Town Planning in Stockholm, she was hired as the director of the Citizens Housing Council in the Los Angeles County Planning Office. She participated in school and recreation planning conferences, and was a member of various city and county committees and commissions. She was the first woman to serve on the Los Angeles Regional Planning Commission, responsible for recreational planning and war housing.

Throughout much of her career, Scott was actively involved with Telesis, a group of architects, landscape architects, urban planners, and critics interested in the development and implications of a socially oriented urban design practice, grounded in scientific methods of investigation. Members included William Wurster, Catherine Bauer Wurster, Vernon DeMars, Thomas Church, Grace McCann Morley, and Garrett Eckbo, among others. They approached design and planning as research disciplines. The group advocated for the belief that "People and the Land make up the environment which has four distinct parts – a place to Live, Work, Play, and the Services which integrate these and make them operate. These components must be integrated in the community and urban region through rational planning, and through the use of modern building technology."[16] It was a critical collaboration for Scott, as Telesis offered the opportunity to fully engage contemporary social issues, while remaining firmly grounded in design practice. Such investigations would increasingly orient landscape architecture, and traces of similar thinking and practice can be identified in the work of many women beyond Bauer, Morley, and Scott.

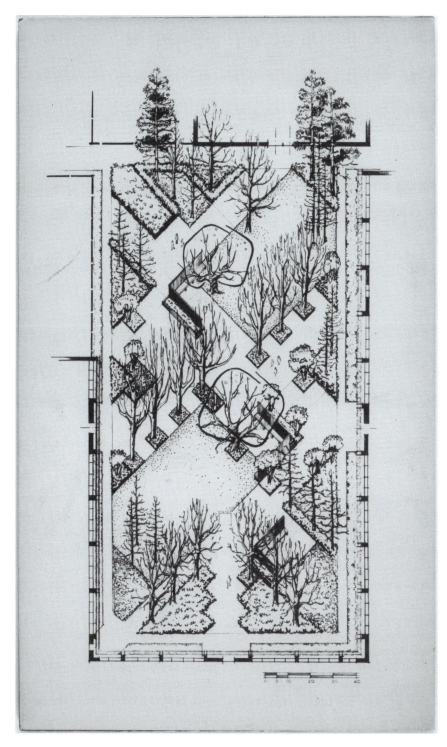

FIGURE 7.2 Food Machinery and Chemical Corporation, plan by Geraldine Knight Scott, landscape architect, no date. Geraldine Knight Scott Collection, Environmental Design Archives, University of California, Berkeley.

FIGURE 7.3   Food Machinery and Chemical Corporation. Photograph by Geraldine Knight Scott,
landscape architect, no date. Geraldine Knight Scott Collection, Environmental
Design Archives, University of California, Berkeley.

Scott opened her office in Berkeley in 1948, and she practiced until 1968, specializing
in designs for housing, schools, private gardens, and professional office parks.[17] Her work
included a significant number of industrial parks and business landscapes, including the Food
Machinery and Chemical Corporation (Figures 7.2 and 7.3) and the Daphne Funeral Home.
While, on the one hand, Scott's work reveals a rich exploration of themes in urban design
and planning, throughout her practice she was most recognized for her plant knowledge. In
addition to this, she was known for her technical skills, reflected in her extensive work on
the Oakland Museum roof garden (Figure 7.4).[18]

The museum had been designed by Kevin Roche and opened in 1969. Daniel Urban
Kiley had originally been commissioned as the landscape architect and he brought on Scott
as a horticultural consultant in 1963, when the project was still in the conceptual phase. As
Kiley's firm was located in Vermont, her local firm eventually oversaw the planting design
and implementation, soil engineering, and the design and placement of the extensive irrigation and drainage systems. Drawing on her knowledge of construction, she supervised the
assembly of the 26,400 square-foot roof garden. The plant palette selected by Scott featured
native plants, such as the redwood tree, as well as a wide range of Mediterranean-type plants,
such as olive trees and Australian bottle brush. The design was shaped by Kiley's modernist
vocabulary of rectilinear geometries, echoing that of Roche's museum building. However,

FIGURE 7.4 Oakland Museum Roof Garden, Office of Dan Kiley, with Geraldine Knight Scott as the local landscape architect for the planting design as well as the lead for the development of the engineered soils and irrigation system. Geraldine Knight Scott Collection, Environmental Design Archives, University of California, Berkeley.

the experience of the garden as an urban retreat was, in large part, a result of Scott's careful plant selections, particularly the trees and shrubs that created small, enclosed garden rooms with dynamic seasonal color and fragrance. The roof garden offered the amenities of an intimate public park with the formal geometries that reflected the character of the modern art museum.[19]

This knowledge of engineering, construction, and plants was evident in Scott's teaching as well. At the University of California, Berkeley, from 1952 until 1968, she was responsible for planting design courses to which she brought deep knowledge and a multidisciplinary approach. She encouraged students to explore and understand movement in space through explorations in the fine arts and dance before challenging them to design space using plants and other materials. Reflecting her practice and involvement with Telesis, she brought a broad commitment to socially relevant design to her teaching, instilling in students the belief in landscape architecture as a socially and culturally oriented practice.

Mae Arbegast[20] (1922–2011) also taught courses in plants and planting design at the University of California, Berkeley. Arbegast graduated from Oberlin College in 1945, earned an M.S. degree in ornamental horticulture from Cornell University in 1949, and concluded her formal education with an M.S. in landscape architecture from Berkeley in 1953. She worked for Geraldine Knight Scott (1951) and Lawrence Halprin (1951 and 1955). She was hired to teach at Berkeley, first as an instructor in 1955–1956, and then as an assistant professor (1956–1967). During this time, she maintained a part-time professional practice that she pursued again full time from 1967 until 2003. Like Scott, Arbegast was known for her extensive plant knowledge and her understanding of how to design both for plant health and aesthetic value.

At the University of Illinois, Elizabeth May McAdams (1881–1967) and Florence B. Robinson (1885–1973) taught most of the plant courses. A 1916 graduate of the University of Illinois, McAdams had worked for Warren Manning and joined the University of Illinois faculty in 1918. She taught design (three years), planting design (six years), and plant identification (nine years) until 1929. She was also responsible for founding the Landscape Gardening Association for professional women and served as secretary for the Chicago club of landscape architects.

Robinson succeeded McAdams. She had attended Kalamazoo College, where she graduated in 1908 with a bachelor of philosophy. After teaching natural and physical sciences in Detroit-area high schools, she enrolled in the University of Michigan, where she completed a degree in architecture and a master of landscape design in 1924. From 1916 to 1926, she led a small practice, while continuing to teach in the local high schools. In 1926, she was hired as an associate teacher in landscape design at the University of Illinois and, in 1929, she was the first woman to be hired in a tenure-track position. While maintaining a small practice, she was promoted to associate professor in 1946 and was awarded a full professorship in 1951.

Robinson was widely respected for her knowledge of plants, ecology, and planting design as a teacher and author. Her courses in plant identification and planting design were considered rigorous and challenging. In addition to teaching, she was a prolific writer for magazines and a series of books on plants and planting design. Her books *Planting Design* (1940) and *Tabular Keys for the Identification of the Woody Plants* (1941) became standard texts in programs throughout the nation. While the first part was focused on "Design Factors," the second was titled "Ecological Factors" and the third was "Applications." Robinson's students, Hideo Sasaki, Richard Haag, and Peter Walker, are recognized for their role in shaping approaches to modernism in landscape architecture.[21]

These teachers would remain influential through the 1950s and into the 1960s. It was only in the late 1960s, with the growing environmental movement, Ian McHarg's *Design with Nature*, of 1969, and the work of Richard Forman in landscape ecology, that the environmental sciences, including ecology, acquired a more prominent role in the landscape architecture programs, now increasingly shaped by male faculty. Among the few female faculty members at that time was Sally Schauman, who had served as the leading landscape architect with the USDA Soil Conservation Service. In 1980, she was appointed the first woman chair of a department of landscape architecture at the University of Washington. Under her leadership, the department focused on ecological design, including wetland restoration and landscape planning and design for urban watersheds. Anne Whiston Spirn joined the Harvard faculty in 1979 and served as director of the Department of Landscape Architecture, from 1984 to 1986.

Spearheading an ecological approach to community-based design, she was then appointed chair of the Department of Landscape Architecture at the University of Pennsylvania. These women have taught multiple generations of designers who are practicing today. Most important has been their success at establishing a strong foundation for plants and ecology within the core curricula of landscape architecture education. This occurred despite many practitioners rejecting such studies and, instead, focusing their attention on explorations of minimalist art, choreography, and large-scale planning.

Constellations of female professionals

Women contributed to shaping modernist landscape architecture as designers as well. They shared many approaches and project types with their male colleagues and, like their female colleagues who were teaching, many practicing women also paid close attention to the role of plants and the importance of ecology in design. With the end of the war, the profession of landscape architecture would shift its focus from estates and private residences to public and civic spaces as well as to corporate landscapes. Initially, there was a decrease in the number of professional women in general. However, by 1960, two out of five women held jobs, many in the broad domain of the professions.[22] In the meantime, women in Europe were being increasingly recognized within the profession of landscape architecture, with the leadership of the International Federation of Landscape Architects and the work of Ulla Bodorff, Brenda Colvin, Susan Jellicoe, and Sylvia Crowe, among others (see Chapters 1 and 2).

In addition to the changes in the profession, the 1950s and early 1960s revealed a very different workforce from women in careers prior to the war, as their lives reflected a new set of assumptions and aspirations. Many of those entering landscape architecture were second-generation professional women. Roberta Wightman's (1912−2011) mother was a physician and supported her daughter as she completed her degree in landscape architecture at the University of Illinois in 1938, from which she went on to practice in Seattle for more than fifty years.[23] Susan Troutman, the daughter of a landscape architect who had worked with Beatrix Farrand, completed a master of landscape architecture degree at Harvard in 1957.[24] A landscape architect in Lawrence Halprin's office for twenty-five years, Jean Walton (1910−ca. 2000) grew up with a mother who worked as a high school home economics teacher. The idea of entering the professions was not new to these mid-century women. Other women were encouraged by their families, including Mary Booth, Dorothy Hussey, and Helaine Kaplan, who was advised to identify a professional career for financial security and self-sufficiency as well as for personal achievement. Mae Arbegast, the oldest of six children, was expected to take over the family's vegetable seed business, although she would instead become a landscape architect and teacher.[25] By mid-century, these women could enter an expanding professional community that no longer viewed them as being ubiquitously out of place in the workforce.

Contributions by women were evident in the modernization of New York City, under the direction of Robert Moses, from the 1920s through the early 1960s. He hired a number of female landscape architects, often putting them in positions that required knowledge of plants. In 1936, landscape architect Clara Stimson Coffey (1894–1982) accepted a position as the Chief of Tree Plantings for the New York City Parks Department.[26] She had worked for Aubrey Tealdi in Michigan, in Warren Manning's Cleveland office, and for Marian Cruger Coffin and Ellen Shipman, both in New York. Each of these practices emphasized the use of plants in design, ranging from Manning's attention to native plants to Coffin's deep knowledge of trees. In addition, Coffey produced topographical maps and surveys to design road systems. She supervised several prominent landscape projects throughout the city, including the plantings on the Hutchinson River and Belt parkways (1941). In these projects, she selected trees that could withstand pollution, neglect, and even abuse, while providing shade, color, and texture to the public spaces.

Coffey left the city department in 1942 to partner with Cynthia Wiley in the design of playgrounds and housing projects, again drawing on her expertise in plant selections for hardy gardens. In 1945, she established her own firm and then the partnership of Coffey, Levine, and Blumberg in New York City, but she continued to work on public projects. Under Mayor John Lindsey, she oversaw significant street tree plantings in New York City and, in 1970, the New York City Parks Department hired her to redesign the Park Avenue malls, by then a prestigious space in the city. For this project, she had older fences and tall hedges removed, city-hardy trees planted, and colorful planting beds installed at the end of each mall. With her firm, she designed a number of playgrounds in Chinatown, Rockaway, and Corona, and she redesigned the Vale of Cashmere in Prospect Park and the Central Park Conservatory gardens near 5th Avenue and 105th Street.[27]

In 1977, Mayor Abraham Beame appointed Coffey as the professional landscape architect in residence to the Art Commission, and she was relied on for her design contributions as well as her knowledge of plants and horticulture. Clara Coffey Park on the East River (at York Avenue between 53rd and 59th Streets) was named in her honor by the Parks Department to recognize her work for New York City's parks and green spaces.[28]

While landscape architects in New York City worked on an urban scale, others were looking at the scale of the region. Genevieve Gillette (1898–1986) developed her career as a landscape architect within the framework of emerging landscape preservation efforts at midcentury, as an advocate and leader more than as a designer. In 1920, Gillette was the first woman to graduate from Michigan Agricultural College in Landscape Architecture. After graduating, she worked in the office of Jens Jensen, where she became involved with The Friends of the Native Landscape. She advocated for the preservation of open landscapes and natural areas throughout the nation and successfully established the Michigan State Parks Association to expand the state park system. She formed the Natural Areas Council and collaborated with P. J. Hoffmaster on housing projects and park designs, and she ran a small design firm. In 1960, she worked closely with Senator Phillip Hart to lobby for a Land and Water Conservation Bill and for the establishment of the Sleeping Bear Dunes National Lakeshore. Shortly thereafter, she was invited to return to Washington to serve on President Johnson's Citizens' Advisory Committee on Recreation and Natural Beauty. In 1976, the E. Genevieve Gillette Nature Center in P.J. Hoffmaster State Park was named to honor her work as a leading conservationist. By the time Gillette died, in 1986, she had established two national lakeshores and over thirty state parks in Michigan and drafted numerous bills for parks and recreation areas.[29] Recognized for her contributions to the conservation movement, Gillette also led landscape architecture's environmental orientation in significant ways.

Publishing books and articles on garden and planting designs, horticulture and gardening was another means of shaping both the practice of landscape architecture and the public's understanding of the profession. Alice Recknagel Ireys (1911–2000) graduated from the Cambridge School in 1935, when the school was affiliated with Smith College. She found work in the office of Marjorie Sewell Cautley, who designed the landscapes for the new garden suburbs, Sunnyside, New York, and Radburn, New Jersey, and other mixed-income housing projects, using native plants and creating what appeared to be natural habitats within the parks.[30] When work in Cautley's office slowed down, Ireys found employment with Charles Lowrie, working on public housing projects, including the Red Hook Housing Project in Brooklyn. After Lowrie's death in 1939, Ireys worked briefly with Cynthia Wiley and Coffey in New York, designing public playgrounds, housing projects, and college campuses, as well as the grounds of the 1939 World's Fair.

Ireys became known for the sophisticated selection of plants in her designed landscapes and gardens and for her publications.[31] The Fragrance Garden at the Brooklyn Botanic Garden, designed in 1955 by Ireys (today Alice Recknagel Ireys Fragrance Garden), became a model of a city garden and the first garden specifically for those with disabilities. The garden was a sensually rich experience of fragrances, textures, and even sounds, as birds and insects were present. This garden expanded the idea of a city garden or park from providing predominantly visual delight to engaging other senses as well. Ireys designed a colonial-revival garden behind the Mount Vernon Hotel Museum and Garden, the former Abigail Adams Smith Museum, in Manhattan. Her planting design established a clear structure for the garden by means of evergreens, particularly boxwoods and trees, and included flowers that highlighted seasonal changes. While it was merely a beautiful garden on one level, it also played an important role in the interpretation of history, similar to the gardens at Williamsburg, Virginia. Ireys' design work expanded the role of the garden from a mere setting to an active participant in the narration of an urban history.

When her first child was born in 1946, Ireys took time off, as there was little support for working mothers with young children. When she returned to professional practice, she focused on garden designs for churches, hospitals, libraries, and schools, the types of public spaces that a young mother would visit. In the 1950s, her commissions included projects for the Brooklyn Museum, Brooklyn Home for Children, and the Brooklyn Botanic Garden.[32] She eventually designed over eight hundred gardens, many private, highlighting her extensive horticultural and plant knowledge as well as her design skills. She used this experience to publish four garden design books and multiple articles on garden design that emphasized the significant contribution of plants to a well-designed landscape.[33] Ireys's books were important for how she addressed design, ecology, and plants.[34]

In addition to those working in the public realm, there were many landscape architects who focused on private gardens and landscapes. The partnership of Arthur Schoene Berger (1903–1960) and Marie Harbeck (later Berger) (1907–1963) in Texas dealt almost entirely with residential design. Harbeck graduated with a bachelor of science in landscape architecture in 1932, from Oregon State University. Initially, she worked for the architect Gardner T. Dailey, from 1938 to 1940, and later in the office of Thomas Church, in San Francisco. Like many of her contemporaries during World War II, Harbeck used her design skills to develop camouflage techniques that she taught at the Camouflage Branch at Fort Belvoir, Virginia. While there, she met Arthur Berger and, by 1945, the two were in partnership in Dallas, Texas. The partners designed 186 projects over their career, of which the vast majority were private residential landscapes, with a handful of projects at a larger scale, including Trinity University, in San Antonio, and the Science Quadrangle for St. Mark's School. Their commercial and corporate projects, while not extensive, included the Texas Instruments Headquarters in Dallas, the offices on Speedway in Houston, the Dallas Furniture Mart, the grounds of the Dallas Morning News, the roof garden of the Dallas Public Library, and resorts in Jamaica and Texas. For many of these projects, they collaborated with San Antonio architect O'Neil Ford.[35]

With residential design an essential part of their practice, their design for *House Beautiful*'s 1955 pacesetter house was important as a model for regional modernism (Figure 7.5).[36] The Bergers paid close attention to the provision of family privacy and the American style of easy living.

FIGURE 7.5   *House Beautiful* Pacesetter House of 1955, Dallas, Texas, Harwell Harris, architect,
Arthur S. and Marie H. Berger, landscape architects. Courtesy of the Huntington
Library.

They celebrated the flow of space from indoors to outdoors that accommodated large areas for
leisure.[37] Understanding the harsh environmental conditions of Texas, they promoted the use
of native plants and regional materials. Drawing on the environmental knowledge Harbeck had
gained at the University of Oregon, they sought to create low-maintenance gardens, knowing
that the climate limited the seasons in which anyone wanted to garden. Foreseeing the popularity of air conditioning in the Dallas climate, they created, with the architect O'Neil Ford, gardens shaded by large trees and gardens that could be enjoyed visually from the inside.

The Bergers were also enthusiastic gardeners at their own home. The writer of an article
in *House Beautiful* noted that "Five years ago, this house [the Berger's own home] was out
in the hot Texas sun [and] now, a leafy canopy of trees and vines, [created] a ceiling over
the entire area, [that] shelters both house and surroundings. Real climate control! All of the
one and a half-acre property was either paved or planted with evergreen groundcovers, paving patterns, and broad, graceful steps defining the entrance."[38] In a much larger project for
Turtle Creek, the Bergers designed the landscape around what was the first luxury high-rise
in Dallas (Figure 7.6). They responded to the scale and materials of the building by designing
a large-scale waterfall and swimming pool, constructed from the same pink-tinted concrete
as the building, surrounded by a softly rolling landscape of lawn and shade trees As with Ireys
and Scott, Harbeck Berger's designs relied on plant knowledge and horticulture as well as their
experience of the social and cultural context of their work. With this knowledge, they created
gardens that were deeply connected to the region's landscapes and lifestyles.

FIGURE 7.6 3525 Turtle Creek, Dallas, Texas, architect Howard R. Meyer with Marie Harbeck and Arthur S. Berger, landscape architects, 1957 (Listed on National Register in 2008). Courtesy of Dianne del Cid.

In the first decades of the twentieth century, most landscape architects worked on the east coast. However, there was an increasingly dynamic community of landscape architects on the west coast. In Los Angeles, Florence Yoch (1890–1972) had established a practice as early as 1918 and was joined by Lucile Council (1898–1964) in 1921. Yoch and Council's excitement over the potential of a range of Mediterranean plants shaped a vision of the Southern California garden as an oasis of luxuriant growth, worthy of the movies, for which they designed a number of film sets. Ruth Shelhorn (1909–2006) established her firm in Los Angeles after working for Yoch and Council. She was eventually responsible for the design of Disneyland as well as the series of Bullock Shopping Malls (see Chapter 8). June Meehan Campbell (1916–2009) joined Thomas Church's San Francisco office in 1940 and remained for twenty-five years. Elizabeth Lord (1887–1976) and Edith Schryver (1901–1984) launched their partnership in 1929 as pioneers in the Pacific Northwest. These designers brought extensive horticultural and environmental knowledge to their landscape designs; they became associated with a Pacific Northwest style using native plants in addition to acclimated plants that could brighten and diversify the landscape. They hosted a radio show on gardens and gardening, sharing their knowledge of horticulture, design, and gardening with the public in the belief that beautiful gardens contributed to a better community.

Barbara Bertha Vorse Fealy (1903–2000) arrived in Portland, Oregon, in 1947. She had grown up on a nursery in Salt Lake City, Utah, run by her father, where she worked in his rose garden. On her father's advice, she enrolled at the University of Illinois, where she studied landscape architecture under Robinson and Stanley White. Jens Jensen led field trips for students, and his tours of the sand dune habitats encouraged her growing interest in native landscapes and plants. In 1947, she moved to Portland, where she opened her own firm, often working in partnership with the architect John Storrs. The Salishan Lodge and Resort on the Oregon coast was a collaborative project with Storrs for the developer John Gray, who believed that a resort that emphasized the native landscape would appeal to a wide audience (Plates 7.2 and 7.3).[39] The resort, as it was constructed, fostered an experience of the Oregon coast with the design carefully inserted into the landscape, allowing humans and the environment to coexist, even nurture each other. While many designers were following Ian McHarg by adapting his environmental assessment methods, women such as Fealy were pushing the boundaries of practice by engaging in a hybrid of design and environmental stewardship. She was designing places that would foster stewardship of the environment through beauty and familiarity. Fealy created places that people would experience as a part of nature, regardless of whether it was a resort or a small private garden.[40] She partnered with craftsmen and gardeners, including the landscape contractor Ron Vandehey and the concrete contractor Roy Haftorson, to construct her designs.

While Fealy worked on mid-sized projects, including the Oregon School of Arts and Crafts, the Catlin Gabel School, Portland's Leach Botanical Garden, as well as one of her last projects – the Timberline Lodge, her most prolific work consisted of residential gardens for many of Portland's most influential families. These gardens featured native plants highlighting the natural beauty of the Pacific Northwest, including magnificent cedar trees and luxurious rhododendrons. Fealy's approach is particularly evident in her garden design for Patricia Lue and William W. Wessinger in Portland, Oregon, begun in 1976. Sometime after the Northwest modernist architect Walter Gordon had designed the house, Fealy was commissioned to produce a landscape design. The Wessingers wanted an elegant space that would evoke the natural beauty of the Pacific Northwest. Fealy designed a series of paths that wandered past the open lawn and into the woods, where native plantings were featured. She designed a small pool with a stone water basin, carefully placed rocks, and a pair of low stone sculptures (Plate 7.4). It was a subtle reference to Japanese gardens, characteristic of the region with its close cultural ties to Japan. The garden brought the natural world to the Wessingers, and their social life to the garden. The work for the Wessingers was the start of a long friendship as well as a collaboration that would lead to the commission for Timberline Lodge, named a National Historic Landmark in 1976. Fealy was elected a Fellow of the ASLA in 1985, the first woman in Oregon to be honored with this title.[41]

Jean Walton (1910–ca. 2000) was the acknowledged plants person and planting designer in Lawrence Halprin's office, which was known for an ecological approach.[42] Walton had worked as a draftswoman for Lockheed and then had the opportunity to work for the landscape architecture firm of Yoch and Council in Los Angeles. She met Halprin when she enrolled at the University of California, Berkeley. In Halprin's office, she worked alongside Don Carter, Sat Nishita, and Richard Vignolo on a range of projects, from residential gardens to civic parks and plazas, providing the planting designs and plant lists. Her plant compositions often appeared natural, even in urban contexts such as the parks the firm designed in Portland. She was responsible for the plant selection and design for Freeway Park, in Seattle, the first covered freeway in the country, where her careful attention to the soils and microclimates allowed the establishment of an urban forest and park (Plate 7.5). Evergreens provided a clear structure for the park, while flowering shrubs contributed seasonal character, even brightness during the grey Seattle winters. Her design appears as a transplant of the Pacific Northwest forest that was edited for the urban setting. As an extension of this work, Walton also taught plant courses and planting design at local educational institutions. She worked with the firm for twenty-five years, until she retired in 1975.

A graduate of the Lowthorpe School, Jane Silverstein Reis (1909–2005) worked briefly for the large architectural firm of Skidmore Owings and Merrill, after leaving her position at the Coast Guard. In 1968, Ries was granted the third certificate ever issued by the Colorado Board of Examiners of Landscape Architects, making her Colorado's first licensed female landscape architect. She practiced for sixty years, engaging in a wide range of projects – from small gardens to large civic projects, including Larimer Square and portions of the Denver Botanical Garden. She has been described as being able to "slip a home into the natural cover and topography without disturbing the existing land. Vistas and native vegetation thus became the garden, yet she would frame the home with comfortable viewing platforms and discrete specimen plantings."[43] Nevertheless, the use of clear geometries and asymmetry produced modernist compositions, and she used modern materials such as metal water sculptures in the Kock/Wheelock garden (Figure 7.7).

FIGURE 7.7 Kock/Wheelock Garden, Denver Colorado, Jane Silverstein Ries, landscape architect, Courtesy of The Denver Public Library, Western History Collection (#C MSS WH1785).

Patricia Carlisle (b. 1928) came to San Francisco, California, and went to work for Royston, Hamamoto, Beck, and Alley in 1961.[44] She had graduated with a BLA from Pennsylvania State University in 1950. Her first job was with the Peoples National Gas Company Engineering Department. For a decade she worked with Simonds and Simonds, where she was named an associate in 1955.[45] At what was then called Royston, Hanamoto, and Mayes, Carlisle was named an associate in 1963 and a principal in 1973. She worked on the design teams for parks, environmental studies, new towns, and campus planning. She contributed to the entire design process, from site analysis to construction oversight. The firm was known for its modernist landscapes, composed of non-axial spaces and asymmetrical arcs and polygons, suggesting the influences of cubism, biomorphic abstraction, or the rectilinear geometry of paintings. Plants were important, both as design elements shaping space and as providing texture, fragrance, and color and in some cases, historical references such as the olive trees in the Santa Clara Valley, Carlisle used primarily native trees, often specifying larger specimens so that they would contribute scale and weight to the design. This can be viewed in parks such as the Santa Clara Central Park and Civic Center Park, both in Santa Clara, California, as well as the Marina Vista in Vallejo. In addition to the plants, Carlisle recalled being proud of how the firm introduced sculpture into the parks, an element that emphasized the modern character of the landscapes.[46] While Carlisle did not receive significant attention for her own work over the course of her career, the firm did.

While most women in practice at mid-century either led a small firm or worked in larger offices, a few established large firms of their own that promoted environmental and ecological design. Two important firms are Carol R. Johnson & Associates and Wimmer, Yamada and Caughey. Carol R. Johnson (b. 1929) graduated from the Harvard Graduate School of Design in 1957, where she studied with Hideo Sasaki, Walt Chambers, Serge Chermeyoff, and Sigfried Gideon, learning an approach grounded in the collaborative process and in environmentally responsive design. Building on her interest in multidisciplinary frameworks, she found work with engineering and planning firms in and around Boston. The Architects Collaborative (TAC), founded by Walter Gropius, hired her as their first landscape architect. However, she left within a year to start her own firm. Between 1959 and 1970, she led the practice from her home, increasingly taking on projects that involved environmental planning and design. As her practice expanded, she moved to larger offices and hired young designers who were now being trained in these areas. In 1970, the firm changed its name to Carol R. Johnson & Associates, revealing the growth of the firm and its collaborative nature.[47] By 2001, with over 40 employees, it was one of the largest landscape architecture firms in the United States, serving a national and international clientele.

While residential gardens comprised the early commissions, Johnson strategically sought out projects that distinguished her practice. Among those projects was the landscape for the United States Pavilion at Montreal's Expo '67, designed by Buckminster Fuller and Cambridge Seven Architects (see Figure 7.1). Johnson also developed a community-based design practice, and in 1972, she was participant in Lyndon Johnson's Model Cities Program for the North Common, in Lowell, Massachusetts. Her firm was commissioned for two visual-impact assessments of the Chevron Oil Refinery, in Perth Amboy, New Jersey (1975), and the Finger Lakes region of New York. In the United States, procedures for visual impact assessments were pioneered by Johnson, and by Jones & Jones, in Seattle, and they later comprised a significant domain of practice. An important project for Johnson was the Mystic River Reserve, an ecological restoration of a wetland landscape that assumed a model function in environmental design and engineering. Johnson became a Fellow of the American Society of

Landscape Architects in 1982, and, in 1998 she was the first American woman to receive the ASLA Gold Medal (Plate 7.6).

Harriet Barnhart Wimmer (1912–1980) studied landscape architecture at the University of Oregon. Returning to her native San Diego in 1932, she launched a small residential design business, while making ends meet by teaching at a high school. In 1954, she was the first female landscape architect to establish a commercial practice in San Diego. As her practice grew, she hired Joseph Yamada, a graduate of the University of California, Berkeley, who became a partner in 1960. The firm grew while working on numerous projects, including the Copley and Kunzel gardens; planning work for the Revelle Campus, the University of California, San Diego; the landscape design for Sea World Marine Theme Park; and the landscape for the Scripps Institution of Oceanography along the coast in San Diego (1963). Each of these designs reflected Wimmer's attention to environmental design and the importance of habitat design to nurture ecological health. Wimmer remained active in the firm until 1967. She was named an ASLA fellow in 1976. The firm is known today as Wimmer, Yamada and Caughey.

FIGURE 7.8   Scripps Institution of Oceanography, San Diego, CA 1963, landscape architect, Harriet Wimmer/Joe Yamada. Courtesy of Robert Glasheen Collection, Mandeville Special Collections, University of California, San Diego.

With Earth Day established in 1970, the environmental movement moved into the mainstream and landscape architects across the nation looked for ways to be engaged. Many women were exploring ecology as a design framework, including Isabelle Green in Southern California, who developed a practice that exemplified a regionalist approach to Southern California that David Streatfield has described as "art . . . completely embedded in nature."[48] Carol Franklin cofounded Andropogon, in Philadelphia, in the 1970s, with Colin Franklin, a firm that used McHarg's analysis methods in ecological design. The city was increasingly the focus of design investigation and in 1984, Anne Whiston Spirn's book *The Granite Garden* revolutionized urban landscape architecture by reframing the city as a place of ecological systems and networks.

Urban ecological design

In 1979, Martha Schwartz installed her Bagel Garden in her small Boston front yard. The garden "earned [Schwartz] a place on the front cover of *Landscape Architecture* magazine as the enfant terrible of landscape architecture."[49] While for many it announced the beginning of the post-modern era in landscape architecture, it also marked a watershed moment for women. Schwartz's willingness to engage the avant-garde and lead as she saw fit challenged women to take on even more visible and ambitious roles.

Generations of women paved the way for her. The situation for those at mid-century had changed as compared with the late nineteenth and early twentieth centuries. But at both times, women's design practices engaged the environmental and horticultural sciences as well as the fine art of design. These landscape architects sought to create urban environments that nurtured social and environmental health. They successfully maintained a knowledge grounded in the sciences, particularly horticulture and ecology, at a time when other professionals chose to set such disciplines aside. When science returned to landscape architecture, in the 1970s, as a legitimate framework for practice, these domains of knowledge were revived and re-engaged by the larger profession. Thus, women were not alone in their efforts to practice landscape architecture as both an art and a science. There were men who shared their orientation. Nevertheless, the number of women who contributed to the effort suggests there is a richer and more nuanced historic narrative to be told than has been told before.

Notes

1 Catherine Howett, "Ecological Values in Twentieth-Century Landscape Design: A History and Hermeneutics," *Landscape Journal* 17, no. 2 (1998): 80–98.
2 Anne Whiston Spirn, "Constructing Nature: The Legacy of Frederick Law Olmsted," in *Uncommon Ground: Rethinking the Human Place in Nature*, ed. William Cronon (New York: W.W. Norton & Co., 1996).
3 See, for example, Mariana (Mrs. Schuyler) Van Rensselaer, *Art Out-of-Doors: Hints on Good Taste in Gardening* (New York: C. Scribner's Sons, 1893).
4 Donna Palmer, "An Overview of the Trends, Eras, and Values of Landscape Architecture in America: From 1910 to the Present with an Emphasis on the Contributions of Women to the Profession" (MLA Thesis, North Carolina State University, 1976), Chapter II: Period of Expansion, 9–23. Catherine E. Koch, "Some Wild Marsh Plants," *Landscape Architecture Magazine* VI, no. 7 (1916). Emma Loines, "Opportunities of the Garden: Some Experiments in Naturalization and Hybridization," ibid.
5 Frank Waugh, "The Physiography of Lakes and Ponds," *Landscape Architecture Magazine* 22, no. 2 (1932): 89–99; "Ecology of the Roadside," *Landscape Architecture Magazine* 21, no. 2 (1931): 81–92.

6 Elsa Rehmann, "An Ecological Approach," *Landscape Architecture Magazine* 23, no. 4 (1933): 239–245.

7 Examples include Marian Cruger Coffin, *Trees and Shrubs for Landscape Effects* (New York: C. Scribner's Sons, 1940); Ruth Dean, *The Livable House, Its Garden* (New York: Moffat Yard and Co., 1917); Martha Brookes Brown Hutcheson and Library of American Landscape History, *The Spirit of the Garden* (Amherst: University of Massachusetts Press, 2001); Elsa Rehmann and Antoinette Rehmann Perrett, *Garden-Making* (Boston and New York: Houghton Mifflin Company, 1926); Edith Adelaide Roberts and Elsa Rehmann, *American Plants for American Gardens: Plant Ecology – the Study of Plants in Relation to Their Environment* (New York: The Macmillan Company, 1929).

8 Dorothée Imbert, "Working the Land: Modernism Assumed Many Forms in Mid-20th-Century Landscape Architecture," *Architecture* 88, no. 11 (1999): 69.

9 See Thaïsa Way, *Unbounded Practice: Women and Landscape Architecture in the Early Twentieth Century* (Charlottesville: University of Virginia Press, 2009).

10 Elizabeth Meade, "Martha Brookes Hutcheson," *Landscape Architecture Magazine* 50, no. 3 (1960): 181–182.

11 As quoted in a letter from Jensen to Mr. and Mrs. Boardman, no date, Morton Arboretum Archives. Robert E. Grese, *Jens Jensen: Maker of Natural Parks and Gardens, Creating the North American Landscape* (Baltimore: Johns Hopkins University Press, 1992), 61.

12 See Way, *Unbounded Practice*.

13 By 1972 only 6 percent are women. It will take until 1984 to return to the earlier numbers. Lamia Doumato, *Women and Landscape Architecture*, Architecture Series – Bibliography (Monticello, IL: Vance Bibliographies, 1986).

14 Garrett Eckbo, Daniel U. Kiley, and James C. Rose, "Landscape Design in the Primeval Environment," *Architectural Record* vol. 87, no. 2 (1940): 73–79; "Landscape Design in the Urban Environment," *Architectural Record* vol. 85, no. 5 (1939): 70–77; "Landscape Design in the Rural Environment," *Architectural Record* vol. 86, no. 8 (1940): 68–74.

15 Ann B. Shteir, *Cultivating Women, Cultivating Science: Flora's Daughters and Botany in England, 1760–1860* (Baltimore: Johns Hopkins University Press, 1996).

16 "Telesis" Wikipedia entry (noted from "The Things Telesis Has Found Important"), accessed August 8, 2013, http://en.wikipedia.org/wiki/Telesis.

17 "Geraldine Knight Scott (1904–89)," accessed August 8, 2013, www.ced.berkeley.edu/cedarchives/profiles/scott.htm.

18 The letters and documents in the Scott files reveal a much more extensive engagement with the project than has been acknowledged by the Museum or Kiley scholars. See Scott above.

19 Memorandum, Oakland Museum Landscaping, December 30, 1965, in "Geraldine Knight Scott (1904–1989)," Environmental Design Archives, University of California, Berkeley.

20 Ronda Skubi, "Women in Landscape Architecture" (MLA thesis, University of Washington, 1975), Mae Arbegast, 253–273.

21 Lillian Hoddeson and Richard Herman, "Florence Bell Robinson and Stanley Hart White: Creating a Pioneering School of Landscape Architecture," in *No Boundaries: University of Illinois Vignettes* (Urbana: University of Illinois Press, 2004), 113–122.

22 David Streatfield, "Gender and the History of Landscape Architecture, 1875–1975," in *Women in Landscape Architecture: Essays on History and Practice*, eds. Louise A. Mozingo and Linda L. Jewell (Jefferson, NC: McFarland & Co., 2012), 5–31.

23 Skubi, *Women in Landscape Architecture*, "Roberta Wightman," 27–70.

24 Palmer, "An Overview," 109.

25 Skubi, *Women in Landscape Architecture*, 12, and individual interviews.

26 She was responsible for directing the Housing Study Group, sponsored by Clarence Stein and Henry Churchill, between 1939 and 1941.

27 Interview with Leonard Mirin on August 10, 2013. He worked for Coffey, Levine, and Blumberg in the 1970s.

28 "Clara Coffey Park," New York City Parks & Recreation, accessed August 8, 2013, http://www.nycgovparks.org/parks/M108P/highlights/12798 and http://www.nycgovparks.org/about/history/women/parks-employees.

29 Miriam E. Rutz, "Genevieve Gillette: From Thrift Gardens to National Parks," in *Midwestern Landscape Architecture*, ed. William H. Tishler (Urbana: University of Illinois Press in cooperation with Library of American Landscape History Amherst, MA, 2000).

30 Thaïsa Way, "Designing Garden City Landscapes: Works by Marjorie L. Sewell Cautley, 1922–1937," *Studies in the History of Gardens & Designed Landscapes* 25, no. 4 (2005): 297–316.

31 Paula Deitz, "Alice Ireys, 89 Dies: Designed Elegant Landscapes Bridging Traditions," *The New York Times* (2000), accessed September 5, 2012, http://www.nytimes.com/2000/12/17/nyregion/alice-ireys-89-dies-designed-elegant-landscapes-bridging-traditions.html.

32 Alice Recknagel Ireys, "Alice Recknagel Ireys Papers" (Sophia Smith Collection: Five College Archives & Manuscript Collections, 1885–2001).

33 *Garden Designs*, 1st ed., Burpee American Gardening Series (New York: Prentice Hall, 1991); *How to Plan and Plant Your Own Property* (New York: Morrow, 1980); *Small Gardens for City and Country: A Guide to Designing and Planting Your Green Spaces, Home Gardening Handbooks* (Englewood Cliffs, NJ: Prentice-Hall, 1978); Alice Recknagel Ireys and W. Atlee Burpee Company, *Designs for American Gardens*, 1st ed. (New York: Prentice Hall Gardening, 1991).

34 Dianne Harris, "Cultivating Power: The Language of Feminism in Women's Garden Literature, 1870–1920," *Landscape Journal* 13, no. 2 (1994): 113–123.

35 Kurt Culbertson and Dianne del Cid, "Biography for Arthur S. And Marie H. Berger (1903–1960)," accessed March 12, 2013, http://tclf.org/pioneer/arthur-berger/biography-arthur-s-and-marie-h-berger.

36 Naomi Ellen Guttman, "Women Writing Gardens: Nature, Spirituality and Politics in Women's Garden Writing" (PhD diss., University of Southern California, 1999).

37 Dianne Susan Duffner Laurence, "A Symbiotic Relationship between Mid-Century Modern Masters: The Collaborative Works of Arthur and Marie Berger Landscape Architects, and O'Neil Ford, Architect" (MLA thesis, University of Texas at Arlington, 2007). Dianne del Cid, "Arthur S. and Marie Harbeck Berger" (MLA thesis, University of Texas, Arlington, 1989).

38 Jean Lawson, "Berger Garden: Five Years Ago, This House Was Out in the Hot Texas Sun," *House Beautiful*, August 1957, 87–89.

39 "Lodge Brings Visitors Close to Nature; Part of Oregon's Heritage, Salishan Receives Medallion Award," DJC Oregon, online as of July 27, 1999, accessed May 15, 2014, http://djcoregon.com/news/1999/07/27/lodge-brings-visitors-close-to-nature-part-of-oregons-heritage-salishan-receives-medallion-award. See also American Society of Landscape Architects, 100th Anniversary Medallion for Salishan Lodge.

40 "Barbara Fealy Landscape Architect Records: 1966–1993, Coll 262" (Eugene Oregon: Special Collections & University Archives, University of Oregon Libraries).

41 Based on the research of Joseph Wessinger, "HALS: The Mr. And Mrs. William W. Wessinger Garden by Barbara Fealy" (HALS No. XX##, 2013).

42 Skubi, *Women in Landscape Architecture*, "Jean Walton," 71–90.

43 Carolyn Etter and Don Etter, "1909–2005: Biography of Jane Silverstein Ries," *The Cultural Landscape Foundation: Pioneers* (2007). Published April 1, 2007, accessed February 10, 2014, http://tclf.org/pioneer/jane-silverstein-ries/biography-jane-silverstein-ries.

44 Skubi, *Women in Landscape Architecture*, 196–201.

45 The first time she applied to the firm she was denied as they did not want to hire a woman. Skubi, *Women in Landscape Architecture*, 196–201.

46 Telephone interview by author with Patricia Carlisle on May 8, 2014.

47 Mary Alice Van Sickle, "Biography of Carol R. Johnson," accessed August 12, 2013, http://tclf.org/pioneer/carol-r-johnson/biography-carol-r-johnson.

48 Kurt Gerard Frederick Helfrich, Isabelle Clara Greene, and University of California Santa Barbara, University Art Museum, *Isabelle Greene: Shaping Place in the Landscape* (Santa Barbara: University Art Museum, University of California, 2005), 23.

49 Leslie McGuire and Nicole Martin, "The Dualities of Reinventing Space/Profile: Martha Schwartz, ASLA, Principal, Martha Schwartz Partners," accessed March 2, 2012, http://www.landscapeonline.com/research/article/11728.

8

RUTH PATRICIA SHELLHORN

Mid-century living in the Southern California landscape

Kelly Comras

Introduction

Ruth Patricia Shellhorn (1909–2006; Figure 8.1) was among the most important Southern California landscape architects of the postwar era. Mid-century Southern California became a major center of development and creativity over the long course of her career. The temperate Mediterranean climate and geographic diversity of the region, along with larger social, cultural, economic, and political factors of the time significantly influenced her work. In this time and in this place, Shellhorn defined and refined the modern Southern California landscape through the design of various small- and large-scale, private and public landscapes.

Shellhorn's success derived from a distinctive combination of abilities that included an aesthetic vision that operated across a wide variety of project types, an indefatigable work ethos, and an unremitting attention to detail that extended from the initial design to the implementation and maintenance of her projects. Between 1933 and 1990, she worked on projects that included award-winning plans for eight Bullock's department stores and Bullock's Fashion Square shopping centers (Figure 8.2); a critical improvement in the original design for Disneyland; large-scale coastal planning; city and regional park designs; a number of university, college, and high school campuses; and more than two hundred private gardens and estates. The breadth of her projects alone is remarkable when we consider that Shellhorn worked as the sole design professional in her practice.

Shellhorn became particularly well known for her development of a landscape aesthetic that was dubbed the "Southern California Look."[1] Her designs reflected a post-war exuberance and appreciation for a lifestyle focused on indoor/outdoor living. This lifestyle demanded designs that blurred the boundaries between the designed landscape and its surroundings; provided ease and comfort in flexible outdoor spaces; manipulated natural light; screened and framed views; and employed modern materials and construction methods. Often set against the clean lines of contemporary architecture or the spare adaptations of Spanish-style buildings, the Southern California Look utilized bold botanical plant forms with glossy, large-textured leaves and exotic, profusely flowering plants to evoke a leisurely, sun-soaked lifestyle. This was a human-oriented view of modern landscape design, and it "reflected the way people really wanted to live."[2]

FIGURE 8.1 Ruth Shellhorn, Los Angeles Times Woman of the Year, 1955. Photographer unknown. Author's collection.

The influence of gender

To date, female landscape architects have received relatively little attention in the scholarly literature of the field. While the work of individual women continues to contribute to our understanding of the profession, the role of gender in these works is often neglected. In some cases, the role of gender has been a determining feature and, in other cases, it may have had only a small influence. A close look at Shellhorn's life and work show that her talent, her creative philosophy, and her formidable work ethic finally superseded gender as a determining factor in her success as a professional landscape architect. In reflecting on her professional career, Shellhorn was always disinclined to cite gender as a challenge to her achievements; instead, she stressed her willingness to acknowledge the needs and wishes of her clients, and her responsiveness to the era and unique locale in which she practiced, as the source of her success.

Shellhorn's landscape designs were driven by empathy. She cared about how her clients would live, work, and play in the outdoor spaces she designed. "In planning for others," she said, "one should try to understand them, realizing that, in a way, you are their means of expression. It is up to the designer, therefore, to mentally project himself into the lives of the clients for a while to try to feel as they do about their problems and wishes for the use of the area to be designed. There is a need here for understanding, sensitivity, and a desire to serve, rather than an opportunity for the designer to express his own ideas exclusively."[3]

On the other hand, however, gender did play a role in Shellhorn's early career prospects. It influenced the manner in which she would establish and run her business, and it had an impact on her landscape designs, in particular, because many of her clients were women. These were the women who, after World War II, moved from leading an independent life working on the home front to settling in the suburbs, rearing children, shopping in Shellhorn's suburban shopping centers, and vacationing with their families at Disneyland. These were also the women who, as middle-class prosperity accelerated, had been able to pursue higher degrees at public universities and colleges whose landscapes were in some cases designed by Shellhorn (see, for example, the campus designs for the University of California at Riverside and El Camino College). These privileged women had already become familiar with Shellhorn's landscape designs as children when they, for example, attended the exclusive Marlborough School for Girls, in Los Angeles. Many of them married prosperous businessmen, devoted their free time to philanthropic and charitable organizations, and acted as the primary link between their families and Shellhorn, who created landscape designs for their estates and their husbands' businesses. A good number of these women became important powerbrokers of the Los Angeles establishment in their own right. Finally, these were also the women who eventually rebelled, or at least pushed back, against the conventional values that prevented equal opportunities. If gender is to provide a meaningful framework at all in considering Shellhorn's landscape designs, we should turn for analysis to her female clients and their roles in the evolving post-war era.

Shellhorn's unconventional marriage and business partnership with her husband also deserves exploration here, and we need to examine the substantial part played in Shellhorn's post-college training by her male mentor, the landscape architect Ralph D. Cornell; the architect Welton Becket; and businessmen such as P.G. Winnett and Walt Disney, who hired Shellhorn early in her career. These men appreciated her design aesthetic, her work ethic, and her attention to detail. Their early support and the later patronage of her female clients enabled Shellhorn to make an indirect but significant contribution to shaping the rapidly evolving mid-century landscape of Southern California.

Early life and education

Shellhorn was born on September 21, 1909. She was the only child of socially progressive, well-educated parents. Both expected their daughter to attend college after high school and undertake a career. Her father, Dr. Arthur L. Shellhorn, was a dentist with a successful practice near their home in South Pasadena. He cherished quiet solitude and introduced young Ruth to the beauty of the California landscape on weeklong camping trips and day trips throughout the Southland. The family was financially comfortable and had a maid. Ruth's mother, Lodema Gould Shellhorn, worked as a volunteer in numerous civic and city beautification organizations. She provided a role model of intellectual independence and conveyed to her daughter the value of a woman's work. Shellhorn grew up knowing that she could, and would, work and make a contribution to society. When she was fifteen years old she sought advice from her neighbor, the landscape architect Florence Yoch, and set her sights on a career in landscape architecture.[4]

FIGURE 8.2 Bullock's Fashion Square Santa Ana, 1969. Photo: Darrow M. Watt. Courtesy of Sunset Publishing.

After graduating from high school, Shellhorn attended the School of Landscape Architecture at Oregon Agricultural State College (today, Oregon State University) from 1927 until 1930. Her coursework adhered to a traditional Beaux-Arts education and she studied primarily classic European landscape design. She was an outstanding student, receiving recognition as the first woman to win the Alpha Zeta Scholarship Cup for the highest marks in the School of Agriculture. In addition, she won the Clara Waldo Prize for Most Outstanding Freshman Woman, was named Phi Kappa Phi (the equivalent of a Phi Beta Kappa for the B.S. degree) in her junior year, and earned a coveted national class prize in a Beaux-Arts competition.[5]

In fall 1930, Shellhorn transferred to Cornell University's College of Architecture to finish her course of study and take advantage of the school's engineering and architecture courses, which had not been available at Oregon, and which Shellhorn believed to be integral to her studies. Again, Shellhorn distinguished herself with academic honors. The only woman in her class of six in the Department of Landscape Architecture (at least two of the men were Rome Prize winners),[6] she won several design awards, served as president of her sorority, Kappa Kappa Gamma, and as its national architect from 1931–1936.

The reality that young women like Shellhorn faced when they sought to study landscape architecture at Cornell was challenging. Women were allowed to matriculate in the school, beginning in 1904, but they faced an administrative unwillingness to treat them on an equal footing with the male students. Women took the same courses, but faculty preconceptions about their ability to perform well in the profession were colored by low expectations: women couldn't achieve the same standard because they were less able.[7] This prejudice was overlaid

FIGURE 8.3 Ruth Shellhorn, Oregon State College, 1928. Photographer unknown. Author's collection.

with a Depression-era sentiment that said women shouldn't work outside the home because they took jobs away from men supporting families.

Women landscape architects during the Great Depression

Considering her progressive upbringing, it is easy to understand why Shellhorn never expected that these attitudes would limit her career. Unlike the first generation of female landscape architects, who were told that making a living as a landscape architect was highly unlikely,[8] Shellhorn believed (rightly, as it turned out) that she would indeed be able not only to support herself, but also do so comfortably in her chosen profession. However, her initial post-college experience was dampened by the economy. She had been sheltered from the effects of the Great Depression during her six years away at college (Figure 8.3). Her return to Southern California in June 1933 revealed that opportunities for inexperienced female landscape architects were hard to find.[9] Undaunted, Shellhorn began her search for work. Emphasizing the significance of Shellhorn's educational credentials, David Streatfield has observed that she was one of a few designers who had been professionally trained.[10] This distinguished her from most male practitioners in the Southland, who had come up through the design departments of the nurseries in the 1920s and 1930s, traveled to Europe to study, or apprenticed with established practitioners.[11] It also distinguished her from most female practitioners working as landscape designers in Southern California, who were not as well trained as she, but still quite successful. Some were self-taught, such as Katherine Bashford;[12] others, such as Beatrix Jones Farrand, had some training that was supplemented by extensive mentoring. Farrand had studied botany with Charles Sprague Sargent on the East Coast, established a bi-coastal practice, and was the only female founding member of the ASLA.[13] Another group of female landscape architects had studied at landscape architecture schools, such as Florence Yoch and Lucille Council, but had not received the same level of technical training in areas such as surveying and engineering as had Shellhorn.[14] Regardless of their level of training, these women were better established than professional women in the field of architecture and engineering.[15] Despite this, however, in 1933, none of the above women was able to offer Shellhorn a place in her office.

Positive attitudes about women working as landscape architects in Southern California were no novelty in 1933. In the 1931 foreword to Winifred Starr Dobyns's book, *California Gardens*, architect Myron Hunt declared his support for professional female landscape architects, writing that

> The profession of landscape architecture is fortunately attracting an increasing number of able, highly-trained, much travelled and experienced women, who handle with firmness and decision those broad background essentials of the good garden, the ground plan and the mass planting. They also have what seems an inborn interest in that other essential element of continuing success, the planting and the yearly renewal of the annuals and perennials whose blending colors make the jewels of a garden.[16]

Hunt may not have fully understood the ability of professionals like Shellhorn, but, nonetheless, his attitude reflected an appreciation for the contributions of women who worked in the field.

When she was later asked if she experienced gender discrimination in the early years of her career, Shellhorn replied with an emphatic, "No."[17] However, it is worth noting that her male colleagues in Southern California had a far less difficult time getting work in offices or nurseries than Shellhorn did. Other men found steady-paying government work through programs funded by Roosevelt's New Deal, but this door was also closed to most women.[18] When Shellhorn inquired about the possibility of a woman being hired for government work, she was told, "No chance."[19] Given her excellent training, her high honors, and her obvious ability, Shellhorn had to have wondered at the unfairness; why were her male friends able to secure these scarce jobs and she was not? Yet, she did not perceive these conditions as discrimination. Her ambition was anchored by the unflappable disposition of someone who kept moving and continued to look elsewhere for opportunities.

Young professional

Shellhorn's first opportunity came from the eminent landscape architect, Ralph Dalton Cornell (1890–1972). Cornell was similarly struck by the effects of the Great Depression, despite a degree from the Harvard Graduate School of Landscape Architecture (1919). However, he maintained a slow but steady one-man practice, primarily working on urban park designs as well as other public works, subdivisions, and residential communities throughout the 1930s and the war years. He also worked on public and defense housing, and he became consulting landscape architect for the University of California, Los Angeles, in 1937. He, too, was unable to offer Shellhorn regular work, but he took a liking to the hopeful young landscape architect. He advised her to "go out on her own," and he made such seemingly preposterous advice possible by taking her under his wing.[20] When he could, he offered her sporadic work in his own office. Cornell insisted that she apply for junior membership in the local chapter of the American Society of Landscape Architects (ASLA), and then sponsored her when she was ready to apply for full membership in 1940. He arranged for her to write a series of articles for *Sunset Magazine*, which addressed common problems encountered by homeowners with small, suburban gardens, and which gave her some needed publicity; he took her to lunch when she needed advice; and he and his wife included her in the dinner parties they hosted with other landscape architectural professionals.[21]

Cornell also taught Shellhorn how to plant for permanence and simplicity.[22] He shared with her his enthusiasm for native plants and their increasingly appropriate use in the urban landscape,[23] and he trained her in the principles of the rapidly expanding field of urban planning. When the opportunity to work on a major county planning initiative came up in 1943, many of her male colleagues who might otherwise have taken the post were away at war or engaged otherwise in the war effort. Grateful for Cornell's tutelage, she was ready, and she got the job. In 1944, she worked with him on plans for the shopping center in Lakewood, California. In 1945, he turned over two Los Angeles city parks for her to design in his office (Verdugo Park, in Glendale (Figure 8.4) and Centinela Park, in Inglewood), and he allowed her to add her name for credit to the plans. Shellhorn discovered she had an aptitude for this type of work and it whetted her appetite for larger-scale landscape design.

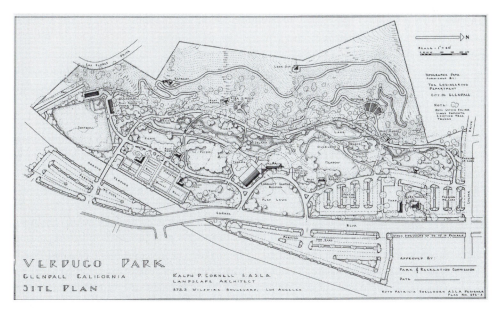

FIGURE 8.4 Verdugo Park, Glendale, California, 1944. Ruth Patricia Shellhorn papers, Department Library Special Collections, Charles E. Young Research Library, UCLA.

The pattern of an older and more experienced male landscape architect offering guidance and support to a younger female landscape architect was not an unusual phenomenon, and it has been the subject of some recent scholarship.[24] In Shellhorn's case, Cornell's influence and support cannot be underestimated. Without it, at the very least, Shellhorn would likely have pursued a practice much narrower in scope than the one she eventually undertook.

Shellhorn's luck in obtaining these opportunities was not as surprising as it might have seemed at the time. The early 1940s marked a turning point in which female landscape architects, especially those with formal training, were gravitating away from residential work and toward design projects on larger scales.[25] Geraldine Knight Scott, educated at the University of California, Berkeley, went to work for the Los Angeles Regional Planning Commission to design wartime housing.[26] Katherine Bashford's office made the transition as well, although it is unlikely she would have completed many of the large-scale garden apartments for the Los Angeles Housing Authority without the leadership of her business partner, Fred Barlow, Jr., who had earned a degree in landscape architecture from Berkeley.[27] The absence of men because of the war facilitated the women's engagement in large-scale public and private projects, but their increasing training and access to formal education also played a role.

Shoreline Development Study

Shellhorn's turn toward larger design projects is exemplified by the 1944 publication of the Shoreline Development Study (Figures 8.5, 8.6, and 8.7), a cooperative planning effort between the Los Angeles City Planning Commission and the Greater Los Angeles Citizens Committee. Led by P. G. Winnett, president of the Bullock's department stores, and architect Carl McElvy, the study was noteworthy for a number of reasons. First, it was commissioned by a private group of businessmen to analyze and make comprehensive recommendations for improving a twelve-mile stretch of public coastal area between Palos Verdes and Playa del Rey. This was done at a time when public–private partnerships of this kind were uncommon. To the extent that these partnerships did occur, they tended to focus on much smaller, commercial projects. Second, Shoreline issued then-prescient political and social proposals that have come to pass. It recommended restrictions on oil drilling in Santa Monica Bay. The study set a precedent for many of the goals of the later California Coastal Act. It advocated the use of public funding for recreation and parkland acquisition, and it paved the way for the installation of Los Angeles' first sewage treatment plant.[28]

In this case, as well, it was the mentoring of older men with established financial and professional connections that provided Shellhorn with the opportunity to expand her own professional expertise. McElvy took an interest in his dedicated and talented employee. He appreciated her keen curiosity in planning and took the time to teach her how to evaluate the qualities of large areas of land and the programmatic recreational needs of the communities along the coast. He also taught her how to track down the tax and ownership status of land parcels for additional parkland acquisition.[29] Shellhorn acknowledged the value of his guidance in her later work and said, "The ability to quickly size up a plan or situation before getting bogged down in details has been invaluable."[30] Her detailed park design for Manhattan Beach and Redondo Beach helped ensure the study's publication.[31] Because of Shellhorn's contribution, we now have the record of an early planning document that sought to balance coastal preservation and development.

FIGURE 8.5 Shoreline Development Study, 1944. Photo: author.

Bullock's department stores and Fashion Square shopping centers

A few months after the publication of *Shoreline*, in 1944, P. G. Winnett hired McElvy to create an original landscape plan for the first suburban post-war Bullock's department store, in Pasadena. McElvy brought Shellhorn in as his junior partner. Soon thereafter, McElvy was appointed as the campus architect for the University of California at Los Angeles and, with Winnett's full approval, turned the Bullock's project over to Shellhorn to complete on her own. Shellhorn did not have the experience or connections to have competed successfully for the Bullock's project by herself, but gaining Winnett's and McElvy's trust and support marked a major turning point in her career. It gave her the opportunity to experiment with early aspects of the Southern California Look; it moved her into the retail milieu as a lead landscape architect; and the character of the project showcased a new type of commission for landscape architects.

FIGURE 8.6 Shoreline Development Study, Master Plan, 1944. Photo: Kelly Comras.

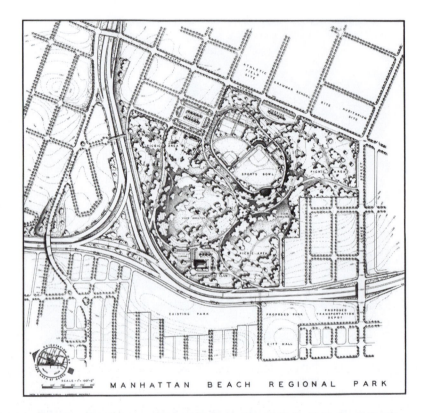

FIGURE 8.7 Shoreline Development Study, Manhattan Beach Park, 1944. Ruth Patricia
Shellhorn papers, Library Special Collections, Charles E. Young Research Library,
UCLA.

P. G. Winnett was the first of the Bullock's presidents to recognize that Shellhorn's
landscape designs promoted business. He knew that his clients were primarily female and
middle or upper class. He made a distinction between buying and shopping, reasoning that
we will always buy the things we need, but we must be enticed to shop for the things we
want. To this end, he directed Shellhorn to design settings for the Bullock's stores to promote
a sense of graciousness and ease, and of a home away from home.[32] Shellhorn used a generous number of profusely flowering trees and wide beds of richly textured evergreen shrubs
and ground covers that formed a buffer between pedestrians and automobiles. Her landscape
designs attracted customers who were, or wished to be, well educated, well traveled and

cultured. Shopping was redefined as a relaxing and pleasant activity for customers from all walks of life.

Winnett specifically forbade the use of deciduous plant material, ordering "nothing Eastern looking,"[33] thereby unwittingly establishing a guideline for Shellhorn's own Southern California Look. Thus restricted, she experimented with a palette of sub-tropical plants, many with large or glossy leaves. Composed like classical paintings, her plantings featured a wide variety of textures and a hierarchical arrangement of sizes. She framed views so that store entrances were visible, but softened them with trees and colorful shrubs. She paid great attention to the details that made shoppers feel like they were on a vacation: climbing vines adorned building walls and fine-textured plantings enhanced shaded seating areas with thoughtfully placed benches (Figure 8.8). Later, in the Fashion Squares, the use of lawn – then a new concept in shopping center design – further invited the shopper to relax and enjoy the experience (Figure 8.9).

As the pace of Bullock's developments accelerated, Winnett began to hire Shellhorn separately from the project architect to avoid the possibility that she would be excluded through underbidding. He encouraged her to start work early on the projects, so that architects had the benefit of her site design skills. He allowed her to box existing trees on site in order to preserve a sense of character in the final design. He intervened if she felt architectural features did not fit with the Bullock's image. Winnett's trust extended to his successor. When Shellhorn suggested changes to the architect's first site plans for Bullock's Fashion Square shopping center in Santa Ana, in 1954, the corporation's president M. E. Arnett asked her to design it herself.[34]

Most important, Winnett shared her aesthetic vision and supported her insistence on the value of long-term maintenance. After installation, Shellhorn visited each site at least twice a

FIGURE 8.8   Bullock's Fashion Square Del Amo. Photo: Darrow M. Watt. Courtesy of Sunset Publishing.

FIGURE 8.9 Bullock's Fashion Square La Habra, 1972. Photo: Dominick Culotta. Courtesy of Dominick Culotta.

year and prepared meticulous maintenance and care instructions for her plantings. She sketched trees, showing each branch to be removed, and trained the gardeners. Again, with Winnett, it was the support of an older professional man who made what would become a signature component of Shellhorn's oeuvre possible. As Streatfield has pointed out, "In Shellhorn's work the world of the immaculately maintained private garden was transferred into the public world of the shopping center – faultless supervision and maintenance. This alone distinguishes her work from that of other modernists."[35]

New business partnership

Bullock's Pasadena established the unconventional business model that became the basis for the practice that Shellhorn developed with her husband, Harry Kueser, during the next thirty-five years (Figure 8.10). Shellhorn never referred to herself as a feminist, but she decided early on that she would marry only if she could find a husband who would let her continue her work. In 1940, she met Kueser when he rented a spare room in her mother's house. He had no college education, but he was a district manager at a local bank and unusual in his support of Shellhorn's ambitions. They married soon after meeting and settled into their own careers. By the time Shellhorn took over Bullock's Pasadena in 1945, Kueser had tired of the constant travel between bank branches, which exacerbated his crippling migraines

FIGURE 8.10   Ruth Shellhorn with husband and business partner, Harry Kueser, ASLA meeting in
San Diego, 1949. Photographer unknown. Author's collection.

that were diagnosed as stress-related. He sought a change that would provide him with the
opportunity to work outdoors. Shellhorn needed a construction manager she could trust to
install her landscape designs, so they decided to try partnering as a design-build team. They
found the experiment so satisfying that they made the arrangement permanent and began
to expand Shellhorn's business. Kueser took over financial management, billing, and correspondence. He worked on a construction crew for six months to gain experience, learned
Spanish in order to facilitate work with the mostly Spanish-speaking labor crews, became
proficient at drafting construction details, and managed installation of Shellhorn's landscape
designs. Without professional training, he became a managing partner and never seemed to
mind that Shellhorn was recognized as the senior partner in their business. Shellhorn was
now free to devote her attention to clients and to the creative aspects of design. Furthermore,
Kueser's support allowed her to assume much larger projects than might be expected for a
professional practicing on her own. Childless, they devoted themselves to the business, often
forgoing vacations and working six or seven days a week. They were constant companions
until Kueser's death in 1991.[36]

Architect Welton Becket

Bullock's Pasadena became an icon of the post-war era (Figure 8.11). It was the first suburban
department store to explicitly celebrate the car. Like its urban sister, Bullock's Wilshire, the
front of the store lost importance and customers approached the store from the parking area
at its side or back. Welton Becket, principal architect of Wurdeman and Becket, created a
streamlined structure that hugged a gently sloping site and emphasized open space and hori-
zontality. Shellhorn's landscape design treated the eight-acre site like an oasis in a suburban
setting. The north parking lot, for example, was landscaped with rows of kumquat trees that
created an orchard protected from the street by bougainvillea cascading over a wall. The link

FIGURE 8.11 Bullock's Pasadena, 1947. Photographer unknown. Author's collection.

between indoor and outdoor living was unmistakable. The strategy spoke to a fresh, new take on California living.[37]

Bullock's Pasadena was the beginning of a productive collaboration between Shellhorn and Becket that continued for a dozen years, during which they completed six Bullock's stores together. Their second Bullock's department store, in Palm Springs, opened in late 1947, just months after the Pasadena store. A third opened at Lakewood Center in 1965. They also completed three Bullock's Fashion Square shopping centers at Sherman Oaks, in 1962, the Del Amo in Torrance in 1966, and another in La Habra in 1968. Their success was not limited to retail. The formidable pair collaborated on the Prudential Insurance Western Home Office in 1949 (Figure 8.12), considered one of the city's major post-war structures and praised by their peers as well as by the general public. Other projects included a new landscape design for Buffum's department store, Santa Ana, and the Santa Monica Civic Auditorium, both in 1956, and the Mutual Savings and Loan Bank in Pasadena in 1964. Their work was so closely connected that when the Los Angeles Conservancy held its "Built by Becket" tribute in 2003, Shellhorn was the only landscape architect and the only woman invited to participate in the panel discussion of Becket's work.[38] Louis Naidorf, architect in the Becket firm who designed the Capitol Records building in Los Angeles, concurred: "With architect Welton Becket, Shellhorn put post-war Los Angeles on the map."[39]

Walt Disney and Disneyland

In March 1955, Walt Disney was rushing to finish his new park, Disneyland, before its opening day in July. Many elements of the park were already under construction but, with

FIGURE 8.12   Prudential Insurance Western Home Office, Los Angeles, 1961. Photo: Douglas M.
Simmonds. Ruth Patricia Shellhorn papers, Library Special Collections, Charles E.
Young Research Library, UCLA.

only four months remaining, major aspects of the plan were still not designed. Disney was
worried that the project would not "hang together."[40] He needed a landscape architect
to design a final layout that would assemble the disparate site features of the entrance,
Adventureland, Frontierland, Fantasyland, and Tomorrowland into a coherent whole.
Disney turned to his friend, Welton Becket, for advice. Becket recommended only one
name.[41]

Shellhorn's ability to quickly appraise the latent qualities of a site led first to a complete
pedestrian plan. Hardscape details for the Town Square, Main Street, and Plaza Hub quickly
followed. She directed grading around the moat to heighten the drama of Sleeping Beauty's
Castle, laid out watercourses, and developed an innovative planting scheme for the Plaza Hub
Garden that distinguished the entrances to each theme park section, but linked them together
with creative repetitions of plant material. Under Walt Disney's direction, she worked directly
with the art directors and was thus part of an elite group of otherwise all male designers who
were responsible for the overall design of the park. She wasn't afraid to challenge Disney
over an issue and he learned, too, to trust her judgment, saying, "I have absolute confidence
in your ability."[42] Shellhorn stood out also because of her engineering skills, which were
acknowledged by the road crews with surprise and appreciation.[43] Among the thousands of
talented people who contributed to the creation of Disneyland, Walt Disney acknowledged

Shellhorn's individual role in creating "the happiest place on earth," singling her out for his personal appreciation in the preface of a Disney publication by Morgan Evans, *Disneyland: World of Flowers* (Plate 8.1).[44]

Female clients

Up until this time, Shellhorn had relied on the support of male architects, landscape architects, and businessmen to provide her with access to larger commercial and retail projects. Her exceptional work was increasingly recognized, however, and she now finally began to secure major commissions without the sponsorship of her early male supporters. After Disneyland had opened in the summer of 1955, Dorothy Buffum Chandler, later the driving force behind the creation of the Los Angeles Music Center and the wife of *The Los Angeles Times* publisher, Norman Chandler, nominated Shellhorn as the newspaper's Woman of the Year. Shortly thereafter, Shellhorn completed a landscape design for the Chandler residence in Hancock Park. The following year, Dorothy Chandler, a regent of the University of California, intervened to award Shellhorn a coveted position as consulting landscape architect for the rapidly growing campus in Riverside. That Chandler convinced the Board of Regents to bypass better-known male contenders for the job, such as Ralph Cornell and Tommy Tomson, speaks to her renown as a premier powerbroker. Indeed, Shellhorn recalled Chandler as a formidable force and said, "She thought it was about time they had a woman landscape architect."[45]

Shellhorn remained in that position for over eight years, creating a landscape master plan that was published in 1964, and designing dozens of specific area plans for buildings, roadways, and open spaces on the campus.[46] The campus plan successfully advocated for the retention of natural gorges and arroyos, which had been slated for filling in to provide for parking. Instead, Shellhorn highlighted the arroyos as scenic features of the overall design, giving the campus an identity that honored the area's natural landscape (Plate 8.2). Other campus design work followed, including a master plan for El Camino College (1970–1978).

In the mid-1960s, Shellhorn's work came to the attention of Nancy Munger and her husband, Charles. Wealthy and prominent Southern Californians, the Mungers appreciated Shellhorn's design aesthetic and her ability to deliver a project on time and on budget. They especially admired her exacting expectation of quality from the designers, engineers, and contractors with whom she worked. Contrary to old-fashioned notions about the feminine inability to direct workmen on construction sites, Shellhorn developed a formidable reputation for unwavering construction standards. If she specified a ground cover to be planted six inches apart, she expected the contractor to use a six-inch ruler to make sure he got it right. If he didn't get it right, she got down on her knees, in a skirt, and showed him how to do the work.[47] On behalf of her clients, Charles said, "Ruth was a quiet fanatic about quality work."[48]

The Mungers were instrumental in recommending Shellhorn as landscape consultant for campus expansion plans for the Marlborough School for Girls in Los Angeles (1968–1993), and the Harvard School in North Hollywood (1974–1990). Shellhorn also created two landscape designs for their home in 1968 and 1980, and Nancy Munger eventually recommended Shellhorn to numerous friends and associates, and to both of her adult daughters. In addition to Dorothy Chandler and Nancy Munger, Shellhorn's female clients included philanthropists, patrons of landscape art, writers, actors, and leaders of charitable organizations and institutions from all over the Southland. They made no secret of their delight in associating themselves with Shellhorn's talent and success. Their pride is evident in the written correspondence between Shellhorn and her female clients over several decades.[49] In recommending her for other commissions and taking an interest in her career, these women were expressing, if not an outright feminism, at least a kind of sisterhood.

Return to a residential practice

Toward the mid-1970s Harry Kueser's health began to decline, and his inability to fully participate in their business pushed Shellhorn to return to an almost exclusively residential practice. A key factor in her successful return to residential design was her acceptance, in 1973, of a position as consulting landscape architect for the City of Rolling Hills Community Association. She met with the design board every other week to review plans and create landscape designs for the association's roadways, parks, and other public areas. She developed a substantial residential practice, based on her connections there. Shellhorn also continued working with past clients as they remodeled or changed residences. During this time and until her retirement in 1992, Shellhorn completed more than sixty residential landscape designs, including two particularly noteworthy Pasadena gardens.

The redesign of the Avery family's garden above the Arroyo Seco in Pasadena was influenced by the presence of magnificent old oak trees, which determined the English, picturesque style of Shellhorn's design. The predominantly green garden invoked memories of gardens that emphasized a passion for green in a dry land. The main lawn recalled spacious qualities of an English landscape park, with shifting tones and contrasts of light and shade to modulate the space. The garden was a superbly understated masterpiece.[50] The Hixon garden, also located in Pasadena, demonstrated how Shellhorn respected and developed designs in response to her clients' interests. The architect A. Quincy Jones remodeled the modern residence to reflect the owner's artistic interest in Oceanic and Pacific culture. Shellhorn's design made continuous references to that water-based culture. Stone walls, encrusted with succulents, evoked a watery grotto. "Streams" of rock and gravel wound throughout the garden, and river-rock stairways cascaded like waterfalls throughout the property. Shellhorn created individual nooks and courtyards to highlight the individual features of each art piece.

Although the designs of the Avery and Hixon gardens were very different, they both succeeded in creating comfortable and leisurely domestic settings that accommodated her client's interests. Rather than adhere to a preconceived design idea, Shellhorn paid much attention to the wishes of her clients. She considered herself an interpreter who responded to her client's desire for easy living and natural respite, and translated the zeitgeist of post-war life into landscape form and space. The wants of her female clients, who belonged to the upper-middle class and the conservative business elite, inspired and guided Shellhorn in her work. However, it would be inaccurate to place much weight on the role of gender in Shellhorn's landscape designs. She herself would have disagreed that her landscape designs were defined or determined by gender considerations. Instead, her collaborative view of the design process, her talent, and her prodigious work ethic played much more important roles in her success, even though she faced hurdles not encountered by her male colleagues in the early part of her career.

During her education, she overcame the gender discrimination she was confronted with in the landscape architecture programs. She also overcame the widespread apprehension during the depression that women were taking work away from their male contemporaries, and she did not let herself get discouraged by the difficulty of finding a regular work assignment during the first decade of her career. Her choice of husband and their unconventional partnership contributed to her ability to run a successful practice, but their childlessness was not a choice, and she would have gladly traded some of her success for the four children she had hoped to have when she was young. She considered some of her best projects, such as Bullock's Fashion Square Santa Ana, to be the children she never had. Working before and during the second-wave era of feminism (first-wave feminism dealt with issues of suffrage before World War II), Shellhorn benefitted from an increasing social acceptance of professional women. Professional training and experience and a high quality of practice, rather than gender, increasingly provided her with access to larger-scale projects.

Afterword

Many examples of mid-century landscape design are disappearing, and only a few of Shellhorn's designs survive today. All of the Bullock's stores have undergone major changes or have been replaced altogether. Only a few private gardens and one or two large projects remain where her installations can still be discerned and appreciated. Disneyland provides us with one of the most enduring and vivid remaining examples of Shellhorn's public oeuvre. Current design and maintenance staff have deliberately preserved a recognizable portion of her landscape design, although that, too, is now diminishing. Shellhorn's contributions are mostly preserved in the archival record of her professional papers and photographs, which she donated to the UCLA Charles E. Young Research Library before her death on November 3, 2006, at the age of 97 years.[51]

Notes

1   This term is derived from a variety of interviews and written articles. Shellhorn referred to the style as "The California Atmosphere," in *Southwest Builder and Contractor*, August 22, 1958, 8. One editor referred to the style as "the California scene." Landscape Design and Construction, *A Study of Ruth Patricia Shellhorn, A.S.L.A Award-Winning Landscape Architect: Her Landscapes Aid Merchandizing*, 13 no. 4 (October 1967): 7. The early president of Bullock's wanted "a California look." Ruth Patricia Shellhorn, interview by author, on November 29, 2004. Also see Molly Johnson, *Interview with Ruth Patricia Shellhorn*, ed. Elaine Zorbas (Pasadena: Pasadena Oral History Project, 2002), 40. The *Pasadena Star-News*, September 9, 1947, featured an article addressing the style as "the spirit of Southern California itself." A Bullock's press release, September 16, 1958, 2, titled "Fashion Square Landscape Plan Creates Garden-Like Effect," referred to "the feeling of early California." While the southern half of the state is not always specified, the semi-tropical plant material of the "Look" is most commonly associated with the climates of Southern California.
2   Wendy Kaplan, "Introduction: Living in a Modern Way," in *Living in a Modern Way: California Design 1930–1965*, ed. Wendy Kaplan (Cambridge, MA: The MIT Press, 2012), 33.
3   Shellhorn, "Thoughts on Landscape Architecture" (personal essay, author's collection, March 23, 1981), 2.
4   Shellhorn (letter to James J. Yoch, April 20, 1981). See also, Johnson, *Interview with . . . Shellhorn*, 32–33.
5   The competition was most likely sponsored by the Beaux-Arts Institute of Design in New York, founded by Lloyd Warren in 1916, which promoted an educational agenda consistent with that of the French École des Beaux-Arts. "The profs are so up in the air they don't know their own name. We got 2 out of 3 prizes given – 10 schools competing and we entered 3. We broke into a ring of Harvard men that's impossible to break!" See Shellhorn (personal diary entry on February 10, 1930, Library Special Collections, Charles E. Young Research Library, UCLA).
6   Daniel Wayne Krall, e-mail message to the author, Oct 1, 2013.
7   Daniel Wayne Krall, "Visions of Outdoor Art: One Hundred Years of Landscape Architecture Education at Cornell" (unpublished manuscript, Cornell University, 2005).
8   Louise A. Mozingo, "Introduction," in *Women in Landscape Architecture: Essays on History and Practice*, eds. Louise A. Mozingo and Linda Jewell (London: McFarland & Company, Inc., Publishers, 2012), 1–4.

9 David C. Streatfield, "Gender and the History of Landscape Architecture, 1875–1975," in *Women in Landscape Architecture: Essays on History and Practice*, eds. Louise A. Mozingo and Linda Jewell (London: McFarland & Company, Inc., Publishers, 2012) 15–17.

10 David C. Streatfield, e-mail message to the author, March 11, 2008.

11 Lockwood de Forest, III, for example, attended landscape architecture school for one year at the University of California, Berkeley, then apprenticed with Ralph Stevens. Exceptions were Ralph D. Cornell, trained at the Harvard Graduate School of Design (1914–1917), and Fred Barlow, Jr., who trained at the University of California, Berkeley (1923–1926).

12 Steven Keylon, "The California Landscapes of Katherine Bashford," *Eden: The Journal of the California Garden and Landscape History Society* 16, no. 4 (2013): 3–13.

13 Farrand moved to Southern California in 1927 when her husband, Max Farrand, became the first director of the Huntington Library, in San Marino. The focus of her practice remained on the East Coast, however, and she did a relatively small amount of work on the West Coast. See Ann Scheid, "Beatrix Farrand in Southern California, 1927–1941," *Eden: The Journal of the California Garden and Landscape History Society* 14, no. 2 (2011): 1–13.

14 Florence Yoch studied for two years at the University of California, Berkeley; for one year at Cornell in the College of Agriculture; and then graduated from the University of Illinois at Urbana-Champaign with a bachelor of science degree in landscape gardening in 1915. Lucille Council studied at the Cambridge School of Domestic and Landscape Architecture and also at Oxford. See James J. Yoch, *Landscaping the American Dream: The Gardens and Film Sets of Florence Yoch, 1890–1972* (New York: Sagapress, 1989), 13, 20.

15 Daniel Wayne Krall, "Were They Feminists? Men Who Mentored Early Women Landscape Architects," in *Women in Landscape Architecture: Essays on History and Practice*, eds. Louise A. Mozingo and Linda Jewell (London: McFarland & Company, Inc., Publishers, 2012), 76.

16 Myron Hunt, "Foreword," in Winifred Starr Dobyns, *California Gardens* (Santa Barbara: Allen A. Knoll Publishers, 1996), 11–12.

17 Shellhorn, interview by author, June 1, 2006. See also, Johnson, *Interview with . . . Shellhorn*, 32–33, 37.

18 Phoebe Cutler, e-mail message to author, November 13, 2013. See also Phoebe Cutler, *The Public Landscape of the New Deal* (New Haven: Yale University Press, 1985), 83–89.

19 Shellhorn (personal diary entry on February 23, 1935, Library Special Collections, Charles E. Young Research Library, UCLA).

20 Shellhorn met Cornell and received this advice on the first day they met. See Shellhorn (personal diary entry for February 5, 1934, Library Special Collections, Charles E. Young Research Library, UCLA).

21 Shellhorn, interview by author, November 3, 2004, transcript pages 7 and 13.

22 Shellhorn, interview by author, November 3, 2004, transcript page 7.

23 Cornell was an excellent photographer, and a former partner and friend of the native plant authority, Theodore Payne. The two spent much time traveling and gathering information for a book that Cornell was preparing. See Ralph D. Cornell, *Conspicuous California Plants With Notes on Their Garden Uses* (Pasadena: San Pasqual Press, 1938).

24 Daniel Wayne Krall, "Were They Feminists? Men Who Mentored Early Women Landscape Architects," in *Women in Landscape Architecture: Essays on History and Practice*, eds. Louise A. Mozingo and Linda Jewell (London: McFarland & Company, Inc., Publishers, 2012), 76–82.

25 Streatfield, *Women in Landscape Architecture*, 16.

26 Waverly B. Lowell, "Geraldine Knight Scott (1904–1989)," in *Shaping the American Landscape*, eds. Charles A. Birnbaum and Stephanie S. Foell (Charlottesville and London: University of Virginia Press, 2009), 309–312.

27 Keylon, "Katherine Bashford," 2. A full list of Bashford's and Barlow's Housing Authority projects can be found on the Los Angeles Conservancy website: https://www.laconservancy.org/sites/default/files/files/issues/ARG%20Garden%20Apts%20%20HCS%2010_17_12%20FINAL%20VERSION.pdf. See also Steven Keylon, "Taming the Car: A Vision for Los Angeles," *Eden: The Journal of the California Garden and Landscape History Society* 16, no. 1 (2013): 1–7.

28 Carl. C. McElvy, *Shoreline Development Study, Playa Del Rey to Palos Verdes: A Portion of a Proposed Master Plan for the Greater Los Angeles Region* (Los Angeles: Greater Los Angeles Citizens Committee, Inc., 1944). See also "Suggested Beach Highway System for an Eleven-Mile Shoreline Development," *Southwest Builder and Contractor*, July 7, 1944, 16–20.

29 McElvy, *Shoreline Development Study*, 31.

30 Shellhorn, letter to Monica Woolner, May 19, 1985.

31 The other studies were unpublished and included "Urban Redevelopment," "Airports," and "Traffic." Shellhorn, interview by author, November 17, 2004, transcript page 6, and November 29, 2004, transcript pages 3–4.

32 Doug Stapleton, "A Study of Ruth Patricia Shellhorn, A.S.L.A. Award-Winning Landscape Architect: Her Landscapes Aid Merchandizing," *Landscape Design and Construction*, October 1967, 4–8.

33 Shellhorn, interview by author, November 29, 2004, transcript page 7.

34 Shellhorn, interviews by author, November 3, 2004, transcript page 1, and November 29, 2004, transcript page 8.

35 David C. Streatfield, email message to author, March 27, 2013.

36 Johnson, *Interview with . . . Shellhorn*, 46. See also Shellhorn, interview by author, November 3, 2004, transcript pages 12, 16, and 17.

37 Louis Naidorf, FAIA, interviews by author, February 2007.

38 Alan Hess, "Adapted from Remarks Delivered at 'Built by Becket: Centennial Celebration,' Los Angeles Forum for Architecture and Urban Design," posted March 4, 2003 at http://www.laforum. org/content/online-articles/built-by-becket-by-alan-hess (accessed August 2, 2013). See also Shellhorn, interview by author, November 29, 2004, transcript page 10.

39 Naidorf, interviews by author, February 2007.

40 Johnson, *Interview with . . . Shellhorn*, 62.

41 Shellhorn interview by author, November 17, 2004, transcript page 2.

42 Shellhorn (personal diary entry on May 24, 1955, Library Special Collections, Charles E. Young Research Library, UCLA).

43 Shellhorn (personal diary entry on July 12, 1955, Library Special Collections, Charles E. Young Research Library, UCLA).

44 Walt Disney, "Preface," in Morgan Evans, *Disneyland: World of Flowers* (Burbank: Walt Disney Productions, 1965), 3.

45 Johnson, *Interview with . . . Shellhorn*, 66.

46 George Vernon Russell, F.A.I.A. & Associates, *Long Range Development Plan* (Riverside: University of California, Riverside, 1964), 12–17.

47 Dan Kaplanak, Sr., telephone interview by author, April 26, 2011.

48 Charles Munger, e-mail message to author, June 9, 2011.

49 Client files include letters from Ernestine Avery, Mrs. Gene Autry, Hannah Carter, Dorothy Chandler, Harriet Doerr, Ann Mudd, Nancy Munger, Antonia Breckenridge Niven, Mrs. Spencer Tracy, and others. See Library Special Collections, Charles E. Young Research Library, UCLA.

50 David C. Streatfield, *California Gardens: Creating a New Eden* (New York: Abbeville Press Publishers, 1994), 147–148.

51 Most of Shellhorn's work is unpublished and relatively unknown to the general public. Her papers include original drawings and plans, letters, invoices, and hundreds of photographs. The collection also includes a diary that Shellhorn wrote over a period of eighty years.

9

CORNELIA HAHN OBERLANDER

A model modern

Susan Herrington

Introduction

Women, Modernity, and Landscape Architecture can be situated within the larger constellation of recovery projects that have sought to reinstate women in the history of art and design. Since Linda Nochlin fatefully asked in 1971 "Why Have There Been No Great Women Artists?"[1] historians have identified the numerous cultural mechanisms limiting women's inclusion in the historical canons of various professions. As the editors of this volume note, histories of landscape architecture have fully participated in this omission. Describing the reasons for this oversight in historical accounts covering the first half of the twentieth century, Thaïsa Way has observed, "women's marginal position in the histories of landscape architecture stems from the assumptions about the breadth of their practice, the number of female practitioners," and scant attention to residential design work, through which many women participated in the profession.[2]

This omission is particularly noticeable when the lens of historical investigation is focused on landscape architectural practice immediately after World War Two. It has been well documented that women were discouraged from professional work after the war.[3] However, the fact that the profession of landscape architecture began to embrace modern design during this time period also created barriers to women's participation in the profession. Hilde Heynen has noted that discourse on *modern* architecture tended to gender it male. This gendering has been due to linkages forged between modern design and critical reasoning – oddly a mental activity deemed more apposite to males than females. In addition, the hero trope found in modern narratives from architectural histories to literature helped gender modernism as male.[4] Moreover, within architectural histories, these heroes were frequently associated with the public realm, an arena seemingly free from the familial and communal obligations that were traditionally tied to women and that, in turn, tied them to domestic spaces. For Heynen, the heroes "function as markers of both modernity and masculinity, and this results in a clearly gendered, and hence biased account of the nature of modernity . . . Not surprisingly, the great modernist artists, authors and architects are predominantly male, and the canons in the different fields comprised of only a limited amount of women."[5]

A more problematic enterprise that historians have wrestled with is *how* a revised history might include women. According to the philosopher Karen Hanson, revisionists have adopted strikingly different frameworks in this regard: essentialist and anti-essentialist. Essentialist notions of the feminine have argued that women are biologically different from men, and thus women's art and experiences of art are identifiably feminine and share similarities across time and space. The anti-essentialist approach contends, "women's art bears a closer kinship to the work of their male counterparts of that era than it does to the work of women temporally and geographically distant."[6]

In this chapter, I analyze the work of landscape architect Cornelia Hahn Oberlander within an anti-essentialist framework. In other words, the fact that she is a woman does not feature in her landscape designs per se. Moreover, since she began her practice immediately after World War Two, I have referred to her as a "model modern," meaning quite literally an example to follow or imitate.[7] Histories of design have described "modern" as embodying male subjectivity.[8] However, it has also been argued that within these histories the "modern woman" has been a recurring theme as a sign of *change*.[9] From the nineteenth-century suffragette to the liberated woman of the 1970s, the modern woman's capacity to epitomize transformation has enabled her to uniquely represent an essential quality of modernity, that of change.[10]

In the following, I describe the design methods employed by Cornelia Hahn Oberlander that mark major shifts in landscape design processes, thus making evident a modern landscape architecture. In particular, I focus on her use of abstract form and space, her employment of a four-fold functionalism, her emphasis on the social agency of design, and her integration of embodied space through syncopation. These approaches have served as hallmarks of modern landscape architecture.[11] For Oberlander, they were forged during her years as a student of landscape architecture at Harvard University, from 1943 to 1947, and refined over the next six decades. It would be remiss, however, to not include her personal history, which also played a formative role in her success as a modern landscape architect.

Beginnings

Oberlander was admitted to the Graduate School of Design (GSD) at Harvard University in 1943. As a member of only the second cohort of full-time female students to be admitted, Oberlander was taking advantage of one of the handful of educational opportunities available to women seeking a professional degree in landscape architecture. Prior to America's involvement in World War Two, full-time enrollment was exclusively reserved for males and women were only enrolled as special students. By January 1942, however, the GSD had lost two-thirds of its student body, and Harvard University's Governing Boards authorized the GSD faculty to admit women.[12]

At the time, Oberlander was enrolled in Smith College's Cambridge School of Architecture and Landscape Architecture. When the United States joined the war effort, the Cambridge School closed and students who had completed two successful years were offered the opportunity to transfer to the GSD.[13] As then-Dean Joseph Hudnut wrote to Oberlander on March 5, 1943, "any of the work which you completed at Smith College and which is also required as part of the work for our Bachelor of Architecture degree here will be credited to you."[14] Oberlander's mother, Beate Hahn, had reservations about her daughter's engagement with design and the technical skills it required. She advised Oberlander to attend the Pennsylvania School of Horticulture for Women (now Temple University Ambler), in Ambler, Pennsylvania.[15] But the opportunity to study at Harvard was too tempting, and Oberlander immediately accepted the invitation.

Despite this remarkable opportunity, many of the female students who enrolled in the GSD did not continue their education during or immediately after the war. In fact, Oberlander was only one of six women in her cohort to graduate in landscape architecture. Based on retention data for students enrolled at the GSD between 1943 and 1949, if you entered as a female, there was a good chance – over 50 percent – that you would drop out (Figure 9.1).[16]

Despite their newfound status as fulltime students, women at the GSD were not treated as equal to their male peers. As Jill Pearlman has noted, Professor John Humphreys wrote in 1944, "The students we have nowadays are an odd lot – mostly 4-Fs or foreigners – the men that is, and of course the women don't count."[17] Oberlander was not only female, but she had also recently emigrated from Germany. So why did Oberlander continue when so many women left?

Undoubtedly, she had confronted greater obstacles than the male professors at Harvard University. Born into an assimilated Jewish family, in Mülheim-Ruhr, Germany, in 1921, Oberlander was part of a long lineage of strong-willed women (Figure 9.2).

On her paternal side, it was a Hahn family tradition that all female members managed their own finances. This idea followed an argument by her paternal grandfather, who had seen too many women who were not prepared to handle money, causing them great hardship.[18] On Oberlander's maternal side, the women received advanced education. Oberlander's mother, Lotte Beate Jastrow Hahn, was a trained horticulturist and an author of children's gardening books. Oberlander helped her mother produce many of the

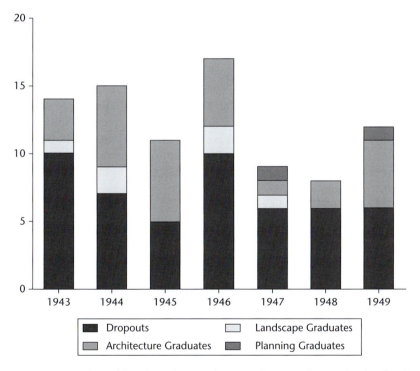

FIGURE 9.1 Retention data of female students at the GSD during and immediately after the war. Information obtained from Mary Daniels, Frances Loeb Library Special Collections Librarian, and Norton Gerenfeld, GSD Alumni Office.

FIGURE 9.2 Oberlander, 1928 (CHO private estate).

drawings for those books. In addition to education, the women on her maternal side also conveyed their awareness of new clothing styles emerging at the turn of the century. A photograph of her maternal grandmother, Anna Seligmann Jastrow, and her sisters from the 1890s shows four young women wearing fashionable day dresses with tailored silhouettes, exaggerated shoulders, and high collars – features that signaled they were keenly aware of the changing times (Figure 9.3).

Oberlander's maternal aunt, Elisabeth Jastrow, was a classical archaeologist who emigrated from Germany to the United States in 1939. She became a faculty member in the Department of Art at the University of North Carolina at Greensboro. From 1937 to 1971, she proceeded with legal claims against Germany for compensation for her parents' estates.[19] Like her aunt, Oberlander would also flee Germany with her mother and sister. Their escape was almost foiled when Nazi officers boarded the train they were leaving on. An officer demanded that Beate Hahn and her daughters vacate the train immediately. Fortunately, they were traveling with a family friend who intervened and reminded him how polite Germans were.[20] The officer jumped off the train and the Hahns continued on to England and eventually New York City, where they arrived in 1939.

Despite her mother's reservations, Oberlander was very interested in the technical dimensions of practice as a student at the Graduate School of Design. Not only were students asked to create cost estimates for their projects, but they were also introduced to the range of technical drawings required to construct a landscape. A pragmatist at heart, she loved her grading

FIGURE 9.3 The Seligmann sisters, circa 1890. From left to right, Minna, Lena, Marta, Ella, and Anna (Oberlander's grandmother) (CHO private estate).

class taught by the landscape architect Walter Chambers. While it is unknown if the other female students enjoyed the technical courses, Oberlander's zeal for grading would most likely have been novel, since women were often labeled as lacking technical prowess.[21] Oberlander even managed to integrate her passion for the technical side of landscape architecture with her admiration for the Vienna-born urban planning student, Peter Oberlander. In 1948, she sent him an unusual card titled "Details for 1948" that mixes coquettish innuendo with technical details (Figure 9.4).

Cornelia and Peter married in 1953 in New York City. The Oberlanders eventually settled in Vancouver, where Peter Oberlander was hired to start Canada's first full professional program in community and regional planning at the University of British Columbia. Even with the birth of their three children (Tim in 1956, Judy in 1958, and Wendy in 1960), Oberlander continued to work as a landscape architect (Figure 9.5).

FIGURE 9.4 A card created by Oberlander for Peter Oberlander (CHO private estate).

Like three generations of women before her, contributing to society, while also having a family, was a given. What was not a given was Oberlander's use of abstraction early on as a student and throughout her career.

Abstraction of form and space

The philosopher Henry Nelson Goodman defined abstraction as "processes of image making in which only some of the visual elements usually ascribed to 'the natural world' are extracted (i.e. 'to abstract')."[22] As early as 1934, the landscape architect Marjorie S. Cautley described, in her book *Garden Design*, the application of abstract design in garden compositions. Interestingly, she identified the principles of abstract design operating in historic and historically inspired gardens.[23] For Cautley, abstraction served as an underlying feature of the garden's formal composition, regardless of the garden's time of creation. Since abstraction was a feature, a distinctive attribute of a garden's design, the novice designer could detect it through observing and sketching built landscapes. As Cautley's book reinforces, principles such as repetition and rhythm, balance, and perspective could be found in a range of works. The exploitation of perspective, for example, is found at the Villa D'Este, where the downward slope makes the garden appear smaller when viewed from the lower (original)

FIGURE 9.5 Oberlander with her son Tim and daughter Judy in 1959 (Wendy was born one year later) (CHO private estate).

entrance.[24] Even asymmetry, the preferred abstract design principle of later modern designers, was demonstrated by Cautley, with a stone pool set off by a mugo pine on one side and a taller Austrian pine on the other.[25]

The process of abstraction was an important dimension of the basic design courses taught to Oberlander and other students at the Graduate School of Design. The course taught by her instructor, George Tyrrell Le Boutellier, never fulfilled Walter Gropius's exact vision to bring the Bauhaus curriculum to Harvard. According to Pearlman, Dean Hudnut's decision to hire Le Boutillier, instead of someone like Bauhaus painter and graphic designer Josef Albers, angered Gropius, who wanted to duplicate the Bauhaus preliminary studio courses at Harvard. Le Boutillier did develop a basic design course for GSD students that was influenced by Bauhaus' teaching methods; however, he was *not* a former Bauhaus faculty member, and so it is unlikely that Gropius would have ever accepted him.[26]

Le Boutillier's instruction played a formative role in Oberlander's early work and her use of abstracted forms. Among Le Boutillier's notes for Design 1, lecture four was dedicated to composing volumetric structures based on basic shapes such as the square, circle, triangle, ellipse, trapezoid, and amoeba. These shapes were given volume by replicating the same form and projecting it spatially. According to Le Boutilliers, "The volume is a function of shape and movement. The volume, to be an economical expression of its generating shape must not contain inaccessible inner forms" (Figure 9.6).[27]

By the 1950s, abstraction had become a key feature of modern landscape architectural design. A 1950s Harvard University exhibition catalogue, which showcased the work of

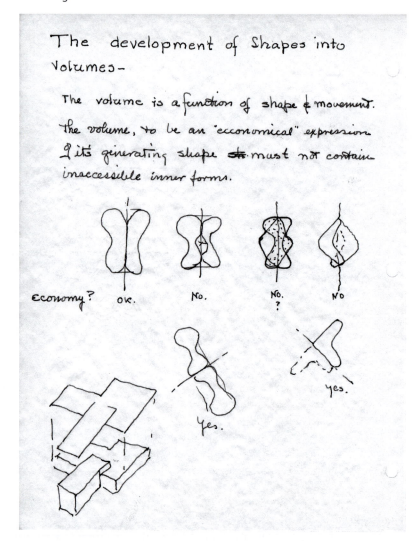

FIGURE 9.6 LeBoutillier's lecture notes for turning spaces into volumes (Courtesy of the Frances
Loeb Library, Harvard University Graduate School of Design).

emerging landscape architects and students, attested to this change in vocabulary from historic
forms to abstract ones.[28] In the chapter "Abstract Art in Landscape Design," Oberlander's
plans for two residential landscapes were shown, as well as the design proposals from Stanley
B. Underhill, Lawrence Halprin, Robert L. Zion, Robert L. Mackintosh, Simonds &
Simonds, and James E. Secord. Likewise, the catalogue featured a group project by students
of Lester Collins for a field laboratory in Massachusetts. Collins stressed the project's connection with modern design, noting, "It was a study in Mondrian balances, a design using color
as well as solids and voids."[29]

The distillation of landscape elements into basic shapes played a social role as well. Garrett
Eckbo contended in his widely read book, *Landscape for Living*, that one of the primary tasks
of the modern designer was to develop a vocabulary that could be understood by everyone,

regardless of education. He thought that the simple shapes and unadorned lines of modern landscape design were more egalitarian than the École des Beaux-Arts designs, where aesthetic appreciation was tied to the user's interpretation of the historical motifs.[30]

Yet, abstract design was still understood to be expressive. Returning to the work of Nelson Goodman, he noted that abstraction, whether in architecture or painting, need not represent anything at all, but it could *symbolize* by calling attention to an exemplary metaphorical feature, which it need not possess.[31] Movement, for example, was such a feature in many modern landscape designs. A walkway or the edges of a swimming pool did not literally move, rather they expressed this dynamism by their form and layout. Modern landscapes that employed asymmetrical layouts, for example, were celebrated for their ability to create movement in the eye, and asymmetry also provided an argument against symmetry, which was equated with elite gardens, and also with stasis.

As distinct from Cautley's examples of abstraction, modern landscape architects distilled basic forms to reinforce abstract features, such as movement or repetition. For example, in the late 1950s, Oberlander collaborated in the design of the Rose Garden on the University of British Columbia campus in Vancouver (Figure 9.7).

FIGURE 9.7 Aerial view of the Rose Garden on the UBC Campus, 1960s. Landscape Architect: Cornelia Hahn Oberlander (University of British Columbia Archives [UBC 1.1/3322]).

While the process drawings are no longer extant, the built work demonstrates the use of abstraction. There, traditional garden beds associated with rose gardens are distilled into an orthogonal circuit of walkways, in conjunction with rows of rose plantings that shift laterally throughout the garden. This system lies within a large amebic form that is cut out from the grass lawn. The garden contained 900 roses and was extremely popular with rose enthusiasts, as the meandering pattern allowed people to weave in and out among the roses – enabling closer inspection and smelling. Unfortunately, it was destroyed in 1997 to create a parking garage. On top of the garage, a new, historically inspired rose garden replaced Oberlander's design.

Oberlander's penchant for abstraction would continue throughout her career. Over forty years after the rose garden she and the architect Moshe Safdie won the design for the Vancouver Public Library. While the library's architecture has been criticized for its overt reference to the Colosseum in Rome, Oberlander's roof garden design has been lauded for its restrained simplicity. Oberlander approached the design of this garden with two objectives: to create an ecological model for storm water storage and retention on high-rise structures and to express this in a design visible from the adjacent buildings and the provincial government offices that rose above it.[32]

To these ends, she planted the 33,000-square-foot roof with 16,000 blue and green fescue grasses and 26,000 kinnikinnick groundcover plants. Avoiding any heavy-handed classical representations, she instead made reference to the Fraser River – the province of British Columbia's longest waterway.[33] This hydrological feature is deeply tied to the region's history. It was the location of one of the earliest recorded First Nation settlements and it became the main transportation route between the Strait of Georgia and the interior, in the nineteenth century. Oberlander's scheme was not a literal waterway. The bands of blue and green fescue grass created a meandering swath around the central light well. The blue fescue referred to the river while an outlying band of the green fescue represented the Fraser's alluvial grasslands. A third band of kinnikinnick plants referenced higher ground (Plate 9.1).

While the roof is not accessible to the public, over the years Oberlander has escorted small groups of designers and journalists into the garden. Now fully mature and viewed from the surrounding towers, the garden creates a distilled image of the river.

A four-fold functionalism

Abstract rather than historic forms could connect more closely with function. Thus, if a client requested a patio space for eating breakfast, for example, Oberlander would not need to worry about matching the patio's design to a specific historical style, which would have ideally echoed the style of the house. She could direct her efforts to determining the size and shape of basic forms to accommodate eating breakfast outdoors, such as the size of the table and chairs, the orientation of the patio in relationship to sun and shade. The role of function in design can be traced back to the eighteenth century Italian architectural theorist Carlo Lodoli, but, as the architectural historian Adrian Forty has contended, in English-speaking cultures between 1930 and 1960, the term became relatively impoverished: "functional became a catch-all term for modern architecture . . . it was the principal term through which the polemic about modern architecture was conducted."[34]

Both Christopher Tunnard and Garrett Eckbo wrote on the importance of function in determining a designed landscape. Tunnard, for example, argued that "use determines form. Garden and landscape must be humanized in accordance with the needs of the twentieth century; they can be made pleasant to live in as well as to look at."[35] Yet, it was the landscape architect Norman T. Newton who described a four-fold approach to function in landscape design. His 1951 book, *An Approach to Design*, described the collaborative teaching methods which he had developed at the GSD since he was hired in 1939. While Newton is commonly associated with his widely read historical textbook, *Design on the Land*, he was actively involved in studio teaching early in his career at the GSD.

In *An Approach to Design* Newton divided the role of function into two categories: natural functions and assigned functions.[36] Natural functions were biological or mathematical and existed without human intervention. The growth of a Douglas fir tree is a natural biological function, for example, while the structural strength of a 4 x 8 Douglas fir beam is a natural mathematical function. Organic processes defined natural biological functions, while physical forces defined natural mathematical functions.

For Newton, assigned functions were produced by conscious human intervention and involved use functions and assigned functions.

Accommodating human uses, like swimming laps in a pool, playing baseball in a park, or parking a truck in a loading dock, were all assigned use functions. Assigned affective functions involved the communicative dimensions of a design, such as a circular form designating to people a place to gather, a form often used by Oberlander. Newton thought that landscape architects should be aware of and employ all four functions. While Oberlander has never claimed that she used Newton's theory, one can observe in her work the range of functions that Newton had described.

For instance, this four-fold approach can be seen in several of Oberlander's residential projects in Vancouver. In 1954, she was hired by the Wong family to plan their new house with the architect Harry Lee of Duncan McNab Architects. The Wong's site contained a huge rock outcropping in the front yard. In fact, Oberlander had to argue with the city to preserve the rock. She won the fight, but the rock constricted the site design and layout substantially. The Wongs requested a Hu-tong layout, a traditional urban pattern of alleyways and courtyards found in traditional Chinese cities. The courtyard was to be the primary social space for the Wong family, so she located it toward the southside yard to capture the most sun (natural biological function). She paved the courtyard with concrete and scored it every four feet to avoid cracking (natural mathematical function). Oberlander created a grass lawn for the children to play on (assigned use function) and she translated the traditional alleyway as an entrance path from the street to the front door at the courtyard (assigned affective function).

Thirty years later, one can still see a four-fold function operating at the residence of Dr. Paul and Josephine Hwang. Designed with architect and long-time collaborator Arthur Erickson, Oberlander transformed a common lot into a unique garden. Similar to the Wong residence, Oberlander and Erickson sought to take advantage of the sun, so they located Erickson's linear-shaped house to the north side of the property, to offer ample sunny spaces in the front yard (natural biological function). Unfortunately, the front yard faced a busy street, so Obelander designed heavily planted earthen mounds to dampen the ambient vibrations generated by passing traffic (natural mathematical function). The Hwangs asked that the house and garden reflect the traditional scholar gardens in Suzhou, China, so Oberlander and Erickson created a continuous veranda from the house that extended over a pond. The veranda was divided into separate areas with white stucco walls, which matched the walls of the internal program spaces on the first floor – living room, dining room, and family room (assigned use function). Between each exterior wall, they placed openings to allow through passage (assigned affective function). Since Oberlander and Erickson were modern designers, they did not try to emulate the traditional forms found in Suzhou. Instead, they used elliptical-shaped openings (Figure 9.8).

Social commitment

The use of abstract, simple forms and an emphasis on a four-fold functionalism also played a social role in Oberlander's and other modern landscape architects' work. The interplay of simple forms in a landscape, for example, would not require an education in art history. In contrast, understanding designs produced by an École des Beaux-Arts architect might require knowledge of history to interpret their forms. For example, in order to determine if a gazebo was inspired by the Baroque or the Neoclassical, a person would need to know the differences between those two styles. For Oberlander, a modern design vocabulary was more egalitarian because it could be understood by all people, and she was quick to employ her modern design language in the social projects she engaged with throughout her career.

Small residential gardens of the middle class provided Oberlander with her first work after graduating from Harvard University. These types of low-cost residential gardens designed by Oberlander eventually became a part of landscape architectural curriculums by the 1950s. Garrett Eckbo wrote in the *Journal of Architectural Education* for the 1956 Annual Convention of the Association of Collegiate Schools of Architecture in Los Angeles that "the private estate is no longer the only problem which the landscape architect will deign to touch."[37] Not only were the private gardens of the middle class an important type of modern practice, but Eckbo also identified larger urban projects, such as housing and recreation areas, that would fulfill

FIGURE 9.8 Hwang Residence garden gateways, Vancouver, circa 1985. Landscape architect: Cornelia Hahn Oberlander. Architect: Arthur Erickson (Photo credit: Stuart McCall/North Light).

the goals of a socially minded landscape architect. "Such programs as urban redevelopment or renewal . . . slum clearance, expanded park, recreation, school and hospital developments have a tremendous potential. They may lead to a filling out of the broad gap between normal city planning procedures and normal architectural and landscape practices."[38]

After graduating in 1947, Oberlander sent numerous letters to emerging modern landscape architects, such as Dan Kiley and Garrett Eckbo, asking if they were hiring. She worked on her own designs for small private gardens and also helped James Rose with the modular gardens that he was developing for a show garden in Great Neck, Long Island. But it was the social potential of landscape architecture that she thought was most important. As she noted in a 1956 publication, "As we well know, the main contributions of the landscape architect lie no longer in the fine art of making gardens, but in site planning, housing projects (public and private), and in playgrounds and parks, small and large; in short, in all the phases of public works."[39]

Oberlander eventually moved to Philadelphia, where she was hired as a community planner for the Citizens' Council on City Planning (CCCP), and by 1949 she finally received a positive response from Dan Kiley, who offered her a job at $40 for five days or $50 for six days of work per week. As Dan Kiley's associate she worked on Oskar Stonorov's design for Schuylkill Falls Public Housing. With Kiley, she also prepared plans for Phase One of the Mill Creek housing project, designed by Louis Kahn. While Kiley determined the overall formal arrangements for these new public housing projects, Oberlander worked on the detailed plans and planting schemes, where she was determined to give every unit in the housing complex the same amount and type of plant material and landscape elements. Each courtyard of the garden apartments at Mill Creek Public Housing, for example, was planted with a small grass lawn, a hedge, a large canopy tree to the north, and a smaller ornamental tree to the south. Unfortunately, the landscape budgets for both Philadelphia projects were cut substantially, and photographs taken after construction show mainly grass and a few small trees.

However, with her move to Vancouver, Oberlander was able to realize the social agenda of her public housing work. Hired as the landscape architect for the McLean Park and Skeena Terrace housing projects in Vancouver, in the early 1960s, she was able to bring to fruition her design plans. The McLean Park and Skeena Terrace were comparable architectural typologies to her Philadelphia public housing work, and Oberlander's landscape plan was installed this time. She also shifted her emphasis from calculating each unit and how many plants they would receive to creating a coherent planting scheme of distinct canopy trees and smaller human-scaled plantings and community gardens. As Oberlander stressed, "It is wise to limit oneself to a few varieties of plants. It is advisable to use fairly large trees; shrubs only when planted in masses; and large areas of grass that can be cut easily instead of hundreds of pocket-handkerchief size. All plant material should be easy to grow and of course indigenous to the region."[40]

Even today, the mature trees at these housing projects stand out with their color and form. At a plaza space in the Skeena Terrace housing project, the broad horizontal branching of the gingko trees contrasts with the verticality of the surrounding buildings (Plate 9.2).

The majestic Crimson King maples that line the parking area suggest a landscape far grander. Likewise, the now-mature Northern pin oaks that line the courtyard at McLean provide complete enclosure for the space. Vegetation is often valued for its ecological contributions to wildlife habitat or for its ability to filter water. These built projects also show the social agency of trees to humanize the landscape, because they contribute positively to the human experience of the site and connect the housing project to the rest of the neighborhood.

While Oberlander would eventually pioneer ecological design in Canada, she continued to maintain her commitment to social projects, such as housing. In 2002, she began work on Wellesley Central Place in Toronto for the Wellesley Institute, a nonprofit research and policy institute. Located on the site of the former Princess Margaret Hospital, this long-term care and outpatient facility for people with Alzheimer's disease and HIV/AIDS was designed to create a residential rather than an institutional atmosphere. As such, the institute knew that the landscape and the natural elements it afforded would be key to its success. The landscape architectural work for the project involved two courtyards and a roof garden. With Diana Gerrard of gh3 architecture, landscape architecture, and urbanism, Oberlander was asked to create a park shared with the public directly north of Wellesley Central Place. The park was to be a space that would physically link residents with the surrounding community.

They designed the one-acre park space with a grid of forty-two London Plane trees in a base plane of crushed granite. In light of Toronto's dramatic weather changes, the trees create varied atmospheres from summer to winter (Figure 9.9).

In contrast to this geometry of trees, large rocks for seating were scattered throughout the park. In 2008, Toronto City Council named it Wellesley Magill Park, honoring Dennis William Magill, a founder of the Wellesley Institute. Today, both Wellesley residents and people living in the surrounding neighborhood, especially those with dogs, use the park.

Syncopation

As Oberlander's career advanced, she began to consider how her conception of abstract space and form, function, and social agency could be deepened by exploring embodied space – a

FIGURE 9.9 Wellesley Magill Park winter, Toronto, 2012. Landscape architect: Cornelia Hahn Oberlander and Diana Gerrard, gh3 (Photo credit: Turner Wigginton).

multidimensional conception of space for human experience. This was a central concern of Lawrence Halprin with whom she had shared a studio space at Harvard. With his wife Anna Halprin, he began to develop design methods that included the consideration of bodily movement, participation, and natural processes. His RSVP cycles were built on their workshops that sought to integrate human movement with architectural space. As Judith Wasserman has pointed out, these workshops both influenced Anna's dancers and informed Halprin's built landscapes. "Anna's dancers opened their senses to the wind, scents, sun patterns, and textures, while practicing on the Dance deck. In turn, Lawrence choreographed experimental elements within his projects to heighten awareness of the physical body in space."[41]

Oberlander borrowed from music rather than dance with what she has called syncopation." In music, syncopation displaced expected beats with anticipation or delay.[42] Translating syncopation to her design work, Oberlander noted that syncopation involved manipulating what people saw, usually with terrain or vegetation, as they moved through a space. By hiding and revealing views, she created anticipation in the experience with her landscapes. According to Oberlander, it was her Harvard landscape architecture professor Lester Collins who introduced her to syncopation. Showing slides of his experiences walking through a Japanese garden he demonstrated how hidden and revealed views of different parts of the garden enticed visitors to explore it further.[43]

Interestingly her initial designs for children's outdoor play spaces did not show syncopation. A rendering for Earl's Court Children's home in Toronto, from 1958, shows flat terrain and play elements (Plate 9.3). Likewise, her design for the play spaces at McLean Park and Skeena Terrace were largely based on play sculptures. Even her highly publicized 18th and Bigler Street Playground in Philadelphia from the 1950s was groundbreaking in her use of sculpture and programming, but there was little consideration of using the landscapes as a means of enticing children to explore the site.

Oberlander first experimented with syncopation in her design for the outdoor play space at the Children's Creative Centre or Expo '67 in Montreal. In contrast to her Philadelphia playground, a flat ground plane was substituted with rolling terrain, looping paths, and a wobble walk. A canal with moving water, a rocking Nova Scotia dory, and giant wooden building pieces replaced static sculptures. Her winding paths and what she has called a series of child-size hills and dales were designed to trigger children's curiosity and entice them to explore the environment on their own. Thus, children were not directed where and how to play. Instead, using their own desires and instincts, they explored materials and space.

The play space was very successful and a post-construction evaluation revealed that Oberlander's play landscape was more popular than the Centre's interior play and learning areas.[44] Oberlander has surmised that this was due to the fact that the outdoor component of the Centre was free for spontaneous play, while the interior had specific classes and activities that were timed by adults. She continued to use syncopation in her numerous play space designs throughout her career, and, in the early 1970s, she brought this method to other areas of her practice.

Syncopation featured in her urban public work, such as Robson Square in downtown Vancouver and the redesigned landscape for the University of British Columbia's Museum of Anthropology. Robson Square's stramps (the blending of steps and ramps) and waterfalls make syncopation evident (Plate 9.4). Early schemes of Robson Square show a straight set of steps ascending the central block of the square. By 1975 (after Oberlander joined Arthur Erickson's design team), the three main stramps and waterfalls were staggered. Walking up from the lower ice-skating rink, you see the waterfall just as you reach the top of the stramps, then you see the next set of stramps to the right, and the process continues with a final set of stramps leading to Oberlander's meandering walkways, where plants and the curve of the path induce curiosity and movement. Syncopation also occurs at the mound area where the height of the hill and the walkway that climbs it keep you in constant anticipation.

Syncopation can also be witnessed in her design of the landscape for the new addition to the University of British Columbia's Museum of Anthropology forty years later in 2010. Using the earth excavated for the building's addition, she sculpted the terrain into six- to eight-foot-high mounds. A winding crushed gravel path weaves through the mounds, leading visitors from the reflecting pool, around the building, and up to the newly constructed courtyard. Meticulously using the mounds and path to hide and reveal the unfolding journey, Oberlander created anticipation and mystery. She planted the mounds with a custom-designed grass seed mix from the Haida Gwaii, an archipelago of First Nation settlements north of Vancouver Island. Since the grass is allowed to grow to two to three feet in height, this volume adds to the syncopation experience (Plate 9.5).

Conclusion

In conclusion, the design methods employed by Oberlander – her use of abstract form and space, her support of a four-fold functionalism, her emphasis on the social agency of design, and her integration of embodied space through syncopation – helped define a modern era of landscape architecture, which unfolded during the decades immediately after World War Two. Over the years, as her career developed, she did not discard these design methods. Rather, she incorporated them into her overall approach as her work became increasingly dedicated to the ecological performance of landscapes. This rich layering of design methods in her landscape architectural practice eventually earned her international recognition, with such accolades as the American Society of Landscape Architect's 2012 Medal, the society's highest honor. It has also enabled her to transcend gender boundaries. Oberlander was the first female to receive the Sir Geoffrey Jellicoe Award, which was conferred on her in 2011.

While it has taken decades for Oberlander to be acknowledged for her unflagging commitment to good-quality landscape architectural design, her work is surely relevant for historians who are recovering the role of women in landscape architecture's contemporary history. Indeed, discourse on modern landscape architecture tended to gender it male by either neglecting women in historical surveys or by diminishing women's participation in the profession to a passing reference. In response, Oberlander has been referred to as a *model modern* in this chapter, because she developed methods to create new ways of designing landscapes after World War Two that exemplified modern ideas. These ideas included the investigation of new forms that did not recycle historical ones, the need to make landscapes useful and for all people, and the manipulation of design features to entice people's exploration of the landscape.

Moreover, by virtue of her gender, she has been uniquely allied to the very concept of modernism itself. As noted earlier, the *modern* woman has been a reoccurring sign, indicating change in North America since the suffragette movement. This distinctive ability to symbolize transformation has allowed Oberlander to present an essential dimension of modernity – that of change. While the features of Oberlander's design work share similarities with her male counterparts, being a woman has made her a more apt model for modern landscape architecture – thus, a model modern.

On a practical level, Oberlander is a logical figure to examine as part of contemporary landscape architecture's history. Given the large number of women in many landscape architecture programs across North America today, she serves as an excellent example of a female landscape architect taking a leading role in the profession. Students often look to historical accounts to find guidance and inspiration for their own professional trajectories. As the feminist Sue Scott has pointed out, "younger women artists working today develop their practice through the lens of art history."[45] Surely it is important that the lens of landscape architectural history disperse light on a model modern such as Cornelia Hahn Oberlander.

Notes

1 Linda Nochlin, "Why Have There Been No Great Women Artists?" *ARTnews* 69 (January 1971): 22–39, 67–71.

2 Thaïsa Way, *Unbounded Practice: Women and Landscape Architecture in the Early Twentieth Century* (Charlottesville: University of Virginia Press, 2009), 135.

3 See Susan Hartmann, "Prescriptions for Penelope: Literature on Women's Obligations to Returning World War II Veterans," *Women's Studies: An Inter-disciplinary Journal* 5, no. 3 (1978); Ruth Milkman, *Gender at Work: The Dynamics of Job Segregation by Sex During World War II* (Urbana: University of Illinois Press, 1987); Joanne Meyerowitz, *Not June Cleaver: Women and Gender in Postwar America, 1945–1960* (Philadelphia: Temple University Press, 1994); Susan Thistle, *From Marriage to the Market: The Transformation of Women's Lives and Work* (Berkeley: University of California Press, 2006).

4 Hilde Heynen, "Modernity and Domesticity: Tensions and Contradictions," in *Negotiating Domesticity: Spatial Productions of Gender in Modern Architecture*, eds. Hilde Heynen and Gülsüm Baydar (New York: Routledge, 2005), 1–29.

5 Ibid., 2–3.

6 Karen Hanson, "Feminism," in *The Routledge Companion to Aesthetics, third edition*, eds. Berys Gaut and Dominic McIver Lopes (New York: Routledge, 2012), 501.

7 *Oxford English Dictionary*, http://www.oed.com/view/Entry/120618?redirectedFrom=modern#eid, accessed September 30, 2013.

8 Heynen, "Modernity and Domesticity: Tensions and Contradictions," 2.

9 Meghan Morris and Naoki Sakai, "Modern," in *New Keywords: A Revised Vocabulary of Culture and Society*, eds. Tony Bennett, Lawrence Grossberg, and Meghan Morris (Malden, MA: Blackwell, 2005), 223.

10 Ibid.

11 They are foregrounded in Marc Treib, "Axioms for a Modern Landscape Architecture," in *Modern Landscape Architecture: A Critical Review*, ed. Marc Treib (Cambridge, MA: MIT Press, 1994), 36–67.

12 Dean Joseph Hudnut, "Report for the Academic Year 1941–42," Harvard University, Graduate School of Design. The GSD History Collection, Administrative Affairs: An Inventory, Frances Loeb Library Special Collections, the Graduate School of Design Harvard University, 292.

13 Dorothy May Anderson, *Women, Design, and the Cambridge School* (West Lafayette, IN: PDA Publishers Corporation, 1980), 150.

14 Cornelia Hahn Oberlander Estate.

15 Interview with Oberlander by author, February 17, 2011, Cambridge, Massachusetts.

16 Obtained from Mary Daniels, Frances Loeb Library Special Collections Librarian, and Norton Greenfeld, the Graduate School of Design Alumni Office.

17 Jill Pearlman, *Inventing American Modernism: Joseph Hudnut, Walter Gropius, and the Bauhaus Legacy at Harvard* (Charlottesville: University of Virginia Press, 2007), 200.

18 Interview with Oberlander by author, February 17, 2011, Cambridge, Massachusetts.

19 See Getty Research Institute Special Collections, Elisabeth Jastrow papers, Series V. Personal papers, 1870–1971, Boxes 53–57.

20 Kathy Stinson, *Love Every Leaf: The Life of Landscape Architect Cornelia Hahn Oberlander* (Toronto and Plattsburgh, NY: Tundra Books, 2008), 9–10.

21 Sophie Nichol Sauve, "Constructing Gender[ed] Outdoor Public Space," in *Women in Landscape Architecture: Essays on History and Practice*, eds. Louise A. Mozingo and Linda Jewell (Jefferson, NC: McFarland & Co., 2012), 210.

22 Nelson Goodman, *Grove Art Online* (Oxford: Oxford University Press, 2009). Accessed September 9, 2013.

23 Marjorie S. Cautley, *Garden Design: The Principles of Abstract Design as Applied to Landscape Composition* (New York: Dodd, Mead & Co., 1935).

24 Ibid., 30–31.

25 Ibid., 25.

26 Jill Pearlman, *Inventing American Modernism: Joseph Hudnut, Walter Gropius, and the Bauhaus Legacy at Harvard*, 206.

27 George Tyrrell Le Boutillier's lecture notes for Architectural Science 3a 1948. Harvard University, Graduate School of Design. The GSD History Collection, Academic Affairs: An Inventory, Frances Loeb Library Special Collections, the Graduate School of Design Harvard University.

28 *Landscape Architecture*, eds. Lester Collins and Thomas Gillespie (Cambridge, MA: Harvard University, 1951).

29 Lester Collins, "Landscape Architecture," in *Landscape Architecture*, eds. Lester Collins and Thomas Gillespie (Cambridge, MA: Harvard University, 1951), 37.

30 Garrett Eckbo, *Landscape for Living* (New York: F. W. Dodge Corporation, 1951).

31 Nelson Goodman and Catherine Z. Elgin, *Reconceptions in Philosophy and Other Arts and Sciences* (London: Routledge, 1988), 40.

32 Linda Lewin Graif, "The Paradox of Public Discourse: Designing Vancouver's Library Square," *The Journal of the Society for the Study of Architecture in Canada* 25, no. 1 (2000): 28.

33 Fax from Moshe Safdie office to Oberlander. Canadian Center for Architecture, Cornelia Hahn Oberlander Archive.

34 Adrian Forty, *Words and Buildings: A Vocabulary of Modern Architecture* (New York, NY: Thames & Hudson, 2000), 187.

35 Christopher Tunnard, *Gardens in the Modern Landscape* (London: Architectural Press; New York: Scribner, 1948), 105.

36 See Norman T. Newton, *An Approach to Design* (Cambridge, MA: Addison-Wesley Press, 1951).

37 Arthur Gallion, Garrett Eckbo and Simon Eisner, "Converging Forces on Design Part 2," *Journal of Architectural Education* 12, no. 1 (Autumn, 1956): 16.

38 Ibid.

39 Cornelia Oberlander, "Parks, Playgrounds and Landscape Architecture," *Community Planning Association of Canada: Community Planning Review* 6, no. 1 (March 1956): 11.

40 Ibid., 10.

41 Judith Wasserman, "A World in Motion: The Creative Synergy of Lawrence and Anna Halprin," *Landscape Journal* 31, nos. 1–2 (2012): 50.

42 Danile J. Levitin, *This Is Your Brain on Music* (New York: Dutton, 2006), 63.

43 Interview with Oberlander by author, July 31, 2008, Vancouver, Canada.

44 H. L. Brown, "1968 Evaluation of the Children's Creative Center." Canadian Center for Architecture, Cornelia Oberlander Archive, Oberlander, 2008 Addition, Play: Vancouver 1969, ARCH252382.

45 Sue Scott, "Domestic Disturbances," in *The Reckoning: Women Artists of the New Millennium*, eds. Eleanor Heartney, Helaine Posner, Nancy Princenthal, and Sue Scott (Munich, London, New York: Prestel, 2013), 127.

10

BEYOND ROBERTO BURLE MARX

Another genealogy of modern landscape architecture in Brazil

Zeuler R. M. de A. Lima

Revising and expanding the Brazilian panorama of landscape architecture

The international awareness of twentieth-century landscape architecture in Brazil has repeatedly placed the iconic work of Roberto Burle Marx in evidence. Though the quality of his skillful creations is undeniable, the almost exclusive attention to his work has limited the recognition of the multifaceted history that constitutes modern Brazilian landscape design and representation. In historiographic terms, the focus on Burle Marx has overshadowed the valuable contribution of innumerable other professionals, including preeminent women, to the development of a field of knowledge and practice that is still in formation in Brazil.

Although the contribution of women to modern and contemporary landscape architecture in Brazil is unquestionable, it is still little studied. Cultural, political, and economic modernization in Brazil made it possible for women – especially those in the educated middle-class – to enter the workforce in the early twentieth century and to excel in it in the post–World War Two period.

This essay is aware of gender, social, geographic, and ethnic identities and differences, but it does not frame women's contributions exclusively within feminist or historical materialist perspectives. Neither does it propose a stylistic analysis of modernism. Instead, it highlights the efforts and achievements of female academics and professionals in landscape architecture in relationship to a field of study and practice that has attracted both men and women equally, both heterosexuals and homosexuals. In addition, this chapter grounds those developments within broader, multidimensional, and shifting contexts of a modernizing nation that stand in dialogue with international artistic and scientific developments and with imagery and imaginaries of a Brazilian landscape in transformation since colonial times.

Modernist gardens in a nationalist landscape

The emergence of modernism in Brazil in the early twentieth century was both the extension of shifting Western cultural mindsets and of a long process of colonization and nation-building that granted landscape representation and native plants meaningful roles. Long before there was landscape architecture in Brazil, there were images and imaginaries of Brazilian landscape. The creation of such constructs – representing simultaneously a place and a nation – developed both by design and by default as the result of different social practices, conflicting political actions, and varying aesthetic dispositions in a vast historical and geographic panorama.[1] While the early system of Portuguese captaincies established a geometric and managerial definition of the Brazilian territory,[2] Dutch settlers and artists created the first pictorial and scientific representations of the Brazilian landscape in the 1700s.[3] In the nineteenth century, Rio de Janeiro became the epicenter of cultural and urban modernization as the imperial capital of a nascent nation.

Landscape design gained a significant role in this process when the French botanist and engineer Auguste Glaziou was hired to serve as the first director of the city's division of parks and gardens.[4] Not only did he help change the capital's appearance between the 1850s and 1880s, as a botanist he also developed a great interest in studying and incorporating Brazilian flora into his projects, an idea that Roberto Burle Marx also built upon some decades later. In the late nineteenth century, the emerging republican state was controlled by rural oligarchies; they used the landscape representations of the late-blooming and robust Romantic artistic movement, promoted by the National Academy of Fine Arts for their own purposes. Picturesque and sublime images of native flora and Brazilian landscapes became virtuous affirmations of the new nation's identity, embedded in the myth of the noble savage and the cosmological grandiosity of nature.[5]

Modernist sensibilities developed during the political and cultural transition from that oligarchic and rural system, which collapsed with the stock market crash of 1929, into an economy based on trade and industry and sustained by massive immigration, with consequential changes in the country's physical, urban, and cultural geography. A new artistic agenda had emerged in Brazil in the late 1910s, culminating in the pivotal Semana de Arte Moderna (Modern Art Week) that took place in São Paulo in 1922, which was led by the younger and well-traveled generation of those rural elites.[6] These developments would eventually have noteworthy repercussions in the conceptions of early twentieth-century Brazilian landscape.

Though not romantic in appearance, the modernist movement stemmed out of a nineteenth-century nationalist aesthetic and merged influences from European avant-gardes with picturesque and popular images of Brazil. The painter Tarsila do Amaral, as well as Anita Malfatti, a pioneer of expressionism in Brazil, helped to renew Brazilian art. Amaral was influenced by the work of her teacher Fernand Léger and by the surrealists, including Pablo Picasso and Joan Miró.[7] As one of the participants in the 1924 "Pau-Brasil" (Brazilwood) movement and of the "Manifesto antropofágico" (Cannibal manifesto; 1926) that was led by her partner, the writer Oswald de Andrade, Amaral produced simple and bright-colored representations of the country's native flora.[8] The group's naturalistic references were not a coincidence. Motivated by a critical approach to primitivism and built on the mythology of sixteenth-century writings, they suggested both metaphorically and politically that, as a cultural norm, European influences should be aggressively digested. From this process, a distinctively Brazilian modernism would emerge, which could be exported just as brazilwood (*Caesalpinea echinata*) had been during colonial times.[9]

In 1928, shortly before de Andrade published his provocative manifesto, Amaral completed one of the most iconic images of Brazilian modernism, her oil painting "Abaporu." Next to a melancholic native with gigantic feet, resting his head on his left arm and sitting on a green mound, this unadorned and distorted composition shows a robust mandacaru cactus (*Cereus jamacaru*) under a bright sun, resembling a slice of lemon. A harbinger of nationalist values,

Amaral's painting heralded – along with images of palm trees, banana trees, and tropical plants recurrent in several of her works – the reinvention of the Brazilian landscape and the invention of modernist landscape architecture.

While Tarsila do Amaral painted "Abaporu," her close friend, the dilettante designer and cultural patron Mina Klabin modernized garden design in Brazil. At the time, the young Roberto Burle Marx was still in Berlin, where he coincidentally, and with great fascination, discovered the tropical flora at the Botanical Garden in suburban Dahlem. By the time Burle Marx returned to Brazil in 1930 to study painting at the National School of Fine Arts in Rio de Janeiro and collect native plants, Klabin had already designed iconic modernist gardens.

Klabin did not develop a professional career or a critical theory about landscape architecture, but, in 1920s São Paulo, she embraced the use of Brazilian plants in the gardens she created for several modernist houses designed by her husband, the Ukranian-Brazilian architect Gregori Warchavchik. Warchavchik was one of the precursors of the introduction of functionalist ideas in architecture and urbanism in Brazil, countering the pervasive neocolonial architectural movement led by the National School of Fine Arts in Rio de Janeiro. Though conforming to the gender and labor divisions of the time, their collaboration significantly helped to renew incipient professional circles in São Paulo and expand the modern design repertory in Brazil.

Klabin's work was less public than her husband's, but no less important. As the educated daughter of a wealthy Jewish immigrant industrialist and real estate investor, she underwrote her husband's professional career. Besides designing gardens for his houses, she supported and sponsored many social and cultural events, for example as a founding member of the Sociedade Pró-Arte Moderna (Pro-Modern Art Society) in São Paulo.[10] Among Warchavchik's many public statements that he likely developed in dialogue with his wife and that resonated among their modernist friends, was his 1926 suggestion that the city would look better if the owners of ornate villas let "jasmines, rose shrubs, wisterias, and other national [sic] plants cover the façades that cost them so much money."[11]

Less-concerned with the native accuracy of the plant material than with geometric simplification, the architect envisioned a close relationship between the design of building volumes and vegetation, according to the modernist formal simplification of regular geometries and lack of ornamentation. In a series of iconic houses built in São Paulo between 1928 and the late 1930s, Warchavchik and Klabin gave private gardens and interior design important supporting architectural roles. Warchavchik's house designs combined a Brazilian vernacular with European rationalism, creating simple volumes surrounded by sizeable gardens. They provided the ground for his wife's figural experiments with native plants. Klabin's compositions had no precedent in Brazilian domestic architecture.

The house the couple built for themselves on a large, flat lot on Santa Cruz Street, between 1927 and 1928, is considered the first modernist house in the country and was declared a public heritage site in 1986 (Figure 10.1).[12] It took Klabin more than two decades to complete her private garden, consisting of regular pathways organized in a symmetrical composition. The garden was initially limited to complement the house's purist façades, but it later grew into a small park. She used large trees, such as guapuruvu (*Schizolobium parahiba*) and copaíba (*Copaifera langsdorfii*), and sculptural tropical plants, such as cacti, agaves, and dracaenas. While these were not always native to the area, they were in tune with the geometric and nationalist allegories of Brazilian modernism. Moreover, her choices expanded the repertoire of Brazilian plants used in private and public gardens, initiated by Auguste Glaziou in the nineteenth

FIGURE 10.1   Mina Klabin, Santa Cruz street gardens, front yard with tropical plants, ca. 1929,
Gregori Warchavchik Collection.

century and continued in the early twentieth century by large nurseries, such as the ones by
Germano Zimber who supplied plants for her projects.[13]

Other houses designed in consecutive years by Warchavchik in São Paulo offered his
wife the opportunity to further explore her interests. Though most of them were smaller
than the estate on Santa Cruz Street, they fully represented the couple's aspirations for a
modern house as *Gesamtkunstwerk*, combining architecture, garden, interior, and furniture
design. Often built on pronounced topography, the houses' cubic geometry allowed for
innovative asymmetrical compositions with transitional porches, large-tiered planters, and
side and back patios that connected interior and exterior spaces and that contained naturalistic allegories of both domesticity and nationalism. Such features are especially visible in two
neighboring houses, built in 1929 and 1930, in the affluent and novel Pacaembú subdivision
of São Paulo, developed a few years earlier, which followed Ebenezer Howard's Garden
City principles.

Involved with promoting the Klabin family's real estate interests, Warchavchik designed
and built a small rental model house on Itápolis Street (Figure 10.2). Built in 1929, the
house stands on a large ascending three-tiered lot. Two large frontal terraces, accessible
from the living room and overlooking the street, contained tropical plants similar to the
ones Klabin had used in her own house, including agaves, dracaenas, and the iconic and
sculptural mandacaru cacti. She divided the side yard that was accessible from the dining
room into two complementary areas – a small lawn with a straight pathway of irregularly

FIGURE 10.2 Mina Klabin, Santa Cruz street gardens, front yard with tropical plants, ca. 1929, Gregori Warchavchik Collection.

placed square paving stones leading toward a statue by the modernist sculptor Victor Brecheret that was placed against the stark white garage wall, and a small patio with a guapuruvu planted at its center and surrounded by a low curved wall lined with calatheas. Inside the house, one of Tarsila do Amaral's iconic paintings, "Cartão Postal" (Postcard), featured a colorful, nationalist, and imaginative composition of Rio de Janeiro's bay, fore-grounding cacti, palm trees, and a large tree on whose branch two monkeys rest languidly (Figure 10.3).

Such intimate details also had a public face. They staged the couple's desire to display a total work of modern art as they opened the property for visitation in 1930. The event, titled "Exposição de uma Casa Modernista" (Exhibition of a modernist house), propelled the renewal of Brazilian architecture that had not been achieved by the anti-Beaux-Arts São Paulo Modern Art Week eight years earlier.[14] The event also attracted international attention among preeminent European members of the International Congress of Modern Architecture (CIAM). This enthusiasm brought Warchavchik commissions for several houses in the following years, which allowed Klabin to continue experimenting with tropi-cal gardens.

The commission that was most significant for modern landscape architecture is a large house, designed in 1930 on Bahia Street, located close to the model house on Itápolis Street (Figures 10.4 and 10.5). Though both still stand, little is left of their original gardens. Built on a steep site with access from the high point of the lot, the backyard of the house on Bahia Street reveals three large terraces, which Klabin incorporated as parterres and tiered gardens

FIGURE 10.3 Mina Klabin, Bahia street house. Bedroom as a tropical garden with "Postcard" painting by Tarsila do Amaral, ca. 1930, Gregori Warchavchik Collection.

(Figure 10.6). They are connected on one side by flights of steps, and they are visible from the residence's large windows and balconies.

The lowest terrace was covered with a lawn and had the largest amount of trees, evoking the impression of a vernacular backyard. Klabin divided the upper terrace, which was accessible from the servant's level, into two main parts. The larger part of the terrace contained a lawn with shrubs and a few guapuruvus. It could be accessed along a central path made out of large, staggered cement pavers that were pervasive in her projects. On one side of the site, she designed a light and geometric metal-frame pergola for vines hovering above a surface of similar pavers separated by grass.

The middle terrace was fully visible from the house. It was the most manicured of the three levels. In addition to laying out a lawn with tropical shrubs and trees, Klabin designed a special feature – a checkered parterre alternating pavers and flowerbeds. Both the parterre mosaic and the pergola evoke the work of the French designer Gabriel Guévrékian. In the former case, as in other projects she would develop with vines a few years later, the light trellis suggests Guévrékian's design for the Heim villa in Neuilly. In the latter case, the ground composition resembles the cubist garden he had devised for the Noailles villa, designed by the architect Robert Mallet-Stevens a few years earlier.[15] Unlike Guévrékian's triangular French garden, Klabin's ground mosaic was completely square and flat. In addition, it was surrounded by vertical hedges on two sides, which gave

FIGURE 10.4 Mina Klabin, Itápolis street gardens, front yard with tropical plants, ca. 1930, Gregori Warchavchik Collection.

the composition spatial proportions comparable to the pergola, one level above. With such a complex project, the couple materialized, with varied references, their own version of cultural cannibalism.

The collaboration of Klabin and Warchavchik helped to propel his career, on both a local and a national scale. Advocating for an artistic avant-garde, Warchavchik galvanized a small circle of affluent, well-educated, well-travelled immigrant clients. However, he struggled to obtain public and large-scale commissions, which were mostly in the hands of local engineers and developers whose interest in technological modernization did not extend to modernist aesthetics. Klabin collaborated with her husband until the late 1930s, but her participation in his projects dwindled as she entered her forties. Simultaneously, São Paulo lost its preeminent role in the modernization of Brazilian culture during the ascendance of Getúlio Vargas' authoritarian regime, and Klabin's dilettante activities as a garden designer yielded to the emergence of Roberto Burle Marx as the de facto representative of modern landscape design in Brazil.

Disseminating modernist gardens

The innovative projects created by Warchavchik and Klabin in São Paulo soon attracted the interest of clients and designers in Rio de Janeiro, then the capital of Brazil and soon to become the new national epicenter of modernism. Warchavchik was building a house for a

FIGURE 10.5 Mina Klabin, Itápolis street gardens, house and back yard terraces ca. 1930, Gregori Warchavchik Collection.

client in Copacabana, in 1930, when architect Lucio Costa, the young leader of a short-lived pedagogical reform movement at the National School of Fine Arts, invited him to reorganize the school's architectural program.[16] Though the reform backfired as a result of confrontations with academic and neocolonial architects, it allowed Costa and Warchavchik to form a design partnership.[17] It also helped to propel the career of several young designers who collaborated with them and who would command the professionalization of modern architecture and landscape design in the following decades.

Such transformation took place against a convoluted background, marked by a political revolution that ended the control of the national government by rural oligarchies and the ascent of Getúlio Vargas' populist and authoritarian regime, between the mid-1930s and 1945. Starting in 1934, the longstanding Minister of Education and Health Gustavo Capanema, along with Lucio Costa, played a leading role in sponsoring modernization projects, absorbing dispersed modernist energies into a nationalist administration, and treating cultural production as an official, state-building affair.[18] Modernist designers, artists, and

FIGURE 10.6   Mina Klabin, Itápolis street gardens, backyard terraces with tropical plants and geometric patterns, ca. 1930, Gregori Warchavchik Collection.

intellectuals who worked under their patronage in search of a synthesis of the arts, presented
themselves as self-elected representatives of Brazilian society, taking responsibility for the
management of the nation's cultural heritage, modernization, and dissemination all at once.[19]
From this time onward, Brazil became progressively more implicated in the global history of
modernism, with the recognition of major Western critics and institutions. However, there
was little room left for independent paths such as the ones pursued by Gregori Warchavchik
and Mina Klabin.

It is no coincidence that Roberto Burle Marx's career developed substantially during this
period. He had joined the National School of Fine Arts in 1930 at age twenty-one, but abandoned his art studies less than three years later to join Costa and Warchavchik, who had established a professional partnership after both had resigned from the school. In Rio de Janeiro,
the young and talented Burle Marx began his career by taking over Klabin's role of creating
gardens for the houses designed by Warchavchik. Burle Marx designed his first gardens for
the Alfredo Schwartz house, producing a Corbusian-style roof garden, and for the Ronan
Borges house. Both houses and gardens were conceived for locations in Copacabana, in 1932
and 1933. They were later demolished and replaced by high-rise buildings.[20] Although Burle
Marx's role was limited to the plant arrangements in flowerbeds and containers, he gained
knowledge about the compositional use of a wide range of native tropical plants – from philo-
dendrons and agaves to frangipanis and tropical almond trees – as seen in photographs taken
of the Schwartz house after its construction.

By 1934, Costa and Warchavchik had ended their collaboration and Burle Marx had lost
his job. However, he soon moved to Recife, where he joined a team of modernist designers,

under the leadership of his former school colleague, the architect Luiz Nunes. The city emerged briefly as a center of modernist experiments until Nunes' premature death in 1937. At the age of twenty-five and without ever having completed his formal education, Burle Marx was appointed director of the city's Department of Parks and Gardens.[21] During his four years of service there, he started to develop his design approach and his independent professional career.

Building on his knowledge of native plants, his fine-arts pictorial sensibilities, and his exposure to evolving design principles, Burle Marx remodeled several public plazas. Although it took him a few more years to abandon the regular, geometric principles of seventeenth-century French gardens, his public gardens for Recife advanced the work of his predecessors such as Auguste Glaziou, along with the professionalization of modern landscape architecture in Brazil. In addition, he followed Klabin and Warchavchik's interest in tropical plants and their desire to integrate garden and architectural design.

In Recife, Burle Marx studied the native flora, striving to increase his compositional palette. For example, his original 1935 design for the elliptical Madalena Cactus Plaza (renamed Euclides da Cunha Square and restored in the early 2000s) stands out as an innovative exercise in the use of uncommon plants in Brazilian public gardens. His central arrangement of cacti surrounded by regional trees seemed out of place on the coast, but it was a tribute to the region's hinterland Caatinga formations of semi-desert xeric scrubland. As in Tarsila do Amaral's paintings and Mina Klabin's gardens, Burle Marx's use of sculptural mandacarus in urban spaces was imbued with allegorical and nationalist meaning.

While the public plazas of Recife gave Burle Marx national notoriety, his organically shaped parterre and roof gardens for the iconic Ministry of Education and Health in Rio de Janeiro gave him international recognition. By the time the ministerial building was completed at the end of World War Two, Brazilian modernism had been legitimized by the state and lost its provocative cannibalistic metaphor. Vargas' regime was peacefully brought down in 1945, but the state apparatus and its cultural policies and practices survived basically unscathed.[22] Modernist designers such as Burle Marx continued to benefit from state-sponsored projects, which furthered the public visibility of his work. Still, this period experienced meaningful changes in artistic and cultural values, along with the United States' increasing geo-political influence in South America. This transformation coincided with the opening of new directions in both modern art and landscape architecture in Brazil and with the emergence of the first generation of professionally trained landscape designers.

Between garden design and urban planning

The years after World War Two in Brazil were characterized by an economic boom, increasing urbanization, and real estate development that culminated during Juscelino Kubitschek's presidency with the construction of the new capital, Brasília. Although international voices criticized modern Brazilian architects who had come of age during Vargas' regime, Burle Marx's career as a designer and artist thrived and continued to attract approval, both nationally and abroad.

The Flamengo Landfill Park, developed between the late 1950s and 1965, stands out as a watershed in Burle Marx's career and as an expression of significant cultural and professional changes in Brazil (Plate 10.1). While Brasília was created following the functionalist principles of urban zoning, with park spaces secondary to transportation and architecture, the Flamengo project gave landscape design a leading role in city planning. The project initiated the exploration of new urban and environmental themes in Brazil, such as the transformation of a hilly area into the first waterfront and parkway, and the idea that public space could counter the urban problems caused by shortsighted transportation projects and profit-driven practices of real estate speculation.

Although Burle Marx's office is generally credited as the author of the Flamengo Landfill Park, it was also the pet project of Lota Macedo Soares, a wealthy aesthete and promoter and, like Burle-Marx, a self-taught modernist. Without her aspirations and leadership, his team's design would not have been possible. A strong-willed woman, Macedo Soares was well connected within the cultural and political elites in Rio de Janeiro. She had sponsored the work of modernist designers, including the architect Sérgio Bernardes, who built the house she shared with her long-time companion, the North-American poet and writer Elizabeth Bishop.

Appointed by the governor as a special advisor to the Parks Department in the Superintendency of Urbanization and Sanitation, in 1960, Lota Macedo Soares was determined to complete the Flamengo Landfill Park, based on a project envisioned by architect Affonso Reidy in the late 1940s. She did not hold a professional diploma, but gathered a small group of friends into a "commission of notables" to revive the project and named herself the group's president. She gained direct access to the governor's office, violating bureaucratic hierarchies.[23] Despite her imperious procedures, she delivered a better vision for urban improvement along the coast than the city's transportation engineers. Her goal was to improve the connection between the historic downtown and the new residential areas. Instead of a plan for four wide thruways, lined with apartment buildings, she suggested two expressways and an extensive public park along the bay. As soon as her vision found support in her social circles, she invited accomplished experts and designers to join her.

Among Macedo Soares' collaborators were the architects Affonso Reidy, Sérgio Bernardes, and Jorge Moreira, who designed structures for the park. She hired Ethel Bauzer de Medeiros, an educator, author, and expert in recreation and leisure with special interest in urban planning to design innovative playgrounds.[24] She also gave Roberto Burle Marx, whose career was already well established by then, a special role. He and his young assistants used the experience of the Parque del Este project for Caracas, Venezuela, to plan and design several gardens for differently sized areas along the bay.

In addition, Macedo Soares hired Luiz Emygdio de Mello Filho, a leading Brazilian expert in tropical plants and soils and director of the state's Parks Department, to organize the collection of seeds and plants and the massive production of seedlings for the project. He pursued the replacement of exotic plants with native plants and developed groundbreaking studies about urban vegetation and the systemic approach to landscape design, which he described as "ecogenesis."[25] While Burle Marx went on regional botanical expeditions, Mello Filho traveled as far as Cuba, where he received tropical species from the Botanical Garden of Cienfuegos, which had, until recently, served as Harvard University's research station on the island. Mello Filho was particularly interested in road landscaping and in the establishment of fruit trees for bird and even human consumption along the bay, which was a challenge, considering the climatological conditions due to the ocean's proximity.

Though Lota Macedo Soares was not a professional designer, her strategic contribution to the advancement of landscape architecture in Brazil was invaluable to the field's development as an interdisciplinary profession. The geographic extension of the institutions involved and the plant palette in the landfill project are testimonies to the growing interest in the aesthetic and botanical diversity of tropical plants as well as the social and ecological awareness among landscape architects in Brazil. The park design is also evidence of the diminishing nationalist sentiment that had driven the first generation of modernist Brazilian designers and artists. In addition, it allowed for a closer dialogue among Brazilian landscape professionals and their colleagues in the United States.

Beyond tropical gardens: infrastructure, the metropolis, and the environment

Lota Macedo Soares died in 1967, before she could see her goals for the Flamengo Landfill Park fully realized. She shared the project's authorship with Roberto Burle Marx, whose career continued to thrive as he approached his sixties. He had also started to organize several naturalist expeditions to different areas of the country, following in the steps of his early mentor, the botanist Henrique Lahmeyer de Mello Barreto. He involved several enthusiasts in his journeys, including Margaret Mee, the British botanical artist who lived in Brazil. She was one of the first environmentalists to draw attention to the deforestation in the Amazon River basin. Burle Marx's legacy encompasses the discovery and cultivation of tropical plants, environmental preservation, as well as landscape design. Above all, he contributed to the informal education of a new generation of landscape architects who have expanded on his work in the last half-century.[26]

During the 1950s, Burle Marx trained two young designers, whose activities would have significant impact on the field. One of them was the architect Fernando Magalhães Chacel, who developed a prominent independent career in landscape architecture. Until his death in 2011, he worked with multidisciplinary groups and served in several public and professional functions. Above all, Chacel pioneered the practice of "ecological landscape design" in Brazil, broadening the scale and purpose of design, ranging from urban plazas to large infrastructural projects such as hydroelectric power plants. The other landscape architect who had a brief association with Burle Marx and contributed to the conceptual and geographic shift of landscape architecture toward North-American influences in the postwar period was Roberto Coelho Cardozo.

A United States native of Portuguese descent, Cardozo moved to Brazil in the early 1950s with his wife, the landscape architect Susan Osborn. The couple had graduated from the University of California and had worked in Garret Eckbo's office.[27] In Rio de Janeiro, the urbanist Luís Inácio Anhaia Mello, dean of the new School of Architecture at the University of São Paulo, hired Cardozo to teach a landscape architecture course. Though limited in scope and taught only to senior students, his garden design classes introduced a new perspective, the notion of environments for living. He transposed the model of Californian modern landscape design into the tropical context of Brazil.[28]

Until he left for England in the 1970s, Cardozo also maintained an active practice in residential garden design, but he did not encourage his wife to pursue her once-promising career in his São Paulo office.[29] Instead, he hired students as interns and educated a new generation of landscape architects. Their work combined elements of Brazilian and North American modernism. More than Cardozo himself, however, two of his female students have assumed professional and academic leadership in the field – Rosa Grena Kliass and Miranda Martinelli Magnoli. With degrees in architecture and urbanism from the University of São Paulo in 1955, both started working with Cardozo and, after a brief collaboration in the 1960s, they embarked on independent careers. Although landscape architecture is not yet recognized as an autonomous field of study and practice in the country and is still claimed by experts in architecture, planning, agronomy, forestry, geography, ecology, and biology, Kliass and Magnoli's invaluable contributions expanded the goals of their modernist predecessors. They ultimately helped to establish landscape architecture as a profession and academic discipline by emphasizing its social, urbanistic, and environmental importance.

A tale of two landscapes

Brazil experienced momentous changes between the 1950s and 1970s, with significant consequences for the design professions. The years of economic prosperity during Kubitscheck's presidency boosted urbanization and agro-industrial expansion, but also created unprecedented environmental problems. In 1964, a military coup d'etat installed an authoritarian regime that implemented a conservative modernization model, based on state-controlled economic development, large urban and infrastructural planning projects, and political repression. It presented landscape architects with both new challenges and opportunities. Some landscape architects, such as Rosa Kliass, engaged in those efforts and renovated practice. Others, such as Miranda Magnoli, resisted them and restructured professional education and research in the field.

Miranda Magnoli, who is known as an austere and deep thinker, gained her first professional experience teaching as an adjunct at the University of São Paulo, while working part time in design offices such as Cardozo's. She also joined a pioneering study of the City of São Paulo. Because the leading engineer refused to have women working in the discussion team, her participation in the study was limited to producing data and mapping surveys. However, she found her way into a few memorable meetings led by Louis-Joseph Lebret, who led the movement "Economy and Humanism," both in Brazil and in his native France, to study the relationship between urban and regional planning and economic and social development.[30]

In the meantime, Magnoli also designed a few private gardens. For a while, she worked in land surveying and subdivision development projects with her brother and father, both engineers. Though she initially expected to pursue a career in building design, she soon dealt with the interface between landscape architecture and urban planning, a field of research and practice in which she became one of the preeminent experts in the country. Between the mid-1960s and 1970s, she pursued post-graduate studies in urbanism in Brazil and in Great Britain until she was hired as a full-time faculty at the University of São Paulo to direct the professional and research programs in landscape architecture.[31]

Rosa Kliass, who is known for her gregarious and energetic temperament, began her career in private practice, after studying with Roberto Cardozo and working as an intern in architecture offices. In 1958, three years after her graduation, she designed her first public plaza for her native town of São Roque, thirty-five miles west of São Paulo, where her parents had moved when they emigrated from Central Europe. As a member of the thriving Jewish cultural circles of São Paulo, Kliass befriended and collaborated with preeminent artists, musicians, and designers. Among them was her life-long collaborator Jorge Wilheim, who brought her attention to urban and environmental issues and work in the public sector. Despite his left-leaning political values, Wilheim secured several public projects and key administrative positions during the military dictatorship. Besides working with him, in 1965, Kliass began to participate in the design of an open-space system for Jaime Lerner's plan for Curitiba. A year later, the mayor of São Paulo commissioned her to design Morumbi Park in an affluent residential area, in collaboration with city officials.

In the early 1960s, Kliass and Magnoli collaborated on a few private gardens.[32] Between 1967 and 1968, they were hired to undertake an open-space study for the city of São Paulo

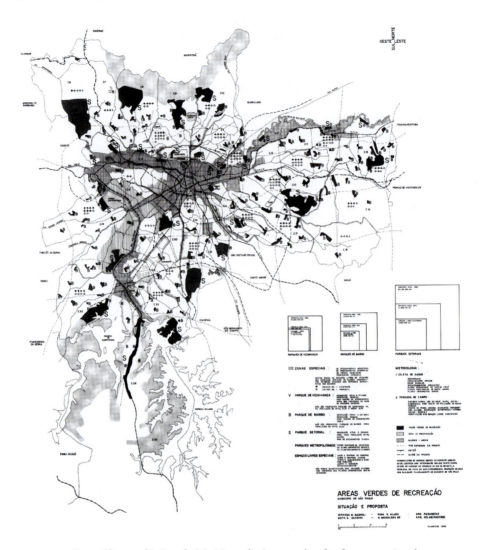

FIGURE 10.7   Rosa Kliass and Miranda M. Magnoli, Survey plan for first recreational open-space
network, São Paulo, City of São Paulo, 1967–68. Rosa Kliass Collection.

(Figure 10.7).[33] They originally designed forty-four new plazas, but only less than a handful
of them – among them Benedito Calixto and Sunset Squares – have survived. In addition,
they organized a large-scale survey of the city's public open spaces, street typologies, trees,
and geomorphology, improvising a mapping methodology because aerial pictures were not
available at the time. During this process, they hired and trained Maddalena Ré, who is now
a leading expert in tropical plants. Once they had concluded the program, Kliass and Magnoli
discontinued their collaboration and took diverging, though equally significant, paths into
professional practice and academic life. Their pioneering work for the city eventually gave rise
to the creation of the city's Department of Parks and Public Spaces (DEPAVE).[34]

Soon after the completion of the city's public-space plan, Kliass received a three-month fellowship from the U.S. Agency for International Development in 1969. She visited landscape

architecture programs at universities, public planning and preservation agencies, and leading design firms on both coasts of the United States. Upon her return to Brazil, she began to pursue a master of science degree in physical geography, at the University of São Paulo. In the early 1970s, she discontinued her studies in order to establish her own practice, which continues to focus on landscape architecture and planning projects throughout Brazil.

While many Brazilian designers, such as Magnoli, saw the persisting military regime as a reason to deepen critical investigation, Kliass, like many confident designers of her generation, saw the possibility of engaging in large, state-run urban planning and infrastructural projects. Beginning in 1971, when Jorge Wilheim was the secretary of planning for the state of São Paulo, Kliass's office participated in a multidisciplinary team for an integrated regional and urban development project for the Paraíba river valley. This experience was followed by further collaborations with geographers and botanists in the creation of statewide environmental protection areas, such as in studies for hydroelectric power plants. Kliass's pioneering streetscape project, done in association with the designers João Carlos Cauduro and Ludovico Martino for the city of São Paulo, in 1973, was also meaningful.[35] Though disfigured over time, their original design transformed Paulista Avenue into today's symbolic boulevard, with wide and accessible sidewalks with patterned pavements, large planters with shrubs and trees separating vehicular traffic, and urban fixtures privileging pedestrian use and public transportation (Plate 10.2).

Aside from working on commissions ranging from private gardens to urban and environmental projects associated with infrastructural development, Kliass played a key role in the professional representation of Brazilian landscape architects. Since the 1972 UN Stockholm conference, many municipal, state, and federal organizations and conservation laws had been created in Brazil that promoted the public awareness of environmental issues.[36] Along with Luiz Emygdio de Mello Filho and Fernando Chacel, she joined the International Federation of Landscape Architects (IFLA), which prompted her to be one of the founders of ABAP, the Brazilian Association of Landscape Architects, in 1976.[37] The association's efforts allowed for the progressive consolidation of professional practice and the dissemination of regional and environmental agendas around the country.

Not only did such resolutions corroborate a paradigm shift in landscape architecture practice in Brazil, with designers such as Burle Marx engaging in preservationist campaigns, but it also led landscape architects to embrace the management of biophysical systems at urban and regional scales. Moreover, landscape architects also significantly contributed to expanding research and reforming education. Miranda Magnoli was at the forefront of those efforts in the School of Architecture and Urbanism at the University of São Paulo.

Hired in 1964 as a part-time assistant to the design faculty, Magnoli became a full-time professor and researcher in 1971. After completing her doctoral degree, a year later, she led a pedagogical reform of the work initiated by Cardozo and his colleagues, by expanding the disciplinary focus of landscape architecture from small-scale projects to urban design and planning, and environmental studies.[38] Self-educated and with fifteen years of professional experience, Magnoli hired a select group of young instructors, including the designers Ayako Nishikawa, Sun Alex, and Benedito Abbud, who later withdrew from the university to dedicate themselves to practice. The group also included the landscape architect Silvio Soares Macedo and the biologist Maria Ângela Faggin, who have continued Magnoli's research and pedagogical mission since her retirement in the late 1980s.[39]

Though Magnoli's work developed mostly within academia and inconspicuously as a professional consultant, her contribution to advancing landscape architecture as a field of knowledge and practice in Brazil is akin to that of Kliass. Although they pursued separate and individual paths with different approaches, both of their voices continue to resound in the country today. While Kliass remains a key reference in the realm of practice, Magnoli's major impact is noticeable in the advancement of theoretical and methodological frameworks that have moved the field away from traditional garden design toward a better understanding of the complex relationships between designed landscapes and their social realities and environmental challenges.

Magnoli developed a profound interest in the social dimension of space, and particularly in fast-growing Brazilian cities and metropolitan areas. Based on discussions with the world-renowned geographer Milton Santos, and critical readings of authors as diverse as Henri Lefebvre and Ian McHarg, she has often insisted that the landscape should be understood as a human environment and not as a scenic territory. Contradicting the modernist idea of the distinction between figure and ground, she has advocated the understanding of landscape as a material product of social and cultural dynamics.[40] Magnoli's main goal was to create a cross-disciplinary theory committed to action based on the convergence between landscape and environment.

Questioning traditional definitions of nature and its opposition to culture, she proposed the notion of the "ecosystemic sphere," described as the relationship between biophysical elements and social practices and as the point of departure for any landscape or urban study or spatial project. In addition, she has continuously advocated that everyday public open space plays an important social role in both urban and regional designs, be it for regular subdivisions and shantytowns or for large environmental remediation projects.[41] Although her theoretical output, which continues to this day in the form of articles and lectures, has not been systematic and has not generated a single book, Miranda Magnoli has educated two generations of landscape designers and researchers, who continue to propagate her scholarly and pedagogical work in professional and academic institutions throughout the country.

Beyond modernism

Between the 1980s and the early 2000s, Brazil has transitioned into a democratic state. This period has also been characterized by economic and social challenges. While postmodernism found little fertile ground in Brazil, the exhausted nationalist agenda and enthusiasm for modernist aesthetics yielded the adoption of values and practices fostered by neoliberal economic policies with meaningful consequences for urbanization, the environment, and landscape architecture practice.[42]

This period saw the increase in real estate development and corporate commissions, but also the spread of environmental consulting and the creation of large urban and ecological park projects. Several of Magnoli, Kliass, and Chacel's younger collaborators, such as Luciano Fiaschi, Maddalena Ré, Mirthes Baffi, Suely Suchodolsky, Jamil Kfouri, Eduardo Barra, and Beneditto Abbud, have since then also established thriving practices.[43] Chacel passed away in 2011, after a long and exemplary career; Kliass continues to work as a landscape architect, and Magnoli has reengaged with professional practice since retiring from the university in the late 1980s, retaining her critical approach.

Always concerned with the relationship between the designed landscape and the environment and guided by a humanistic approach, Magnoli has participated in innovative urban planning and design teams, calling conventional planning strategies into question. Among them, two public projects, realized in the last decade, deserve attention. A public commission realized in 2003 for the Lapa district in São Paulo consisted of a critical analysis and proposal regarding the region's urban and environmental planning. Lapa developed in the early twentieth century as one the main industrial neighborhoods of São Paulo, occupying a wide area along the Tietê river valley and on its adjacent hills to the south. In the last three decades, since most train lines and factories have become inactive, this working class area of small row houses has developed into a middle- and upper-middle-class neighborhood, with large-scale high-rise and commercial development.

Magnoli's proposal rejects mere embellishment solutions, such as streetscape renovations and tree planting that bolster real estate interests. Instead, her project takes into consideration the visual and spatial continuity between the different urban typologies and the topography on and around the site. The design emphasizes land use control and storm water management. It also promotes the coordination of transportation networks, residential pockets, and commercial areas. Her proposal also anticipates a long-term implementation, based on a careful evaluation of social, geological, hydrological, and geomorphological factors, which will require strong and continued political will to mature into a dynamic regional landscape.

She developed the other large regional project in the early 2000s, in cooperation with Botti-Rubin Architects. Their proposal focused on regulating a controversial plan for public–private development along Água Espraiada creek, a tributary of Pinheiros River and one of the city's two largest waterways.[44] This project was among the experiments related to the creation of the City Statute, an innovative federal law, based on many years of popular struggle for egalitarian and democratic urban governance. This legislation, which has been incorporated into new urban master plans, aims at fostering the social purpose of land uses and urban spaces associating the control of real estate development, low-cost housing projects, and environmental sustainability.

Magnoli and Botti-Rubin's main goal was to minimize several challenges in a large area of low-density residential neighborhoods and a sizeable shantytown. Though the project was eventually rejected because of complex public and private alliances, it represents Magnoli's aspiration to design self-sustainable projects and to challenge traditional real estate development. This initiative is a testimony to her life-long theoretical claim that urban renewal should begin with the creation of public open spaces and low-income housing, and that it should respond to complex social and environmental dynamics.[45]

While Magnoli's work has been dedicated to research, teaching, and practice at the intersection of landscape architecture and urban planning, Kliass's contribution has consisted mostly of serving in public positions and in developing landscape architecture projects with varied scopes and scales. The many projects her office has worked on since its creation in the 1970s include private gardens, public parks, urban landscape plans, and projects for environmental protection areas.

In addition to the projects already mentioned, some recent designs deserve special attention for their methodology and significance. Among them are the Heron's Mangrove Park, on Guamá River in Belém, state of Pará, and the urban landscape project for São Luís, capital of the state of Maranhão. Completed in 1999, in the delta of the Amazon River, the Belém project merges ecological preservation with education and urban recreation (Plate 10.3).

The large riverfront is divided into two complementary parts: an urbanized area, which includes traditional park infrastructure and pavilions, and an educational and conservation area dedicated to representing the state's wetlands, dry land woods, and prairies, and to the restoration of a mangrove habitat with native aninga-açus (*Montrichardia arborensces*).[46] Completed in 2003, the urban landscape project in Maranhão, aimed at balancing out geophysical, economic, and social spheres of a metropolitan region that houses 1.5 million residents close to a large mining area, is especially concerned with controlling land occupation that has, like in many Brazilian cities, moved toward valley areas containing fragile ecosystems. The project combines planning and zoning strategies with specific urban and environmental projects (Plate 10.4).

Kliass also developed projects that combined urban planning and environmental and historical preservation, such as the Fortress Park in Macapá, in the northern state of Amapá in the Amazon region (Plate 10.5). The Vauban-style São José Fortress, built in the mid-1700s, is the centerpiece of a large park that reconnects the historic riverfront with the urban grid, which was developed indiscriminately during the twentieth century. The project that was completed in 2004 cleared a large paved area and ordinary buildings and transformed it into a park with leisure infrastructure for adults and children, a pathway along the shoreline, reconstituted vegetation, and an archeological site.

Another significant recent project in Kliass's large portfolio is the Youth Park, completed in São Paulo in 2006 (Plates 10.6 and 10.7). Located on the site of the once-notorious Carandiru penitentiary, demolished after human rights violations, this competition-winning proposal was designed in partnership with the architecture firms Aflalo-Gasperini and Purarquitetura. Aside from dealing with the convoluted memories that some of the remaining buildings evoke, the park project aims to restore Carajás Creek, increase biodiversity, and create recreational areas that connect the surrounding neighborhoods.

The irregular site geometry allowed for three strips for phased interventions. The ensemble consists of a sports park to the east; a central, secluded wooded area with the repurposed remains of an unfinished building; and public gardens accessible from the subway station on the west side. This area also includes the main buildings and public facilities that constitute the cultural sector.[47] The project is part of a series of urban initiatives to recover degraded areas in the floodplain of the Tietê River. It also integrates a large, formerly disconnected site into the urban fabric and offers a park in a large mixed-use area, previously deprived of public open space. The provision of park space for underprivileged citizens is a goal that Kliass has pursued since the beginning of her career.

Historical legacies and future challenges

Landscape architecture as a field of knowledge and practice in Brazil in the twentieth century is the result of economic, social, and artistic developments that, since colonial times, have generated a genealogy of different forms of visual representation, the appropriation of biophysical resources, and urbanization. Until recently, the idea of landscape – *paisagem* in Portuguese, following the Latin etymology – was associated with the representation of a nation under construction.

The invention and reinvention of a pluralistic Brazilian landscape is perceptible as much in sixteenth-century land demarcations and eighteenth-century paintings as in the experimental modernism of Mina Klabin and the iconic tropical gardens of Roberto Burle Marx. In the last few decades, however, the wishful association between landscape and national identity that came with intense economic and cultural development in Brazil has yielded to concerns about the flipside of those advances – an environmental crisis that has posed new demands on contemporary and future generations of designers.

The field of landscape architecture in Brazil grew out of the work of self-taught enthusiasts who practiced as artists, botanists, and designers, and it still waits to be recognized as an independent profession. However, thanks to the pioneering efforts of Roberto Burle Marx and Roberto Coelho Cardozo, and especially to several of their followers, including Rosa

Grena Kliass and Miranda Martinelli Magnoli, who expanded their teachers' legacies, Brazilian landscape architecture has advanced considerably since the 1970s.

Women's leadership in the profession and in landscape architectural education, and their contribution to the field in Brazil, are unquestionable. Women have been involved in pioneering, dilettante, and experimental work, both individually and as part of a multifaceted group of specialists devoted to enabling and organizing professional practice and its institutions as well as to promoting policies, education, and research. At the beginning of the twentieth century, the prevalent social division of labor limited the opportunities for women, even if they were as cultured as Mina Klabin. Her work was limited to collaborating in commissions obtained by her husband and she did not develop an independent professional career. The economic and social changes after the 1950s in Brazil increased access to university education and the emergence of a professional middle class that included a considerable number of remarkable, independent, and industrious women. Their coming of age, during a period of robust modernization and convoluted political conditions, offered opportunities and challenges that allowed them to broaden their professional and intellectual influence by either associating themselves with governmental agencies and private investors or by taking the opposite stance and developing influential activist and academic practices.

Female landscape architects have substantially helped to give new meanings to the modern Brazilian landscape and to the role of designers and planners. They have contributed to shaping a professional figure aware of Brazil's variable geography, natural resources, and urban and social realities, who can link urban, regional, and environmental projects with planning and preservation. In a country that still contains most of the world's biodiversity, in a global context that is characterized by a tension between diminishing natural resources, on the one hand, and expanding social and cultural practices, on the other, the challenges and opportunities for landscape architects are paramount. As a complex discipline, landscape architecture depends on dialogue and interdisciplinary contributions. It may, thus, not be a coincidence that it has been more accessible to women than other design professions. As landscape architecture evolves in Brazil, women continue to contribute to this field of knowledge and practice, which leaves behind the modernist search for a nationalist synthesis of the arts and seeks, instead, new relationships between changing social and environmental realities and artistic projects.

Notes

1   Ana Maria Belluzzo, "A propósito d'O Brasil dos Viajantes," *Revista USP* 30 (June–August 1996), 15–16.
2   Eduardo Bueno, *Capit, do Brasil: a saga dos primeiros colonizadores* (Rio de Janeiro: Objetiva, 1999), 24.
3   J. L. Mota Menezes, "O Urbanismo Holandês no Recife, Permanências no Urbanismo Brasileiro," Colloquium *A Construção do Brasil Urbano*, Lisbon (2000), 20.
4   Lilia Moritz Schwarcz, *Romantismo Tropical: A estetização da política e da cidadania numa instituição imperial brasileira* (São Paulo: Instituto de Artes, UNESP, 2000), 15.
5   Belluzzo, "A propósito d'O Brasil dos Viajantes," 18.
6   Marta Rossetti Batista, *Anita no tempo e no espaço: biografia e estudo da obra* (São Paulo: Editora 34/EDUSP, 2006), 45–46.
7   Amaral, Aracy A. *Tarsila: Sua Obra e Seu Tempo* (São Paulo, Tenenge, 1986), 104.
8   Nadia Batella Gotlib, *Tarsila do Amaral: a Modernista* (São Paulo: SENAC, 2000), 27–30.
9   Oswald de Andrade, "Piratininga Ano 374 da Deglutição do Bispo Sardinha," *Revista de Antropofagia* 1, Year 1 (May 1928): 1.
10 Tatiana Perecin, *Mina Klabin: Paisagismo e Modernismo no Brasil* (São Carlos: EESC-USP, 2003), 119.
11 Ibid., 149.
12 José Lira, *Warchavchik, Fraturas da Vanguarda* (São Paulo: Cosac Naify, 2011), 143–167.

13 Perecin, *Mina Klabin*, 50.

14 Lira, *Warchavchik*, 197–198.

15 Dorothée Imbert, "Unnatural Acts: Propositions for a New French Garden, 1920–1930," in *Architecture and Cubism*, eds. Eve Blau and Nancy J. Troy (Montréal: Centre canadien d'architecture, 1997), 167–186.

16 Zilah Quezado Deckker, *Brazil Built: The Architecture of the Modern Movement in Brazil* (London: Spon Press, 2001), 15.

17 Lira, *Warchavchik*, 277–282.

18 Teresa A. Meade, *A Brief History of Brazil* (New York: Facts on File, 2003), 145.

19 Sergio Miceli, *Intelectuais e classe dirigente no Brasil (1920–1945)* (Selectuais e classe dirigente no Brasil) (São Paulo: Difel, 1979).

20 Lira, *Warchavchik*, 302–303.

21 Vera Beatriz Siqueira, *Roberto Burle Marx* (São Paulo: Cosac Naify, 2005), 117.

22 Derek Williams, *Culture Wars in Brazil: The First Vargas Regime (1930–1945)* (Durham, NC: Duke University Press, 2001), 89.

23 Carmen L. Oliveira, *Rare and Commonplace Flowers: The Story of Elizabeth Bishop and Lota Macedo Soares* (New Brunswick: Rutgers University Press, 2003), 66–67.

24 Ibid., 84.

25 Ana Rita Sá Carneiro, "A produção paisagística brasileira entre 1930 e 1976," in org. Ivete Fahra, Mônica B. Schlee, and Raquel Tardin, *Arquitetura paisagística contemporânea no Brasil* (São Paulo: SENAC, 2010), 68.

26 Claudio Cavalcanti, Farès el-Dahdah, and Francis Rambert, eds. *Roberto Burle Marx: The Modernity of Landscape* (Barcelona, Basel, New York: Actar Birkhäuser, 2011), 331–332.

27 Omar de Almeida Cardoso, "Roberto Coelho Cardozo: A Vanguarda da Arquitetua Paisagística Moderna Paulistana," in *Paisagem e Ambiente, Ensaio 4* (São Paulo: FAUUSP, 1992), 173.

28 Rossana Vaccarino, "The Inclusion of Modernism: *Brasilidade* and the Garden," in *The Architecture of Landscape (1940–1960)*, ed. Marc Treib (Philadelphia: University of Pennsylvania Press, 2002), 208.

29 Rosa G. Kliass, interview with the author, November 19, 2013.

30 Miranda Martinelli Magnoli, "Entrevista," in *Paisagem e Ambiente. Ensaios 21: Miranda Magnoli* (São Paulo: FAUUSP, 2006), 13–42.

31 Miranda Martinelli Magnoli, *Currículo Lattes*, Conselho Nacional de Pesquisa e Desenvolvimento Tecnológico, http://lattes.cnpq.br/2115921880311848 (November 28, 2013).

32 Euler Sandeville Júnior, "Miranda Martinelli Magnoli: Contribuição Fundamental para uma Teoria e Ação do Arquiteto na Paisagem Brasileira. Uma Aproximação de seus escritos," in *Paisagem e Ambiente. Ensaios: Miranda Magnoli* (São Paulo: FAUUSP, 2006), 81–100.

33 Rosa Grena Kliass, *Desenhando paisagens, moldando uma profissão* (São Paulo: SENAC, 2006), 61.

34 Ibid., 17.

35 Ethel Leon, *Design Brasileiro: Quem fez, quem faz* (São Paulo: SENAC, 2005), 44.

36 Ivete Farah, "Arquitetura Paisagística no Período entre 1976 e 1985," in org. Ivete Fahra, Mônica B. Schlee, and Raquel Tardin, *Arquitetura paisagística contemporânea no Brasil* (São Paulo: SENAC, 2010), 79.

37 Kliass, *Desenhando paisagens, moldando uma profissão*, 204.

38 Miranda Martinelli Magnoli, "Entrevista."

39 Silvio Soares Macedo, "O Ensino de Paisagismo na FAUUSP e a Figura de Miranda Magnoli," in *Paisagem e Ambiente. Ensaios 21: Miranda Magnoli* (São Paulo: FAUUSP, 2006), 43–55.

40 Eugenio F. Querioga, "Por um Paisagismo Crítico," in *Paisagem e Ambiente. Ensaios 21: Miranda Magnoli* (São Paulo: FAUUSP, 2006), 55–64.

41 Sandeville Júnior, "Miranda Martinelli Magnoli: Contribuição Fundamental para uma Teoria e Ação do Arquiteto na Paisagem Brasileira. Uma Aproximação de seus escritos," 83.

42 Mônica Bahia Schlee, "O (Re)desenho Paisagístico das Cidades Brasileiras (1985–1996)," in org. Ivete Fahra, Mônica B. Schlee, and Raquel Tardin, *Arquitetura paisagística contemporânea no Brasil* (São Paulo: SENAC, 2010), 79.

43 Ivete Farah, "Arquitetura Paisagística no Período entre 1976 e 1985," in org. Ivete Fahra, Mônica B. Schlee, and Raquel Tardin, *Arquitetura paisagística contemporânea no Brasil* (São Paulo: SENAC, 2010), 80–83.

44 Alberto Botti, Marc Rubin, and Renée Otmar, eds. *Botti Rubin Arquitetos, Selected Works* (Victoria (Australia): Images Publishing, 2002), 233.

45 Vladimir Bartalini, "Fazer, ensinar, saber-ensinar-fazer," in *Paisagem e Ambiente. Ensaios: Miranda Magnoli* (São Paulo: FAUUSP, 2006), 135–140.

46 Kliass, *Desenhando paisagens, moldando uma profissão*, 212–213.

47 Ibid., 211–212.

BIBLIOGRAPHY

Adams, W. H. *Grounds for Change: Major Gardens of the Twentieth Century*. Boston: Little, Brown, 1993.

Allen, Marjory, and Mary Nicholson. *Memoirs of an Uneducated Lady*. London: Thames and Hudson, 1975.

Alpert, Natalie, and Gary Kesler (edited by Dianne Harris). "Florence Bell Robinson and Stanley Hart White: Creating a Pioneering School of Landscape Architecture." In *No Boundaries: University of Illinois Vignettes*, edited by Lillian Hoddeson, 113–123. Chicago: University of Illinois Press, 2004.

Amaral, Aracy A. *Tarsila: Sua Obra e Seu Tempo*. São Paulo: Tenenge, 1986.

Anderson, Dorothy May. *Women, Design, and the Cambridge School*. West Lafayette, IN: PDA Publishers Corporation, 1980.

Andrade, Oswald de. "Piratininga Ano 374 da Deglutição do Bispo Sardinha." *Revista de Antropofagia* 1, no. 1 (May 1928): 1.

Annuaire des Anciens Elèves de l'ENSH et de l'ENSP, 1994. Versailles: Association des ingénieurs horticoles et anciens élèves de l'école nationale supérieure d'horticulture et de l'école nationale supérieure du paysage, 1994.

Appleyard, Donald, Kevin Lynch, and John R. Meyer. *The View from the Road*. Cambridge, MA: MIT Press, 1964.

Architektur und Bautechnik 20, no. 5/6 (1933).

Arminius. *Die Grosstädte in ihrer Wohnungsnoth und die Grundlagen einer durchgreifenden Abhilfe*. Leipzig: Duncker & Humblot, 1874.

Backhouse, William. "Welkom – a Town Planned to Serve the New Gold Mines." *Optima*, March 1952, 12–17.

Barraqué, Bernard. "Le paysage et l'administration." Research report, Ministère de l'Urbanisme, du Logement et des Transports, Mission de la Recherche Urbaine, Paris, 1985, 2005. Available online at <http://www.developpement-durable.gouv.fr/IMG/9-Paysageetadministrationvl.pdf>. Accessed April 9, 2014.

Batista, Marta Rossetti. *Anita no tempo e no espaço: biografia e estudo da obra*. São Paulo: Editora 34/EDUSP, 2006.

Beil, Ralf, and Regina Stephan, eds. *Joseph Maria Olbrich: 1867–1908: Architekt und Gestalter der frühen Moderne*. Ostfildern: Hatje Cantz Verlag, 2010.

Beinart, William, and Peter Coates. *Environment and History: The Taming of Nature in the USA and South Africa*. London: Routledge, 1995.

Belluzzo, Ana Maria. "A propósito d'O Brasil dos Viajantes." *Revista USP* 30 (June–August 1996): 15–16.

Ben-Joseph, Eran. *Against All Odds: MIT's Pioneering Women of Landscape Architecture*. Cambridge, MA: MIT, School of Architecture and Planning, 2006.

Berman, Marshall. *All That Is Solid Melts into Air: The Experience of Modernity*. New York: Simon and Schuster, 1982.

Berrizbeitia, Anita. "Amsterdam Bos: Modern Public Park and the Construction of Collective Experience." In *Recovering Landscape: Essays in Contemporary Landscape Architecture*, edited by James Corner, 186–203. New York: Princeton University Press, 1999.

————. *Roberto Burle Marx in Caracas: Parque del Este, 1956–1961*. Philadelphia: University of Pennsylvania Press, 2005.

Berrizbeitia, Anita, and Linda Pollak. "Materiality." In *Inside/Outside: Between Architecture and Landscape*, 48–49. Gloucester, MA: Greenwood Press, 1999.

Beveridge, Charles E., Paul Rocheleau, and David Larkin. *Frederick Law Olmsted: Designing the American Landscape*. New York: Rizzoli, 1995.

Blanchon, Bernadette. "Public Housing Landscapes." *Landscape Research* 36, no. 6 (Dec. 2011): 683–702.

————. "Pratiques et compétences paysagistes dans les grands ensembles d'habitations, 1945–75." *Strates* 13 (2007): 149–167.

————. "Les paysagistes en France depuis 1945: l'amorce d'une indiscipline ou la naissance d'une profession." In *Les espaces publics modernes*, edited by Virginie Picon-Lefebvre, 121–210. Paris: Le Moniteur, 1997.

Boddam Whetham, Ruby. *A Garden in the Veld*. Wynberg, Cape Town: Speciality Press, 1933.

Bodorff, Ulla. "Industri och människor: Stora Vika – bostadsområde för Skånska Cementaktiebolaget." *Hem i Sverige* 44 (1951): 128–129.

————. "Landskapsplaneringen." *Byggmästaren* 26 (1947): 269–270.

————. "The Swedish Society of Landscape Architects: Brief Statement on Professional Practice in Sweden." *Landscape Architecture* 38, no. 3 (1948): 91–94.

————. "Från den internationella trädgårdsarkitektkonferensen i Bryssel." *Havekunst* 16 (1935): 134–136.

Bonomo, Bruno. "'On Holidays 365 Days a Year' on the Outskirts of Rome." In *Urban Planning and the Pursuit of Happiness: European Variations on a Universal Theme (18th–21st Centuries)*, edited by Arnold Bartetzky and Marc Schalenberg, 168–197. Berlin: Jovis, 2009.

Born, Wolfgang. "Schöne Wiener Privatgärten." *Die Bühne* 285 (August 1930): 29–30.

Borrmann, Norbert. *Paul Schultze-Naumburg. Maler, Publizist, Architekt 1869–1949. Vom Kulturreformer der Jahrhundertwende zum Kulturpolitiker im Dritten Reich*. Essen, Germany: Bacht, 1989.

Botti, Alberto, Marc Rubin, and Renée Otmar, eds. *Botti Rubin Arquitetos: Selected Works*. Victoria, Australia: Images Publishing, 2002.

Bourne, Michel, and Ingrid Bourne. *1956–1996: 40 ans de pratique du Paysage*. Paris: Pleine Vie, 2000.

Brigada ASNOVA [Viktor Balikhin, Militsa Prokhorova, Mikhail Turkus, P. V. Budo, Romual'd Iodko, Flora Sevortian]. "ASNOVA: Drovets Sovetov." *Sovetskaia Arkhitektura* 4 (1931): 52–55.

Britz, Bannie. "Reflections on Being a Young Architect in South Africa: 1965–70." Unpublished paper. Available online at <www.artefacts.co.za/main/Buildings/archframes.php?archid=2123>. Accessed July 2012.

Brown, Catherine R., and Celia Newton Maddox. "Women and the Land: 'A Suitable Profession'." *Landscape Architecture* 72, no. 3 (1982): 64–69.

Brunier, Yves. *Yves Brunier: Landscape Architect*. Bordeaux: Arc en rêve/Birkhauser, 2001.

Buckley, Craig. "Interview with Isabelle Auricoste, Utopie: Sociologie de l'Urbain, Editor, 1967–1978. Interview by Craig Buckley, Poitiers, October 7, 2007." In *CLIP/STAMP/FOLD: The Radical Architecture of Little Magazines, 196X to 197X*, edited by Beatriz Colomina and Craig Buckley, 197–200. Barcelona: Actar, 2010.

Buckley, Craig, and J.-L. Violeau, eds. *Utopie: Texts and Projects, 1967–1978*. Los Angeles: Semiotext, 2011.

Bueno, Eduardo. *Capitães do Brasil: a saga dos primeiros colonizadores*. Rio de Janeiro: Objetiva, 1999.

Burmil, Shmuel, and Ruth Enis. *The Changing Landscape of a Utopia: The Landscape and Gardens of the Kibbutz: Past and Present*. Worms, Germany: Wernersche Verlagsgesellschaft mbH, 2011.

Butler, Russell H., and Loutrel W. Briggs. "The International Conference with the Institute of Landscape Architects as Hosts." *Landscape Architecture* 39, no. 2 (1949): 72–75.

Caldwell, Melissa. *Dacha Idylls: Living Organically in Russia's Countryside*. Berkeley: University of California Press, 2011.

Cane, Percy S. *Modern Gardens, British and Foreign*. Special Winter Number of *The Studio* 1926–1927. London: The Studio, ltd., 1926.

Cardoso, Omar de Almeida. "Roberto Coelho Cardozo: A Vanguarda da Arquitetua Paisagística Moderna Paulistana." *Paisagem e Ambiente, Ensaio* 4 (1992).

Cautley, Marjorie S. *Garden Design: The Principles of Abstract Design as Applied to Landscape Composition*. New York: Dodd, Mead & Co., 1935.

Cavalcanti, Claudio, Farès el-Dahdah, and Francis Rambert, eds. *Roberto Burle Marx: The Modernity of Landscape*. Barcelona, Basel, New York: Actar Birkhäuser, 2011.

"Ce que les femmes font à l'architecture." *Criticat* 10 (2012): 36–87.

Çelik, Zeynep. "Kinaestheisa." In *Sensorium: Embodied Experience, Technology, and Contemporary Art*, edited by Caroline Jones, 159–162. Cambridge, MA: MIT Press, 2006.

Champy, Florent. "Les architectes, les urbanistes et les paysagistes." In *La Ville et l'Urbain: l'État des savoirs*, edited by Thierry Paquot, Michel Lussault, and Sophie Body-Gendrot, 215–224. Paris: La Découverte, 2000.

Chelpanov, Georgii. "Glazomer i illiuzii zrenia" ["Eye-balling and visual illusions"]. *Voprosy filosophii i psikhologii* [*Issues in Philosophy and Psychology*] 17, no. 2 (1893): 45–54; 18, no. 3 (1893): 1–13.

Chemetoff, Alexandre. *Visits*. Basel: Birkhäuser, 2009.

Christopher, A. J. "Mining Landscapes." In *South Africa: The World's Landscapes*, 119–133. London: Longmans, 1982.

Cicé, Chantal and F. Dubost, "La profession de paysagiste." Research report. Paris: Centre de Sociologie des Arts, EHESS, Mission de la recherche urbaine, 1986.

Cid, Dianne del. "Arthur S. and Marie Harbeck Berger." MLA Thesis, University of Texas Arlington, 1989.

Claesson, Ester. "Trädgårdsanläggningskonst som kvinnligt verksamhetsfält." *Stockholms Dagblad*, June 24, 1918.

Clay, Grady. "Shapely Women and Cities. An Editorial: What's the Urban Equivalent of '38–24–34'?" *Landscape Architecture* 49, no. 1 (1958–1959): 7.

Coetzee, J. M. *White Writing: On the Culture of Letters in South Africa*. New Haven, CT: Yale University Press, 1988.

Coffin, Marian Cruger. *Trees and Shrubs for Landscape Effects*. New York: C. Scribner's Sons, 1940.

Collens, Geoffrey, and Wendy Powell, eds. *Sylvia Crowe*. Reigate, Surrey, England: Landscape Design Trust, 1999.

Collins, Lester, and Thomas Gillespie, eds. *Landscape Architecture*. Cambridge, MA: Harvard University Press, 1951.

Conan, Michel, ed. *Environmentalism in Landscape Architecture*. Washington, DC: Dumbarton Oaks Research Library and Collection, 2000.

———. "The Hortillonages: Reflections on a Vanishing Gardener's Culture." In *The Vernacular Garden*, edited by John Dixon Hunt and Joachim Wolschke-Buhlmann, 19–46. Washington, DC: Dumbarton Oaks Research Library, 1993.

Conekin, Becky E. *"Autobiography of a Nation": The 1951 Festival of Britain*. Manchester and New York: Manchester University Press, 2003.

Cornell, Ralph D. *Conspicuous California Plants with Notes on Their Garden Uses*. Pasadena, CA: San Pasqual Press, 1938.

Corner, James. "Paradoxical Measures: The American Landscape." *Architectural Design Profile* 124 (1999): 46–49.

Cosgrove, Denis. "Gardening the Renaissance World." In *Geography and Vision: Imagination, Landscape, Mapping*, 51–67. London: I. B. Tauris, 2008.

Cresswell, Tim. "Landscape and the Obliteration of Practice." In *Handbook of Cultural Geography*, edited by Kay Anderson, Mona Domosh, Steve Pile, and Nigel Thrift, 269–281. London: Sage, 2003.

Crowe, Sylvia. *Forestry in the Landscape*. London: Her Majesty's Stationery Office, 1966.

———. *The Landscape of Roads*. London: The Architectural Press, 1960.

———. "Power and the Landscape." *Journal of the Institute of Landscape Architects* 52 (Nov. 1960): 3–7.

————. "The Landscape of Power." *Landscape Architecture* 49, no. 2 (1958–1959): 106–109.

————. "Landscape USA: Impressions of an English Visitor." *Landscape Architecture* 49, no. 2 (1958–1959): 120, 122.

————. *The Landscape of Power.* London: The Architectural Press, 1958.

————. "Recreational Landscape in England." *Landscape Architecture* 49, no. 1 (1958): 32–35.

————. "Presidential Address." *Journal of the Institute of Landscape Architects* 40 (Nov. 1957): 3–5, 20.

————. "Landscape Architecture in the New Towns." *Journal of the Institute of Landscape Architects* 18 (July 1950): 4–6.

Crush, Jonathan. "Power and Surveillance on the South African Gold Mines." *Journal of Southern African Studies* 18, no. 4 (1992): 825–844.

————. "The Compound in Post-apartheid South Africa." *Geographical Review* 82, no. 4 (1992): 388–400.

Cutler, Phoebe. *The Public Landscape of the New Deal.* New Haven, CT: Yale University Press, 1985.

Daniels, Stephen. "Landscape History: Material and Metaphorical Regimes." *Journal of the Society of Architectural Historians* 65, no. 1 (2006): 16–17.

————. *Humphrey Repton: Landscape Gardening and the Geography of Georgian Britain.* New Haven, CT: Yale University Press, 1999.

————. "Marxism, Culture, and the Duplicity of Landscape." In *New Models in Geography: The Political-Economy Perspective*, Vol. 2, edited by Richard Peet and Nigel Thrift, 196–220. London: Unwin Hyman, 1989.

Dean, Ruth. *The Livable House: Its Garden.* New York: Moffat Yard and Co., 1917.

Deckker, Zilah Quezado. *Brazil Built: The Architecture of the Modern Movement in Brazil.* London: Spon Press, 2001.

Deitz, Paula. "Alice Ireys, 89 Dies: Designed Elegant Landscapes Bridging Traditions." *New York Times* (2000). Published electronically December 17. Available online at <http://www.nytimes.com/2000/12/17/nyregion/alice-ireys-89–dies-designed-elegant-landscapes-bridging-traditions.html>.

DeSilvey, Caitlin. "Cultivated Histories in a Scottish Allotment Garden." *Cultural Geographies* 10 (2003): 442–468.

De Vico Fallani, Massimo. *Parchi e Giardini dell'EUR. Genesi e sviluppo delle aree verdi dell' E42.* Rome: Nuova Editrice Spada, 1988.

Dewes, Dudley. "Coaxing a Garden from the Veld." *Country Life*, June 20, 1963, 1480–1482.

Didier, Béatrice, Antoinette Fouque, and Mireillle Calle-Gruber, eds. *Le dictionnaire universel des créatrices.* Paris: des femmes, 2013.

Disney, Walt. "Preface." In *Disneyland: World of Flowers* by Morgan Evans, 3. Burbank: Walt Disney Productions, 1965.

Dokuchaev, Nikolai. "Arkhitektura i tekhnika" ["Architecture and technology"]. *Sovetskoe iskusstvo* [*Soviet Art*] 8–9 (1926).

Dolff-Bonekämper, Gabi, and Franziska Schmidt. *Das Hansaviertel. Internationale Nachkriegsmoderne in Berlin.* Berlin: Verlag Bauwesen, 1999.

Donadieu, Pierre, and M. Bouraoui, "La formation des cadres paysagistes en France par le ministère de l'Agriculture 1874–2000." Research report. Ministère de l'Ecologie et du Développement Durable/Cemagref Bordeaux, 2003.

Doumato, Lamia. *Women and Landscape Architecture.* Architecture Series – Bibliography. Monticello, IL: Vance Bibliographies, 1986.

Dubost, Françoise. "Les nouveaux professionnels de l'aménagement et de l'urbanisme." *Sociologie du travail* 27, no. 2 (1985): 154–164.

————. "Les paysagistes et l'invention du Paysage." *Sociologie du travail* 25, no. 4 (1983): 432–445.

Dümpelmann, Sonja. "The Art and Science of Invisible Landscapes: Camouflage for War and Peace." In *Ordnance: War + Architecture and Space*, edited by Gary Boyd and Denis Linehan, 117–135. Farnham: Ashgate, 2013.

————. "The Landscape Architect Maria Teresa Parpagliolo Shephard in Britain: Her International Career 1946–1974." *Studies in the History of Gardens and Designed Landscapes* 30, no. 1 (2010): 94–113.

————. "Breaking Ground: Women Pioneers in Landscape Architecture: An International Perspective." In *CELA 2006 Shifting Grounds Proceedings*, edited by Patrick Mooney, 45–50. Vancouver, 2006.

————. *Maria Teresa Parpagliolo Shephard (1903–1974): Ein Beitrag zur Geschichte der Gartenkultur in Italien im 20. Jahrhundert*. Weimar, Germany: VDG, 2004.

————. "Maria Teresa Parpagliolo Shephard (1903–74): Her Development as a Landscape Architect between Tradition and Modernism." *Garden History* 30, no. 1 (2002): 49–73.

Duncan, James. *The City as Text: The Politics of Landscape Interpretation in the Kandyan Kingdom*. Cambridge: Cambridge University Press, 1990.

Durth, Werner, and Niels Gutschow. *Träume in Trümmern*, Vol. 1. Braunschweig, Wiesbaden, Germany: Friedrich Viehweg & Sohn, 1988.

Düwel, Jörn, and Niels Gutschow. *Städtebau in Deutschland im 20. Jahrhundert*. Stuttgart, Leipzig, Wiesbaden, Germany: Teubner, 1965.

Düwel, Jörn. "Hamburg: Two Catastrophies in 1842 and 1943." In *A Blessing in Disguise: War and Town Planning in Europe 1940–1945*, edited by Jörn Düwel and Niels Gutschow, 194–261. Berlin: Dom Publishers, 2013.

Eckbo, Garrett. *Landscape for Living*. New York: F. W. Dodge Corporation, 1951.

Eckbo, Garret, Daniel U. Kiley, and James C. Rose. "Landscape Design in the Primeval Environment." *Architectural Record* 87 (Feb. 1940): 73–79.

————. "Landscape Design in the Urban Environment." *Architectural Record* 85 (May 1939): 70–77.

————. "Landscape Design in the Rural Environment." *Architectural Record* 86 (Aug. 1939): 68–74.

Edensor, Tim. "Entangled Agencies, Material Networks and Repair in a Building Assemblage: The Mutable Stone of St Ann's Church, Manchester." *Transactions of the Institute of British Geographers* N.S. 36, no. 2 (2011): 238–252.

"Ein Garten." *profil* 2, no. 4 (1934): 116.

"Ein Haus im Wienerwald." *profil* 2, no. 1 (1934): 64–67.

Eliot, Charles W., ed. *Charles Eliot Landscape Architect*. Boston and New York: Houghton Mifflin, 1902.

Eliovson, Sima. *Garden Beauty in South Africa*. Johannesburg: Macmillan South Africa, 1979.

————. *The Complete Gardening Book for South Africa*. Cape Town: Howard Timmins, 1962.

————. *South African Flowers for the Garden*. Cape Town: Howard Timmins, 1955.

"En blomma åt en dam." *Idun* 42 (1944): 22.

Enis, Ruth. "Zionist Pioneer Women and Their Contribution to Garden Culture in Palestine 1908–1948." In *Frauen und Hortikultur*, edited by Heide Inhetveen and Mathilde Schmitt, 87–114. Hamburg: LIT-Verlag, 2006.

Enstam, Elizabeth York. *Women and the Creation of Urban Life: Dallas, Texas, 1843–1920*. College Station: Texas A & M University Press, 1998.

Ernst Epstein 1881–1938. Exhibition catalog. Edited by Karlheinz Gruber, Sabine Höller-Alber, and Markus Kristan. Vienna: Jüdisches Museum Holzhausen, 2002.

Etter, Carolyn, and Don Etter. "1909–2005: Biography of Jane Silverstein Ries." *The Cultural Landscape Foundation: Pioneers*. Published electronically April 1, 2007.

Fahra, Ivete, Mônica B. Schlee, and Raquel Tardin, eds. *Arquitetura paisagística contemporânea no Brasil*. São Paulo: SENAC, 2010.

Fairbridge, Dorothea. *Gardens of South Africa*. London: A. & C. Black, 1924.

Forty, Adrian. *Words and Buildings: A Vocabulary of Modern Architecture*. New York: Thames and Hudson, 2000.

Foster, Jeremy. *Washed with Sun: Landscape and the Making of White South Africa*. Pittsburgh, PA: University of Pittsburgh Press, 2008.

————. "From Socio-Nature to Spectral Presence: Re-imagining the Once and Future Landscape of Johannesburg." *Safundi: The Journal of South African and American Studies* 10, no. 2 (April 2009): 175–213.

————. "The Wilds and the Township: Articulating Modernity, Capital and Socio-nature in the Cityscape of Pre-apartheid Johannesburg." *Journal of the Society of Architectural Historians* 71, no. 1 (March 2012): 45–59.

Frank, Josef. "Über die ursprüngliche Gestalt der kirchlichen Bauten des Leone Battista Alberti." PhD diss., Technische Hochschule Wien, 1910.

Fürth, Paula. "Gärtnerinnen sprechen über ihre Gärten." *Österreichische Kunst* 7 (1932): 29–30.

———. "Stein und Beton als Gartenwerkstoffe." *Innendekoration* (1937): 177–182.

Gallion, Arthur, Garrett Eckbo, and Simon Eisner. "Converging Forces on Design Part 2." *Journal of Architectural Education, 42nd Annual Convention of the Association of Collegiate Schools of Architecture* 12, no. 1 (Autumn, 1956): 15–18.

"Gartenarchitekt Wilhelm Wolf." *Gärtner-Kurier* 12 (1954): 3.

Geelhaar, Christiane. "Ein Stück lebendiger Kunst. Olbrichs Gartengestaltungen." In *Joseph Maria Olbrich, 1867–1908: Architekt und Gestalter der frühen Moderne*, edited by Ralf Beil and Regina Stephan, 313–319. Ostfildern, Germany: Hatje Cantz Verlag, 2010.

Gibberd, Sir Frederick. "Harlow New Town." *Architectural Review* 117 (May 1955): 311–329.

Gibson, Sylvia. "Institute of Landscape Architects och dess utredningar." *Havekunst* 29 (1948): 57–59.

———. "IFLA:s verksamhet 1948–1966." *Havekunst* 48 (1967): 22.

———. "IFLA:s rapport om fackskolor för trädgårdsarkitekter." *Havekunst* 49 (1968): 126–127.

Gibson, Trish. *Brenda Colvin: A Career in Landscape*. London: Frances Lincoln, 2011.

Glan, Betti. *Prazdnik vsegda s nami*. Moskva: Soiuz teatral'nykh deiatelei, 1988.

———. "Za sotsialisticheskii park" ["For a socialist park"]. In *Za sotsialisticheskii park. Obzor proektov general'nogo plana Tsentral'nogo parka kul'tury i otdykha Mossoveta* [*For a Socialist Park. Review of Projects for the General Layout of the Central Park of Culture and Leisure of the Moscow Council*], edited by Betti Glan, 7–21. Moskva: Izd. Mosoblispolkoma, 1932.

———. "Tri goda raboty parka," *Park kul'tury i otdykha*, August 12, 1931.

Go, Jeong-Hi. "Herta Hammerbacher (1900–1985): Virtuosin einer Neuen Landschaftlichkeit-Der Garten als Paradigma." PhD diss., Technische Universität Berlin, 2004.

Goodman, Nelson, and Catherine Z. Elgin. *Reconceptions in Philosophy and Other Arts and Sciences*. London: Routledge, 1988.

Gotlib, Nadia Batella. *Tarsila do Amaral: a Modernista*. São Paulo: SENAC, 2000.

Graif, Linda Lewin. "The Paradox of Public Discourse: Designing Vancouver's Library Square." *Journal of the Society for the Study of Architecture in Canada* 25, no. 1 (2000): 18–32.

Green, Louise. "Changing Nature: Working Lives on Table Mountain, 1980–2000." In *Imagining the City: Memories and Cultures in Cape Town*, edited by Sean Field, Renate Meyer, and Felicity Swanson, 173–190. Cape Town: HSRC Press, 2007.

Grese, Robert E. *Jens Jensen: Maker of Natural Parks and Gardens*. Creating the North American Landscape. Baltimore: Johns Hopkins University Press, 1992.

Groening, Gert. "Teutonic Myth, Rubble, and Recovery: Landscape Architecture in Germany." In *The Architecture of Landscape, 1940–1960*, edited by Marc Treib, 120–153. Philadelphia: University of Pennsylvania Press, 2002.

Gröning, Gert, and Joachim Wolschke-Bulmahn. *Grüne Biographien, Biographisches Handbuch zur Landschaftsarchitektur des 20. Jahrhunderts in Deutschland*. Berlin: Patzer Verlag, 1997.

Grunert, Heino. "75 Jahre Planten un Blomen, Hamburgs Niederdeutsche Gartenschau von 1935." *Stadt + Grün* 11 (2010): 51–59.

Guttman, Naomi Ellen. "Women Writing Gardens: Nature, Spirituality and Politics in Women's Garden Writing." PhD diss., University of Southern California, 1999.

Halprin, Lawrence. *Freeways*. New York: Reinhold Pub. Corp., 1966.

Hammerbacher, Herta. "Gartenarchitekten planen im Hansaviertel." *Garten und Landschaft* 67, no. 10 (1957): 263–265.

———. "Japanische Städte-heute und morgen." *Garten und Landschaft* 74, no. 10 (1964): 326–335.

———. "Über landschaftsbezogene Bauplanung," *Garten und Landschaft* 77, no. 1 (1967): 12–14.

Hammerbacher-Mattern, Herta. "Neues Bauen und Neues Gartenwesen: Der Garten Poelzig." *Gartenschönheit* 12, no. 2 (1931): 26–30.

Hannig, Georg. "Der Wettbewerb für Erweiterung des Südlichen Friedhofes zu Stockholm." *Die Gartenkunst* 28, no. 9 (1915): 118–119.

Harris, Dianne. "Cultivating Power: The Language of Feminism in Women's Garden Literature, 1870–1920." *Landscape Journal* 13, no. 2 (Fall 1994): 113–123.

Hartmann, Susan. "Prescriptions for Penelope: Literature on Women's Obligations to Returning World War II Veterans." *Women's Studies: An Inter-disciplinary Journal* 5, no. 3 (1978): 223–239.

Harvey, David. *The Condition of Postmodernity.* Cambridge, MA, and Oxford: Blackwell, 1990.

Hayden, Dolores. *The Grand Domestic Revolution.* Cambridge, MA, and London: The MIT Press, 1981.

Helfrich, Kurt Gerard Frederick, Isabelle Clara Greene, and the University of California Santa Barbara. *Isabelle Greene: Shaping Place in the Landscape.* Santa Barbara: University Art Museum, University of California, 2005.

Helphand, Kenneth I. *Dreaming Gardens.* Santa Fe, NM: Center for American Places, 2002.

Helphand, Kenneth I., and Nancy D. Rottle. "Cultivating Charm: The Northwest's First Female Landscape Architecture Firm Created a Lasting Legacy at Deepwood Gardens." *Garden Design* 7, no. 3 (Autumn 1988): 26–33, 88.

Herbst, Christopher. "Architecture and Town Planning of Western Deep Levels Village: Integrating Landscape and Buildings to Construct a Sense of Home." In *Carletonville: Explorations of a Small South African Mining Town*, edited by Melinda Silverman, 77–83. Johannesburg: University of Witwatersrand, 2010.

Hermelin, Sven A. "Inger Wedborn." *Landskap* 50 (1969): 41.

Herrington, Susan. *Cornelia Hahn Oberlander: Making the Modern Landscape.* Charlottesville: University of Virginia Press, 2014.

Heynen, Hilde. "Modernity and Domesticity: Tensions and Contradictions." In *Negotiating Domesticity: Spatial Productions of Gender in Modern Architecture*, edited by Hilde Heynen and Gülsüm Baydar, 1–29. New York: Routledge, 2005.

Hill, Jonathan. *Weather Architecture.* Abingdon, England: Routledge, 2012.

Hofmeyr, Isabel. "The Spoken Word and the Barbed Wire." In *"We Spend Our Years as a Tale That Is Told": Oral Historic Narrative in a South African Chiefdom*, 59–77. Portsmouth, NH, Johannesburg: Heinemann/Witwatersrand University Press, 1993.

Homann, Katharina, and Maria Spitthöver. "Freiraum- und Landschaftsplanerinnen: Ein Beitrag zur Disziplingeschichte von 1900 bis 1945." *Stadt + Grün* 12 (2007): 26–33.

Howett, Catherine. "Ecological Values in Twentieth-Century Landscape Design: A History and Hermeneutics." *Landscape Journal* 17, no. 2 (1998): 80–98.

———. "Careers in Landscape Architecture: Recovering for Women What the 'Ladies' Won and Lost." In *Feminist Visions*, edited by Diane L. Fowlkes and Charlotte S. McClure, 139–148. Tuscaloosa: The University of Alabama Press, 1984.

Hudnut, Joseph. "Report to the President of Harvard University on the Graduate School of Design for the Academic Year 1941–42." Available online at <http://oasis.lib.harvard.edu/oasis/deliver/~hua08002>. Accessed February 1, 2011.

Humboldt, Alexander von, and Aimé Bonpland, *Essay on the Geography of Plants.* Edited by Stephen T. Jackson. Translated by Sylvie Romanowski. Chicago and London: University of Chicago Press, 2009.

Hunt, Myron. "Forward." In *California Gardens* by Winifred Starr Dobyns, 11–12. Santa Barbara, CA: Allen A. Knoll, 1996.

Hutcheson, Martha Brookes Brown, and the Library of American Landscape History. *The Spirit of the Garden.* Amherst: University of Massachusetts Press, 2001.

Hyslop, Jonathan. "An Anglo-African Intellectual, the Second World War and the Coming of Apartheid." In *South Africa's 1940s*, edited by Saul Dubow and Alan Jeeves, 212–226. Cape Town: Juta & Company, 2005.

"IFLA News." *Anthos: Zeitschrift für Landschaftsarchitektur* 3 (1964): 3, 33.

Imbert, Dorothée. *Between Garden and City: Jean Canneel-Claes and Landscape Modernism.* Pittsburgh, PA: University of Pittsburgh Press, 2009.

———. "Landscape Architects of the World, Unite! Professional Organizations, Practice, and Politics." *Journal of Landscape Architecture* 2, no. 1 (spring 2007): 6–19.

———. "Unnatural Acts: Propositions for a New French Garden, 1920–1930." In *Architecture and Cubism.* Montréal: Centre Canadien d'Architecture, 1997.

———. "Working the Land: Modernism Assumed Many Forms in Mid-20th-Century Landscape Architecture." *Architecture* 88, no. 11 (1999): 69–73.

————. "On Site and Time: French Landscape Architecture in the Twentieth Century." In *Het landschap [The Landscape]*, 53–75. Antwerp: De Singel, 1995.

Interbau Berlin 1957: Amtlicher Katalog der Internationalen Bauausstellung Berlin 1957. Berlin: Graphische Gesellschaft Grunewald, 1957.

Ireys, Alice Recknagel. *Garden Designs*. Burpee American Gardening Series. New York: Prentice Hall, 1991.

————. *How to Plan and Plant Your Own Property*. New York: Morrow, 1980.

————. *Small Gardens for City and Country: A Guide to Designing and Planting Your Green Spaces*. Home Gardening Handbooks. Englewood Cliffs, NJ: Prentice-Hall, 1978.

Ireys, Alice Recknagel, and W. Atlee Burpee Company. *Designs for American Gardens*. New York: Prentice-Hall Gardening, 1991.

Isnenghi, Marta, ed. *Donne di fiori: paesaggi al femminile*. Milan: Mondadori Electa, 2005.

Jacobs, Jane M., and Peter Merriman. "Practising Architectures." *Social & Cultural Geography* 12, no. 3 (2011): 211–222.

Jensen, Jens. *Siftings*. Chicago, IL: R. F. Seymour, 1939.

Johnson, Molly. *Interview with Ruth Patricia Shellhorn*. Edited by Elaine Zorbas. Pasadena, CA: Pasadena Oral History Project, 2002.

Kaplan, Wendy. "Introduction: Living in a Modern Way." In *Living in a Modern Way: California Design 1930–1965*. Edited by Wendy Kaplan, 27–59. Cambridge, MA: The MIT Press, 2012.

Keylon, Steven. "The California Landscapes of Katherine Bashford." *Eden: The Journal of the California Garden and Landscape History Society* 16, no. 4 (2013): 3–13.

————. "Taming the Car: A Vision for Los Angeles." *Eden: The Journal of the California Garden and Landscape History Society* 16, no. 1 (2012): 1–7.

Khan-Magomedov, Selim. *Pervye vypuski molodykh storonnikov arkhitekturnogo avangarda: MPI-MIGI (1920–1924 gg.) [First graduates of young supporters of architectural avant-garde: MPI-MIGI (1920–1924)]*. Moskva: Architectura, 1997.

Kliass, Rosa Grena. *Desenhando paisagens, moldando uma profissão*. São Paulo: SENAC, 2006.

Koch, Catherine E. "Some Wild Marsh Plants." *Landscape Architecture* 6 (July 16): 184–197.

Kolodney, Annette. *Lay of the Land: Metaphor as Experience and History in American Life and Letters*. Chapel Hill: University of North Carolina Press, 1975.

Korzhev, Mikhail, "Doklad o tvorcheskom puti parkovogo arkhitektora, chlena SSA i chlena sektsii ozelenenia goroda Moskvy Prokhorovoi Militsy Ivanovny" ["Report on the professional path of landscape architect, member of Soviet Union of Architects and member of the Section of Greening of the City of Moscow Militsa Ivanovna Prokhorova"]. Unpublished manuscript. March 1960.

Krall, Daniel Wayne. "Were They Feminists? Men Who Mentored Early Women Landscape Architects." In *Women in Landscape Architecture: Essays on History and Practice*, edited by Louise A. Mozingo and Linda Jewell, 76–82. London: McFarland & Company, Inc., 2012.

————. "Visions of Outdoor Art: One Hundred Years of Landscape Architecture Education at Cornell." Unpublished manuscript, Cornell University, 2005.

Krinskii, Vladimir. "Vozniknovenie i zhizn' ASNOVA" ["Emergence and life of ASNOVA"]. *Sovetskaia arkhitektura* 18 (1969): 20–28.

Krippner, Ulrike, and Iris Meder. "Cultivating, Designing, and Teaching: Jewish Women in Modern Viennese Garden Architecture." *Landscape Research* 36, no. 6 (2011): 657–668.

Kuchenbuch, David. "Circles within Circles: Visions and Visualizations of the City of Tomorrow." In *A Blessing in Disguise: War and Town Planning in Europe 1940–1945*, edited by Jörn Düwel and Niels Gutschow, 52–65. Berlin: Dom Publishers, 2013.

Kunert, Friedrich. *Hampels Gartenbuch* für *Gärtner und Gartenliebhaber*. 6th ed. Berlin: Verlagsbuchhandlung Paul Parey, 1929.

Ladovskii, Nikolai. "Moskva istoricheskaia i sotsialisticheskaia" ["Historic and socialist Moscow"]. *Stroitel'stvo Moskvy* 1 (1930): 17–20.

Lange, Willy. *Gartengestaltung der Neuzeit*. 3rd ed. Leipzig: Verlagsbuchhandlung J. J. Weber, 1912.

Laurence, Dianne Susan Duffner. "A Symbiotic Relationship between Mid-Century Modern Masters: The Collaborative Works of Arthur and Marie Berger Landscape Architects, and O'Neil Ford, Architect." MLA thesis, University of Texas at Arlington, 2007.

Lauterbach, Iris. "Gärtner, Virtuoso, Gartenkünstler – Zum Berufsbild des Gartenarchitekten in der Frühen Neuzeit." In *Der Architekt. Geschichte und Gegenwart eines Berufsstandes*, Vol. 2, edited by Winfried Nerdinger, 727–743. München, London, New York: Prestel, 2013.

Lavrov, Vitalii. "Park ku'tury i otdykha v Moskve po proektam diplomnikov VKhUTEINa" ["The park of culture and leisure in Moscow in the projects of VKhUTEIN graduating students"]. *Stroitel'stvo Moskvy [The Construction of Moscow]* 10 (1929): 13–18.

Lawson, Jean. "Berger Garden: Five Years Ago, This House Was Out in the Hot Texas Sun." *House Beautiful*, August 1957, 87–89.

"Laying the Dust on Mine Dumps and Slime Dams." *Optima* 16, no. 3 (1966): 159–160.

Leatherbarrow, David. *The Roots of Architectural Invention: Site, Enclosure, Materials*. Cambridge: Cambridge University Press, 1993.

————. "Leveling the Land." In *Recovering Landscape: Essays in Contemporary Landscape Architecture*, edited by James Corner, 170–184. New York: Princeton Architectural Press, 1999.

Le Corbusier. *La Charte d'Athènes*. Paris: Editions de Minuit, 1957.

Le Dantec, Jean-Pierre. *Le Sauvage et le régulier: Art des jardins et paysagisme en France au XXe siècle*. Paris: Le Moniteur, 2002.

Lefebvre, Henri. *Le droit à la ville*. 2nd ed. Paris: Anthropos, 1968.

Leon, Ethel. *Design Brasileiro: Quem fez, quem faz*. São Paulo: SENAC, 2005.

Levitin, Daniel J. *This Is Your Brain on Music*. New York: Dutton, 2006.

Lingner, Reinhold. "Die Stadtlandschaft." *Neue Bauwelt* 3, no. 6 (1948): 83–86.

Lira, José. *Warchavchik, Fraturas da Vanguarda*. São Paulo: Cosac Naify, 2011.

"Liubov' Sergeevna Zalesskaia." *Arkhitektura SSSR*, no. 3 (1968): 43.

Loines, Elma. "Opportunitites of the Garden: Some Experiments in Naturalization and Hybridization." *Landscape Architecture* 6 (1916): 198–202.

Lowell, Waverly B. "Geraldine Knight Scott (1904–1989)." In *Shaping the American Landscape*, edited by Charles A. Birnbaum and Stephanie S. Foell, 309–312. Charlottesville and London: University of Virginia Press, 2009.

Lunacharskii, Anatolii. "O narodnykh prazdnenstvakh" ["On popular festivals"]. *Vestnik teatra* 62 (April 27–May 2, 1920).

Lunts, Leonid. "Opisanie proektov general'nogo plana Tsentral'nogo parka kul'tury i otdykha Mossoveta" ["Description of projects of the general plan of the central park of culture and leisure of Mossovet"]. In *Za sotsialisticheskii park: Obzor proektov general'nogo plana Tsentral'nogo parka kul'tury i otdykha Mossoveta [For a Socialist Park: Review of Projects for the General Layout of the Central Park of Culture and Leisure of Mossovet]*. Moscow: Izd. Mosoblispolkoma, 1932.

————. *Parki kul'tury i otdykha*. Moscow: Gosstroiizdat, 1934.

————. "Parki kul'tury i otdykha gorodov-novostroek." *Arkhitektura SSSR* 5 (1934): 20–29.

Madsen, Karen, and John F. Furlong. "Women Land Design: Considering Connections." *Landscape Journal* 13, no. 2 (1994): 88–101.

Major, Judith K. *Mariana Griswold Van Rensselaer: A Landscape Critic in the Gilded Age*. Charlottesville: University of Virginia Press, 2013.

Makhulu, Anne-Maria. "The Conditions for after Work: Financialization and Informalization in Post-transition South Africa." *Proceedings of the Modern Languages Association* 127, no. 4 (October 2012): 782–799.

Mallgrave, Harry Francis, and Ikonomou, Eleftherios, eds. *Empathy, Form and Space: Problems in German Aesthetics, 1873–1893*. Los Angeles, CA: Getty Research Institute, 1994.

Massey, Doreen. *Space, Place, and Gender*. Minneapolis: University of Minnesota Press, 1994.

Matless, David. *Landscape and Englishness*. London: Reaktion, 2000.

————. "Action and Noise over a Hundred Years: The Making of a Nature Region." *Body & Society* 6, no. 3/4 (2000): 141–165.

Mbembe, Achille. "The Aesthetics of Superfluity." In *Johannesburg: Elusive Metropolis*, edited by Sarah Nuttall and Achille Mbembe, 37–67. Durham, NC: Duke University Press, 2008.

McElvy, Carl C. *Shoreline Development Study, Playa Del Rey to Palos Verdes: A Portion of a Proposed Master Plan for the Greater Los Angeles Region*. Los Angeles: Greater Los Angeles Citizens Committee, Inc., 1944.

McGuire, Diane Kostial, and Lois Fern, eds. *Beatrix Jones Farrand (1872–1959): Fifty Years of American Landscape Architecture*. Washington, DC: Dumbarton Oaks, Trustees for Harvard University, 1982.

McGuire, Leslie, and Nicole Martin. "The Dualities of Reinventing Space/Profile: Martha Schwartz, ASLA, Principal, Martha Schwartz Partners." Available online at <http://www.landscapeonline.com/research/article/11728>.

Meade, Elizabeth. "Martha Brookes Hutcheson." *Landscape Architecture* 50, no. 3 (April 1960): 181–182.

Meade, Teresa A. *A Brief History of Brazil*. New York: Facts on File, 2003.

Meder, Iris. "'Natur und Architektur werden hier ineinandergeschoben' – Haus und Garten in der Werkbundsiedlung." In *Ein Manifest des Neuen Wohnens. Werkbundsiedlung Wien 1932*, edited by Andreas Nierhaus and Eva-Maria Orosz, 96–101. Exhibition catalogue. Wien Museum, Salzburg: müry salzmann, 2012.

———. "Offene Welten – Die Wiener Schule im Einfamilienhausbau 1910–1938." PhD diss., Stuttgart University, 2004.

Merchant, Carolyn. *Reinventing Eden: The Fate of Nature in Western Culture*. New York: Routledge/Taylor & Francis Group, 2013.

———. *Earthcare*. New York: Routledge, 1996.

———. *The Death of Nature: Women, Ecology, and the Scientific Revolution*. San Francisco: Harper & Row, 1989.

Meredith, Anne. "Horticultural Education in England, 1900–40: Middle-Class Women and Private Gardening Schools." *Garden History* 31, no. 1 (2003): 67–79.

Merriman, Peter. "'"Beautified" Is a Vile Phrase': The Politics and Aesthetics of Landscaping Roads in Pre- and Postwar Britain." In *The World Beyond the Windshield*, edited by Christoph Mauch and Thomas Zeller, 168–186. Athens: Ohio University Press, 2008.

Merrington, Peter. "Cape Dutch Tongaat: A Case Study in Heritage." *Journal of Southern African Studies* 32, no. 4 (2006): 683–699.

Meyer, Elizabeth. "The Expanded Field of Landscape Architecture." In *Ecological Design and Planning*, edited by George F. Thompson and Frederick R. Steiner, 45–79. New York: John Wiley & Sons, Inc.

Meyerowitz, Joanne. *Not June Cleaver: Women and Gender in Postwar America, 1945–1960*. Philadelphia, PA: Temple University Press, 1994.

Miceli, Sergio. *Intelectuais e classe dirigente no Brasil (1920–1945)*. São Paulo: Difel, 1979.

Migge, Leberecht. "Der neue Hausgarten." *Deutsche Kunst und Dekoration* 20 (1907): 221–230.

Milkman, Ruth. *Gender at Work: The Dynamics of Job Segregation by Sex during World War II*. Urbana: University of Illinois Press, 1987.

Miller, Kristine F. *Almost Home: The Public Landscapes of Gertrude Jekyll*. Charlottesville: University of Virginia Press; Amsterdam: [published] by arrangement with Architectura & Natura, 2013.

Mozingo, Louise A. "Introduction." In *Women in Landscape Architecture: Essays on History and Practice*, edited by Louise A. Mozingo and Linda Jewell, 1–4. London: McFarland & Company, Inc., 2012.

Mumford, Eric. *The CIAM Discourse on Urbanism, 1928–1960*. Cambridge, MA: MIT Press, 2000.

Murray, Martin. *Taming the Disorderly City: The Spatial Landscape of Johannesburg after Apartheid*. Ithaca, NY: Cornell University Press, 2008.

Neckar, Lance. "Recovery into Prosperity." *Landscape Journal* 16, no. 2 (1997): 211–218.

Nevins, Deborah. "The Triumph of Flora: Women and the American Landscape, 1890–1935." *Magazine Antiques* 127 (April 1985): 904–922.

Newton, Norman T. *An Approach to Design*. Cambridge, MA: Addison-Wesley, 1951.

Nochlin, Linda. "Why Have There Been No Great Women Artists?" *ARTnews*, January 1971, 22–39, 67–71.

Nolin, Catharina. "Ulla Bodorff, landskapet och industrin." In *Berättelser från markerna. En antologi om järnet, skogen och kulturarvet. En vänbok till Gert Magnusson*, edited by Ing-Marie Pettersson Jensen, Lena Berg Nilsson, and Catarina Karlsson, 297–306. Norberg: Skrifter från Bergslagens medeltidsmuseum 1, 2013.

——— "Publicering och professionalisering: Om kvinnliga trädgårdsarkitekters författarskap som en väg till etablering och legitimering." *Bebyggelsehistorisk tidskrift* 60 (2010): 7–21.

———. "Ester Claesson und die deutsch-schwedische Beziehungen am Anfang des zwanzigsten Jahrhunderts." *Die Gartenkunst* 21, no. 2 (2009): 257–280.

Nowotny, Claus and Bengt Persson. *Ulla Bodorff: Landskapsarkitekt 1913–1982*. Stockholm: Arkus, 1988.

"Ob'edinenie arkhtitektorov-urbanistov." *Arkhitektura i VKhUTEIN* 1 (January 1929): 8.

Oberlander, Cornelia. "Parks, Playgrounds and Landscape Architecture." *Community Planning Association of Canada: Community Planning Review* 6, no. 1 (March 1956): 4–12.

Ogborn, Miles. "Spaces of Modernity." In *Spaces of Modernity: London's Geographies 1680–1780*, 1–28. London, Guilford Press, 1998.

Oliveira, Carmen L. *Rare and Commonplace Flowers: The Story of Elizabeth Bishop and Lota Macedo Soares*. New Brunswick, NJ: Rutgers University Press, 2003.

Olmsted, Frederick Law, Charles E. Beveridge, and David Schuyler. *Creating Central Park, 1857–1861*. Baltimore, MD: Johns Hopkins University Press, 1983.

O'Malley, Therese, and Marc Treib, eds. *Regional Garden Design in the United States* Washington, DC: Dumbarton Oaks Research Library and Collection, 1995.

Ormos, Emmerich. "Zwei Hausgärten, Zu Arbeiten der Gartengestaltung Helenium." *Architektur und Bautechnik*, 1931, 316–319.

———. "Von den Arbeiten des modernen Gartengestalters, Zu den Arbeiten der Firma Helenium, Abteilung Gartengestaltung." *Architektur und Bautechnik*, 1930, 100–112.

———. "Ein Miethausgarten." *Architektur und Bautechnik*, 1930, 426–429.

Ottillinger, Eva, and August Sarnitz. *Ernst Plischke: Das Neue Bauen und die Neue Welt. Das Gesamtwerk*. Munich, Berlin, London, New York: Prestel, 2003.

Oxley, John. *Down Where No Lion Walked: The Story of Western Deep Levels*. Johannesburg: Southern Book Publishers, 1989.

Paisagem e Ambiente, Ensaios 21. *Miranda Magnoli*. São Paulo: FAUUSP, 2006.

Palmer, Donna. "An Overview of the Trends, Eras, and Values of Landscape Architecture in America: From 1910 to the Present with an Emphasis on the Contributions of Women to the Profession." Master's thesis, North Carolina State University, 1976.

Parpagliolo-Shephard, Maria Teresa. "Eindrücke beim IFLA-Kongress in Japan." *Garten und Landschaft* 74, no. 10 (October 1964): 343–344.

Pearlman, Jill. *Inventing American Modernism: Joseph Hudnut, Walter Gropius, and the Bauhaus Legacy at Harvard*. Charlottesville: University of Virginia Press, 2007.

Perecin, Tatiana. *Mina Klabin: Paisagismo e Modernismo no Brasil*. São Carlos: EESC-USP, 2003.

Persson, Bengt, Eivor Bucht, and Peder Melin. *Svenska landskapsarkitekter: Glimtar från branschen 1920–1960*. Stockholm: Arkus, 1991.

Pevsner, Nikolaus. "Johannesburg." *Architectural Review*, July 1953, 361–364, 381.

Pim, Joane. *Beauty Is Necessary: Creation or Preservation of the Landscape*. Cape Town: Purnell, 1971.

———. "African Gold: The New Mining Landscape." *Landscape Architecture*, April 1968, 192–195.

———. "The Deepest Gold Mine in the World: Life on the Surface." Typescript of article submitted to Anglo American Corporation for review, May 1967. Historical Papers Archive, William Cullen Library, University of Witwatersrand.

———. "Industrial Landscape: The South African Mines." In *Shaping Tomorrow's Landscape, Vol. 2: The Landscape Architects Role in the Changing Landscape*, edited by Silvia Crowe and Zvi Miller, 90–94. Amsterdam: Djambatan, 1964.

———. "Creating a Landscape for a Mining Town." *Optima*, March 1956, 26–31.

Plishke, Anna. "A Garden for Pleasure." *Design Review* 6 (1951): 139–143.

Plischke, Ernst A. "Gegen Vereinfachungen." *Die Furche* 51/52 (1967): 12.

Plischke, Ernst A., and Anna Plischke. "Sunrooms and a Garden." *Design Review* 4 (1952): 82–85.

Pousin, Frédéric. "Projeter la grande échelle. L'aménagement du littoral aquitain (1967–1988)." In *L'emprise du vol*, edited by Nathalie Roseau and Marie Thébaud-Sorger, 147–160. Genève: MetisPresses, 2013.

Powers, Alan. "Landscape in Britain." In *The Architecture of Landscape, 1940–1960*, edited by Marc Treib. Philadelphia: University of Pennsylvania Press, 2002.

Preussisch Grün: Hofgärtner in Brandenburg-Preussen, edited by Stiftung Preussische Schlösser und Gärten Berlin-Brandenburg. Berlin: Henschel Verlag, 2004.

Racine, Michel, ed. *Créateurs de jardins et de paysages en France du XIXe siècle au XXIe siècle.* Arles, France: Actes Sud/Ecole Nationale Supérieure du Paysage, 2002.

"Recent Designs in Domestic Architecture." *The Studio* 55 (1912): 132.

Rehmann, Elsa. "An Ecological Approach." *Landscape Architecture Magazine* 23, no. 4 (July 1933): 239–245.

Rehmann, Elsa, and Antoinette Rehmann Perrett. *Garden-Making.* Boston and New York: Houghton Mifflin Company, 1926.

Roberts, Edith Adelaide, and Elsa Rehmann. *American Plants for American Gardens: Plant Ecology; the Study of Plants in Relation to Their Environment.* New York: The Macmillan Company, 1929.

Rumelhart, Marc. "Eco-logiques pour les projets de paysage. Autobiographie d'un héritage." *Les Carnets du Paysage* 20 (November 2010): 179–197.

Russell, George Vernon, F.A.I.A. & Associates. *Long Range Development Plan.* Riverside: University of California, Riverside, 1964.

Rutz, Miriam E. "Genevieve Gillette: From Thrift Gardens to National Parks." In *Midwestern Landscape Architecture*, edited by William H. Tishler, 215–230. Urbana: University of Illinois Press in cooperation with Library of American Landscape History, Amherst, Massachusetts, 2000.

Sargent, Charles Sprague. "Taste Indoors and Out." *Garden and Forest* 5, no. 233 (1892): 373–374.

Sauve, Sophie Nichol. "Constructing Gender[ed] Outdoor Public Space." In *Women in Landscape Architecture: Essays on History and Practice*, edited by Louise A. Mozingo and Linda Jewell, 195–216. Jefferson, NC: McFarland & Co., 2012.

Schalaster, Frank. "Zum Zusammenwirken der Landschaftsarchitekten Gustav und Rose Wörner im Büroalltag: Was verraten Akten und Pläne?" *Die Gartenkunst* 21, no. 2 (2009): 171–186.

Scheid, Ann. "Beatrix Farrand in Southern California, 1927–1941." *Eden: The Journal of the California Garden and Landscape History Society* 14, no. 2 (2011): 1–13.

Schekahn, Antje. *Spurensuche 1700–1933: Frauen in der Disziplingeschichte der Freiraum- und Landschaftsplanung.* Kassel: Universität Gesamthochschule Kassel, 2000.

Schenker, Heath. "Feminist Interventions in the Histories of Landscape Architecture." *Landscape Journal* 13, no. 2 (Fall 1994): 107–112.

C[amillo]. S[chneider]. "Um den kommenden Garten." *Die Gartenschönheit/Gartenwerk* 11, no. 1 (1930): 3–5.

Schneider, Camillo. "Ester Claesson †." *Die Gartenschönheit* 13, no. 4 (1932): 58.

Schulz, Stefanie, and Carl-Georg Schulz. *Das Hansaviertel. Ikone der Moderne.* Berlin: Verlagshaus Braun, 2007.

Schwarcz, Lilia Moritz. *Romantismo Tropical: A estetização da política e da cidadania numa instituição imperial brasileira.* São Paulo: Instituto de Artes, UNESP, 2000.

Scott, David. "New Towns." In *Sylvia Crowe*, edited by Geoffrey Collens and Wendy Powell, 47–67. Woking, England: Landscape Design Trust, 1999.

Scott, Sue. "Domestic Disturbances." In *The Reckoning: Women Artists of the New Millennium*, edited by Eleanor Heartney, Helaine Posner, Nancy Princenthal, and Sue Scott, 118–127. Munich, London, New York: Prestel, 2013.

Shephard, Marie T. "Landscape of Work and Leisure." *Building*, September 1948, 271–274.

Shepheard, Peter. "The Setting for Industry in the Landscape." In *Landscape and Human Life: The Impact of Landscape Architecture upon Human Activities*, edited by Clifford R. V. Tandy, 91–95. Amsterdam: Djambatan, 1966.

Shteir, Ann B. *Cultivating Women, Cultivating Science: Flora's Daughters and Botany in England, 1760–1860.* Baltimore, MD: Johns Hopkins University Press, 1996.

Sitte, Camillo. *Der Städtebau nach seinen künstlerischen Grundsätzen.* Vienna: Graeser & Kie, 1922.

Skubi, Ronda. *Women in Landscape Architecture.* Seattle: Department of Landscape Architecture, University of Washington, 1975.

Smith, Alan Huw. *The Brenthurst Gardens.* Houghton, SA: Brenthurst Press, 1988.

Sohn, Elke. *Zum Begriff der Natur in Stadtkonzepten.* Hamburg: Lit Verlag, 2008.

Southard, Tony. "Maria Shephard Talks to Tony Southard, On design No. 6." *Landscape Design* 11 (1971): 11–14.

Southwest Builder and Contractor. "Suggested Beach Highway System for an Eleven-Mile Shoreline Development." *Southwest Builder and Contractor* 104, no. 1 (July 7, 1944): 16–21.

————. "Santa Ana Has Beautiful New Fashion Square." *Southwest Builder and Contractor* 132, no. 8 (August 22, 1958): 6–8.

Spain, Daphne. *Gendered Spaces*. Chapel Hill: University of North Carolina Press, 1992.

————. *How Women Saved the City*. Minneapolis: University of Minnesota Press, 2001.

Spark, Jeremy, and Peter Gawn. "Reassessment 2: Harlow New Town." *Journal of the Institute of Landscape Architects* 86 (May 1969): 22–23.

Spirn, Anne Whiston. "Constructing Nature: The Legacy of Frederick Law Olmsted." In *Uncommon Ground: Rethinking the Human Place in Nature*, edited by William Cronon, 91–113. New York: W.W. Norton & Co., 1996.

"Standesnachrichten." *Die Gartenkunst* 45, no. 3 (1932): 5

Steele, Fletcher. *The House Beautiful Gardening Manual*. Boston: The Atlantic Monthly Press, 1926.

Stilgoe, John. *Alongshore*, New Haven, CT: Yale University Press, 1994.

Stinson, Kathy. *Love Every Leaf: The Life of Landscape Architect Cornelia Hahn Oberlander*. Toronto and Plattsburgh, NY: Tundra Books, 2008.

Stratigakos, Despina. "The Good Architect and the Bad Parent: On the Formation and Disruption of a Canonical Image." *The Journal of Architecture* 13, no. 3 (2008): 283–296.

————. *A Women's Berlin: Building the Modern City*. Minneapolis and London: University of Minnesota Press, 2008.

Streatfield, David C. *California Gardens: Creating a New Eden*. New York: Abbeville Press Publishers, 1994.

————. "Gender and the History of Landscape Architecture, 1875–1975." In *Women in Landscape Architecture: Essays on History and Practice*, edited by Louise A. Mozingo and Linda Jewell, 5–31. London: McFarland & Company, Inc., 2012.

Strnad, Oskar. "Neue Wege in der Wohnraum-Einrichtung." *Innendekoration*, 1922, 323–328.

"A Study of Ruth Patricia Shellhorn, A.S.L.A Award-Winning Landscape Architect: Her Landscapes Aid Merchandizing." *Landscape Design and Construction* 13, no. 4 (October 1967): 5–15, 21–23.

Tabor, Grace. *Come into the Garden*. New York: Macmillan, 1921.

————. *Old-Fashioned Gardening: A History and a Reconstruction*. New York: McBride Nast & Company, 1913.

————. *Suburban Gardens*. Outing Handbooks. New York: Outing Pub. Co., 1913.

Tang, Dorothy, and Andrew Watkins. "Ecologies of Gold: The Past and Future Mining Landscapes of Johannesburg." *Places Journal*, http://placesjournal.org/article/ecologies-of-gold-mining-landscapes-of-johannesburg.

Tankard, Judith B. "Women Take the Lead in Landscape Art." In *Women in Landscape Architecture*, edited by Louise Mozingo and Linda Jewell. Jefferson, NC, and London: McFarland & Company, 2012.

————. *The Gardens of Ellen Biddle Shipman*. Sagaponack, NY: Harry N. Abrams, 1996.

Thistle, Susan. *From Marriage to the Market: The Transformation of Women's Lives and Work*. Berkeley: University of California Press, 2006.

Tolstoy, Vladimir, Irina Bibikova, and Catherine Cooke, eds. *Street Art of the Revolution: Festivals and Celebrations in Russia, 1918–1933*. New York: The Vendome Press, 1990.

Treib, Marc. "Landscapes Transitional, Modern, Modernistic, Modernist." *Journal of Landscape Architecture* 8, no. 1 (2013): 6–15.

————. "Axioms for a Modern Landscape Architecture." In *Modern Landscape Architecture: A Critical Review*, edited by Marc Treib, 36–67. Cambridge, MA: MIT Press, 1994.

Tromm, Ilse. "Beispiele schwedischer Gartenkunst." *Die Gartenkunst* 41, no. 3 (1928): 35–37.

Tunnard, Christopher. *Gardens in the Modern Landscape*. London: Architectural Press; New York, Scribner, 1948.

Ukhanov, Konstantin. "V bor'be za kul'turu (K organizatsii v Moskve 'Parka kul'tury i otdykha')" ["In a fight for culture (To the organization in Moscow of 'Park of culture and leisure'")], *Pravda* [*Truth*], March 21, 1928.

Urbanism 41, no. 130 (1972).

Van der Spuy, Una. *Ornamental Shrubs and Trees for Gardens in Southern Africa*. Cape Town: Juta, 1954.

Van Rensselaer, Mariana (Mrs. Schuyler). *Art Out-of-Doors: Hints on Good Taste in Gardening*. New York: C. Scribner's Sons, 1893.

"Vår första kvinnliga trädgårdsarkitekt." *Idun* 20 (1907): 522.

Vera Beatriz Siqueira. *Roberto Burle Marx*. São Paulo: Cosac Naify, 2005.

Vaccarino, Rossana. "The Inclusion of Modernism: *Brasilidade* and the Garden." In *The Architecture of Landscape, 1940–1960*, edited by Marc Treib, 206–237. Philadelphia: University of Pennsylvania Press, 2002.

Vietsch, Willi. "Der Weg zum schönen Garten." *Das Wüstenroter Eigenheim*, 7, no. 7/8 (1937): 250–252.

Waldheim, Charles. "Landscape as Urbanism." In *The Landscape Urbanism Reader*, edited by Charles Waldheim, 35–54. New York: Princeton Architectural Press, 2006.

Wasserman, Judith. "A World in Motion: The Creative Synergy of Lawrence and Anna Halprin." *Landscape Journal* 31, no. 1–2 (2012): 33–52.

Waugh, Frank. "Ecology of the Roadside." *Landscape Architecture* 21, no. 2 (January 1931).

———. "The Physiography of Lakes and Ponds." *Landscape Architecture* 22, no. 2 (1932).

Way, Thaïsa. *Unbounded Practice: Women and Landscape Architecture in the Early Twentieth Century*. Charlottesville and London: University of Virginia Press, 2009.

———. "Designing Garden City Landscapes: Works by Marjorie L. Sewell Cautley, 1922–1937." *Studies in the History of Gardens & Designed Landscapes* 25, no. 4 (2005): 297–316.

———. "Women as a Force in Landscape Architecture, 1893–1942," PhD diss., Cornell University, 2005.

Wedborn, Inger. "Anna Weber: Kvinden som Gartner og Havebruger." *Lustgården* 14 (1933): 167–168.

———. "Från en engelsk trädgårdsskola." *Allmän Svensk Trädgårdstidning* 4 (1932): 12–14, 43–45.

———. "Mitt bästa trädgårdsminne." *Hem i Sverige* 49 (1949): 20–209.

———. "Tysk väg- och landskapsvård." *Lustgården* 18–19 (1937–38): 51–59.

Weilacher, Udo. "Entre naturalisme et minimalisme, évolution de l'architecture paysagère suisse du 20ᵉ au 21ᵉ siècles." In *Guide suisse de l'architecture du Paysage*, edited by Udo Weilacher and Peter Wullschleger, 26–55. Genève: Presses Polytechniques et universitaires romandes, 2005.

Wiesmeyer, Esmé Moseley. *Joane Pim: South Africa's Landscape Pioneer*. Edited by Pat Widdas. Pinegowrie Natal: South African Horticultural Society, 2007.

Williams, Daryle. *Culture Wars in Brazil: The First Vargas Regime (1930–1945)*. Durham, NC: Duke University Press, 2001.

Wimmer, Clemens Alexander. "Der Garten- und Landschaftsarchitekt in Deutschland ab 1800." In *Der Architekt. Geschichte und Gegenwart eines Berufsstandes*, Vol. 2, edited by Winfried Nerdinger, 745–751. Munich, London, New York: Prestel, 2013.

———. *Die Preussischen Hofgärtner*. Edited by Stiftung Preussische Schlösser and Gärten Berlin-Brandenburg. Berlin: Hentrich, 1996.

Wolf, Helene. "Blühende Stufen." *Der getreue Eckart* 7, no. 2, appendix *Heim und Geselligkeit*, 1929/30, 54–55.

Wolf, Willy. "Schöne Zweckgärten." *Der getreue Eckart* 6, no. 2, appendix *Heim und Geselligkeit*, 1928/29, 52–54.

———. "Friedhofsgestaltung." *Architektur und Bautechnik*, 1930, 66–70.

Wolf-Pollak, Helene. "Von Steingärten und ihrer Bepflanzung." *Architektur und Bautechnik*, 1930, 71–77.

Wolschke-Bulmahn, Joachim. "The Nationalization of Nature and the Naturalization of the German Nation: 'Teutonic' Trends in Early Twentieth-Century Landscape Design." In *Nature and Ideology: Natural Garden Design in the Twentieth Century*, edited by Joachim Wolschke-Bulmahn, 187–207. Dumbarton Oaks Colloquium on the History of Landscape Architecture: Washington, DC, 1997.

Wolschke-Bulmahn, Joachim, and Peter Fibich. *Vom Sonnenrund zur Beispiellandschaft: Entwicklungslinien der Landschaftsarchitektur in Deutschland, dargestellt am Werk von Georg Pniower (1896–1960)*. Hannover: Institut für Grünplanung und Gartenarchitektur, 2004.

Wylie, John. *Landscape*. London: Routledge, 2007.

Yoch, James J. *Landscaping the American Dream: The Gardens and Film Sets of Florence Yoch, 1890–1972.* New York: Sagapress, 1989.

Yves Brunier, Landscape Architect. Bordeaux: Arc en rêve/Birkhauser, 2001.

Zaitzevsky, Cynthia. *Long Island Landscapes and the Women Who Designed Them.* New York: Society for the Preservation of Long Island Antiquities, in association with W. W. Norton & Co., 2009.

Zeller, Thomas. *Driving Germany: The Landscape of the German Autobahn, 1930–70.* New York and Oxford: Bergahn Books, 2006.

Ziegler, Volker. "Les autoroutes du IIIe Reich et leurs origines." In *Les années 30: L'architecture et les arts de l'espace entre industrie et nostalgie*, edited by Jean-Louis Cohen, 207–213. Paris: Editions du Patrimoine, 1997.

INDEX

Headings in italics denote document title and locators in italics refer to material within a photograph or illustration.